NINE MONTHS TO GETTYSBURG

NINE MONTHS TO GETTYSBURG

Stannard's Vermonters and the
Repulse of Pickett's Charge

★ ★ ★

HOWARD COFFIN

★

FOREWORD BY EDWIN BEARSS

THE COUNTRYMAN PRESS

WOODSTOCK, VERMONT

Copyright © 1997 by Howard Coffin
First Edition

The publisher and author gratefully acknowledge permission to reprint excerpts from
the following: *Gettysburg, The Second Day*, by Harry W. Pfanz, copyright 1987 by the
University of North Carolina Press; *Terrible Swift Sword*, by Bruce Catton, copyright
1963 by Doubleday, a division of Bantam Doubleday Dell Publishing Group, Inc.; *The
Memoirs of Colonel John S. Mosby*, copyright 1917 by Little, Brown and Company.

Library of Congress Cataloging-in-Publication Data

Coffin, Howard, 1942–
Nine months to Gettysburg : Stannard's Vermonters and the
repulse of Pickett's charge /
Howard Coffin : foreword by Edwin Bearss.
p.   cm.
Includes bibliographical references (p. 299) and index.
ISBN 0-88150-400-9 (alk. paper)
1. United States. Army. Vermont Brigade, 2nd (1862–1863)—History.
2. United States—History—Civil War, 1861–1865—Regimental histories.
3. Vermont—History—Civil War, 1861–1865—Regimental histories.
4. Middle Atlantic States—History—Civil War, 1861–1865.
5. Gettysburg (Pa.), Battle of, 1863. I. Title.
E533.4.C64   1997
973.7—dc21
97-20031
CIP

Text and cover design by Glenn Suokko
Cover painting "Stannard's Vermonters"
copyright Michael J. Middleton/The Champlain Collection

Maps by Paul Woodward, © 1997 The Countryman Press

Published by
The Countryman Press, PO Box 748, Woodstock, VT 05091

Distributed by
W. W. Norton & Company, Inc., 500 Fifth Avenue, New York, NY 10110

Printed in the United States of America

10 9 8 7 6 5 4 3 2 1

DEDICATION

Hughes Oliphant Gibbons, Dartmouth class of 1930, servant of his country and lover of books, was a devotee of Civil War history. Born April 13, 1909, in Farragut Terrace, Pennsylvania, Gibbons, an English major at Dartmouth, studied at the University of Edinburgh before earning a degree in library science from Drexel University. He worked in the Georgetown Public Library in Washington and the Trinity College Library in Hartford, Connecticut, then for nine years as a librarian in Cairo, Egypt, where he gained an understanding of the Middle East. Turned down for military service because of health reasons at the outbreak of World War II, he went to work in army intelligence. For the remainder of his life he served the National Security Agency as a Middle East expert.

A quiet man who cared deeply about his family, Gibbons spent most of his leisure hours reading, particularly from his considerable Civil War library. That interest continued unabated until his sudden death, in 1973, of a heart attack. His knowledge of the Civil War was widespread and deep, with a particular focus on military activity in his native state of Pennylvania. With a special thanks to his niece Mary Stewart Baird, for her generous support and tireless help, I dedicate this book to Hughes Gibbons, hoping that in remembering the soldiers of the Second Vermont Brigade who served so well at Gettysburg, I also do honor to the memory of a good and decent man who lived a rich and valuable life.

In the *Boston Journal* of July 7, 1865, appeared the following account by war correspondent Carlton Coffin of his return to the Gettysburg battlefield: "Now leaving this line [Harrow's Brigade] and walking directly west . . . six or eight rods toward Cadori's house, we find a shallow ditch, yet remaining partly concealed by small scrub oaks. There were the nine months Vermont boys under Stannard . . . The Green Mountain State won for herself on that day a laurel which never will fade.

"Oh how it stirs one's blood," wrote Coffin, "to stand here upon this spot, to recall that scene, walk over the ground, trace the yet visible outlines of the conflict and read the historic record—that there the hopes of the confederacy began to wane—that there the future of our country began to brighten.

"I hope that no vandal hand will ever be permitted to touch one of those trees, that no other growth will ever be permitted to rise, that the fences may never be removed or others erected, but that through the coming years the features may remain as they are. As the years roll on we shall understand more fully than now how great were the issues involved, and how momentous the decisions of that hour."

CONTENTS

ACKNOWLEDGMENTS

I owe great thanks to very many people, living and dead, for their help on this book. Foremost among those departed are George Grenville Benedict, private and then lieutenant in the 12th Vermont, who wrote his wonderful two-volume *Vermont in the Civil War* and followed it with shorter accounts of his service in the Second Vermont Brigade; and Ralph Orson Sturtevant, a private in the 13th Vermont, who assembled the *Historical and Biographical History of the 13th Regiment*. Much is also owed to other brigade members, such as Edwin Palmer, Pvt. John Williams, and Cpl. John Williams, who kept diaries and turned them into books. The collected letters of Roswell and Mary Farnham, along with her diary, were invaluable, as were the letters of Wheelock Veazey and the Hammond family (copies of which were generously given me by Sidney Hammond), and the illustrations of William Henry Jackson. Special thanks go to Clifford Heustis, Elizabeth Bordeaux, Larry and Allan Keyes, and Vernon Turner, who provided family letters. And great thanks are due all the families who preserved letters, many of which now reside in the wondrous collections of the Vermont Historical Society and the University of Vermont's Special Collections.

Mary Stewart Baird, dear friend, has given me generous support, unfailing help, and constant good-hearted encouragement through the high and low points inevitably encountered while researching and writing a book. I hope that this effort is an adequate tribute to her uncle, Hughes O. Gibbons. I thank Edwin Bearss, friend, battlefield savior, and former co-member of the Civil War Sites Advisory Commission, for his support and advice, for reading the manuscript, and for accompanying me on explorations of northern Virginia. During those travels, Tersh and Sally Boasberg time and again opened their Washington home to me and offered welcome advice, at the same time waging their tireless fight to save the Brandy Station battlefield. Historian and preservationist James McPherson, friend and also a former fellow member of the Civil War Sites Commission, provided valued advice, as did friend Robert Krick, also a defender of battlefields, without whose help, it seems, few Civil War books would be written. Historians Harry Pfanz and Scott Hartwig walked with me the hallowed ground of Gettysburg. The staff of the library at the Gettysburg National Battlefield was most helpful. At the Vermont Historical Society, Barney Bloom and Paul Carnahan rendered very patient and inspired support. There, historian Edward Hoyt offered sage counsel. The same was true at the University of Vermont's Special Collections, where Connell Gallagher and Jeffrey Marshall and staff were always helpful. David Blow at UVM's Archive also advised. Peggy Daniels at the Fairbanks Museum in St. Johnsbury made available the wonderful William Herrick diaries. Brad and Sue Limoge, in Morrisville, Vermont, tirelessly sought material and made their collection available, while offering constant good-natured support. Elliott and Florence Morse, of Montpelier, Vermont, provided valuable information. Nicholas Picerno of Springfield, Vermont, offered books and suggestions. Vincent Vellucci, in Woodstock, Vermont, solved my computer problems. Robert Manasek and Dean

Knudsen, respectively acting superintendent and historian of the Scotts Bluff National Monument in Nebraska, made available the William Henry Jackson sketches and photos. Glenn Suokko, again, ably designed a Coffin book. Phyllis Lavelle at the Bradford Historical Society provided the photos of the Farnhams. The late Frank Teagle, of Woodstock, generously supported the book, as did Susan Audy, through a gift of reference books, in memory of her husband Stephen Audy. John Stevenson, of George Mason University, showed me the parklands along the Occoquan and Bull Run that preserve places where Vermonters served. My friend Peter Jennison, as with my book *Full Duty: Vermonters in the Civil War,* edited and advised. Helen Whybrow and the staff of Countryman Press were ever helpful and patient, and made great efforts to bring this book to completion on time. Jack Anderson and Atty. Charles Martin walked the Gettysburg battlefield with me, read this manuscript, and offered valuable advice. To others, such as my daughter Anya Coffin and my friends Marjorie Pierce and Cathy Pearse, who offered letters, books, tips, criticism, and encouragement, I say a sincere "thank you." And I offer thanks to, and deep admiration for, the nearly 5,000 men who served in Stannard's brigade. I believe their story to be one of the most intriguing of the Civil War.

FOREWORD

My interest in the Civil War was sparked during the bitter Montana winter of 1935–36 when I was in the seventh grade and my father read to me and my brother from John Thomason's *J.E.B. Stuart,* but it would be the summer of 1949 before I made my first visit to the Gettysburg battlefield. My 40-year National Park Service career began at Vicksburg, more than 1,000 miles southwest of Gettysburg, in 1955.

Following my April 1966 reassignment as a staff historian to the park service's Washington D.C. office, I made my first official trip to the Gettysburg National Military Park. In 1967 I returned to prepare a Historic Structures Report on the Snyder house. Located west of the Emmitsburg Road, on ground over which left flank units of Brig. Gen. Joseph Kershaw's South Carolina brigade advanced to participate in Lt. Gen. James Longstreet's July 2 onslaught—which for a while threatened the Union army with disaster—the Snyder house was restored in the 1970s to its Civil War appearance. From 1969 to 1972, I spent more than a month all told in Adams County, walking the grounds and interviewing people familiar with lands included in the Eisenhower National Historic Site. The research resulted in a document titled *Historic Resource Study and Historical Base Map, Eisenhower Farm, 1762–67.*

In the spring of 1978 I led my first tour of the Gettysburg battlefield for the popular Smithsonian Resident Associates program. Not then recognizing the public's desire for in-depth tours of the site of this three-day battle, the tour spent only seven hours on the field. Following publication in paperback of Michael Shaara's *The Killer Angels,* however, interest in Gettysburg burgeoned, and the format for my Resident Associates tours was changed to provide one day on the site for each day of the battle. The highlight for day-three participants is to walk in the steps of history by following the route taken by Maj. Gen. George E. Pickett's Virginians as they crossed three-quarters of a mile of hell to pierce The Angle and then—along with the soldiers of Maj. Gen. Isaac R. Trimble's and Brig. Gen. J. Johnston Pettigrew's divisions—suffered a crushing repulse.

To prepare myself to lead this walk, I familiarized myself with Edwin B. Coddington's *The Gettysburg Campaign: A Study in Command;* George R. Stewart's *Pickett's Charge;* and Kathleen Georg Harrison and John W. Busey's *Nothing but Glory: Pickett's Division at Gettysburg.* Coddington's book provided a context, and the latter two sufficient detail, for me to interpret what occurred during the charge that was to become a synonym for heroism and gallantry. It was then that I became aware of the important, perhaps critical, role played by Brig. Gen. George Jerrison Stannard and the three nine-months regiments of his Vermont brigade.

In the spring of 1989, my friends Robert and Mary Younger of Morningside Bookshop informed me that they planned to publish a biannual periodical devoted to the reading public's favorite Civil War campaign and battle under the name *Gettysburg Magazine.* I was honored when Bob asked me to be a contributing editor and, as such, to read and comment on the articles selected for publication in an introduction headed "Gettysburg Revisited." In the eight years that have rushed by since the first issue of *Gettysburg Magazine* went to press, three monographs have centered on Stannard and his Vermonters. The first of these, in issue No. 2, was "Paper Collars: Stannard's Brigade at Gettysburg," by Tony Trimble; issue Nos. 16 and 17 featured articles by Christopher C. Dickson: "The Flying Brigade: George Stannard and the Road to Gettysburg," and "Co. Francis Voltaire Randall and the 13th Vermont Infantry." Only one other brigade—Strong Vincent's, heralded by many as the savior of the Little Round Top—in the 17 issues of *Gettysburg Magazine* has commanded such attention.

When I prepared the foreword for Howard Coffin's critically acclaimed *Full Duty: Vermonters in the Civil War* a few years ago, he shared with me his dream of following it up with a unit history featuring Stannard's nine-months brigade. I was enthusiastic for a number of reasons: First, I wanted to know more about Stannard and his people beyond what three of the five regiments did at Gettysburg; second, I was curious as to what manner of men were those citizen soldiers; third, there are few, if any, satisfactory histories of the nine-months units that answered "Father Abraham's" August 4, 1862, call for 300,000 men to meet the crisis following the dramatic turn of the tide of war beginning in mid-June 1862; and fourth, I knew that Coffin's skills as a researcher and writer would ensure a publication of lasting value.

On a cold, blustery day in late January 1993, the Civil War Sites Commission visited Gettysburg and toured the battlefield. There, Coffin and I spoke of the significance of the Vermonters' actions, which on July 3 saw them first savaging Brig. Gen. James L. Kemper's Virginians and then turning on Brig. Gen. Cadmus M. Wilcox's Alabamians and David Lang's Floridians, sending them running. Later, I visited Fairfax Court House in Virginia with Coffin and pointed out extant sites connected with what for Vermonters was an embarrassment: the capture of handsome brigade commander Brig. Gen. Edwin H. Stoughton by then Captain John Singleton Mosby, destined to become known as the "Gray Ghost of the Confederacy." We also visited Fairfax Station and Wolf Run Shoals, sites where the Vermonters camped and pulled guard and fatigue duty in the weeks and months while they unknowingly awaited their date with destiny. Fairfax Station has been engulfed by subdivisions, but the Wolf Run Shoals area, on what was the Union side of the Occoquan, is as rural and devoid of modern intrusions as when the Green Mountain Boys experienced these scenes 130 years ago.

In this book, as in *Full Duty,* Coffin combines his skills as a journalist and historian with those of a dedicated preservationist and battlefield stomper to tell a compelling story of Civil War soldiers and their brigade. He separates the important from the trivial and repetitive, and he integrates these voices from the past into a narrative that captivates the reader. Coffin wisely chose to employ a light hand as he let the soldiers and their families long dead describe what their experiences were like. His efforts are enriched by the high literacy level found among Vermonters of the 1860s, most of whom were blessed by the state with a good education. Consequently, primary accounts of participants survive in large numbers in letters to local newspapers, letters to and from loved ones, journals, reminiscences, and unit histories written and published during the first 30 years after the cannon ceased to roar.

As a World War II marine—an 18-year-old who enlisted in the spring of 1942—I found many of these soldiers' experiences familiar, and others foreign. The call to arms for the volunteers of Stannard's brigade came more than 15 months after the guns of Fort Sumter spoke, and much of the innocent enthusiasm that gripped the men and boys who in April and July 1861 answered their nation's call was absent. Once organized, mustered, and sent to help defend the nation's capital, long months in camp and on guard and picket duty ensued. During this time, the Vermonters became aware of an experience common to most infantrymen and marines of World War II: "Hurry up and wait." These were important months, however, in molding character and preparing them for the arduous march from Bull Run to Pennsylvania and the battle of Gettysburg.

Thanks to Howard Coffin, we may now appreciate and know these men, their hopes and fears, their love of the Union, and their reasons for taking up arms. Apprised of these factors, it will come as no surprise to learn that when summoned, three of the five regiments of Stannard's Second Vermont Brigade left a significant mark on what many of us perceive as one of the climactic events of our nation's history. Thank you, my friend.

Edwin C. Bearss
Historian Emeritus, National Park Service

PREFACE

In 1864 Edwin Palmer, an attorney and former sergeant in the Second Vermont Brigade, published a book on his nine months of military service titled *The Second Brigade, or Camp Life*. He began with a description of his first hours as a soldier and then looked ahead to the brigade's rendezvous with history:

"The boys, rolled in their blankets, are lying in their straw bunks, and the day is ended. In the afternoon of the next day, we are inspected by the governor and adjutant general, with knapsacks, haversacks and all on, for the first time. Around we go, each carrying thirty to fifty pounds—swaying this way and that way, especially as we wheel. One jogs his neighbor, and he his, the momentum increasing as the jogging passes along, till the left of the companies is quite broken. The knapsack don't hang quite easy. It is the first time. Now you see one of the weaker ones—his head half down to his knees—raising it higher on his shoulders; half are getting them in new positions. An old soldier that moves with such steadiness, though he has been through the same process, would smile and mutter, 'You'll lighten those knapsacks before you march far.' But is it strange? The farmer is made lame the first day he mows. Can the scholar or merchant use the sickle or swing the scythe? Are they poor soldiers? I saw them nine months later, when our thinned and shattered ranks were giving way, charge down the plain a hundred rods in front, and capture eight cannon from the foe; I saw them on the third of July, long ere the sun had risen, roused from sleeping on their guns, by hostile cannon, in the front line of battle, till nine o'clock at night, not withstanding the furious onslaughts of the enemy, till they were rolled in frightful heaps, and not a man breathed in their front, that dared to flaunt a rebel flag in their faces, and now he, who looks upon the tattered banner they bore on that victorious day, may read 'Gettysburg' inscribed for their signal bravery."

The citizen soldiers of Brig. Gen. George Jerrison Stannard's Second Vermont Brigade, hours and days from termination of their nine-months enlistments and engaged in their first fighting, were in the thick of the Civil War's greatest battle, Gettysburg. On the second day, as Gen. James Longstreet's flank attack threatened to shatter the Union line, the brigade came onto Cemetery Ridge, stabilized part of the line, and counterattacked to recapture a battery near the Emmitsburg Road. The next day, as Pickett's Charge drove against Cemetery Ridge, Stannard swung his brigade out into a no-man's-land of shot and shell to shatter the flank of perhaps the most important assault of the entire war.

Across the century and a third that has passed since the Civil War, the nine-months regiments have generally been forgotten. No book has ever attempted to summarize their service. Indeed, only one book—with the exception of postwar regimental histories—seems to have been written about any of the regiments. That book, *Shower of Stars*, concerns a Maine outfit whose members were awarded Medals of Honor as an incentive to prolong their enlistments a few days after Gettysburg. In researching this book, I contacted several Civil War historian friends, and few could recall anything about those regiments—save for the Second Vermont

Brigade. It seems that the veteran units and their commanders had little confidence in the short-term soldiers, and therefore called on them for few important tasks. Veteran soldiers, enlisted for two or three years, saw them as men who were trying to get through their service as quickly and safely as possible. Apparently most of the units did their time and went home without having accomplished anything of note. They have faded into history.

According to Wilbur Fisk, a private in the First Vermont Brigade who served nearly four years, most of his fellow soldiers in the First also had little use for the short-term men, particularly for those who were briefly made part of their brigade. "The 26th New Jersey regiment belongs to this brigade," Fisk wrote on April 26, 1863, "a regiment of nine months men who came out here with big bounties, and, of course, has seen more hardships, endured more privations, and suffered more generally than any of the old soldiers ever dreamed. The boys call them 'two hundred dollar men,' and take wicked delight in playing their pranks on them whenever they get the chance."

Though the Second Vermont Brigade served with distinction and received wide acclaim, as the years have passed its five regiments have been somewhat forgotten, even in Vermont. The best-known story of Vermont and Gettysburg concerns the First Vermont Brigade, which was positioned behind Big Round Top and did not fight. Legend has it that on the way to Gettysburg, Sixth Corps commander John Sedgwick sent the following order after being told to hurry his troops toward the fighting: "Put the Vermonters in the lead and keep the column well closed."

Yet, to have grown up in Vermont and know of its part in the Civil War is to have a sense that something very important occurred concerning the Green Mountain State on the shot-torn fields of Gettysburg. In 1972 a Vermonter, Newton Burdick, put it well in a little book he wrote and published: "The view from my window from my desk corner is as old as the hills. The view looks like an old painting with Ascutney, forty miles south, rising in the centre of it. Beyond that in the subdued twilight of reminiscence looms Gettysburg, five hundred miles south, except that part of it lodged here."

The men of the Second Vermont Brigade were proud of their achievements and believed them to have been of singular importance. In the introduction to his history of the 13th Vermont, regimental historian Ralph Sturtevant wrote: "As long as civilization shall last will the heroic charge of the Second Vermont Brigade stand as the most important and far reaching in its result of any during the Civil War."

Certainly in the immediate aftermath of the great battle, the Vermonters got their due. According to the *New York Times:* "A Vermont brigade held the key position at Gettysburg and did more than any body of men to gain the triumph which decided the fate of the Union." Maj. Gen. Abner Doubleday, who commanded the division in which the nine-months Vermonters fought, told the Committee on the Conduct of the War: "The prisoners stated that what ruined them was Stannard's brigade on their flank, as they found it impossible to contend with it in that position; and they drew off, all in a huddle, to get away from it." Lt. Col. C.H. Morgan, on the staff of Maj. Gen. Winfield Scott Hancock, said, "Stannard's fire was more than the hard pressed enemy could stand, and thousands of them sought safety by themselves on the ground, and holding up their handkerchiefs or a piece of white paper in token of surrender."

The importance of the Vermonters' flank attack is well appreciated by modern-day historians. James McPherson, author of *Battle Cry of Freedom*, has said "Union veterans in three-year regiments had a low opinion of most nine-months regiments. But the outstanding performance of the Second Vermont Brigade at Gettysburg, which helped turn the tide of battle, changed their minds insofar as the Vermonters were concerned." Edwin Coddington, one of the foremost authorities on the battle, wrote in his *The Gettysburg Campaign: A Study in Command:* "The important thing is that the 13th Vermont, followed by the 16th Vermont on its left, pivoted ninety degrees to the right and fired a succession of volleys at pistol range on Pickett's right flank. Despite the efforts of five Confederate guns advanced beyond Alexander's line by Major J.C. Haskell to break up this movement, the Vermonters persisted in their attack. The effect of their assault cannot be precisely gauged, but without a doubt it was largely responsible in destroying the ability of the Confederates to exploit their gains (to the north). The Vermonters exacted a heavy toll from the Virginians in lives and prisoners and threatened to cut them off completely." Gettysburg historian Kathleen Georg Harrison, who has studied the flank attack in depth, wrote: "Stannard's Vermont Brigade began its flanking movement during the attack phase of the Confederate assault, and was responsible not only for a major part of the repulse of the Virginians which was to follow, but was the major factor in driving Pickett's Division into each other and compressing them into a confused and disorganized mass." She has also said of Stannard's attack, "It definitely was the most important infantry maneuver, bold and decisive, and tactically perfect." Edwin Cole Bearss has said that "Stannard's flank attack was the most important infantry maneuver directed against the Confederate assault. It was so important that Winfield Scott Hancock tried to claim credit for it."

In 1959 historian George R. Stewart produced a book called *Pickett's Charge,* a 350-page account of the climactic event at Gettysburg. He wrote of Stannard's moment of decision: "Stannard suddenly realized that his Vermonters might become agents of the destiny of the nation. It was a time to be measured in seconds . . . At that moment, the battle hung in the balance . . . Hancock had decided to throw the Vermonters on Pickett's flank. Stannard, himself, had the same idea, and by the time that Hancock spurred up, shouting orders, Stannard already has his men in motion. Now the long months of tedious close order drills suddenly paid off for the Vermonters . . . The three nine-months regiments of Vermonters, their time having expired, were mustered out days after the battle. They went home and were received—not entirely incorrectly—as the heroes of Gettysburg."

The introduction to Stewart's book begins: "If we grant—as many would be ready to do—that the Civil War furnishes the great dramatic episode of the history of the United States, and that Gettysburg provides the climax of the war, then the climax of the climax, the central moment of our history, must be Pickett's Charge."

The men of the Second Vermont Brigade contributed mightily to that "central moment," delivering a withering flank fire into the ranks of Robert E. Lee's brave boys. As was noted on the Medal of Honor awarded Col. Wheelock Veazey, commander of the 16th Vermont, the Vermont troops were "new troops in their first battle."

As the century in which the Civil War veterans died out nears its close, the soaring Vermont monument on Cemetery Ridge, the first large state monument erected at Gettysburg and still among the most prominent on the battlefield, does not seem oversized. Indeed, it seems a most appropriate pedestal from which General Stannard may ever gaze over the ground that he and his nine-months boys of the Second Vermont Brigade did so much to defend and thereby—in the words of Lincoln—to dedicate, consecrate, and hallow, in those mighty days of July 1863. And they have left us their story.

Civil War soldiers were prolific letter writers, particularly in the early stages of their enlistments when the military experience was new and they were unused to being away from home. The writing of the soldiers of the Second Vermont Brigade, who served less than a year, hardly waned from the day they left home to the day they returned. This book is the saga of the brigade's nine months of service, told in their own words.

This book is without footnotes, but the sources of information are identified. A quotation not attributed in the list of sources is generally from an unsigned letter to a newspaper or—if it is from a member of the 13th Vermont Regiment—from that unit's official regimental history.

I have long been fascinated by the individual experiences in the Civil War, and have tried to learn what being at war was like for both Northerners and Southerners. I have been particularly interested in what happened to Vermonters, for my people go back six generations in the state and my great-grandfathers fought in the Civil War. I have also been drawn to the places where they drilled, camped, marched, and fought, and I describe how those places look, and feel, today.

More than 34,000 Vermonters served during the Civil War, and more than 5,000 gave their lives. The farm boys, store clerks, quarry workers, hired hands, schoolteachers, and lawyers generally volunteered willingly, many leaving home for the first time. Most were the products of farm upbringings; duty was inbred, hard work was the way of life, and the Bible was read after supper, teaching its lessons of faith and eternal life. With such a background the Vermonters proved to be excellent soldiers, and the First Vermont Brigade, time and again placed in critical positions on major battlefields, suffered more casualties than any other brigade in the Union armies. Then came the nine-months Second Vermont Brigade, some 5,000 strong, who shone in one of the war's most severe tests.

When you look at the dull and faded photographs the men of Stannard's brigade once sent home to loved ones, remember that those Vermont men and boys were not as they appear. The slow cameras of the day required that they be still for some considerable time—too long to hold a smile. Recall that they were not all grim and sober faced, stiff necked and rigid. They were full of life and laughter. Their faces were deeply tanned, and their blue, green, brown, or gray eyes sparkled. They were young, full of chatter and pranks and sometimes quiet tears. They knew the same hills and valleys, rivers and mountains, that we do.

They knew beauty and terror, and loved life as much as we do, though because of their strong faith they did not so much fear to die. They hurt and bled, they loved and yearned, and at times they were lonesome, or rough and mean. They played and worked hard, despaired, and shirked. They went to war and came to know more of the range of life's experiences in their often too short years than many of us will in our full lifetimes. And now they are all gone. It is a pity that we did not know them. It is a blessing that we know what we do of these people who, in a time of fire, knew Wolf Run Shoals and Fairfax Station, Bull Run, the rivers Occoquan and Potomac, the long roads of Maryland and Pennsylvania, and, most especially, the fury and agony of Gettysburg.

PART I

Disaster on the Peninsula:
Lincoln Calls Up
the Militia

Vermont Gov. Frederick Holbrook urged Abraham Lincoln to call hundreds of thousands more men into the Union armies.

I

On March 30, 1862, a soldier in the Army of the Potomac, Joseph Spafford, took pen in hand to write a letter to his sister in the little valley village of Perkinsville, Vermont; it read, in part: "This hospital life grows rather dull after one gets to feeling pretty well. Rainy days when passes are not given to go out, I sit in my room all day long reading, writing, and thinking. I hear from my room from the time I first wake in the morning till I go to sleep at night the clank, clank, clank of the soldiers' swords as they rattle on the sidewalks as they are passing up and down. That sound is almost as regular as the ticking of a clock, from morning till night. Every little while we hear a band, and look from our window to see the Regts. as they come in here to go 'down to the river' . . . Many boats are at the wharves today."

Spafford's letter, from a military hospital in Alexandria, Virginia, provides a glimpse of the huge army that Maj. Gen. George Brinton McClellan led in the late winter of 1862 down to the Peninsula of Virginia. Hopes in the Union states were high that Richmond, the Confederate capital, would fall quickly and that the fearful Civil War would soon be over.

In the early summer of 1862, another Vermont soldier, Col. Wheelock Veazey, wrote to his wife, "Thursday, June 26, Jackson appeared on our right flank and made an attack. Since then it has been fight, fight almost daily . . . Nothing can equal the desperation with which the rebels tried to annihilate us. As soon as one force was repulsed they would press us with another and so on for 6 or 8 times until their dead blocked the way."

Between the two letters, the Peninsula Campaign ended in dismal and bloody failure. McClellan's army of 100,000 had moved ponderously, but with the power of a glacier, to the outskirts of Richmond. Then, on May 31, Confederate Gen. Joseph Johnston brought the advance to a standstill, hitting McClellan at Seven Pines, amid the woods and fields bordering the Chickahominy River. Johnston was seriously wounded, and Confederate President Jefferson Davis quickly named Robert E. Lee as his replacement.

There were a few days of quiet, the Union soldiers able to set their watches by the sound of clocks striking in Richmond. Then Lee brought in Stonewall Jackson's army from the Shenandoah Valley and struck on June 26. In seven days of fierce fighting, Lee battered the Union army at Beaver Dam Creek, Gaines's Mills, Savage Station, and Glendale. McClellan finally brought the killing to a close, bloodily repulsing a heavy but futile rebel attack up the long slope of Malvern Hill. Still, McClellan's attempt at seizing Richmond had ended in a staggering reversal.

In Washington, Abraham Lincoln took the news hard. Many years later, Carl Sandburg wrote: "Slowly, at last, the whole story had to be told to the country of the Seven Days' battles. Out over the country, in homes where had been faith, doubts crept in. The national mood reached the White House, where the president sat in the library writing, 'with directions to deny him to everybody.' Senator Browning stepped in a moment and in the evening wrote, 'he looked weary, care-worn and troubled. I shook hands with him, and asked him how he was. He said "tolerably well" and remarked that I felt concerned about him—regretted that troubles crowded so heavily upon him, and feared his health was suffering. He held me by the hand, pressed it, and said in a very tender and touching tone—"Browning, I must die sometime." I replied, "your fortunes Mr. President are bound up with those of the Country, and disaster to one would be disaster to the other, and I hope you will do all you can to preserve your health and life." He looked very sad, and there was a cadence of deep sadness in his voice. We parted I believe both of us with tears in our eyes. The Army of the Potomac, its sick and wounded, its cannon and horses, its farm hands, shopmen, college boys, store clerks, was brought back from the Peninsula to old places on the Potomac River within sight of the Capitol.'"

Before the defeated army came back north, Colonel Veazey wrote from "Camp Near Harrison's Landing" on July 17, 1862: "I wish the war would end & we could go home. It might be ended this Autumn, but only by an immediate draft of a half million men. Waiting for enlistments will miss campaigns. 300,000 will not be enough raised."

Veazey's letter was prophetic; in the coming weeks Abraham Lincoln, never one to let his deep sadnesses prevent action, called on the nation to send 300,000 three-year soldiers to the Union armies. Little more than a month later, on August 4, 1862, the president summoned 300,000 more men to serve for just nine months. Nearly 5,000 Vermonters would answer the latter call, filling five regiments to constitute the Second Vermont Brigade. Spafford and Veazey, originally members of regiments in the First Vermont Brigade, would return home to serve in the new short-term outfits. Those regiments' brief terms of enlistment would, just barely, include the Civil War's greatest battle—Gettysburg. No state—on a per capita basis, at least—would be harder hit by the organizing of the nine-months regiments than Vermont. No nine-months regiments from any other state would make a contribution equal to that of those sent to war by Vermont.

•　　•　　•

In 1863, preacher and abolitionist Henry Ward Beecher delivered a speech at Boston's Music Hall on the subject of New England. He began, "There lies, between the St. Lawrence and the Atlantic Ocean, a little gore of land, a few hundred miles wide and long, that seems to have been made up of fragments and leavings, after the rest of the continent was made. Its ribs stick out beyond all covering, it has sand enough to scour all creation; there are no large rivers, but there are many nimble little ones, that seem to have been busy since the floods, in taking exercise over rifts and rocks."

In the northwestern corner of the six states that make up New England lies the state of Vermont, scarcely 9,000 square miles, longer than it is wide, rather wedge shaped, and lying between 120-mile Lake Champlain on the west and the Connecticut River on the east. Vermont's most prominent summits poke up from the long Green Mountain Range running north–south down its center. More or less level farmlands fill the Champlain Valley, becoming increasingly hilly as they rise toward the Green Mountains. On the northern border, the great plain of Canada touches down into Vermont and makes the landscape comparatively level, at least in the far northwestern corner. But along the international border to the east, the terrain bumps up and a near wilderness of thickly forested hills and mountains emerges. South from the borderlands, all the way to Massachusetts, Vermont is a jumble of steep hills and mountains, with rocky farm fields cleared along the narrow valleys and up the hillsides. Here and there, where the swift streams come to falls, there were, as the Civil War approached, mill towns, here and there a village allowed by the slight parting of the hillsides to be a street, or two or three, wide. Vermonters have always been tempted to believe the adage that if the state were flattened out, it would be larger than Texas.

Vermonters are proud that their state had existed as an independent republic for 14 years before it was granted, in 1791, admittance as the 14th state of the United States of America. The republic's Constitution, adopted in 1777, had been the first in America to at least partially outlaw slavery. In the years preceding the breakup of the Union, abolitionists such as Frederick Douglass, William Lloyd Garrison, and Wendell Phillips visited Vermont time and again and generally were listened to by enthusiastic audiences. The Underground Railroad routed many escaped slaves through the state, providing them with safe passage, making good on the famed decree of a Vermont judge, in nullifying the Fugitive Slave Act, that the only acceptable proof of one person having ownership of another would be "a bill of sale from God almighty."

As the Civil War neared, patriotic fever gripped the Green Mountain State. Pro-war rallies were held in almost every town, and militia companies formed in virtually all communities of any significant size. With the firing on Fort Sumter, Gov. Erastus Fairbanks called the Vermont General Assembly into special session, already having replied to an inquiry from President Lincoln as to what might be expected of his state: "Vermont will do its full duty." Fairbanks opened the session by asking the lawmakers to appropriate half a million dollars to support Vermont's war effort. They responded, after fervent nonpartisan discussion, by voting a full million dollars, a huge sum for the times and the size of the state.

Before receiving any legislative sanction, Fairbanks ordered a Vermont infantry regiment formed, the First Vermont Infantry. That unit, 1,000 strong, went south on May 9, and soon fought in the war's first battle, the confused shoot-out at Big Bethel, Virginia. By that time, the Second Vermont Regiment—a three-year unit—had been organized and sent south to fight in the first big battle, Manassas. Four more three-year regiments, the Third, Fourth, Fifth, and Sixth

Vermont, joined the Second Vermont in the ranks of the Army of the Potomac in time for the Peninsula Campaign. With special permission from General McClellan, sought and received by Vermonter William Farrar (Baldy) Smith, those five regiments were assembled into one command, the First Vermont Brigade. It would be the only brigade in the Union army composed entirely of the regiments of one state that would serve throughout the war. Vermont first experienced heavy casualties on April 16, 1862, when General McClellan ordered the brigade to make an unsupported attack across the Warwick River near Yorktown, Virginia. Two months later, in the Seven Days' battles, the Fifth Vermont sustained the heaviest casualties of any Vermont regiment during the entire war in a rearguard action at Savage Station: 65 killed, 148 wounded.

Governor Fairbanks's single-year term ended in the fall of 1861. A farmer and inventor with a musical bent, Frederick Holbrook, was then elected Vermont's chief executive. A resident of Brattleboro, a prosperous manufacuring community on the Connecticut River near where Vermont, New Hampshire, and Massachusetts join, Governor Holbrook was a Massachusetts native. He promptly called up the Seventh and Eighth regiments, which were sent to Louisiana in the New England Division of Gen. Benjamin F. Butler. Then the Ninth Vermont was formed, destined to be captured en masse by Stonewall Jackson at Harpers Ferry. (Its moments of glory would come later.)

When the news reached him of the losses at Lee's Mills, Holbrook badgered the federal government into allowing him to build military hospitals in Vermont. Eventually three such hospitals were opened. Holbrook also urged his fellow governors to raise troops for the war effort. Many years later Holbrook recalled: "The call in 1862 for 300,000 three-year volunteers, followed very soon after in that year for 300,000 nine-months men, resulted from a letter I wrote to the president earnestly and frankly setting forth the fact, well known to us, from my point of outlook, that a very large additional force was immediately needed to crush the rebellion, and urging him at once to call for 500,000 three-year volunteers, assuring that the people of the loyal states would respond to such a call . . . On receiving the letter, the President, Secretary of War [Edwin M. Stanton] and Provost Marshall General Simon Draper, had a session over it at the secretary's office, the president taking out my letter and saying, 'I have a letter from Governor Holbrook of Vermont which solves all my doubts and difficulties about calling for more men.'

"General Draper was immediately dispatched to Vermont to call on and confer with me, and have such a paper formulated as I thought the loyal governors would be willing to sign, recommending and endorsing such a call for men, and General Draper appearing in my office two days later, such a paper was agreed upon."

Holbrook noted that a letter asking Lincoln to order a call-up of troops was circulated to the northern states' governors for their signatures: "While preparations for issuing the call were in progress at Washington, Governor Yates of Illinois, not yet knowing what steps were being taken to reinforce the Union army, wrote a desponding letter to President Lincoln about the discouraging aspects of the war. He was a brother lawyer and intimate friend of Mr. Lincoln's and so the president, in his characteristic way, at once telegraphed this reply to Governor Yates' letter—'Wait a little, Dick, and see the salvation of the Lord.' Within a day or two after, Governor Yates received the call for more volunteers.

"Upon receiving the call I at once wrote to the president again, thanking him for the call, but expressing the opinion that it should have been for a larger number of men, and hoping it would be succeeded very soon by another call, for I felt certain they would be needed to bring the war to a close. Very soon the call for 300,000 nine months men did come."

The governors' letter was printed in the Woodstock newspaper, *The Vermont Standard:*

> To the President,
>
> The undersigned, governors of the States of the Union, impressed with the belief that the citizens of the States which they respectively represent are of one accord in the hearty desire that the recent success of the federal arms may be followed up by measures which most speedily ensure the speedy restoration of the Union . . . we respectfully request, if it meets with your entire approval, that you will at once call on the several states for such number of men as may be required to fill up all military organizations now in the field, and add to the army heretofore organized such additional numbers of men as may, in your judgement, be necessary . . . All believe the decisive moment is at hand.

Though the governors were stretching the facts by referring to the Peninsula Campaign, despite the repulse at Malvern Hill, as a "recent success," 18 chief executives signed the letter, Holbrook being the third. His reminiscences, crafted more than 40 years after the war, today seem a bit naive. Obviously, he was involved in mustering support for raising more troops. But Lincoln was well ahead of the governors. The call for 300,000 three-year men had, indeed, come after receipt of that letter, but the president had apparently had members of his cabinet at work drumming up enthusiasm for it, and it came as no surprise. Indeed, as Pulitzer Prize–winning historian James McPherson has written, "Seward hastened to New York and conferred with the northern governors. They agreed to issue an address (written by Seward) to the president urging him to call on the states for new volunteers." Lincoln made the missive public before issuing the call for volunteers, telling General McClellan that he had been "offered" 300,000 men by the governors. Placing the impetus for bringing more men into uniform and putting them at risk on the loyal states rather than the administration was a clever strategy.

Lincoln certainly knew that many more men would be needed. On July 17, Congress had passed a "Militia Law," which provided that all able-bodied men between the ages of 18 and 45 were legally part of the militia, and empowered the president to call the militia into federal service for nine months. Civil War historian Bruce Catton wrote, "As the law stood, the president could not compel citizens to go into the United States army. He could, however, draft the state militia for nine months . . . This authority, cut and stretched to fit the emergency, was now put in use. On August 4 the president called on the states to enroll 300,000 militia, adding the provision that if by August 15 any state failed to meet its quota under the previous call for volunteers, men would be drafted from the militia to make up the deficiency."

More than a century later, historian McPherson called the militia call-up "a quasi-draft."

In Vermont, a state about to be ordered to fill five of the new regiments, the governor was sure that his constituents would meet the new call. Holbrook, the only Vermont governor to serve two full (single-year) terms during the Civil War, had made clear from the start where he stood. In his first inaugural address at the State House in Montpelier in the fall of 1861, he had assessed the feelings of Vermonters regarding the growing conflict. "They are willing to expend their blood and treasure, if need be," he said, "to the fullest extent of their means to aid the national government in crushing this causeless rebellion." Holbrook, during his 24 months in office, put that resolve sternly to the test; calling up 12 infantry regiments and two artillery batteries would be his principal legacy.

In 1860, the year before the Civil War began, Vermont had a population of 315,000. In the summer of 1862, with nine regiments in the field and the first dead and wounded having come home, Vermont had already made a major commitment of its flesh and treasure. Now another 4,898 men were being asked to volunteer.

Catton wrote, "In August of 1862 America's tragedy was that it was caught between the madness of going on with the war and the human impossibility of stopping it." By the time the war ended, in the spring of 1865, Vermont had sent 34,238 men to the Union armed forces, more than a tenth of its entire population.

★

2

As spring turned to summer in 1862, Vermont still wore the look of peace. True, some 10,000 native sons had already gone to war, and hundreds had come home in caskets (many more dead of disease than of wounds). Many communities were bustling, such as Windsor on the Connecticut River, where rifle-muskets were being manufactured; nearby Felchville, where the woolen mill was turning out military uniforms; and Brattleboro, where the railroads brought still more men for training, just before going south to war. Most of the more than 30,000 farms still functioned, though with their lads gone, a far heavier burden fell on father, mother, and daughters.

In Burlington, on northern Lake Champlain, junior editor George Benedict, publishing the daily *Burlington Free Press* alongside his father, regularly editorialized in support of a vigorous war effort to subdue the seceded states. In the valley town of Cavendish, 100 miles to the south, Redfield Proctor was home from the war and on the family farm, recuperating from tuberculosis and eager to return to the army. Over a few ridges in West Windsor, Daniel Hammond, with the help of his six sons, was running his farm and providing the services of hearse driver and general jack-of-all-trades to the town. But four of his boys were old enough to serve, and no doubt their endless chatter about things military had him believing that some would soon be leaving home.

To the west, on a high hill farm in the shadow of Pico and Killington Peaks, the question of whether the time was coming to volunteer his services weighed heavily on the mind of William Doubleday. But there were four young children to think about; besides, like most Vermont men raised on farms, he had never really been away from home. Wheelock Veazey, fresh from service on the Peninsula, was in New Hampshire at the home of his wife's family, enjoying the company of his bride of half a year. Veazey had recently opened a law practice in Springfield, Vermont, but was determined to return to the armies. He had high hopes of getting command of a new Vermont regiment, as did his best friend over in Cavendish, Redfield Proctor.

In Hinesburg, near Lake Champlain, members of the Mead family were making plans for spending some of the hot July days at the hotel near the top of Vermont's highest summit, Mount Mansfield. Meanwhile, Charles Mead had decided to enlist in one of the new regiments. Also back in Vermont, after a failed try at raising a company for the Second Vermont, was John Lonergan, by no means

*Wheelock Veazey returned from the Peninsula seeking
command of a nine-months Vermont regiment.*

ready to return to his dry goods business in Winooski. He was talking with many young Irish lads about joining him in a predominantly Irish company to fight in the armies of his adopted country.

In Waterbury, Edwin Palmer, fresh out of Dartmouth, was serving a clerkship in the office of Atty. Paul Dillingham. But Palmer, too, had decided to enlist, and would soon wear a sergeant's stripes in the 13th Regiment.

In the northwestern Vermont town of Swanton, Stephen Brown, 20 years old and with distinctly Native American features, a schoolteacher since age 16 now studying Latin and Greek in preparation for college, had long been ready for war. But his first attempt at enlistment had been foiled by his parents. A year before, when his 44-year-old father was as impatient to enlist as he was, Brown's mother had stepped in, saying she could not spare them both, and held two straws for them to draw. Her husband drew first, took the long one, and was off to war. Stephen worked the farm until his father returned. Now the son was about to sign up.

In the northern town of Fairfield, 24-year-old Ralph Sturtevant, a descendant of some of Vermont's earliest settlers, decided to enlist. That meant setting aside the two jobs he held part time—teaching and house painting.

In Brattleboro, Governor Holbrook ran the affairs of state in a downtown office, except when the legislature was in session and he roomed in Montpelier. He was an inventor and made notes on ideas concerning some new and improved

Woodstock, Vermont, site of the Vermont adjutant general's office in which the state's Civil War effort was administered, seen just before the war began.

farm implements. He also directed a local church choir and, when time permitted, liked to slip away to Boston for an opera performance.

Thinking of bigger things, and still in the army, with the Fourth Vermont Regiment under his command, was Col. Edwin Stoughton. The remarkably handsome young warrior and ladies' man, infatuated with a New York woman, had set his sights on a general's star and on the command not of a regiment, but of a brigade.

The long days were bringing forth a good second crop of hay, and the sap buckets had been washed and put away for the season. Though the papers daily brought more and more news of war, life went on generally unimpeded in Vermont, 500 miles and more from the thunder of the guns. But there was growing cause for concern that the faraway events would soon call forth more young men not yet sent to war. And that call would come from Woodstock, one of the state's lovelier and more peaceful-appearing villages.

Located slightly south and east of the center of Vermont, in the foothills of the Green Mountains where the valley of the gently flowing Ottauquechee River is met by a brook with the biblical name Kedron, there the hills opened to accommodate a village that in 1860 was home to more than 3,000 Vermonters. Because of its beauty, with neat redbrick and white-frame homes set on quiet elm- and maple-shaded streets and around a distinctive boat-shaped green, the village was already attracting travelers and people seeking summer refuge from the hot cities. Woodstock has always been a town of outsized importance to Vermont, and the Civil War years were no exception. Before the war it had been a hotbed of abolition and a stop on the Underground Railway. As the war began, it was the home of the influential U.S. Sen. Jacob Collamer. Peter Washburn, a lawyer of statewide prominence with a flair for soldiering, had drilled the Woodstock Light Infantry to be the finest military company in the state, and he and the company had gone off to serve in the First Vermont Regiment. Washburn had led some 500 Vermonters into the fight at Big Bethel, and took pride in the fact that, in defeat, his men had advanced closest to the Confederate entrenchments. Washburn had come home to run successfully for election, by the legislature, as adjutant general and inspector general of Vermont, to administer Vermont's war effort. He set up shop in an office overlooking the village square, and thus most of the business of Vermont at war was being handled in Woodstock. Indeed, in the parlance of a later age, the town might have been called the "Pentagon" of Vermont.

On August 8, a Woodstock newspaper, the *Vermont Standard,* carried the following notice, as did most Vermont papers:

> WAR DEPARTMENT, WASHINGTON, D.C., AUGUST 4—Ordered, first, that a draft of three hundred thousand militia be immediately called into the service of the United States, to serve for nine months, unless sooner discharged.

The same day, the *Bellows Falls Sentinel* ran the following headline:

GOOD NEWS
ANOTHER 300,000 CALLED FOR

On August 10, Governor Holbrook received instructions from Secretary of War Edwin M. Stanton setting Vermont's quota at 4,898 men. The next day, with recruitment still under way for the three-year 10th and 11th regiments, Holbrook issued a general order for a new enrollment of the Vermont militia, to comprise all able-bodied men between the ages of 18 and 45. Washburn promptly set enlistment quotas for each town in the state. In most, rallies were held to encourage enlistments and to raise money for bounty payments as a further stimulus for local lads to sign on.

On August 15, in Woodstock, the adjutant general issued General Order 11, which was printed in most Vermont papers: "In pursuance of directions issued by the President of the United States, dated the ninth day of August, A.D. 1862, it is hereby ordered as follows:

"1. The Listers of the several towns in the State will forthwith enroll all elegible able-bodied male citizens, between the ages of eighteen and forty-five, in their respective towns, giving the name, age and occupation of each, together with remarks, showing whether he is in the service of the United States, and in what capacity, and say other facts, which may determine his exemption from military duty.

"The following diseases and imperfections are proper causes of military disability;—Wounds of the head, which impair the faculties or cause convulsions,

Peter Washburn, the Woodstock lawyer and combat veteran
who served as Vermont adjutant general.

serious impairment of hearing, speech, or vision; Anchylosis, or active disease of any of the larger joints; the presence of pulmonary disease, or organic disease of the heart; hernia; fistula in ano; large hemorrhoids; large and painful variocele, or varicose veins, which extend above the knee; the loss of a limb, or of the thumb and forefinger of the right hand; any marked physical imperfection, which would unfit for active service."

On August 13 came a general order from Governor Holbrook: No recruiting officers would be appointed, but town officers and patriotic citizens would be expected to enlist men and form companies. "The commander in chief confidently expects," Holbrook wrote, "that before the time for a legal draft shall arrive, every man necessary to complete the requisition upon the State will be furnished; and he trusts to the people of the State to carry out his wishes, in their own way, without the intervention of recruiting officers or other official agencies."

The *Vermont Standard* observed on August 22: "Those who imagine that our State authorities, upon whom it devolves to put into the field Vermont's quota of troops, have an 'easy time' ought to have spent a little time last week in observing the workings of the Adjutant General's Office. Notwithstanding that he has four assistants it was only by unceasing labor night and day that he could issue the requisite orders, and the instructions . . . Number of letters received per days averages between seventy-five and one hundred."

There was much work to be done, for the Vermont militia by the summer of 1862 amounted to anything but a formidable military entity. Indeed, 15 years before the war, all state laws requiring the maintenance and equipping of local companies had been repealed. By 1856, there were no active militia companies in any of Vermont's towns. But in 1858, with trouble brewing in the border states, abolitionist Gov. Ryland Fletcher had attempted to revive the militia, and by the end of 1860 state records showed 22 organized companies. Then came war, and by May 1861, 56 companies had been organized and reported themselves ready for war. Many of their members enlisted and went off with the early Vermont infantry regiments, so that by midsummer of 1862, again only 22 companies were listed on state rosters. Nine of those units had formally disbanded; thus, when the call went out for nine-months men, only 13 companies were able to respond. New companies quickly began assembling. A few of the larger towns were able to form companies on their own. Burlington, the state's most populous community, mounted two companies, the Howard Guards and the Emmett Guards. Most units formed in the largest town in a particular locale and drew members from surrounding hamlets and farms. The Middlebury Company in the Champlain Valley also included men from Salisbury, Addison, Cornwall, Whiting, Shoreham, Weybridge, and Ripton. The McIndoe Falls Company in northeastern Vermont drew volunteers from Barnet, Peacham, Ryegate, Danville, Coventry, Greensboro, Barton, Waterford, and a few from well-populated St. Johnsbury, which had already turned out its own unit.

The companies gave themselves jaunty names that would last only until they went to war, at which time the militia units became Company A, Company B, Company C, and so on, of the various regiments. Brandon had its Allen Greys; Rutland, the Rutland Light Guard; Northfield, the New England Guards; Coventry, the Frontier Guards; Calais, the Lafayette Artillery.

Soon 30 new companies had organized and were steadily building their rosters to the required 100 men. From the capital city came the Montpelier Company, and from the nearby Mad River Valley came the Moretown Company. Towns near the Canadian border in northwestern Vermont and the islands of Lake Champlain provided men for the Highgate Company. The Bakersfield and Bristol Companies formed up from communities along the northern Green Mountains. The northern Connecticut River Valley brought forth the St. Johnsbury Company. From the northeastern section came the Barton Company. In hilly central Vermont, the Bethel and Barnard Companies organized. Southwestern Vermont, from towns along the Taconic Range, sent the Bennington and Wallingford Companies. The Springfield and Ludlow Companies came from the valleys of southeastern Vermont. The Waits River Company was made up of men from along the splashing trout stream that feeds the Connecticut at Bradford. The great recruiting device that was the war meeting was still obtaining results and, remarkably quickly, 43 companies had organized.

★

3

Vermont's town halls drew townspeople in August 1862 to drum up support—and enlistsments—for the new nine-months regiments. Since the towns had just finished meeting quotas to fill three-year regiments, the task of suddenly turning out nearly 5,000 more men (preferably volunteers) was daunting. War meetings had lately been held in almost every village and hamlet, but a new round was quickly organized. Within the white-clapboard town halls, proudly regarded by Vermonters as temples of liberty, the finest orators in town and the local brass bands did their best. In Berlin, bordering Montpelier, according to the *Green Mountain Freeman:* "At 2 o'clock the meeting war [sic] called to order. Rev. J.F. Stone was called out and made a brief and most telling speech. The meeting then enthusiastically passed a resolution directing the Selectmen to pay from the town treasury FIFTY DOLLARS BOUNTY to each man who should volunteer to fill up the quota of Berlin . . . and space was opened in front of the stand, for recruits to come forward."

The article continued: "Five young men immediately stepped into the area and enrolled their names as soldiers for the Army of the Union. Jona A. Woodbury, Esq.—a man with his heart in the right place, and who never goes into anything by 'halves'—now passed up $10 to be divided among the next five who should enlist. The clerk caught the inspiration and proposed himself to add another $10 to the sum. J.E. Bosworth, Esq., of the firm of Bosworth & sons, in a few most touching and fitting remarks, pledged the company to pay $2 each to those, and it was voted to put all contributions into a general fund, to be equally divided among all who should enlist . . . The scene became most interesting and inspiring. Young men were constantly pressing up to enroll their names for the grand Army of Freedom. On all sides men were rushing to the stand with one, three, five or ten dollars . . . Cheer upon cheer shook the Hall to its foundations; the living mass swayed to and fro like the waves of the mighty ocean, as men and money came forward, and the wildest enthusiasm prevailed.

"It was soon announced that the quota—fourteen men—was filled, but as others were on their way to the stand, it was voted to receive them all, and three more enrolled . . . The meeting adjourned with the full assurance that Berlin was ready to do her duty, and her whole duty."

In the capital, Montpelier, the *Freeman* gave this account: "The war meeting Monday night was a rouser. The hall was crowded to the utmost capacity, and the door and entry-way were packed full back to the the street. More than a hundred ladies were present, to urge, by their smiles and praises, brave men to fight for the flag . . . Mr. Heaton spoke earnestly, forcibly and effectually, urging men to enlist. Rev. Mr. Carpenter, of Barre, was next called upon, and he made a stirring and warm hearted speech, which aroused the enthusiasm of the audience. Father Droun, the Catholic priest, was next called out, and 'brought down the house' continually by his sharp, clear, and forcible exposition of the situation of the country, and the necessity that it be rescued from its present peril. In the midst of Father Droun's speech the Barre Brass Band marched into the Hall. After Mr. Droun, Rev. Mr. Ballou made some most stirring remarks. Mr. Stockwell, of Moretown, an old Democrat, and soldier of 1812, in a few strong sentences pressed home upon those present the duty of fighting in defense of the country."

The account went on: "Mr. Carter, one of the volunteers from Waterbury, already enlisted, was called out, and standing before the audience, in a few thrilling words asked others to do as he had done, to leave father, mother, and sweetheart to stand under the Stars and Stripes and fight for the Republic. Mr. Stetson, the Recruiting Officer, then came forward, and the BUSINESS of the evening commenced. Recruits were called for and two young gentlemen, Henry M. Bradley and Albert J. Aher, sprang forward to the platform and put their names on the roll of heroes, the ladies, meanwhile, testifying their appreciation of this patriotism by showering bouquets upon these young men who led the way. Others followed suit, faster than the papers could be made out.

"Mr. James R. Langdon offered to give $10 each to the first twenty-five recruits from Montpelier. S.M. Walton offered $5 each, for the same number, Mr. Collamer and other gentlemen then followed, pledging to guarantee a bounty of $50 to each accepted volunteer. And thus the good work went bravely on, men of means giving freely of their money, and the unselfish ones offering themselves, the Band, meanwhile, playing patriotic airs, until 27 men had enrolled their names in this new war for Republican government. While the enlisting was going on, it was stated that J. Monroe Carr, the third volunteer who stepped forward, left four small children at home while he went into the service of his country, and the ladies unanimously voted that those children be their especial charge while the father was away.

"It was getting late, and some were leaving the Hall, Mr. Brown moved a vote of thanks to the Barre Brass Band, which was voted with a cheer. Three cheers were then proposed and given with a will for those who could go and would go to war. The audience then slowly went away, though the Hall was not empty till nearly or quite midnight."

Several days later the following letter appeared in the *Freeman:*

Brattleboro August 20

The people of Montpelier and adjacent towns have my warmest thanks for their prompt and patriotic response to my proposition for supplying the quota of nine months troops. I called for three cheers in my office today, and some dozen persons gave them with right good will.

FREDERICK HOLBROOK, GOVERNOR

thirty eight of those on the spot, and the sun only set once more before they had fifty, making three to spare.

　—War meeting in Grafton—$4,500 raised by subscription . . . all of their quotas are now full.

But not all went smoothly. The *Sentinel* ran this account of a gathering in the south-central Vermont mountain town of Whitingham: "A war meeting was held at Whitingham Center, on Saturday, the 23d inst. for making some provision for the soldiers who should enlist as volunteers who make up the quota of the 300,000 men called for by the War Department to serve nine months:—The town voted to pay each volunteer for nine months $100 bounty . . . Twenty-six men enrolled their names as volunteers for nine months, the quota of the town being but twenty-two. At the close of business, John Corkins offered the following resolution:

"'Resolved, That John Gates, by voting against paying any bounty, or making any appropriation to aid volunteers who enlist in the service of the United States, has forfeited all claim to the right of citizenship of the town of Whitingham, and ought to be transported to Haystack Mountain, where he could enjoy his selfish propensities unmolested.'

"The motion passed unanimously with loud acclamation."

In Bellows Falls, the *Sentinel* reported, "There has been quite a rush of business at the doctors' offices in this town, this week, by a large number of persons in various parts of the County for certifications of exemption from military duty . . . It is proper to add that many got certificates that they were able to do military duty, which was somewhat different from those they applied for."

Up north, on the western side of Camel's Hump, according to the *Burlington Free Press:* "HONOR TO HUNTINGTON—Huntington has filled her quota, both for three years, and of nine months. Love of country pervades the hearts of her people. Money has been pledged to those who defend our Constitution. These are good men,—those who forsake good business to go at the call of their country. Huntington has furnished over sixty men to the war. Our men say that a draft shall never be made in Huntington."

In Vermont's second largest community, the *Rutland Daily Herald*—the state's oldest newspaper—reported on war meetings in surrounding towns. From little West Haven, on the New York border, the *Herald*'s correspondent wrote: "We are an agricultural people and somewhat removed from the great thoroughfares of our State, and therefore may not as readily catch the enthusiasm of the passing moment as many more highly-favored towns; but when real danger is apprehended, we think no people can boast of a more self-sacrificing devotion to the common weal, than can the citizens of this town . . . After some deliberation and discussion as to the amount of the bounty that should be offered, it was voted that the Selectmen be authorized to pay each volunteer that should be mustered into the service of the United States, the gratuity of fifty dollars."

But in Rutland itself, things were not going so smoothly, much to the chagrin of the local daily. The *Herald* had enthusiastically supported Lincoln's call for nine-months men and had so editorialized on August 15. But a week later, the paper printed the following editorial with the headline, WHERE ARE ALL THE BRAVE MEN: "We cheerfully give place to the following communication from one of our citizens, and we commend it to the thoughtful perusal of our young men:

"Are there none to make sacrifices in Old Rutland? Are the young men all cowards—indifferent spectators to the grand conflict which is raging? Are they waiting for the gray-headed men, of a past generation to shoulder the musket and defend the LIBERTIES of a pusillanimous race of young men? . . . Other towns all around us are nobly responding to the call of their country, and their citizens scorn to be drafted. We hear from every section of the State that Vermont's quota will be filled without a draft, UNLESS IT BE IN RUTLAND! Shall RUTLAND have the notoriety of being the only town in Vermont from whence soldiers were dragged along to war as CONSCRIPTS? It is to be wondered at, as stated by one of the speakers in the war meeting Saturday evening, that the young ladies of the town of Rutland are making aprons for the young men who linger at home without sufficient excuse?"

Despite that fiery challenge, a draft began in Rutland before the big town's quota was met. In the end, those drafted agreed to list themselves as volunteers, and Rutland did not show a single draftee on the roll of its new militia company.

Among those in Rutland who went voluntarily was William Jackson. Just 19, with an artistic nature and working as a touch-up expert in the studio of a local photographer, he noted in his diary August 18, "Made an application in the Rutland Light Guard—Capt. Kingsley Commanding. I had previously made up my mind to enlist. God knows that the country needs me and I regard it as the duty of every able bodied man who can possibly do so to enlist at once the sooner the better and it is better by far to enlist voluntarily than to be dragged into the army a conscript. Nothing to me would appear more degrading."

So Vermont met its quota. By mid-September, 43 companies with about 4,000 men in the ranks had signed on. By September 20, the Island Pond, Vergennes, McIndoe, Lyndon, Danby, and Felchville Companies, and a second Montpelier company, told Washburn they were ready. They were the final seven units to organize, meeting Vermont's quota of 50 companies and 4,898 men. In the end, throughout Vermont, some 50 men were drafted, but like the men in Rutland, they officially signed on as volunteers.

All 50 units were greeted warmly by the state's military authorities, with one considerable exception. That was the Emmett Guards of Burlington (named for a martyred Irish patriot), and the origins of the controversy predated the calling up of the nine-months regiments. The man who led the Guards was John Lonergan, the eldest son of Thomas and Mary Lonergan of Carrick-on-Suir, County Tipperary, Ireland. Schooled early in the local Catholic school, young Lonergan's education was cut short when his family fled the potato famine, immigrating to America and settling in Burlington in 1848. Lonergan was fascinated by the military as a boy and joined a militia company, the Brandon Greys, well before the war. By 1860, he had established himself in the grocery business in Winooski, just across the river from Burlington. With the firing on Fort Sumter, Lonergan promptly reported to Col. George Stannard and was given permission to recruit a company for the Second Vermont Regiment. He quickly collected 65 men and brought them to the old fairgrounds at Burlington, where the regiment was organizing. But on June 18, 1861, an order came from Governor Fairbanks disbanding the company for lacking the requisite number of men and for not having been properly authorized.

Lonergan was furious and protested vigorously, thinking a great injustice had been done. His words fell on deaf ears; his 65 men, having been sworn in, were sent off to serve in other companies. Undaunted, Lonergan followed the Second Vermont to Virginia and found himself under fire at least once. But lacking any official position with the regiment, he went to Washington to protest his situation directly to Secretary of War Simon Cameron. Adj. Gen. Peter Washburn was ordered to put Lonergan to good use, and after still further protestations he was again given permission to raise a company, this one of 101 nine-months men. Lonergan traveled first to Rutland and quickly signed up a man who would become his best friend, John Sinnott, a schoolteacher and also a native of the Old Sod. He and Sinnott went into the marble quarries nearby, where many Irish were employed, and procured several recruits. They also attended war meetings in and around Burlington and filled more than 75 percent of the company with Irishmen. Lonergan was subsequently elected captain, and Sinnott first lieutenant, of Company A, 13th Vermont Regiment.

John Hanlin, a soldier in the Irish Company from Burlington, talked years later about his enlistment: "I was only 16, but quite large, rugged and strong and

John Sinnott, a schoolteacher and native of Ireland,
joined the Irish Company of the 13th Vermont.

was bubbling over for a chance to fire a gun and help put down the wicked rebellion. Though born in Ireland I knew no land or home except the United States of America and though a mere boy was anxious to go to war and fight for my adopted country. I read the papers and could see the rebels were whipping us in every fight, and unless we all pitched in to help, those fellows that wanted to buy and sell niggers would soon conquer and make a government to suit themselves and come North and tell us what we must do. I thought this a good country and was ready and willing to do what I could to save it."

In Montpelier, in mid-September, another war meeting was held. The *Freeman* reported: "Tuesday evening the Village Hall was filled to repletion to witness the presentation of an elegant Sword, with belt and sash, procured by the citizens of this village for Capt. Brown, the commander of the company of nine months men raised in the towns of Montpelier, Barre and Waterbury. At eight o'clock, Capt. Brown, 1st. Lieut. Thatcher, 2nd Lieut. Bancroft, and S.B. Colby Esq., appeared upon the platform, and were greeted with tumultuous applause. After the cheering subsided, S.B. Colby presented the Sword in the following graceful and eloquent speech:

"'Captain Brown:—Many of our citizens, friends to you, and to the gallant members of your company, have delegated me to the agreeable duty of presenting you this sword; a token as well of personal regard as of their deep devotion to the sacred cause in which you are enlisted. You cannot mistake its use. Wear it in defense of the best Government ever founded; against the most dangerous rebellion ever conceived by man . . . May victory go with your banner wherever it floats on the breeze . . .'"

Captain Brown responded (in part) as follows: "It shall be used to strike terror to the hearts of traitors; and I pray my arm may be made strong to wield it in the maintenance of the best government that the light of the sun ever shone upon. Its polished blade is now untarnished, and I hope to be able to return it to you, stained with no dishonor, and unsullied, save by the blood of traitors. May the day speedily come when this unholy rebellion shall be crushed to earth, and we be enabled once more to return to our usual peaceful avocations—when swords shall be beaten into plowshares, and spears into pruning hooks, and the nations of the earth shall learn war no more."

In Burlington, on September 24, a similar event was held for the Howard Guards, soon to leave for war. The *Burlington Times* reported: "The Town Hall was thronged at an early hour last evening, on the occasion of the presentation to Capt. Page of the Howard Guards, of an elegant sword, sash and belt, revolver and field glass . . . The presentation was made by Mr. G.G. Benedict of the *Free Press,* and a member of the Howard Guards. 'We trust whatever befalls the rest of us, that you will return from the war in safety. You SHALL so return if these stout arms and faithful hearts can protect you from injury and capture. We trust that you may return unharmed, in days to come, when peace is restored, when our country is again one, when a New England man can go from Maine to Texas, and express his honest, honorable opinions, without fear of tar and feathers.'"

Benedict was a private in the company, and it seems peculiar that a man not elected an officer would be chosen to speak at so grand an occasion. But George

Grenville Benedict was no ordinary private. At the time of his enlistment, the recent University of Vermont graduate, along with his father, edited and published a local daily newspaper. Father and son had significant other interests. At 24, young Benedict was postmaster of Burlington and president of the Vermont and Boston Telegraph Company. Obviously, Private Benedict was well connected politically, and his star, not surprisingly, would rise in the Second Vermont Brigade.

Thus were formed the companies that would make up the brigade. At one particular war meeting in southern Vermont in early August, a notable speech was given. Addressing the meeting in his hometown of Bellows Falls, Col. Edwin Stoughton, just home from service on the Peninsula, was quoted by the *Bellows Falls Argus* in an article later discussed by the *Burlington Times:* "Colonel Stoughton, of the Fourth Vermont Regt., made a speech at a war meeting in Bellows Falls . . . the *Argus* says that in the course of his remarks he briefly depicted the state of affairs on the Peninsula, and ascribed the blame of all our defeats to the radicals in Washington, intimating that if the army could have reached Congress after the Richmond fight they would have made short work with the abolitionist nest."

The *Burlington Times* editorialized on August 4, "Whose servant is Col. Stoughton? Whose livery does he wear? Whose bread and meat does he eat? Whose money does he spend while he is absent from his post of duty . . . When soldiers, officers, or other malcontents talk about turning the bayonets of the army against the chosen representatives of the people the treason is as flagrant as that of the vilest traitor that declaims on confederate rostrums against the 'Lincoln Government.'"

Young Stoughton had come home, it was widely believed, to assume command of the new nine-months brigade about to go south from Vermont. One prominent Vermont newspaper, at least, believed he had already made a most serious error in judgment.

★

*In the summer of 1862 Abraham Lincoln called 300,000 men
to serve in nine-months regiments.*

4

If the man destined for command of the new Vermont brigade had
misspoken, the governor of the state also soon committed a considerable faux pas. In mid-August 1862, Frederick Holbrook took it upon
himself to appoint officers for the brigade's five regiments. In early September, the following letter appeared in the *Burlington Times,* signed with the
fictitious name "Amicus":

> To the editor of the *Times,*
>
> I see by your columns Governor Holbrook has already announced the
> appointments of officers of our nine months regiments. Will you, or some-
> body who knows, inform the public by what authority or right, or by virtue
> of what act, his Excellency the Governor appoints these officers of our militia
> regiments? If we have reached a point where LAWS are of no consequence,
> and usurpation is the order of the day, many people would like to know it.

Two days later, the *Times* stated: "Governor Holbrook has appointed most
of the field and staff officers of the nine months militia regiments. For some time
the question has been raised in private circles here whether this course of action
was legal and proper . . . The question having been brought to Governor Holbrook,
after taking advice from eminent legal gentlemen—he has determined to retrace
his course. We suppose, then, that all appointments made in those regiments are
void. The officers will now be appointed in accordance with the provisions of the
state Constitution which declares that the several companies of militia shall as often
as vacancies happen, elect their Captains and other officers, and the Captains and
subalterns shall nominate and recommend the field officers of their respective regiments, who shall appoint their own officers."

The governor saw the error of his ways, and the Vermont Constitution prevailed. The 50 companies met to elect their officers, and those officers then met
to elect regimental field-grade officers. Pvt. Ralph Sturtevant of the Highgate Company, soon to be Company K of the 13th Vermont, gave an account of its election of officers. He first gave a rather rosy profile of the company: "None of us
had seen much of the world, and hardly had even been out of sight of the green
hills and fertile valleys of our beloved state. Nearly all of us were horny handed

farmer's sons, mere boys, mostly between the ages of fifteen and twenty-two, a few older. John Chapel, the oldest of our company, and in the regiment, was fifty-three. Since the firing on Fort Sumter in April, 1861, we had heard much and learned something about war and some of us had brothers and fathers who had volunteered, and therefore were intensely interested and knew what we were doing when we volunteered, though soldier life, the camp, the march, the battle, the killed and wounded, the dreaded hospital, the prison pens, were visions to us now, and yet we expected soon that these visions would become realities. The average age of this company was twenty-three, Yankee born, mostly, and from the best families, active, healthy and strong, good height, good sized, good natured and good looking, happy and jolly always, generous and kind, brave and courageous, many devoted Christians who wore their religion as they did their uniforms, where it could be seen and read by all. None were coward as I am aware of, only a little timid at first in battle. Indeed we were a happy family, and like brothers, ever anxious for the welfare and happiness of each other."

He then described the company's election of officers: "Between about the 20th of August and the 10th of September, possibly some before and a few after, the boys who joined Company K volunteered, and the towns from which they came, Swanton, Highgate, Franklin, Alburg, North Hero and Grand Isle were saved the humiliation of a draft, with the exception of Grand Isle, which furnished one drafted man and a number of substitutes for Company K. These towns were duly notified that those who had enrolled under the call of August 4th were to meet at Highgate on September 11th to organize a company, elect officers, and commence to drill, etc., etc. There had been more or less talk among a few, as to officers to be chosen, but on the whole, but little thought or consideration had been given the question of officers. September 11th, 1862, was a most delightful day, and during the forenoon a large number had arrived and the park in front of Landlord Johnson's hotel was literally covered with boys and men, women and children, to witness the important event of the day, election of company officers.

"There were present 126 volunteers, selectmen from the several towns, fathers, mothers, brothers and sisters, wives and sweethearts, relatives and friends of those that had enlisted, numbering as many more, all anxious and curious to see and hear, for nothing of the kind had occurred in this quiet village before. None were officers yet, and all stood on a level and all were very cordial and greeted each other like old friends. We met, the most of us, for the first time, but after a little freely mingled in a friendly way, and soon knew each other, and began to talk about war, battles, and the election of officers. It was soon ascertained that quite a number were willing to serve as officers, and a good many were well qualified, but we were to have only a captain and two lieutenants, and there could not be commissioned officers enough to go around, and some must be satisfied with non-commissioned positions . . .

"It was generally understood that Highgate, Swanton and Franklin should have the commissioned officers, namely, captain, first and second lieutenants, and that captain L.D. Clark who had served as captain of Company A, 1st Vt. Regiment for three months, and because of experience, age, valor and other qualities ought to be made captain, and the majority rather acquiesced in this view, and in fact he was a man of good presence and military bearing. There was good material from other towns for Captain, and they were quite willing to furnish it. From Franklin there were Orloff Whitney and Edward Hibbard and Carmi L. Marsh . . . but the Franklin boys were quite modest and did not urge any one for captain, and said [they] would be satisfied with a lieutenant's position, and would agree among themselves who they would name as their choice. There was finally a sort of an understanding between Highgate and Swanton that Captain Clark of Highgate should be elected captain, and when the question of who should have the honors had been arranged and agreed upon by the managers (which took a good while) a man appeared on the piazza of the hotel, waved a flag to call attention, and then said, 'All is ready, forward your votes for captain.' All the boys started at once, for it was now mid-afternoon and all had been waiting a long time, but we all went pell mell, helter skelter, ballots in hand . . . each crowding and pushing to get his vote in first, very much after the manner of voting at town meetings in those days. The votes were quickly cast and counted, and Captain Clark was chosen by a handsome majority, and declared by the officer in charge duly elected captain, whereupon all commenced to cheer and clap their hands. Soon Captain Clark appeared and the speech he made I shall never forget. It was eloquent and patriotic . . .

"In a few moments, announcement was made to forward votes for first lieutenant, and away we went again, ballots in hand, but not so well agreed, and there was considerable excitement and anxiety, for Captain Clark's friends who had kept quiet until he was elected, were now more out-spoken in their preferences . . . but the count gave my friend [Stephen] Brown a good majority and he was declared elected first lieutenant. In short order we were told to forward our votes for second lieutenant, the vote was cast and counted quickly, and Carmi L. Marsh of Franklin, was the unanimous choice for second lieutenant. Both Brown and Marsh made nice little speeches, and thanked the boys for the honor, and promised to do their best.

"The facts are that the boys did not have much to do about this election, and still they were generally pleased and satisfied. It was really pretty much arranged by the leading citizens and selectmen of the several towns there represented, before we commenced to vote, and the boys were given the great privilege of ratifying the selections made for us. Some resented this way."

The men of the newly organized company were then dismissed, but ordered to report back to Highgate on September 16 for medical examinations and drill. Pvt. Ralph Sturtevant recalled: "Tuesday, September 16th was a lovely day, and the boys were all on hand for the medical examination. As a rule we were a little timid and anxious, for we knew not how rigid the examination would be, or how many of us would be rejected. Dr. Hiram Stevens, of St. Albans, had been appointed . . . He looked and appeared like a kind hearted gentleman of the old school . . . he assured us no one would be harmed. We were taken one by one into the parlor of the hotel . . . This took all day for there were 126 for examination . . . some blushed when asked to strip to the skin. The doctor was full of fun and joked as he carefully handled and looked us over, taking from three to five minutes in each case. Only a few were rejected, thirteen out of the 126 . . . The selectmen of the several towns were present on this occasion, and deeply interested, for unless enough of their enlisted men passed the examination, they would be quickly obliged to find others to fill up their quotas."

Drill began the next day: "The captain undertook to form us in a straight line," Sturtevant remembered, "but after repeated trials gave it up . . . He finally divided us into squads of some twenty in each and placed us in charge of Blake, Whitney, Smith, Church and Sisco, and they took us out on the Common to receive our first military lessons . . . George Blake took us up to opposite the village cemetery where stood a good stretch of fence and placed us up against it, and in this way formed a pretty good line, placing the tallest at the head of the line and then asked us to count by twos. This was Greek to us. None in this squad knew what to do, but were told and did it then all right . . . After a little the order was given 'right dress.' No one moved, but were told what to do and how, and soon had that. Then came instruction how to march and keep step, stepping off first with the left foot then the right, and so we started down the road, Sergeant Blake marking time by saying, 'Left, right, left, right,' and keeping watch to see if all were doing as told. This was the first lesson, and it lasted about two hours. It was hot and the boys began to look red in the face and wanted to rest. It was about noon, and down to the hotel we all went to dinner, well satisfied with the first lesson necessary to fit us for soldier."

The company remained at Highgate, drilling until September 26. All around the state, the companies that would make up the five nine-months Vermont regiments were learning the basics of soldiering. The 13th regiment would consist of Captain Lonergan's Irish Emmett Guards of Burlington; the Moretown, East Montpelier, Colchester, Morristown, Richmond, Bakersfield, Montpelier, and Highgate Companies; and the Lafayette Artillery of Calais (with no cannon, they would be assigned to the infantry).

To the capital city, on September 24, came commissioned officers from each company in the regiment, for the purpose of electing regimental officers. Sturtevant described it: "After arrival at Montpelier, looking over the situation, it was found that the election of Francis Voltaire Randall as Colonel was conceded and for Lieutenant Colonel and Major a number of candidates were talked of, and the officers of Highgate company with Whitney and others of our company, who went down to watch the proceedings, decided to try and elect Captain Clark as Major. Lieutenant Stephen F. Brown was quite an aggressive wire puller, and Marsh and Whitney were not slow, and Captain Clark understood the ways of the world and was a shrewd man, and on finding out the situation at once made friends with the Montpelier and Barre Company, suggesting to them they bring forward A.C. Brown for Lieutenant Colonel, and Captain Clark as Major, and it worked like a charm and they were duly elected. Sergeant Orloff H. Whitney was also made Adjutant of the regiment, which was quite a compliment to this company."

The commander of the 13th, Col. Francis Voltaire Randall, was born in the central Vermont town of Braintree, the son of parents fond of christening their children with grand names; a brother was named Jean Jacques Rousseau Randall. When Francis was a child, the family moved to Northfield, just south of Montpelier. He attended school there in winter; summers he spent working on the farm and

28

George Grenville Benedict, of the 12th Vermont, the soldier and war correspondent who wrote Vermont's official Civil War history.

carpentering with his father. He later taught school, studied law with a local attorney, and was admitted to the Washington County Bar, where he quickly won a reputation as a highly competent lawyer. In his spare time he sometimes practiced the violin. He grew tall and muscular, with thick dark hair and a prominent mustache. He enlisted in 1861, serving with the Second Vermont and seeing action at Bull Run and on the Peninsula. He returned to Vermont in the early summer of 1862 to help raise men for the nine-months regiments. When he led his 13th Vermont to war, he took two sons with him, 16-year-old Charles and 17-year-old Francis V. Randall Jr., a musician the men called Jim.

The 12th Vermont Regiment had met in Bellows Falls on September 19 to elect officers. Chosen colonel was Asa P. Blunt, of St. Johnsbury, an executive of the big manufacturing company of E & T Fairbanks, a maker of industrial scales and owned by the family of Vermont's first war governor, Erastus Fairbanks. Esteemed as an expert horseman, Blunt, 34, had already served as adjutant of the Third Vermont Regiment and as lieutenant colonel of the Sixth Vermont. It should be noted that Roswell Farnham, of Bradford, was chosen lieutenant colonel. Farnham had served in the 90-day First Vermont Regiment, and there was soldiering in his lineage, a grandfather having fought at Lexington and Bunker Hill. A graduate of the University of Vermont, he was a lawyer. When the war began, he was state's attorney of Orange County. He and his wife, Mary, also ran the local and well-regarded Bradford Academy. Blunt and Farnham led a regiment that consisted of the West Windsor Guards, Woodstock Light Infantry, Howard Guards of Burlington, Tunbridge Light Infantry, Ranson Guards of St. Albans, New England Guards of Northfield, Allen Greys of Brandon, Bradford Guards, Saxtons River Light Infantry, and Rutland Light Guards. The 12th was the veteran regiment among the five nine-months units; all its companies had served in the First Vermont. However, few veterans of that unit's service in Virginia remained in the ranks, most having already enlisted in other regiments.

The officers of the 10 companies designated to make up the 14th Vermont assembled in Rutland on September 25. The companies came from Bennington, Wallingford, Manchester, Shoreham, Middlebury, Castleton, Bristol, Rutland, Vergennes, and Danby. William T. Nichols of Rutland was chosen colonel. Nichols, also a lawyer, had served in the First Vermont and had been under fire, briefly, at Big Bethel. On returning home with his regiment, Nichols ran for, and was elected to, the Vermont House of Representatives. He was 33 and serving his second term when he resigned to seek command of the 14th.

From northeastern Vermont towns along the Connecticut River came the companies that formed the 15th Vermont Regiment. They included the West Fairlee, Danville, West Randolph, Wait's River, Island Pond, McIndoe Falls, Lyndon, Barton, and St. Johnsbury Companies, and the Frontier Guards of Coventry. Meeting at St. Johnsbury on September 26, the officers elected Redfield Proctor of Cavendish as their commander.

Proctor, too, had an ancestor who had served in the Revolution—with George Washington at Trenton and at Monmouth. Capt. Leonard Proctor had then settled along the Black River in southeastern Vermont, and helped found the town of Cavendish. The family farm prospered, and the Proctors proudly sent the grandson of the old patriot to Dartmouth College, across the Connecticut River in Hanover, New Hampshire, where he was known not only as a fine student, but also for his "irregular behavior." Proctor, years later, recalled, "Being the college 'bad boy' had benefit of more frequent supervision by the faculty as well as the privilege of many personal interviews with the college president." One of Proctor's pranks was the painting of a portrait of Satan above the pulpit of the college chapel. Despite it all, he graduated in 1851 and went on to attend Albany (New York) Law School.

Lean at six feet, with a deep and powerful voice, Redfield Proctor was a born leader and, on enlisting in June 1861, was commissioned a lieutenant in the Third Vermont. Soon assigned to the staff of Gen. William F. "Baldy" Smith, also a Vermonter, Proctor contracted tuberculosis and missed the fighting of the Peninsula Campaign. Near death, he was sent to a military hospital in Philadelphia, where he was placed in a bunk beside another young Vermont officer, Samuel Pingree. (Both men recovered and both would one day serve as governor of Vermont.) Proctor returned to Cavendish to convalesce. His health restored, he joined in recruiting men for the 15th Vermont. His election as colonel was unanimous. While at Albany Law School, Proctor had met a fellow student who was also a Dartmouth graduate. The two became fast friends; in fact, Proctor called Wheelock Veazey his best friend.

Veazey, a native of Brentwood, New Hampshire, was an 1859 graduate of Dartmouth. He was awarded a law degree by Albany in 1860 and moved to Springfield, Vermont, in that year to set up his practice. In June he returned to New Hampshire to wed his sweetheart, Julia A. Beard, of Nashua. Soon thereafter, Veazey enlisted in the Third Vermont. Also a natural leader, he was within a month promoted to major and lieutenant colonel of the regiment. Then he joined his friend Proctor on the staff of General Smith, the first commander of the First Vermont Brigade. On the Peninsula, Veazey commanded the Fifth Vermont. He returned home after the failed campaign to recruit men for the 16th and aiming to be chosen colonel. When the company officers of the 16th gathered on September 27 in Bellows Falls, Veazey was promptly elected commander. The regiment was from southeastern Vermont, with companies from Bethel, Brattleboro, Ludlow, Townshend, Springfield, Wilmington, Barnard, Felchville, Williamsville, and Chester.

The five regiments of the Second Vermont Brigade were thus formed and their officers selected. On September 18, newspapers throughout the state carried a message, forwarded from the War Department to Washburn's office in Woodstock: "As the sudden call for volunteers and militia has exhausted the supply of blankets, fit for military purposes, in the market, and it will take some time to procure by manufacture or importation a sufficient supply, all citizens who may volunteer or be drafted are advised to take with them to the rendezvous, a good stout woolen blanket."

As the regiments were organizing, word reached Vermont of some momentous events. The Union cause had suffered another disaster, on the heels of the Peninsula failures, in late August with the rout of Gen. John Pope's Army of Virginia on the old Manassas battlefield. Robert E. Lee, with James Longstreet and

Stonewall Jackson, had trounced a big new federal army in three days of vicious fighting. The victory sent Lee on the march north into western Maryland. The Army of the Potomac, under beleaguered General McClellan, came face to face with Lee's spirited though outnumbered Army of Northern Virginia near the Potomac River along Antietam Creek. The fighting lasted just one day, the bloodiest of the entire war. When it was over, 23,000 casualties lay upon the green and amber autumn fields, and Lee's northern invasion had been firmly halted. Though McClellan failed to pursue and batter Lee's mangled army, Abraham Lincoln found the impetus in the Confederate repulse to issue, on September 22, the preliminary Emancipation Proclamation.

The *Rutland Herald* responded to the declaration of intent to free slaves in large areas of the seceded states with these words: "We hail the process as the unequivocal manifestation of the people, at home and abroad, of one of the most important steps ever undertaken toward consummating the true end of all governments,—freedom to all within their sway."

But the *Burlington Sentinel* said that Lincoln "has taken a step which will do no good, and which may do infinite harm to the National cause."

The *Brattleboro Phoenix* said the declaration "brings glad tidings of great joy." And in Montpelier, C.W. Willard of the *Freeman* (later to be a congressman from Vermont) penned the following editorial on September 23, 1862:

THE PRESIDENT'S EMANCIPATION
PROCLAMATION

The decisive step has at last been taken by President Lincoln. The issue on which the war is to be hereafter waged has been stated. The policy of the campaign has been authoritatively announced. Emancipation, as a war measure, has at length been resorted to, and the mighty word which will make this Republic free, has been spoken . . . This is the greatest victory of the war, the most damaging blow which the rebellion has yet received, and the grand utterance which will thrill the north like inspiring bugle notes, rallying to the government millions whose eyes had grown weary watching for the dawning light of the day of freedom. Let us, with devout Thanksgiving, praise the deep Disposer of human events, that he has put it into the heart of Abraham Lincoln to this great, crowning, and beneficial act of the 19th Century . . . The great truth, that it is only through the destruction of Slavery that this Republic can be preserved, has now taken national expression.

Just underneath the editorial, fresh from the office of Adjutant General Washburn in Woodstock, was a list of the companies making up the five Vermont nine-months regiments.

Clearly those regiments were about to depart for a war that threatened to become more vast and terrible, with every prospect that the smoke and din of battle would envelop them. Those who watched the companies as they learned the military disciplines knew the test would be awesome, and wondered if the raw recruits would ever be ready for action. Redfield Proctor recalled: "A captain was drilling his company, who was more conspicuous for his perseverance and energy than for his knowledge of infantry tactics. He was marching his recruits by company front, when he reached a fence which he could not pass by the flank. He therefore issued the following unique order: 'Halt—order arms. Company will break ranks; and when they form, form t'other side of the fence.'"

★

5

"Farming is my favorite occupation," wrote Cpl. Edmund Clark, "but I felt it my duty to come here and contribute my mite towards putting down this unholy rebellion." Those words appear in a letter sent home to Georgia, in northwestern Vermont, at the beginning of Clark's service in the 12th regiment. The 12th was the first to leave home for soldiering, departing September 25 for intense drilling in Brattleboro. Corporal Clark wrote of the "local companies getting on at the different stations until the whole regiment was aboard. We reached White River Junction about noon. We staid there about 20 minutes to get some dinner. There was a grand rush for the table you may believe and Henry and I being a little behind we stood for slim chances but Henry at last got a pie and some cheese & He and Calvin and I sat down on the floor of the depot and made away with it."

G.G. Benedict, who throughout his nine-months service sent letters home for publication in the family newspaper, the *Burlington Free Press,* wrote from camp: "Our ride to Brattleboro was a pleasant one. We were joined at Brandon by the Brandon company, at Rutland by the Rutland company, and at Bellows Falls by the long train with the remainder of the regiment. At every station, the people seemed to be out in multitudes, and from the doors and windows of every farmhouse on the way the handkerchiefs were fluttering . . . I am told that the arrival of a whole regiment, in camp, on the day set, is something unprecedented here."

The Fourth and Eighth Vermont Regiments had already camped in Brattleboro on their way to war. Barracks stood on the plateau on the south side of town overlooking the Connecticut River. Brattleboro had been a natural choice as a rendezvous for new regiments. It was the southernmost large Vermont community on a major railroad line that led directly south, and the high plateau above the village provided a fine campground. A writer said of Brattleboro at the time, "It was still a village of white houses and with but few exceptions, buildings of every kind were painted white; all property was surrounded by fences; sidewalks were made of the natural soil or Guilford slate; there were crossings of slate at intervals the length of Main Street . . . Cows, pigs and hens were kept within the village limits."

A keen observer of her hometown was Mrs. Levi K. Fuller. "The games of the children on the streets during those war days partook of the war spirit," she wrote. "Amputating arms and legs; carrying each other about on an improvised stretcher, in case of a difference of opinion, battles were fought between the 'Yankees and Secesh.' Often you would see children drawn up in line, and if you inquired what was going on they would tell you that the Company was being 'busted out.'"

It was a community built on three levels. On the lower one, beside the Connecticut River, was the railroad station, where the forming regiments arrived and from which the drilled and organized regiments departed for war. On the second level was the village, with its various stores, manufacturing firms, and most of its homes. Up on the third level, south of the village, on a plateau overlooking the valley, was the campground to which, in 1863, would be added a military hospital.

In 1862, at Brattleboro's Camp Lincoln, Col. Edwin Stoughton greeted the new regiments. As G.G. Benedict noted, he was "commandant of the post, having been taken from his regiment under the understanding that after drilling the new regiments while in the State he should command the brigade when it took the field." Though just 23, Stoughton had already commanded the Fourth Vermont; in less than two months he would be promoted to the rank of brigadier general, becoming, at the time, the youngest general in all the Union armies.

The 12th reached Brattleboro about 4 PM September 25 and, as Pvt. William Jackson, the artist, noted, ". . . marched to the camping ground about a mile

Edwin Stoughton (center), the first commander of the Second Vermont Brigade, his brother Charles (left), and fellow officer Harry Worthen, during the Peninsula Campaign.

35

distant. Talk about dust. I never knew what dust was until we undertook that march. It was almost impossible to breathe and when we arrived in camp several were so weak that they had to be carried."

Benedict reported: "The regiment . . . after considerable exertion on the part of Col. Blunt, it was finally formed into line, in front of the barracks. The companies are, most of them, deficient in drill, and the men have in fact, about everything to learn. We broke ranks just at dark, received our blankets, woolen and india-rubber, selected our bunks, and marched off to supper, which was abundant and good enough for anybody, sauced as it was with a hearty appetite. The barracks are houses of plain boards, ten in number, within which wooden bunks are ranged for the men, in double tiers. I cannot speak from experience, as yet, as to their comfort, your humble servant having been among the fortunate individuals who, constituting the first eight (alphabetically) of the company, were the first detailed for guard duty. This I found to mean a couple hours of rest as could be extracted from the soft side of a hemlock plank in the guard house, with sergeants and corporals and 'reliefs' coming in and going out, and always in interested conversation when not in active motion; then two hours (from 11 to 1) of pacing a sentry beat, musket on shoulder, over what by this time is a path, but then was an imaginary, and in the darkness, uncertain, line on the dew-soaked grass of the meadow; then about three hours more of that 'rest' I have alluded to, but this time I found the plank decidedly softer, and slept in spite of the trifling drawbacks mentioned; then two hours more of sentry duty; and then—volunteers having been called for special guard duty—two hours more of the same. By now it was well into the morning.

"Not a rebel broke in," he wrote, "nor a roving volunteer broke out, over my share of the line, and if there was no sleeping there was a good deal of other things. There was, for instance, a fine opportunity for the study of astronomy . . . I read in the bright planets success for the good cause, and glory for the Twelfth Vermont . . . This was one of the finest opportunities to see the Connecticut Valley mist rise from the river and steal over the meadows, giving a shadowy veil to the trees, a halo apiece to the stars, and adding to the stature of my comrade sentinels till they loomed like Goliaths of Gath through the fog-cloud. There was also the opportunity to see the morning break, not with the grand crash of bright sunrise, but cushioned and shaded by that same fog-bank."

Jabez Hammond, a 20-year-old private in the 12th, wrote home to his parents on the family farm in West Windsor of his arrival in camp: "The boys was pretty wide awake but we had A good nights rest without much sleep this morning we went down to the frog pond to wash."

On October 5 he wrote, "I have for the first time in my life attended church out doors . . . our Chaplins name is Brestow I think. He is about the size of Elder Wight. We talk now (if there can a couple get a pass to the village) of having some oysters for supper. I think Ira, S.F., U.H. & I shall get our pictures taken together to day or tomorrow and send it home we get them taken for $1.75." Hammond was referring to this brothers Ira, 27, Stephen, 26, and Ulysses, 20, also privates in the 12th.

*A Civil War encampment at Brattleboro, on the field where
the Second Vermont Brigade's regiments drilled*

The next day, October 6, was a happy one for Private Jackson, who reported, "Were paid our bounty of $110.00 and back state pay amounting to $10.70. Makes some of us feel pretty rich."

"The last day of September, 1862, the Thirteenth Vermont Regiment went into camp at Brattleboro," wrote lawyer-turned-sergeant Edwin Palmer. "The frost had come and turned the leaves to a golden yellow just so as to remind us that autumn was near by." Among those who had enlisted in Company F of Colonel Randall's regiment was 21-year-old farm boy Simeon Palmer, the mainstay of his parents' Underhill farm. He had a younger brother, Cornelius, who had been sickly when young, but whose health had improved with the years. As the time for Simeon's departure neared, Cornelius determined that he, not his older brother, should be the one to go to war, for the parents could not do without the stronger Simeon to handle the chores. Cornelius studied his father's handwriting, and when he hitched up the buckboard to take Simeon to Richmond for the company's departure, he had in his pocket a bogus permission to enlist. The company slept that night on straw thrown down on the dance-hall floor in J.H. Ransom's hotel. Cornelius rose early the next morning and donned his sleeping brother's uniform. When Simeon wakened, an hour-long argument ensued. But the words "I am going to war and you are going to stay with father and mother" held sway. When the company was ordered to fall in, young Cornelius stepped into ranks, and when Simeon's name was called, Cornelius answered. Off he went for Brattleboro, headed for war, while Simeon turned the buckboard north, toward Mount Mansfield and the family farm.

Pvt. Ralph Sturtevant wrote of the trip: "Met the train at St. Albans, having come over from Egypt in the town of Fairfield that morning. It was a long, heavy

Sgt. Edwin Palmer, of the 13th Vermont, a Waterbury lawyer-turned-soldier,
wrote a book on his wartime experiences.
LIMOGE COLLECTION

train, moved slow, and did not arrive until late in the afternoon . . . On our arrival in Brattleboro, we were received by Colonel Blunt with his regiment, the 12th, and escorted to the camp ground called Camp Lincoln, where the 12th Regiment had been for several days . . . The barracks were 74 by 22 feet, each designed for one company of 100 men, doors at each end, a narrow hall through from end to end and on either side bunks built about 4 by 6 feet, two stories high, each calculated for two persons, and made out of boards, simply a box six inches deep nailed up to posts, just space enough between for one at a time to pass and climb over in and when in, just lie down, no room to sit up or would hit their heads on the bottom of the bunk above, or the roof overhead. Some had straw for their bunks and others not . . . We were soon marched over to a long, low wooden building with stationary tables running through, benches for seats and into these all pushed rapidly along jostling each other, anxious for something, anything to eat . . . No bread and butter with strawberry preserves, doughnuts and cheese, pies and cakes, hot biscuits and honey, jelly tarts, tea and coffee with cream are anywhere to be seen . . . Silently and sullenly the boys ate because hungry and returned to their sleeping barracks for the night."

Sergeant Palmer recalled, "At half-past eight the roll is called; at nine the order is given— 'No talking.' This is not heeded. As soon as the officer retires, some show their skill by cackling like the rooster, others imitate the feline, canine and taurine animals all at once."

Sturtevant added, "All night long the boys were turning over from one side to the other to change positions, and the curses and imprecations that some uttered showed on what they were sleeping, and how they were covered. Some in their mid-night efforts attempted to sit up for a rest and change, but in so doing hit their heads against the bunk above, or the timber and roof overhead. The night was long, the wind whistled through the cracks, and there was commotion all about, some were taken suddenly sick and hurried out into the black darkness . . . Daylight, to the relief of all, finally came and we crawled out with sore backs and sides, aching heads, shaking with cold, and this was our first night in camp as a regiment.'"

The next morning Pvt. Samuel Dana, of the 13th, wrote to his wife in Warren, "I feel first rate this morning but yesterday I had the headache hard. We arrived here at four o'clock and drawed our blankets and canteens and then went to supper. Our supper consisted of bread and meat and poor coffee, but I can go that."

Sergeant Palmer wrote, "The cooks are making their first attempts at cooking, who were as ignorant of the art as we of the military; neither knowing anything of either. The former, no doubt, had seen his mother boil beef and beans; we, in our childhood, had witnessed a June training."

Sturtevant recalled that the day "opened with lowering clouds, drizzling rain, and a dense fog and it was cold. The boys ran up and down the hall to limber up their stiffened limbs and to warm their bodies, whooping and jumping like wild Indians, caring but little for appearance and utterances . . . Quite a few of the more curious and restless secured passes and went over to the village stopping on their way to look over the village cemetery. During the afternoon the clouds broke and cleared away, and everything appeared more pleasant in and about camp, and as we looked to the south and west the wooded hills and mountains beyond and the beautiful and thriving village with its white painted houses on the high banks of the broad Connecticut River on its way to the sea made an attractive picture.

"In the afternoon," he continued, "officers were busy, moving rapidly from place to place . . . to distribute blankets and guns, straps, etc., to be ready for drill, guard duty and dress parade, medical examination and inspection, and a thousand and one little details necessary to bring order to the ranks of this regiment of raw recruits . . . Late in the afternoon orders came to get ready for regimental parade, and soon we heard the bugle call and then the fife and drum."

On October 1 Sergeant Palmer noted, "The morning came foggy, drizzly. The boys spent most of the day in making their barracks more comfortable—nailing narrow pieces of boards on the cracks. We succeeded in getting a little more straw; also a stove, just before night, by carrying it a mile on a wheel-barrow, through the mud and rain. The boys gave three cheers for the stove, and the same number for those that got it. We are soon sitting around a good fire—some talking, some laughing, some smoking, others singing; all in good spirits."

The 12th received its equipment, as reported by Private Benedict: "The overcoats, knapsacks, belts, cartridge boxes and haversacks were distributed yesterday morning, completing our equipment . . . The whole form an amount of harness which strikes the unsophisticated recruit with a slight feeling of dismay.

Is it possible, he says to himself, that all this pile of straps is only my share, and is all to be carried on my devoted shoulders? Why have they made them all so heavy? What earthly reason now, for cutting these straps out of such an almighty thick side of harness leather, and making them so broad, too?"

The 13th's first drilling was described by Private Sturtevant: "Springfield rifles had been given out . . . and when it did not rain, there was company and squad drill in the forenoon and battalion drill in the afternoon. The boys had to be told how to carry their guns, though most were quite familiar with the old shot guns that hung on the walls at home, with which, as boys, they had hunted and killed squirrels, skunks, woodchucks. Springfield rifles were heavier and different, and had bayonets attached that were dangerous in the hands of raw recruits . . . Occasionally some one was accidentally pricked with a bayonet."

On October 4, it was officially announced that Edwin Stoughton had been appointed commandant of the post. This was occasion for a grand review by Governor Holbrook, who rode up to Camp Lincoln from his home just down the hill. Sturtevant noted, "Our camp was thronged with visitors from all parts of the State of high and low degree, beautiful women and red cheeked girls and their anxious faces revealed the cause of their presence, doting mothers and loving brides were there to make farewell visit and say good bye, and some had come from distant homes that the nuptial agreement might be solemnized by the sacred rites of the church before it was too late."

According to Benedict, "The review was considered quite a fine affair by the numerous array of spectators . . . We of the rank and file did not think it so fine. At two o'clock, then, each private hoisted on to his shoulders his knapsack, packed as above, slung around him his haversack and canteen, buckled on his cartridge belt, and musket in hand, took his place in the ranks. The sun has come out hot . . . He straightens up manfully, and endeavors, when the order comes, to step out with his customary light step. He is LOGY. He weighed 145 pounds half an hour ago, now he weighs 190 . . . There is drumming and fifing and stepping into place of officers; but you notice little of what is going on. Your attention is mainly directed to a spot between your shoulder blades . . . it aches. The sensation gradually spreads through your back and shoulders . . . The perspiration bursts from every pore. You hear a groan from a comrade on the left, and are comforted to know that you have company in your misery . . . And now you are conscious of a sharp pain in the hollow of your right arm, from holding your musket at the shoulder for three-quarters of an hour. Why can't they let us order arms for five minutes? But instead comes the order to wheel into platoons, and around the grounds we are marched for a weary hour. We don't 'dress right' and 'dress left' good, we don't 'wheel' good, and we don't 'feel' good."

Colonel Stoughton took up residence in the village, as Pvt. John Harmon of Milton and the 13th Vermont recalled: "I was placed on guard in front of General [sic] Stoughton's headquarters way down under the hill towards the village of Brattleboro." Choosing not to camp with the men in the ranks was a habit that would cost Stoughton dearly.

Despite their earlier company physicals, everyone had to undergo a second checkup soon after arrival at Camp Lincoln. Recalled Private Sturtevant: "We were marched by companies to a commodious hall on the camp ground, one of the many buildings recently built, and about fifty at a time were admitted and the doors shut, and then we were told to remove all our clothing as quick as possible and stand in line up and down the hall. This was a new deal that we had not been told of, and some demurred, but no use, strip we must and so we did, and when we were all lined up in a row we hardly knew ourselves and especially each other. Though there were two surgeons we thought them very slow, the room was cold and no fire and we were growing chilly. This examination was critical and reminded me of the careful and scrutinizing examination of the horse buyer when about to purchase a valuable animal for market. Eyes, ears, teeth, arms, thumbs and fingers, legs, feet and toes and required to go through various motions with hands, run and jump over a common empty flour barrel laid down on the floor, and many similar antics, nothing escaped their attention. If symptoms of hernia of any kind appeared, their fingers would press hard upon the spot . . . The boys' teeth chattered and they shivered with cold long before the surgeons finished their scrutinizing task, but the running and jumping warmed them up and none took cold. None of Company K was thrown out, nor of the regiment to my knowledge. Corporal H.P. Bullard had a defective eye, and Cadmus S. Gates was not a good high jumper. The eye of Corporal Bullard they did not see and comrade Gates' sprawling jump lighting on the barrel and his ride on it almost across the hall, so amused the surgeons that they said, 'You are all right.'"

Soon thereafter, men with experience as carpenters were taken from drill and put to work building barracks for the soon-to-arrive 14th, 15th, and 16th regiments. Later, clothing was issued to the 13th. Recalled Sturtevant: "Some were very tall and others very short, some were large, broad shoulders, long arms and legs, and some very corpulent, and to secure good fits for such was found quite impossible. The Government did not have in mind the stalwart Yankee boys of the Green Mountain State when giving out the contract for the manufacture of army clothing, for a number could not find dress coats large enough, nor trousers long enough."

Men adjusted to camp life and in the evening and on weekends found time to relax. The organ factory in town was of particular interest to the mechanically minded farm-boy soldiers. According to John McMahon, from Bakersfield, a private in the 13th: "While at Brattleboro we had a wrestling match one evening, when I threw 17 men. We wrestled the old fashioned 'collar and elbow' hold . . . That evening seems to be the best work I ever did in that line."

Pvt. Benjamin Hatch, in the 12th regiment, was troubled by soldier morality. He wrote to his wife in Hartland, "Is as much as 20 playing cards and gambling every night . . . Last night I went along the line of camps, some were gambling, some were swearing, some were dancing and everything else you can think of."

Religious services were held on Sunday. One soldier in the 13th remembered, "The regiment was formed into a hollow square, and addressed by the Chaplain from the center, who reminded us that life was fleeting and admonished us to be prepared, for no one could tell the hour that would be our last, and likely some there present who would never see home and friends again. These statements were literally true and yet not consoling and encouraging in these early days of our service."

According to Sergeant Palmer: "Now comes a few hours rest, and then evening, the shadows lengthening eastward. On the thinly grassed plain in front of the barracks are many soldiers, strolling arm in arm . . . One, sad, shows me a letter, scarcely dry from the tears of his wife at home; another, a fiery nature, tells over the Kansas forays; the Nebraska iniquity; the wrongs inflicted on Northern men; the firing on Fort Sumter; the great uprising in the North . . . A few hours more, a third comes along, and laughing, 'Have an apple Sergeant,' tells how he ran the guard, and 'hooked the old man's fruit down by the river.' Still, a fourth, a sly one, had overheard the countersign, and so he gets out; but at nine the countersign is changed to catch the rogues; and 'poor Jim, you are shut out, and the heavy dew on your coat and cap, the next morning, tells that you were poorly housed last night'; and away on the right is a prayer meeting."

On October 10, the 12th became the first nine-months Vermont regiment to head for the war zone. Colonel Stoughton was on hand, resplendent in his new uniform, tall and handsome, riding a magnificent horse. What he did that day would be long remembered by the troops. G.G. Benedict reported: "By eleven o'clock every knapsack was packed and the regiment in line, and at half-past eleven—the time set to a minute, it marched out of Camp Lincoln. The day was a very hot one, and the sun blazed down with midsummer power. The Thirteenth, Colonel Randall, escorted the Twelfth to the railroad station. Col. Stoughton, commanding the post, took the head of the column, and in order to show the regiment to some of his Brattleboro friends, took it by a circuitous route through the streets to the station. The march of two miles in the hot sun was a pretty hard one for the boys."

Pvt. George B. Barnett, from Newbury on the Connecticut River, wrote home: "[M]arched through the city of Brattleboro two or three times and down about a mile which about tuckered us out for it was very warm and we had everybody on our backs."

Benedict said: "Through some misunderstanding or neglect on the part of the railroad companies, though the day and hour of departure had been set for nearly a week, no cars were in readiness, and we had to wait until they were brought from below. The regiment was accordingly marched half a mile down the river to a shaded meadow and allowed to lie off for the remainder of the day. A barrel of good things, sent from Burlington by Mr. Beach, supplied our company with all they could eat and some to spare to the rest, and the afternoon passed comfortably away. At six o'clock, a train of empty cars arrived, and the work of embarkation commenced at seven. The cars were too few in number, however, and some freight cars had to be rigged with seats manufactured on the spot . . . It was ten o'clock before we were fairly under way. Before this, our kind friends who had come to Brattleboro to see us off, had taken their leave, and the actual departure was as quiet as that of any train of thirty loaded cars could be."

Back at Camp Lincoln, Colonel Nichols's 14th arrived on October 6 and was met at the depot by the 13th. According to Private Sturtevant: "[E]scorted them over to camp with drum and fife, to the music of the 'Girl I Left Behind Me,' which brought tears to the eyes not yet dry from the home parting of the morning." On October 8, Colonel Proctor's 15th chugged in. Joel Glover, a private from Topsham, wrote to his wife of the trip: "We stopped at White River Junction and got Lunchion then stopped at Windsor and the ladies gave us some good apples to eat and some watter. The train wass half a mile long." Wheelock Veazey's 16th arrived October 9.

Obviously, in a large army camp, not all was camaraderie and cheerfully shared travails. Joseph Spafford, now with the 16th Vermont, wrote to his sister soon after arriving in Brattleboro:

> Dear Sister,
>
> We are still here, and do not know anything more about going than we did the day we came. Now they tell us we are going tomorrow, but we have heard that same story for some time. They say we are going to be mustered into the service today but I do not believe that either for it is now 3 o'clock PM and no signs of it yet. There is a great deal of feeling towards the Col. in the Regt. He got d—d to his face by a number of privates last night, and a great many men in a number of the companies say they will never take the oath. The guard house was full last night of men who had run the guard some of our boys among the number. The Adjt. drew his revolver on one fellow who insulted him last night but concluded not to fire.
>
> YOUR BROTHER

If Colonel Veazey was having trouble with the troops, he got a respite from it just before the regiment departed. His wife came to visit and the two checked into a hotel in Brattleboro. Judging from what Veazey wrote in later letters home, they had a fine old time, and as a result the colonel was even more hopelessly in love.

The 14th Vermont left by train for Washington on October 22, and Cpl. John Williams, from the mountain town of Danby, who kept a diary throughout his army career, noted: "We are to leave for 'Dixie,' and can hardly find time, amid the din and bustle of camp, to write. We are to bid farewell for the present to our Green Mountain home, to dwell in the tented field surrounded by dangers and hardships. We are to part with friends whom we hold dear, and what a sad thought it is that many of us will not return. But the ways of Providence are mysterious, and we poor mortals cannot lift the veil which hides the future." (Cpl. John Williams, by the way, was one of two John Williamses in the 14th Vermont to keep a journal. The other, a Welshman from Fair Haven, will be heard from later.)

Among those caught up in the enlistment fever of August had been William Doubleday, who decided to take temporary leave of his wife, Asceneth, and his four sons to join the 14th. Soon after William walked up the Elbow Road in Sherburne to get the stage and head off to the army, Asceneth and the boys moved to the White River Valley, near Sharon, where some of her husband's relatives lived, to await William's return. Private Doubleday wrote from Camp Lincoln shortly before his regiment departed: "There is quite an excitement here in regard to our nine months commencing. The Officers say it will not until we are mustered into the United States service. The most of the boys say they will never hold up their right hand to take the oath unless they can have their time commence the 10th of Sept. We can't get any furloughs and there has 12 of our boys left without leave and more agoing. I lent my last dollar to my bedfellow to go home."

A hot topic in the regiments concerned just when terms of service began and when they would end. The authorities held that the nine months commenced only with the official mustering of the regiments, but many in the ranks felt the nine months should begin when they reported to their companies or, at least, on their arrival at Brattleboro. Mustering occurred, with the ceremony of a regimental review, on the drill field of Camp Lincoln. The official mustering officer for each regiment was Maj. William Austine, of Brattleboro. The 12th was mustered October 4, the 13th on October 8, the 14th and 15th October 22, and the 16th on October 23. One now wonders how many men noted that the first regiment to go home would be the 12th, and its day of departure would fall on the next Fourth of July, 1863. That Fourth would be one of the most fateful dates in the history of the nation.

★

•❖ Near the entrance to Brattleboro High School stands a monument marking the location of the campground where the Vermont regiments assembled and drilled before going south to war. It also notes that a military hospital was located nearby. This is the site of Camp Lincoln, where the Second Vermont Brigade assembled in the fall of 1862. The plateau now contains the high school, its athletic fields, and a sizable number of houses. Some soldier accounts of the Brattleboro encampment mention tall pines, and children or grandchildren of those trees still stand in the field's southeastern corner. I went there very early one autumn morning, well before sunrise, and found that housing construction and tree growth blocked my view of the Connecticut, which Private Benedict had seen while walking guard his first night in the army. But a mist lay over the ground, as it had when Private Benedict saw his fellow soldiers as "Goliaths of Gath."

PART II

We Are Coming, Father Abraham,
300,000 More

6

The time had come for the Second Vermont Brigade to depart for the war zone. Colonel Blunt's 12th led the way, and Pvt. G.G. Benedict wrote of the trip: "The night was a splendid one, and the ride down the beautiful valley of the Connecticut, which seemed doubly beautiful in the liquid moonlight, was a notable one for every man who had a particle of sentiment in his soul. At Springfield, Mass., where we arrived about one o'clock, we were received with a salute of fifty guns. On the supposition that we should arrive about supper time, preparations had also been made to supply refreshment to the troops; but the delay upset the kind of arrangement. We made little stop there or anywhere, but swept on down the river. We reached New Haven at 5 o'clock, AM, spent an hour in changing the men and the baggage from the cars to the 'large and splendid' steamer *Continental*, and were off for New York. The boat barely touched at Peck Slip, and then went to Jersey City, where it debarked about noon. Col. Howe [the state agent of Vermont at New York] had provided soup and bread, which was served promptly, and we were off again by rail for Washington . . . [F]rom New York to Washington we had the customary wavings of handkerchiefs and flags, all along the way, and the usual— and it is all the more praise-worthy because it IS usual—substantial welcome, in the shape of hot coffee, good bread and butter, and other substantials, served by the kind hands of the ladies and gentlemen of the Union Relief Association, in Philadelphia.

"Up to our arrival at Baltimore," he continued, "we made steady and reasonably rapid progress, reaching there at six o'clock Thursday morning. Then came a march of a mile and a half across the city, and six hours of tedious standing with stacked arms, near the Washington depot, varied by breakfast at the Relief Rooms. Then we were stowed away in freight cars and started out of the city. The train took 600 other troops besides our regiment, and numbered thirty-four heavily loaded cars, the men covering the tops of the cars as well as filling them inside. We made slow progress, waiting three or four hours at Annapolis Junction, and reached Washington at 9 o'clock Thursday night. Supper was given us in the now sweet or savory halls of the 'Soldiers' Rest' near the Capitol, and in the huge white-washed barns attached thereto, the boys finally laid themselves down to sleep as best they might, on the hard floors, many preferring to take their blankets and sleep on the ground outside. Today we are to go into camp somewhere about Washington."

Another perspective on the trip emerges from a letter sent from Annapolis Junction by the 12th's second in command, Roswell Farnham. Writing to his wife in Bradford, he reported, "We passed the *Great Eastern* near Ft. Schuyler & had a fine view of her. She is a monster indeed . . . About two o'clk we left [for] Philadelphia. We reached Camden opposite the city between six and seven o'clk in the evening. We were ferried across the river & had a good lunch at the Soldiers Relief . . . We had some trouble with the boys there were so many girls about. Some of them were rather loose in their manners but their free & easy style suited many." And he wrote, "We are now stopping near Annapolis Junction for trains to pass . . . The men have behaved themselves nobly. None have got drunk & all are doing just as well as they can."

In Springfield, Massachusetts, the *Springfield Republican* noted the 12th's passing through: "The regiment numbers 1004 men fully equipped with the Springfield gun . . . A regimental dog that bears the sobriquet 'Old Abe' goes with the 12th. He is the best that the Green Mountain State could furnish, and is truly a splendid fellow."

Four days behind the 12th, on Saturday, October 11, the 13th Vermont left Brattleboro. Just before it boarded the trains, someone in Company H noticed that Pvt. Charles Smith was missing. Later, Cpl. Theodore Snow said, "A man by this name enlisted in several regiments and deserted." (Throughout the Union armies there were men who collected bounties, deserted, then enlisted again and again.)

Private Sturtevant wrote: "Many citizens from the village and from up the State were in camp through the forenoon, though cold and damp and looked like rain, but no one seemed to care for weather. The majority of those who came, found their way to the location of the Thirteenth Regiment where the boys, some had come so far to see, were anxiously waiting their arrival . . . There were quite a number now donned in blue here and there to be seen, affectionately holding the trembling hand of a sweet faced girl of sixteen or twenty summers whose cheeks blushed in changing colors as she, with eyes cast down, listened to the renewed vows of abiding love and promised marriage on return. Some were brides of a day shedding tears of sorrow . . . Mothers too . . . would throw their arms around the neck of an only son and impart the accustomed kiss as if it were the last."

Among the young couples married in Brattleboro were Sgt. Edwin Reed and Miss Sarah Williams, both of the northern Vermont town of Bakersfield. After three days of marriage, she was there to see him off to war. "The sound of bugle, fife and drum suddenly changed the scene," wrote Sturtevant, ". . . and soon [we] were keeping step to the stirring strains of martial music as they moved from Camp Lincoln through the village to the Railroad Station."

"Citizens, fathers, mothers, brothers and sisters, who have come a long way, are there too," wrote Sgt. Edwin Palmer. "They have sober faces. They speak with trembling lips. They shed tears. They shake hands, and say, 'God be with you!' We are off to the South."

A private wrote to Morrisville that day, "We are all confusion, and it is impossible to glean much information as to our destination, which would be

*Ralph Orson Sturtevant, a private in the 13th Vermont,
who assembled the official history of his regiment*

authentic, but I GUESS we are going to Washington and garrison the forts around the city." The train departed nearly on schedule, in daylight, and that made quite a difference. Private Sturtevant wrote: "The whole town turned out, old and young boys, and girls . . . On either side of the long train from end to end stood the citizens of Brattleboro, Gov. Holbrook and his Staff, the escort from Camp Lincoln, and our relatives and friends soon to return home and all busy in earnest conversation, handkerchief in hand ready to wave the last good-by . . . Colonel Randall was fully satisfied all was ready, walked up to the Governor, saluted and reported. They clasped hands, and then the Colonel waved his hand to the Conductor."

Sergeant Palmer remembered, "'We are bound for Dixie,' shout a dozen jolly fellows, as they ascend the car steps. 'John Brown's knapsack is strapped upon his back,' sing half the company; and the iron wheels begin to rattle, and the engine to scream."

"The whistle blew, the cars moved and then the cheers loud and long from the assembled multitude filled the air and resounded up and down the valley," Sturtevant wrote. "The waving of hands and handkerchiefs seemed the spontaneous action of all, and as far as we could see, the white handkerchiefs were still fluttering in the breeze as we passed down the valley out of sight on our way to New Haven."

"As we pass down the valley of the Connecticut river, the fishermen in their little boats take off their hats; the farmers in the fields, too, show their sweaty brows and raise their sickles; the women and children flutter their handkerchiefs from the windows and doors of the white cottages," Palmer recalled.

Sturtevant added: "The boys . . . rode in silence for miles absorbed in thought of the past and future. But on passing through the Massachusetts villages of Holyoke and Chicopee, the boys were now rested and eager to see the new places and the long line of beautifully dressed girls with flags and handkerchiefs in hands on both sides of the cars singing patriotic songs and waving banners . . . Our first stop when permitted to leave the cars was at the city of Springfield, and here we remained for some twenty minutes or more. Our coming had been announced, and the city was out, factory girls . . . they cheered and sang and waved their tiny flags of stars and stripes as we slowly rolled into the station and extended their hands of welcome as we jumped from the cars as if we were old friends just returned."

Sturtevant wrote of "bewitching smiles and enchanting eyes . . . so animated, cordial and solicitous . . . Sandwiches and coffee, cake and fruit in abundance freely offered. Love's swift arrow pierced many a throbbing heart at first sight, a dangerous place long to linger at . . . manhood and devotion only kept us on our way . . . The signal was sounded, clasped hands held tight until the last moment, and with speaking eyes and rosy lips some (not all) sealed the parting salute. Many cast long lingering tokens of love and regret as the train passed from sight, and looked forward to promised letters from soldier heroes in the army and their return."

Gilman Foster, a drummer from Moretown, recalled, "Our train made a short stop at Hartford, where our car was surrounded and we were captured by the ladies and presented the best that the city afforded in the line of eatables. We thanked them, but one of the boys said, 'You have done nobly, but not quite as well as the girls of Springfield.' They wanted to know wherein they had failed . . . the answer was, 'They kissed us.' And the girls said, 'We will not be beaten by Springfield.'"

If George Benedict's description of the 12th's trip south seems somewhat perfunctory, a trip to Washington was a common thing for him. But most of the new Vermont soldiers had hardly been away from home, certainly not to Massachusetts or faraway New York. Private Sturtevant, like most of his comrades, was on an adventure. "This was the first experience of nearly all on the briny sea," he wrote, "and though protected by Long Island, the waters were rough and some were sick."

Palmer wrote, "Though not half had been on the water before, after a little observation, sleep overcomes curiosity, nor stars, nor moon, nor splashing waves, or anything connected with the sea, nor thought of friends behind were much to us."

"We arrived in the harbor of New York in the early gray of the morning and the great masts and bars fluttered in the breeze and greeted our astonished gaze, and we were entranced with wonder and amazement . . . The whole regiment were up and well spell-bound at the sight," Sturtevant wrote.

The regiment, he said, docked at Jersey City and marched through streets "cold and breezy, the thick dust filled the air." Presently a halt was called, and soon several wagons bearing large barrels arrived. "It must be, they are the fellows that gather up the morning swill of the city for the hogs," one soldier remarked, and apparently was not far wrong. Wrote Sturtevant: "They, stopped, took off the heavy wooden covers of the barrels and with long handled dippers in hand announced, 'Hot soup, boys, come right up and we will fill your tin cups with nice hot soup' . . . It was porridge, a combination of vegetable and animal, so blended, cooked and mixed that none of us could make out what to call it . . . It looked like a mixture of potatoes, sweet and Irish, rice, barley, peas and beans, calf, lamb and ram, pork and fish, cooked and cooked, warmed over and over again, evidently from the same barrels had been dipped day after day the supply for other troops passing through the city. Some ate of it sparingly, others disgusted threw it out on the ground saying it was no better than home made swill that filled the troughs of the pig sty at home."

Kimball Cross, from Montpelier, a private in the 13th, wrote, "We called it Jersey Soup and the taste and smell we never forgot. In Philadelphia the 13th, like the 12th, and the three regiments yet to come south, received a warm welcome and good food. Then back on the cars."

Lyman Seeley wrote to the Morrisville paper, the *Lamoille News Citizen,* about Philadelphia: "After dinner we marched through the city to the depot and went on board the cars and waited an hour. While we were waiting, the Lamoille County company sang some comic songs which kept the crowd in laughter till the bell rung."

Sturtevant recalled: "The ride to Baltimore was cold, slow, hard and dismal, some of us had not forgotten the attack on the Sixth Massachusetts Regiment in the streets of Baltimore on their way to Washington, April 19, 1861 . . . some feared we might be attacked in Baltimore. We arrived . . . about three o'clock in the morning. Engines detached and moved by horse power across the city . . . We left the cars and marched with fixed bayonets in close order in wind and rain along the dismal, slippery streets to a large brick building and up a flight of winding stairs where we were served with soft bread and boiled ham and hot coffee. We remained in Baltimore until mid-forenoon, before we commenced our journey to Washington."

Pvt. Henry Fassett, from Enosburg, remembered that the men in his company "were ordered to load weapons when the train passed through Baltimore."

In Company B, as departure time came, 17-year-old Pvt. Levi Weaver, a Waitsfield lad, failed to respond to roll call. A friend remembered: "It was thought that he might be asleep but every corner was searched without avail and the whistle sounded 'all aboard,' but just as the wheels began to move, Levi appeared on the track in front of the train all out of breath, coming as fast as he could run. He said, 'There were some passenger cars standing in the depot and I went into one of them and the seats looked so comfortable that I sat down . . . next thing I knew the cars were in motion and we were already out of the city. The conductor stopped the train and let me off and I hurried back as fast as I could, but I found so many tracks as soon as I got to the city I had a hard time to get the right one sometimes.'"

Private Sturtevant reported: "The train from Baltimore to Washington moved slowly and cautious, soldiers were on guard along the railroad in some places, to guard against raids and surprise, the battles of second Bull Run, Crampton's Gap, South Mountain and Antietam were fresh in memory still."

On October 22, the 14th left Brattleboro. The regiment was given pies and cakes as it passed down the Connecticut Valley, then it went by boat from New Haven to New York City. Corporal Williams said, "Such contemptible treatment as we received in this city—the greatest in America—is outrageous and shameful . . . The food presented to us was not fit for a dog to eat. Great God! what a dish to set before human beings—soup alive with maggots."

On October 24, Williams continued: "If there is ever a want of comfort attendant upon such a journey as this, we experienced it last night. It would be impossible for the government to treat cattle and hogs any worse than it does soldiers in transporting them to the seat of war . . . At Amboy we took the cars for Camden, where we arrived just at daylight this morning, and such a night of suffering and misery is far beyond the power of any pen to portray. Suffice it to say the night was very cold . . . there was no fire aboard the cars, our sufferings were almost beyond human endurance." But the 14th was accorded the usual warm welcome and food in the City of Brotherly Love, and the rest of the journey went well.

The 15th departed on October 23, arriving in Washington the morning of the 23rd, remembering the kindness of the Massachusetts and Philadelphia people.

"At 12 or midnight our cars came in and we loaded in the wet and darkness into some dilapidated cattle cars for Washington," wrote Lt. Col. Charles Cummings to his wife in Brattleboro as his regiment, the 16th, moved south. Cummings was, not surprisingly, a prolific writer of letters; in civilian life he edited the *Brattleboro Phoenix*. He had a taste for soldiering, having already served briefly in the 11th Vermont, and would later enlist in still another regiment.

"It rained all night," he continued, "and the water ran in between every crack and between every two boards on the roof until all within were wet nearly through . . . Everyone was cheerful, and songs—we have a few singers within our regiment—and stories kept us in good humor during the EIGHT HOURS ride from Baltimore to Washington—a distance of ONLY FORTY FIVE MILES."

Though every mile brought them closer to war, men in all the regiments seemed glad when the long trip ended. As Private Sturtevant reported, "When within a few miles of Washington, Butterfield of Company K, whose head had been out most of the way night and day, cried out, 'Boys see there, that must be the capitol,' every head was out and we for the first time saw that grand imposing building, a beautiful and magnificent structure of stone, iron, marble and glass."

Palmer noted, "As the cars halt we look for the marble capitol; we see a long line of poor mules mounted by negroes, who are lashing them terribly, as I fancied THEY had been ere they were 'contrabands.'"

Sturtevant again: "We arrived in Washington late in the afternoon and were placed in a building called the Soldier's Retreat for the night, a large wooden building near the grand and imposing structure where were assembled the wisdom of the Nation divising ways and means to carry on the war. Hot coffee and chocolate was here furnished, and with the remaining contents of our haversacks we made a fairly good supper, and then spread down our rubber blankets on the bare floor, knapsacks for pillows, overcoats and woolen blankets for covering, laid down for rest and sleep, all in the same building. We were weary and had had but little sleep since leaving Brattleboro, and therefore were soon sound in sleep, oblivious of the tumult of moving cars and screeching engines and constant marching all about, tramp, tramp, tramp, throughout the night."

★

7

Members of the Second Vermont Brigade were quick to report their arrival in Washington to the home folks—most of whom had never seen the nation's capital. A soldier in the 13th wrote: "Cows, pigs, geese and dogs seem to grow spontaneously in this part of the world, for we are annoyed with them both day and night, and they actually become so bold that they steal our rations in the dark hours of the night when poor volunteer lies helpless and asleep."

If the first sight of the Capitol had inspired and excited the Vermonters, they were soon writing letters complaining about the city along the Potomac. "The Twelfth left its temporary quarters at the Soldiers' Rest, on Friday at 11 o'clock, and moved to our present camp," wrote Pvt. G.G. Benedict to the *Free Press,* "something over a mile to the east of the Capitol. It is upon the wide, high, level plain called Capitol Hill. To the south of us, but hidden from our sight, runs the eastern branch of the Potomac, and across it are the Virginia heights, with four or five forts crowning the more prominent elevations. The ground on which we are encamped had but two or three trees in a square mile, and having been the site of numerous camps, is not overstocked with grass. Some of the men looked a little blank as they saw the bare, cheerless surface of Virginia clay on which they were to pitch their tents, and some blanker yet when they took in the length and breadth of the little strips of canvas which were to be our only shelter from sun and storm . . . We got our little tents pitched by dark, and officers and men were by that time hungry enough to enjoy their supper of three hard army biscuits apiece,—there was no fuel to cook anything with, and our cooked rations had spoiled on the journey—and tired enough to drop off quickly to sleep, with but their blanket between them and the ground. Most of us, however, were waked at midnight by the rain driving into our little tabernacles. My bedfellow turned out and hung rubber blankets so as to keep out the most of it from us, and we dropped to sleep again, to sleep soundly till morning."

Washington, D.C., in 1862 was indeed a primitive capital city. Margaret Leetch, in her estimable book *Reveille in Washington,* looked back most of a century: "Immediately north of [Pennsylvania] Avenue, between the Capitol and the Executive Mansion, was the only part of Washington which was sufficiently built up to warrant the description of a city. Here were houses and churches and a few inadequate school buildings, and here, on Seventh Street, was the principal business section

Pennsylvania Avenue and the Capitol with its unfinished dome, which greeted Vermonters on their arrival in Washington

. . . Ugly blocks of offices had been hastily run up as a speculation. Shabby boardinghouses, little grocery shops, petty attorneys' offices and mean restaurants and saloons served the fifteen hundred clerks who were employed in the departments . . . It was a Southern town," she wrote, "without the picturesqueness, but with the indolence, the disorder and the want of sanitation. Its lounging Negroes startled Northern visitors with the reminder that slaves were held in the capital. Hucksters abounded. Fish and oyster peddlers cried their wares and tooted their horns on the corners. Flocks of geese waddled on the avenue, and hogs, of every size and color, roamed at large, making their muddy wallows on Capitol Hill and in Judiciary Square. People emptied slops and refuse in the gutters, and threw dead domestic animals into the canal."

The 12th arrived in Washington on October 8. The next day it was temporarily placed in a brigade with the 25th New Jersey Regiment and the nine-months 27th New Jersey, all under the command of a Colonel Derrom. The brigade was within the overall command of Maj. Gen. Silas Casey's Division of the Reserve Army Corps, charged with protecting the capital city. Casey, 55, white haired with sideburns and a hooked nose, was an old army regular, a veteran of the Seminole and Mexican wars. He had suffered bad luck during the Peninsula Campaign, his division having been overrun at the battle of Seven Pines. Destined for administrative duty through most of the rest of the war, he nonetheless left his mark, for his three-volume *System of Infantry Tactics* was widely referred to by inexperienced officers learning how to lead troops.

After a day of hardtack, rations of bread, beef, pork, and potatoes arrived, as did A-tents. "They are not the biggest things in the world—are in fact the simplest form of tent proper," wrote Private Benedict, "wedge shaped and holding six men apiece lying closely side by side; but they are TENTS, and can be closed against the weather. When we take the field, we must take the others again."

The 13th Vermont chugged in on October 13, setting up camp a half mile west of the 12th, also assigned to Colonel Derrom's brigade. Roswell Farnham wrote home, "Before [the tents] were pitched it began to rain & they passed a very uncomfortable night of it as the tents are so short that those who sleep in them get wet either at one end or the other." Farnham, as second in command of his regiment, had much better accommodations. "I have a good sized tent to myself," he noted. "Last night the Maj. & I rode down into the city and bought a mess chest & a lot of provisions so that we can now live."

Capt. Orcas Wilder of Waitsfield remembered, "It was the next morning after a severe rain storm had struck us in the night, blowing down more than half of our tents, that the surgeon making his morning rounds, remarked as he found the boys shivering from the cold, that he pitied them, whereupon one of the soldiers replied that he didn't, if anyone was dam fool enough to come down there he didn't deserve any pity."

Lieutenant Colonel Farnham wrote, "The unfinished capitol is just west of us. The dome is a magnificent structure. In every other direction is a barren plain, stripped of every portable thing by the thousands of troops that have encamped here. There is hardly a blade of grass under our feet and men have to go more than a mile to get limbs of trees for bedding in their tents."

Cpl. Edmund Clark of the 12th wrote to his future wife, Mary, in Georgia, Vermont: "One year ago I would have gone 20 miles to see a regiment of soldiers but I would not now go that number of rods . . . We are encamped on a large level field & the trenches on all sides of us & the marks of a thousand camp fires tell us that the ground has been occupied by other soldiers many of whom it may be are now numbered among the silent dead. You would laugh to look into our tent & see us great fellows lying sprawled out asleep like so many hogs. Last Saturday we had a Brigade review . . . Mary, as I marched down the streets & heard the praises which were bestowed upon us on all sides I must say I FELT PROUD to think I was in the army of the Union & a member of the 12th Vt."

Benedict wrote, "The troops, after review, were marched down to the city, through Pennsylvania Avenue to Gen. Casey's headquarters near Long Bridge, then back to camp, making in all a march of six miles or more. The boys stood it well. They are getting toughened pretty rapidly, although many suffer from diarrhoea and colds. The list of sick men in hospital, however, does not average over twenty, none of them being very sick."

As the Vermonters settled in at Washington, it was learned that a member of the 12th Vermont, a chaplain on a mission of mercy in south-central Pennsylvania, had caught first sight of the enemy. Benedict wrote of the incident: "Our chaplain returned to us to-day after an absence of four days, having been under rebel rule at Chambersburg [Pennsylvania] in the meanwhile. He left us at Baltimore to accompany a Vermont lady on her way to her brother, an officer in the Third Vt. who was lying at the point of death at Hagerstown; and was returning by way of Chambersburg when the rebels (under Gen. J.E.B. Stuart) occupied

A wartime view of the White House, as seen by the nine-months Vermont soldiers

the town. He thinks there were about 1,500 of them. They were well mounted, and well clothed as far as their captured U.S. clothing went—the men under strict discipline and perfect control of the officers, who conducted themselves in a gentlemanly way. Private persons and property were greatly respected. They left in a great hurry, amounting almost to a panic. The chaplain being with us, the order for evening prayer was observed this evening."

Sergeant Palmer was on guard duty the night of October 20. "Towards midnight faces grow sober," he wrote. "'This is pretty raw,' says one; 'little tough,' another; 'one must be drunk or mad,' continues a third, 'to enlist.' But the sun returns, with it smiling faces and good feelings. 'Soldiering is not very hard after all,' say the same. 'Not half as hard as I thought it,' etc."

On October 23 Benedict recorded: "Quite dusty for a day or two . . . yesterday morning the wind began to blow. It commenced before light with a furious gust, which woke our thousand sleepers, and many other thousands around us, to find the dust pouring in upon us through every opening and crevice. We sprang up and with blankets and over-coats closed the openings; but the dust was still there, kept in constant motion by the slatting of our canvas walls, and the only way was to lie down and take it as came. What a dirty crew crawled out of the tents that morning. You open your mouth, it is as if some one had put in a spoonful of pulverized clay. You put your hand to your hair, it feels like a dust brush. You touch your cheek, it is a clod . . . The dust penetrates every fiber and article of clothing; you feel dirty clear through."

Two days later he added, "The dust storm is over. The frost lies this morning thick and white on the ground. The sick are all doing well, except Captain Savage of Company A, who has been delirious and ran out of camp in his shirt and drawers last evening. He was found after a while in the barracks of a neighboring regiment . . . We had a soaker today—hard rain all day, tents soaked through, camp ground swimming; mud five to fifteen inches deep . . . The Fourteenth Regiment was sent up to Chain bridge night before last, which shows that the Vermont regiments are not to be brigaded together at present."

Private Williams wrote from the 14th Vermont on October 25, "Here at last at the Capitol, nearly worn out by fatigue, having had little or no rest since leaving Brattleboro. This is a very warm day and, while awaiting orders, three soldiers were sun struck."

The next day the 14th marched up the Potomac and across the river about a mile, becoming the first nine-months Vermont regiment to tread Virginia soil. There it was put into another of Casey's brigades, with some Maine troops. The campground was on Arlington Heights, near the stately former home of Robert E. Lee. "We here begin to see the devastating effects of war," said Williams. "Wherever I turn my eye I behold its ravages. I can see pleasant homes and fair fields, that have been left only to be ravaged and laid waste by the relentless hand of war."

A day later, the 15th Vermont reached Washington and was immediately moved across the Potomac to join the 14th and the Maine troops. Two days later, the 14th and 15th marched back to Capitol Hill and went into camp with the 12th, 13th, and the 16th, just in from Vermont. Wheelock Veazey, commander of the 16th, wrote to his wife, who had just informed him that she was pregnant:

> My own Angel Wife,
>
> We got into camp on Monday on East Capitol Hill . . . Should think you were getting weighty indeed. You think it is a sure thing, do you? Well I guess you have the hardest nine months before you. I wish I could be with you & be with my own angel. What a good time we had together . . . It is too bad to have such a splendid wife and be away from her.

Private Williams also wrote home: "On Wednesday, before the order to pitch our tents was hardly completed, a new order came, rebrigading the five Vermont regiments by themselves, under Col. Blunt of the 12th, the ranking colonel, constituting it the 3d Brigade, Casey's Division."

Cpl. Edmund Clark wrote, "We have just got some great news the 12, 13, 14, 15, & 16 Vt. Regts are to be brigaded together."

While in and near Washington, the Vermonters had eagerly sought passes for sight-seeing in Washington. George Barnett wrote home to Newbury: "I with some of the boys went into the Capitol of the United States and saw such a splendid building as I never imagined, it is built entirely of marble, it has one temple and 2 wings covering in all nearly 4 acres of land. I went through most every part of it except one of the wings which was full of sick soldiers . . . I never thought I should have a chance to go into the Capitol. I almost feel myself honored."

Lieutenant Colonel Cummings informed his wife: "Today I rode down Pennsylvania Avenue past Willard's Hotel and the Presidential mansion . . . The tenement occupied by 'Old Abe' is respectable in appearance, and I shall judge decently comfortable. It is large enough for his family, I presume, but not so large as I had supposed."

Private Jackson described the Smithsonian Institution: "It is a splendid building built of red sandstone. It is a curious building abounding in turrets and towers and any quantity of wings."

Corporal Clark: "We left the Capitol & took the horse cars and rode through some of the principal streets of the city passing on our way the Treasury Department & the WHITE house. We visited a life like statue of Washington mounted on a monument 20 feet square. Oh Mary I can't tell you anything about it. I tell you it will pay any body well to come here to see what is to be seen."

Sergeant Palmer noted, "Many soldiers are in the Capitol, who move about as if they were on their own farm. I hear arguing in this wise: 'We've as much right here as anybody; Abe Lincoln has no more. We are freeborn Americans, and have come here to defend our won property.'"

Pvt. John Wallace in the 15th wrote to his sister in the Connecticut Valley town of Barnet: "I was detailed to go to the city and buy a stove for the company . . . I took the whole afternoon for it and saw a great many fine sights that I never saw in Barnet. I went into the public gardens and saw some of the finest plants I ever read of and then went into the greenhouse and such a display I never imagined could be brought together as there was there from every country in the world. If I had had a book I would have confiscated some of the leaves and flowers and sent you some . . . Washington would be a handsome place if it was situated anywhere in the north where they would clean up the streets and clear out the hogs. You would sometimes see a hundred of them walking the streets as deliberately as if they were the sole occupants of the place, and niggers are as plenty as the white folks."

Jabez Hammond told his family: "Yesterday was the first day I have done duty since you and mother left Brattleboro. Having had the diarhea since that day and it still follows me up. To day I have taken some cholera medicine and several powders that the Sergeant gave me and feel better to night . . . The order of the day is as follows. Roll Call five Oclock AM Police of camp five thirty. wash squads from five thirty to six Breakfast six thirty Squad drill seven thirty or eight thirty guard mount eight thirty Company drill ten to eleven Battalion drill two thirty to four PM. but it is bed time and I must stop."

As Hammond noted, men in all the regiments were getting sick; the rain and chill, the crowded conditions, and the inconsistent quality of food were certainly factors. Here and there, a case of typhoid fever was diagnosed. Benedict noted that many boys suffered from homesickness. And there were accidents. Private Irwin wrote: "We have had but one death in our Co. Geo. Collamer from Shelburne he went with me and two others two miles down in the City after mules and one of them kicked him and he was sick from that time till he died he was a fine fellow and we miss him very much."

There were other unpleasant matters. Cpl. Thomas T. Snell of the 13th, from Enosburg, near the Canadian border, recalled: "My duty as corporal of the guard was the saddest of my army life. One of the boys without the password knocked down a comrade on guard duty, and ran to the city. He was arrested and landed in the guard house, and I was directed to hang him up by his thumbs to the ridge pole; so he was obliged to stand on tip toe. It was not for me to say when he was punished enough. The colonel soon left us. The culprit was soon in actual pain, and begged me to let him down. I found the colonel to get permission to relieve him. He finally told me I could cut him down when he became limber in the knees and not till then. I felt bad for the fellow, but think he got no more than he deserved. It was a warning to us all, and I'm glad to say it was the only case of the kind I knew of in the regiment."

Word of the incident spread quickly through the brigade, and it was generally believed that Colonel Stoughton had ordered such harsh punishment.

David Hard, a private from Burlington, had problems on the streets of Washington. "They made a teamster of me and in about two days the quartermaster went with us to get our teams," he said. "Well, we arrived safely to where the horses and wagons were. I got my rig consisting of four horses, wild as hawks, never had a harness on. Well after about two hours of work with four or five men we succeeded in getting the animals hitched to the wagons. I mounted the seat which consisted of a rough board without springs or cushion. I was ordered to take a load of bread to camp and after considerable manipulating I got started with my rig and bread, pretty soon my steeds wanted to go faster and I had to let them go, kept them headed towards camp. The patrolmen were after me with drawn sabers, ordering me to drive slower, but I stuck to the wagon and let them go. When I got into camp my bread was scattered all along the road for three miles. I turned my team over to the quartermaster and resigned my position."

Hard also noted, "At the request of the surgeon, Dr. Nichols, I was detailed to drive ambulance. They managed to keep me going from camp to the city every day . . . When I found anything loose in the streets that my tentmates would like I would pick it up and take it in."

One night a local man came into camp and serenaded the 13th Vermont with patriotic songs. The men took particular delight in a tune that ended with the chorus, "From many a spire in Richmond."

As October waned, illness began to take the final toll. A private in the 13th wrote, "During the first days of our encampment First Lieutenant Nathaniel Jones Jr. [of Moretown] was taken sick and died October 30. His death was the first break in our ranks and it cast a gloom over the whole company."

Hammond wrote home, "I suppose that you have heard of the death of E. Hopkins before this time. There was a paper circulated in the company this afternoon for the purpose of raising money to effray the expenses of imbalming and transportation of the body home there was upwards of thirty five dollars raised and there is still more to sign."

Writing to his mother and sister in Burlington in late October, Private Irwin of the 12th said, "You will see by the heading of my letter . . . we were formed in a brigade with the 13, 14, 15, 16th Vermont Regts and supposed that we would stay in Washington some time if not all winter so we went to work and fixed our tents up so that they were very comfortable some of the men spent four or five dollars in fixing them and all went merry as a marriage bell. But oh the uncertainty of war . . . " Irwin also wrote, "If you want to hear from the Regt get a copy of the *Free Press* when you can as Mr. Benedict's letters are very interesting and they tell the thing just as it is."

The 12th and 13th had just stockaded their tents when Second Vermont Brigade Commander Blunt, on October 29, received orders to be ready to march the next morning. The previous evening there had been a celebration in the camps of the Vermont regiments. Private Benedict wrote: "The brigading of these Vermont regiments is particularly satisfactory to us, and we of the Twelfth were also gratified that command of the brigade should fall to our colonel. Co. C first got the news, just after dark last evening, and turning out, they filed down to the colonel's tent, led by Captain Page, and gave three cheers for the Second Vermont Brigade, and Colonel Blunt commanding. This called out the colonel who made one of the little speeches which he makes so happily . . . He congratulated the men on the brigading of these five fine Vermont regiments, which, he felt sure would fight side by side like true comrades. He explained that the command fell to him by virtue of his rank as senior colonel; that it was merely temporary and could last only till a brigadier general should be placed over us, as he trusted a good one soon would be.

"'We have hitherto, my boys,' he said, 'seen but the pleasant part of a soldier's life. Thus far we have known little of trial and suffering, and nothing of danger. The rough times are yet to come. When they do come we must meet them like men, each doing the very best he knows how to do, for the cause of the country, the honor of our State, and for the credit of the Twelfth, and looking to God to grant us success.' Other companies came up in succession, each to cheer the colonel and call him out for a speech, the drum corps winding up the series with a salute and Yankee Doodle."

★

8

Within sight of the Vermont camps on Capitol Hill lay the Confederate States of America, just across the wide Potomac to the south, in Virginia. The time to move into hostile territory had arrived. On the last night that the Second Vermont Brigade camped on friendly land, Private Hatch, of the 12th Vermont, wrote to his wife: "We have got to move tomorrow morning we have got to go over the river into Virginia . . . I wish you could be here tonight to see this camp and hear the noise . . . there is so many fires burning all around that it is light as day and the men are hallowing in every direction and it makes a perfect bedlam."

With Colonel Blunt temporarily commanding the brigade, leadership of the 12th went to Roswell Farnham, who wrote to his wife on October 30, "We left camp at eight o'clock Thursday morning, marched down through the city in fine style and across long bridge, past Arlington Heights."

While Farnham rode the new horse recently presented by his soldiers, Private Irwin was in the ranks. "The whole brigade started down by the Capitol and through the city," he reported, "and I tell you it was a splendid sight to see those five thousand stalwart sons of old Vermont marching down Pennsylvania Avenue."

Albert Clarke, a Montpelier lawyer, now a lieutenant in the 13th, said the brigade "marched down Pennsylvania Avenue to the tune of 'The Girl I Left Behind Me.'"

According to George Benedict, the brigade "crossed the river by Long Bridge, and moving out five miles into the country back of Arlington Heights, halted near Munson's Hill and camped in the edge of a stretch of oak timber, where fresh green grass, near a stream of clear water." He wrote, "Our present camp bids fair to be a great improvement on our late one, as far as the ground and nearness to wood and water are concerned." He added, "You have heard before this of the death of young Collamer of Shelburne. It is the first gap made by death in the ranks of Company C, we feel it keenly. He was an amiable and excellent young man . . . His disease was uncontrollable. For a day or two the doctors thought he might rally, but he did not agree with them. 'I shall die in three days,' he said one night, and in three days he died, peacefully, even happily, for he had made his peace with God."

The entire brigade spent its first day and night on Confederate soil. At the same time, back in Montpelier, US Sen. Solomon Foot, home from Washington,

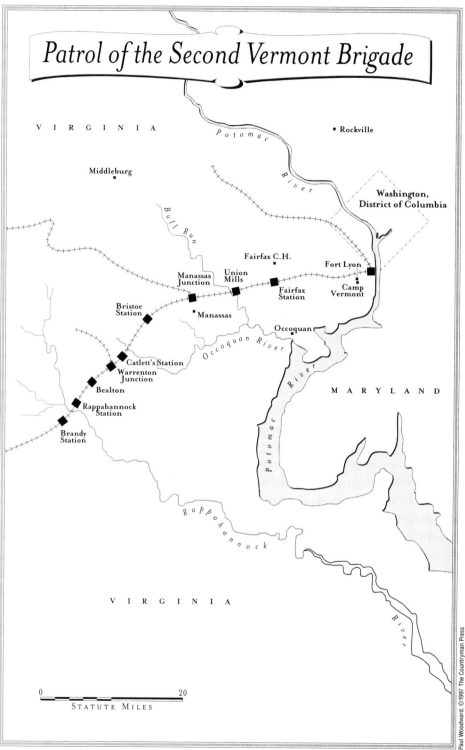

Patrol of the Second Vermont Brigade

VIRGINIA

Potomac River

• Rockville

Middleburg

Washington, District of Columbia

Bull Run

Fairfax C.H.

Fort Lyon

Manassas Junction

Union Mills

Fairfax Station

Camp Vermont

Bristoe Station

• Manassas

Occoquan River

Occoquan

Catlett's Station

Warrenton Junction

Bealton

Rappahannock Station

Potomac River

MARYLAND

Brandy Station

Rappahannock

VIRGINIA

River

0   20
STATUTE MILES

rose in the State House to address the General Assembly. "My fellow citizens," he began, "this rebellion must be crushed. It must be done in the briefest possible period, and if one million men is not enough to do it, call two millions; and if two millions will not do it, then let every loyal man and woman who can shoulder a musket, or wield a mop handle, come to the rescue, and then, my life upon it, our country will be saved. I will speak for my own, and pledge for her that she will never be behind any one in the day of her country's need.

"If the 16 regiments are not the full proportion," he went on, ". . . if the twelve or fourteen thousand who have gone forth robed for the sacrifice are not enough, let the blast of war be echoed along these hills, and every man and every woman will hasten from their homes to fill up the hospitals of the sick, and every mother will make haste to offer her son, rather than that the bright orb of this republic shall go down in perpetual darkness and night."

In Virginia, the Vermonters christened their new campground Camp Seward. Private Hatch told his wife the troops were having a fine time chasing rabbits. "It would please you to hear the boys run and hollar after them," he said. "There is lots of black snakes and rattle snakes around . . . there is cannon balls all about here on the ground that has been shot at somebody."

The Vermonters' stay at Camp Seward was to be brief. The next day the 12th and 15th regiments moved down the south bank of the Potomac to Arlington,

Camp Seward in a sketch by William Henry Jackson, of the 12th Vermont

where an important Union supply base was located. From Arlington they continued toward historic Mount Vernon, the home of George Washington. Their stopping point was a spot south of Hunting Creek, and south of some heavily fortified heights that protected Arlington and Washington, where they established another campground. George Benedict wrote that the two regiments "were sent to the south by ten miles' march through Alexandria, to a spot south of Hunting Creek, on the road to Mount Vernon, to take the places of [Daniel E.] Sickles's [Excelsior] brigade, which had marched the day before, with other troops, to join General [Franz] Sigel at Centreville. The two regiments bivouacked there for the night and the next day moved another mile-and-a-half south, to a spot the brigade would occupy the next four weeks. The three other regiments followed on November 5 and the camp was christened 'Camp Vermont,' the brigade headquarters being established in a wing of the mansion of a Mr. George Mason—an old Virginian who declared himself 'neutral' on the war issue."

Private Benedict, in his first minutes at Camp Vermont, was detailed for picket: "We were marched off rapidly two or three miles farther to the brow of the high ground which looks off on the valley of the Potomac, stretching many a mile to the south," he reported, "in a varied scene of meadow and timber, now glowing with the bright colors of the American autumn . . . Away below winds the Potomac through a magnificent valley, woodland and meadow varying the prospect and evergreens relieving the bright coloring of the oak forest. Directly in front lies Mount Vernon, the house hidden by the interposing ridge, but the estate plainly in view."

Private Hatch wrote, "If we can go a little ways from our camp we can look back down into Alexandria onto Washington and fairfax seminary and can see the shipping on the Potomac for miles it is quite a scenery. There is once in a while a rabid old rebel on his plantation there is one within 10 rods of our tent we keep the old scamp a fretting all the time we steal his wood then he will run to the colonel."

The Vermonters were truly in Old Virginia, in a land of plantations. Besides Mr. Mason's Spring Bank, just down the road was the most revered of all the old homes, George Washington's Mount Vernon, which quickly become a favorite tourist stop for off-duty Vermonters.

Roswell Farnham wrote home from "beyond Hunting Creek" on November 2: "We are camped near a plantation owner's house that was once a fine establishment but is now going to ruin. He hangs out a white flag—but is evidently secesh in his feelings."

George Mason, born in Virginia in 1797, had become alarmed about the invading Yankees as soon as federal forces began to arrive in large numbers in and around Washington in 1861. He had written to Robert E. Lee, reminding the Confederate commander that he had known him when he was a boy, and noting that Washington was filling with "armed thousands." He went on to say that the new arrivals were not "regular and distinguished soldiers, but fanatics and lawless ruffians ready for every outrage and violence."

Soon from Spring Bank to Farnham came a letter from Mason that was quickly forwarded to Brigade Commander Blunt:

Colonel,

In my Note of thanks to you this morning for your kindness in placing Guards around my House to preserve my sick Family from annoyance, I took occasion to state that under some misapprehension of orders, on yesterday my Family Physician coming to visit my sick Daughter, & a Neighbor to bring her some sustenance & medicine had been arrested & prevented access to the House.—This morning on going out, I find myself & Family prisoners; as the Guards will not allow us to pass beyond their immediate circle, even to the wood pile & Barn.— This, of course, is from a misapprehension of the purpose for which they were placed here; but the interruption and confine-ment is exceedingly annoying, as even if one of my Cows or Horses were to get out, we cannot go bring them in, or for any other necessary business about the premises.—I have but a single man servant hired, & during his absense from the House, we have no means of looking after anything.—I pray you Sir, to correct this evil, as early as possible; I should be greatly obliged, that you would send me a written order, that I may hold & show to any one on post, allowing myself and Family and visitors free ingress & egress to my House.—During all the Encampments around us, during the last Eighteen months, this has been always allowed us, without the slightest interruption.— I am very sure, Colonel, it will be your pleasure to accord to us the same.— Our situation is sad enough at best; & I am convinced it is entirely contrary to your wishes to place us under any constraint or inconvenience that is un-necessary.

Colonel Blunt responded:

Sir:

In reply I have only to say that your loyalty to the United States Gov-ernment is strongly suspected not only by the troops in this immediate vicin-ity but also at Head Quarters. And altho' I shall not permit my troops to destroy your property unless necessary for government purposes or to disturb your family, still I cannot make arrangements for the comfort of yourself & family with the same cordiality that I could if I felt that you stood by the flag under which I serve, which has so long protected you.

My advice to you is, that in the place of the non-committal emblem which now hangs over your dwelling you unfurl the stars and stripes, and if you have not already done so that you take the oath of allegiance to our Gov-ernment at once.

Eventually, Mason took the oath of allegiance.

On November 7, Farnham wrote to his wife: "In the first place it has snowed hard all day & blown a hurricane & the boys have had a hard time in their tents . . . We are encamped near an old Virginia mansion owned by G. Mason Esq . . .

65

He is a secessionist at heart. His house is a two story one & things were once in good shape, but his slaves have all run away & the troops have ruined him . . . We have occupied his barn with our horses and today Col. Blunt, who has command of this brigade moved his headquarters into the house—into two vacant rooms in one wing . . . His plantation is a desert & his mansion will soon be in the condition of hundreds in the vicinity . . . I have just come from a visit to Col. Blunt at his new headquarters. He has two big fire places & looks as cheerful as possible. Rather different from our tents, tho' we are comfortable. Soon we shall have comfortable huts made & then we can bid defiance to the weather."

Private Benedict noted on November 7: "We are enjoying a veritable snow storm. It began at 7 o'clock this morning, has fallen steadily, and now at 7 PM, at least five inches of snow lies upon the ground.—But there is little suffering in this regiment. Not that a small tent . . . soaked with moisture from damp snow, is the most warm and cheerful habitation imaginable; but it can be closed tight enough to keep the snow from actual contact with its inmates, and by piling on what woolen clothing he has, in all shapes, a healthy man can keep up the warmth of his body, and by snuggling close to his comrades can sleep with some approach to comfort."

Benedict also noted that the soldiers were finding ways of rigging up little stoves for their tents: "A piece of sheet iron," he wrote, "a foot or two square, bent as to the edges so as to form a shallow pan, was inverted over a hole in the ground for corresponding size; a tube of bent sheet iron, leading from the outer air to the bottom of the hole provides air, and a joint or two of rusty stove pipe, eked out with one or two topless and bottomless tin cans, makes a chimney which draws like a blister plaster."

On November 5, frustrated by the lack of aggressiveness in pursuing Robert E. Lee's army in its retreat from bloody Antietam, Abraham Lincoln relieved George McClellan as commander of the Army of the Potomac. Word quickly spread through the ranks, though the men of the Second Vermont Brigade took little interest since few had served under "Little Mac." Private Benedict said, "There has been no mutiny in the Second Vermont brigade in consequence of General McClellan's removal, and any change that promises more active and efficient service for the army, will have our hearty approval."

Jabez Hammond wrote, "We have received orders from Colonel Blunt to rig up winter quarters our huts to be made of small poles and are to be about sixteen feet square there is to be a fireplace in each there is to be six number to each company . . . Have been to work on a fort about 100 rods from here today."

Not far north of Camp Vermont was high ground, fortified against any rebel attacks from the south. There a new fortification, Fort Lyon, was under construction. It overlooked the old Telegraph Road, which led deep into Virginia—eventually to Fredericksburg and Richmond—and was a likely route of approach for any Confederate raiders. The Vermonters were assigned to build its earthen parapets, and they hated the work. "The fort building business, the boys resented, saying they were ready to fight, but digging Virginia clay in mud and water was not in their contract, and some were sullen and ugly, and contrary, and were not a success in building forts with spade and pick," said Private Sturtevant. "Some three hundred a day from the Thirteenth, and I assume an equal number from the other regiments,

SCOTTS BLUFF NATIONAL MONUMENT

Vermont soldiers reluctantly march off to work on the ramparts of Fort Lyon,
as sketched by Private Jackson.

for a number of days were detailed to work on this fort."

A corporal in the 13th, Thomas Snell, said: "I told my 16 men if I caught one of them sweating I would send him to camp and detail the other 15 men to take him there. I am of the opinion there is but one place you can get a soldier to do much with a spade and pick, and that is when he is placed at night on guard near a rebel picket line and has to dig a hole before day light to protect himself or loose his head."

Working on forts "made me tired," wrote Pvt. Martin Pope, from Highgate, adding, "there are plenty of niggers around who knew how to build forts."

More snow fell. "The unpleasant thing for the boys," said Private Sturtevant, "was guard and picket duty, which must be attended to; a large detail was made each day for the picket line, a mile or more south of our camp, extending from the Potomac low lands westward for a number of miles, and on this picket line for twenty-four hours in such a storm was not so pleasant an experience . . . we were not even allowed to make fires on the picket line."

A homesick William Doubleday wrote:

Dear Asceneth,

Asceneth I am sorry I caused you to feel bad. I must leave off writing such letters, but can you blame me. You don't know how anxious I was to get a letter from you. I will tell you all about what a good time I had out on picket when I get home to Vt. One of our men was shot the first night we were out. He was shot by one of our own men by accident, was shot through the right breast. The ball went in just above the nipple and came out between the shoulders. They thought he could not live but he is alive yet & is better tonight. It rained all the time we out on the lines . . . There was 12 or 15 acres of stout corn that had not been husked, some not cut up. I will send father a few kernals of it to plant.

The earliest Virginia winter in memory was beginning, and in the first days of November considerably more snow lay on the ground than the folks back home were reporting in Vermont. On November 8, Lieutenant Colonel Cummings told his wife in Brattleboro: "Yesterday we had a regular Vermont snowstorm. It snowed all day and blew in such fitful, driving gusts that I could not make my stove draw; so I wrapped in my great coat all day. The snow piled in drifts 12 to 18 inches deep . . . Thursday I was field officer of the day and as such had charge of the pickets. These consist of four companies, and are stationed from 2 to 3 miles from camp, the chain extending from the Potomac irregularly 8 miles westward. I visited all the posts twice in the day time and once in the night. In the 24 hours I rode from 40 to 50 miles horseback, through forests, ravines, pastures and brush and brier. The night visit was pleasant in the extreme . . . My only draw back was a persistent diarrhaea that caused me frequently to dismount. The night was light as the moon was near her full and the excitement of espying the pickets, of riding up hill and down, jumping fences, ravines, ditches and dodging boughs, &c. I cannot portray."

The same day Pvt. Joel Glover wrote to his wife, "Tell John not to worry at all about home for I know who is there. If you and John see fit to sell the oxen you may but get all you can for them . . . Tell Emily and Willy to be good children for I think of them every day . . . If anybody wrongs you in [a] deal I will see to it when I get home.

"There is two men in our company who is going to be discharged in a few days and there is another one that has fits and will be discharged this is a hard place for a man to be sick but anybody that is as tough as I am can get along nicely."

At Camp Vermont, the soldiers were beginning to settle into a routine. Writing to the *Green Mountain Freeman* from "Hunter's Creek, Va.," a soldier reported, "Our orderly, Chas. White, is now complaining of tobacco smoke, which is quite thick in our little tent to-night . . . Our camp is merry to-night; some of the boys are singing John Brown; some hymn tunes, while others are dancing & playing the elephant."

On November 14, Private Benedict sent to the *Free Press* a letter he titled "An Ordinary Day in Camp." He wrote: "In absence of any thing especially exciting, let me try and describe, briefly, an ordinary day in camp . . . The tents of the colonel and his staff are commonly disposed in a line at the rear of the camp. In a parallel line with them are the tents of the officers, each captain's tent fronting the street of his company. The company streets run at right angles to the line of the officers' tents, and are of variable widths, in different camps, according to the extent of the ground. In our present camp they are about twenty-five feet wide. On each are the company tents, nine on a side, facing the street on the same side. At the inner end of the street, on one side, is the cook tent, occupied by the company

A camp sutler sketched by Private Jackson

cooks and stores, and in front of it is the 'kitchen range' . . . It is composed of a trench, four feet long and two deep, dug in the ground. In the bottom of this the fire is kindled. Forked sticks at the corners, support a couple of stout poles, parallel with the sides, across which are laid shorter sticks on which hang the kettles . . .

"The first signs of life, inside of the lines of the main camp guard, are to be seen at these points. The cooks must be up an hour or two before light, to get their fires started and breakfast cooking. The fires on cold mornings, and most of the mornings are cold, are objects of attraction to those of the soldiers who for any reason have lain too cold to sleep. These come shivering to the fires, and watch the cooks and warm their shins, till reveille. There are stoves now, however, of some sort, in most of the tents, and almost all can be as warm as they wish at any time."

He described the morning routine: "At daybreak the drum major marshalls his drum and fife corps at the centre of the line, and the reveille, with scream of fife and roll of drum, arouses the sleeping hundreds, lying wrapped in their blankets under the canvas roofs . . . The men tumble out for the most part just as they have slept, some with blankets wrapped about them, some in slippers and smoking caps, some in overcoats. They fall into line and the orderly sergeant calls the roll and reads the list of details for guard, police, fatigue duty, etc. After roll call, many dive back into their tents and take a morning nap before breakfast; others start in squads for the brook which runs close by camp, to wash. The fortunate owners of wash basins—there are two in our company—bring them out, use them, and pass them over to the numerous borrowers; others wash in water from their canteens, one pouring on the hands of another.

"'Police duty' comes at 6:15, and is performed by a squad under direction of a corporal . . . In camp 'police duty' corresponds to what, when I was a boy, was called clearing up the door yard . . . At half past six comes the 'surgeon's call.' This is not a call made by the surgeon, who is not expected to appear in company quarters unless for some special emergency; but of the orderly sergeant, who calls for any who have been taken sick in the night, and feel bad enough to own it and be marched off to the surgeon's tent, where, after examination, they are ordered into hospital or on duty, as the case may require.

"Breakfast takes place at 7, by which time, in well ordered tents, the blankets have been shaken, folded and laid away with the knapsacks in a neat row at the back of the tent, and the soldiers start out, cup in hand, for the cook tent, where each takes his plate with his allowance of bread and beef or pork, and fills his cup with coffee. Some sit and eat their breakfast on the wood pile near the fire, but most take their meals to their tents . . . Our meals do not differ greatly, the principal difference being that for dinner we have cold water instead of tea or coffee. The rations are beef, salt and fresh, three-fifths of the former to two of the latter, both of fair quality; salt pork, which has uniformly been excellent; bread, soft and hard . . . rice, beans, both good, and potatoes occasionally; coffee fair, and tea rather poor. Butter, which when good is one of the greatest luxuries in camp, cheese, apples, which with most Vermonters are almost essential, and other knicknacks, are not furnished by government, but may be bought of the sutlers at high prices. Our men are great hands for toast; and at every meal the cook-fires are surrounded with a circle of boys holding their bread to the fire on forked sticks or wire toast racks of their own manufacture, and of wonderful size and description. So we live, and it shows to what the human frame may be inured by practice and hardship, that we can eat a meal of good baked or boiled pork and beans, potatoes, boiled rice and sugar, coffee and toast, and take it not merely to sustain life, but actually with a relish—curious isn't it?

"Dinner is at 12," he continued, "dress parade at 4:30, and supper at 5:30. The heavy work of the men fills the intervals. This varies. At Capitol Hill it was company and militia drills. Here it is digging in the trenches of Fort Lyon, and cutting lumber in the woods near by, for our winter quarters. Evenings are spent very much as they would be by most young men at home, in visiting their comrades, playing cards and checkers, writing letters, and reading. A common occupation of a leisure hour, with the smokers, is the carving of pipes from the roots of the laurel, found in profusion in the woods here . . . Another common, but not so delightful pastime, is the washing of one's dirty clothes. Many of our men have learned to be expert washers, and that without wash-board or pounding barrel. Those who have pocket money, however, can have their washing done by the 'contraband' washerwomen, who have been on hand at every camp we have occupied.

"At half-past eight PM the tattoo is sounded by the drum and fife corps, playing several tunes at reveille, when each company is again drawn up in its street and the roll called. At nine comes 'taps,' when every light must be out in the tents, and the men turn in for their night's rest. The ground within the tents is covered with straw or cedar branches, on which are spread the rubber blankets; this is the bed, the knapsack is the pillow. There is no trouble about undressing; our blouses, or flannel fatigue coats, pantaloons and stockings, sometimes with overcoat added, are the apparel of the night, as of the day. We slip off our boots, drop in our places side by side, draw over us our blankets; and sleep, sound and sweet, soon comes to every eyelid."

On November 24, Private Benedict wrote: "We have had four days of rain and I have the facts for an essay on Virginia and mud, whenever I get time to write it, and I assure you it is a deep subject. Orders were put out on Thursday for a grand review at Fort Albany, six miles from here, of all the forces on this side of the river. It was the third and hardest day of the storm. A countermand was expected; but none came, and the Twelfth, with three other regiments, took up its line of march . . . It was a hard march. The foot planted in the red salve alluded to, is lifted with some difficulty, and comes up a number of sizes heavier and three or four pounds lighter."

Benedict noted that a mile past Alexandria a courier rode to the head of the column with orders to return to camp. "The substance of the proceeding," he wrote, "was that four thousand men had a march of eight miles in a storm . . . Perhaps 'somebody blundered.'"

The previous fall, in 1861, when the First Vermont Brigade had first come south, a private was found asleep while on picket duty and, after a court-martial, was sentenced to be shot. But William Scott's life was spared on orders from Abraham Lincoln, and the private from Groton was known throughout the remainder of his brief life (he was killed in April 1862 at Lee's Mills) as "the Sleeping Sentinel." In the first days at Camp Vermont, according to Capt. Aro Slayton, from Calais, one night while checking picket outposts, he and a lieutenant found some Second Brigade members asleep at their posts. A friend of Slayton's recalled: "After consulting a moment they crept up to the tree and having secured the guns, retreated a short distance and gave a wild yell. Instantly the pickets sprang to their feet for their guns which to their consternation were not to be found. After a few moments the officers made themselves known and after administering a sharp reprimand, informed the men that while the penalty for the offense was death, on account of their previous good records and fatigue from over work they should say nothing about it unless the men themselves spoke of it, in which case all would be liable to court marshall. To this one of the men replied, 'Guess if you don't say anything about it, Captain, we sha'nt,' and he never did."

A private in the 13th Vermont, John Dwyer, from Richford, one day strayed beyond camp and knocked on the door of a house that proved to be the home of a doctor and his family. "There were two nice appearing young ladies at home," said Dwyer. "They said their father was in Capitol prison because he would not take the oath of allegiance. Also they had four brothers in the Confederate army they wished they had five."

Wilson Winter, from Chittenden, a private in the 14th, wrote to his wife from Camp Vermont about his plans to have a photograph taken. "You wanted me to send my picture," he said. "I don't know when I can for they haint paid us any thing yet and the money I've not got I will try [to] get it and send it quick as I can and when they pay I will try and send you some."

On November 11, Private Hatch wrote to his wife, "How do you and Leslie get along there alone we have the same sun and moon and stars to look at that you do. I have thought a great many times when I have been out in the evening looking at the moon and stars if you was not looking at them at the same time."

Within Camp Vermont, Colonel Veazey—now married a year—hunkered down in his tent each day and wrote one or two letters to "my angel wife." He wrote on November 8, "If you could get into my arms my sweet love how happy I would be. Oh my own darling, you don't know how dearly I love you, what a splendid time we had together." This was followed a few days later with another fond reminiscence of their farewell at Brattleboro: "It is dreadful cold sleeping alone after being at home so long. What a good time I had while at home. Do you remember when you first went to the hotel at B?"

On November 22, a soldier in the 14th Vermont wrote home, "I think Elias Baker of Company B will make the best shot of any man in the regiment. A wild duck came flying along and alighted in the stream nearby where the reserve was stationed. Two of the boys fired their pieces at it, scaring it up without hurting it. But Baker, drawing his 'Manhattan' revolver from his pocket, shot the duck through the breast, while at considerable height in the air."

In early November, the brigade heard the first sounds of war. They came from the west, cannon fire—not the roar of big guns close up, but a distant rumble, the sound of skirmishing at Snicker's Gap in the Blue Ridge Mountains. Then all was silent and fighting again seemed rather far away. In mid-November, Brigade Commander Blunt extended an invitation to his wife in St. Johnsbury to join him in camp.

On November 19, Veazey penned still another love letter, which also contained the following line of real military substance, and referred to his best friend, the commander of the 15th Vermont: "Proctor and I are ordered to be ready to move at notice."

★

9

The relative quiet on the eastern battlefields was nearing an end as winter settled on Virginia. The Army of the Potomac, now commanded by Maj. Gen. Ambrose Burnside, was massed along the Rappahannock River opposite Fredericksburg. As soon as pontoons arrived, the army would go over the river to move against the Army of Northern Virginia, which was manning the well-fortified heights just east of town. The Second Vermont Brigade moved forward to replace units gone down to Fredericksburg.

"Last Tuesday evening the Brigade was called upon for 3 Regiments to go to Bull Run at Union Mills," wrote Charles Cummings on November 28. "They left about 9 o'clock in the evening the rain coming down abuntantly. It was pitchy blackness and unpleasant."

Orders had arrived to divide the Second Vermont, for the time being. The Vermonters were called on to strengthen the outer line of the Washington defenses and on November 26 the 13th, 14th, and 15th regiments were sent to picket along the Occoquan River and Bull Run, and to guard the Orange and Alexandria Railroad. Colonel Randall, of the 13th, was put in charge of those regiments, with Colonel Blunt to remain at Camp Vermont with the 12th and 16th. Lieutenant Spafford wrote, "It is very dark and begins to rain. I can hear the 14th just marching off to the tune of 'Old Shady' or 'Away, Away, I Can't Stay With You Longer.' They will have a wet time before morning."

Private Benedict reported: "The night was dark and rainy, and as the other regiments passed on the double quick through our camp, their dark columns visible only by the light of the camp fires, our boys cheering them and they cheering lustily in response, the scene was not devoid of excitement. Every man in the ranks believed that such a sudden night march to the front meant immediate action, and the haste and hearty shouting showed that the prospect was a welcome one."

"Officers carrying lanterns rode at the front and the rear, but our progress was painfully slow," according to Pvt. John Forest, of the 13th, from Colchester. "We kept together fairly well until midnight when the line broke at a cross-road, and in the darkness and rain about half of the regiment wandered down the wrong track. After what seemed ten hours we found our comrades again."

Private Glover, in the 15th, said of the march, "We started we know not where it was dark as Egypt and we marched till four in the morning."

Corporal Williams, in the 14th, wrote afterward: "In camp near the

Occoquon Creek, Va. After leaving Camp Vermont . . . we marched until four o'clock the next morning, when the column halted, and was ordered to stack arms and rest. It being very dark and muddy, our march was very slow. Fires were built to dry our clothes, and we lay down to rest, making ourselves as comfortable as circumstances would allow. When daylight came, we found we were within six miles of Fairfax Court House, and at eight o'clock we resumed our march, our place of destination still being a mystery to us. We halted again one mile the other side of the Court House, to take dinner, after which we again took up our line of march. At Fairfax Station we again halted and pitched tents— such as we carry when on the march. We rested well that night, being fatigued with our marching. At about ten o'clock this morning, we resumed our march, each man again being supplied with one day's ration of hard bread. We marched until about noon, when the regiments separated, the 13th and 15th going off in the direction of Bull Run, and the 14th being ordered to its present camp."

The 13th's tents lagged well behind on wagons, so, according to a private, "We made bough houses . . . everywhere, no regularity being observed in their arrangement . . . It was 10 days before the tents arrived."

The Vermonters were now much closer to the front. The territory on the far sides of the Occoquan and Bull Run were most decidedly rebel, although with few if any Confederate regulars in the vicinity. Williams wrote: "False alarms are very frequent to soldiers stationed near the enemy. Last night, the first of our arrival, the 14th was formed in line of battle about midnight, firing being heard near by, which signalized the approach of the enemy. The regiment was formed in line with great alacrity. Our officers praised us highly. The firing proved not to proceed from the enemy however. We have part of a battery of artillery with us, and also a squad of cavalry, which go out scouting every day."

The move by the three regiments had placed them near Manassas, along Bull Run, where two big battles had been fought. Pvt. Samuel Dana wrote to his wife and children in Warren, "There is a lot of rebel graves around here. Some of them are buried so near the top of the ground that some of the boys kicked off a little dirt and their feet stuck out." He added, "The Col. says if we see anything that looks lovely to make love to it, so some of the boys killed three beef cattle and some hogs and brought them into camp, but I didn't get any."

Back at Camp Vermont things were quiet, and several officers took a break. Lieutenant Colonel Cummings, the Brattleboro newspaper editor, went to Washington, where he knew some people in rather high places. He wrote, ". . . going up from Alexandria by a steamboat—nine miles. I arrived in the city at six o'clock, and put up at Willard's . . . The next day at 12 I went to the Capitol, saw our Members of Congress & Senators besides sundry other notables, saw Congress opened, heard the President's message part through and left. Among other things and the main occasion of my visit, I went to Brady's and sat for a photograph, of which I am to have a dozen cards-de-visite."

Lieutenant Colonel Farnham also took brief leave of the camp: "Yesterday I rode down to Mount Vernon the home of Washington," he told Mary. "I wish you could have been with me. It is about six miles from here & we had a delightful ride. The day was warm and now the roads are good . . . Mt. Vernon looks as I had expected it would, tho' there was more of a forest in the vicinity than I supposed . . . The buildings have been kept in nearly the same form in which they were at the time of Washington's death. The grounds are however much overgrown with trees and shrubs. The garden is laid out as it was by Washington himself . . . But every thing looks dilapidated. The tomb is open with an iron grating in the front . . . The key to the Bastile France still hangs in the passage. In the dining room was an old harpsichord, shaped like a grand piano, something like that old piano that we had at Franklin . . . In the same room were his holsters and some good sized saddle bags to carry stores while in the army. I wish you and Laura could have been with me. I had a very interesting time."

By early December, Colonel Blunt's wife had joined her husband at Camp Vermont, the first of several officers' wives who would come south. Wheelock Veazey urged his wife to join him: "You had better bring a straw tick, mine is only single width and would hardly accommodate two unless we laid pretty near together."

Roswell Farnham wrote to his wife on November 28 that his log hut had been completed by the troops: "I wish you were here very much indeed if we should move forward and you had no chance to come to me this winter I should feel bad." He added, "You must write me how you get along with your teeth . . . Can you get a temporary set that will look well and last while you are here?"

At Camp Vermont, sickness was taking an increasing toll. Cpl. Edmund Clark told his fiancée, Mary: "Since I wrote you I have had the opportunity of learning something of what it is to be sick in camp. The beginning was a cold which terminated in a fever. Oh how thirsty I was day and night. It seems as if I drank more water than two men but it did not relieve me at all . . . Yesterday morning the water began to pour into our tent wetting everything . . . The boys say I have grown poor dreadfully. There are some 20 sick ones in there [the hospital] now. A private in Co. C. died this week also. It is sad to die 'a stranger in a strange land.'"

Two days later, Clark wrote, "Went to the surgeon's this morning and the rascal reported me fit for duty."

Not so fortunate was Pvt. Joel Bliss. He was taken sick and placed in the hospital. A friend recalled: "His father, hearing of his sickness, hastened South and was soon at his bedside. Thinking he would recover sooner at home than in a hospital, he hastened to Washington to get his discharge, if possible. In his absence his nurse, Comrade Wells, saw that he was failing. On the father's return he said to him, 'I think you had better stay with Joel for he will soon obtain his discharge.' In a few days the discharge came. It became the sad duty of the grief stricken father to take to his home in Enosburg the lifeless body of his only son."

Out near Bull Run with the 13th, 14th, and 15th regiments, Pvt. Joseph Travisee of Winooski observed, "This ain't much like being home sitting on Frank Allard's steps drinking beer."

Soldiering was also beginning to wear on Private Glover, who wrote to his wife, "If government should send round a Company of Sharpshooters and shoot three quarters of the Officers it would do more toward putting down the Rebellion than anything." He added a few days later, "I am well and rugged and hope you at home are the same."

Matters at home weighed particularly heavy on the farm boys. Glover wrote,

The Bull Run battlefield soon after the battle

"I wish you would write how many of the cows are going to have calves and if you have got any oatmeal made and all about things at home and how mother's health is and all about the neighbors and everything else."

Corporal Williams wrote on December 4, "Our company has just returned from picket duty, and an order has just been issued for the regiment to get ready to march in ten minutes, each man to be supplied with three days rations. It has been made known to us that we are going to Camp Vermont, and shouts of joy are heard all through the camp . . . We are forty miles from Camp Vermont, and hope it is not the intention to march us through in one day."

At Camp Vermont, Private Hatch instructed his wife, "I want that you should go up and kill grandmother's old cat she says that she steals her butter out of the jar and hides it in the wood pile and puts the cover on again and steals her sheets out of her wash tub and carries them up toward Dan Morgan's. Such a cat ought to die."

In West Windsor, Daniel Hammond received a letter written November 14 from son Jabez at Camp Vermont. It said, in part: "On the sacred soil of Va. sits Jabez with his feet curled up under him and his knapsack resting on his knees for a desk on it lays some paper in his hand he holds pen trying to scratch a few lines to you to let you know that we are all alive and for the most part well I was on guard last night which makes me rather cross and sleepy and to make it worse I have got a large boil under my arm."

Father replied by writing one letter to be shared by the four boys: "Three minutes before 8 oclock sits Dan pretty tired writing A few Lines to his 4 little boys in the Great Big Army . . . Yesterday it was warm and the snow pretty much disappeared in the Valleys the hills are still white with snow. I got up yesterday Morning and found the Old Cow all Bloated up as big as A small shit house, turned her out, finished My chores eat my Breakfast give the old cow 1 lb of Butter went up the hill and got the Hearse come home rigged up and went up to Sanders Funeral Parlor there at 10 oclock waited until 11 oclock took the corpse carried it to the church at Brownsville where the services were conducted . . . the corpse was as fair as any I ever saw . . . Mother says follow your hand and write often as you can.

"Well Stephen and Jabez we received A Letter from each of you to Night. Mailed the 10th giving a description of Mules and Niggers. Now Bogus I guess if My hogs new that you compared them to Mules you had better be drawing your Ass out of their way and as for Niggers they are Just About as much consequence as so many Rattlesnakes the less we have to do with them the better we be off."

Back home went a letter from Jabez: "I wish you could come out here before the season sets in so as to see how the war has affected this part of Va . . . do you have any conception of the ruin it has produced . . . I had not there is not a fence to be seen."

Daniel replied, "My prayer is that you all have your health until the President shall unlock the doors, and Let you all out of Prison, and let you all return to your Homes and Friends where you will all be greeted with warmth and friendship that never was before dreamed of . . . I have been into the kitchen and got a good meal of Butternuts and been to the barn and done my chores . . . The Black Charger that chased the bear is in fair working order . . . the hogs are doing well. they are about ripe enough to lay up for Winter. Jabez calf is fat as a skunk . . . Misses Stowe sends her love, and if measured by size you have a lot of it."

Jabez wrote: "[I]t stopt snowing about midnight it cleared off then and a clearer pleasanter morning I never saw . . . A good many men are troubled with the jaundice."

Replied father, "Yesterday morning I went up and helped kill Kendalls hogs the Heaviest weighed 390 lbs. come home got Dinner and helped your Mother in the Afternoon and Evening to try out her Tallow Cut up and salted my beef . . . I shall send the Windsor papers tomorrow and this letter if I get it done . . . It had been reported that the 16 Regiment has left you and that the 9th and 10th Vermont have come to assist you, but I consider it all moonshine and shall until I hear more About it. How far is Camp Vermont from Washington how far is Fredericksburg from Camp Vt how far to Harpers Ferry How far to Manassas how far to Centerville. Does any of the 12th Vermont when out on Picket see any Rebels . . .

"Boys I have taken A good deal of comfort in reading your letters to myself and Neighbors. we did not receive but two Last week and glad to get them. hope you will be Able to send us 4 or 5 a week we feel anxious to hear from you Every Day . . . Ira your Black Horse looks first rate I have not drove him but once since Puddlford commenced Drawing wood the Colts look first rate. I guess I will stop and as Ira used to say go to the Barn and go to bed."

Jabez responded: "The distance from here to Washington is ten miles the route that we take that is by water from Alexandra The distance to Fredericksburg from here as near as I can find out is about fortyfive miles next the distance to harpers ferry is variously estimated from fifty to seventy miles. fourth the distance Manassas is about twentyseven or thirty miles to Centreville thirtyfive miles. from here to Alesandra is two miles you wanted to know if the 12th vt see any Rebbels while out on picket. In answer I will say i have seen nothing of a rebel."

And Daniel Hammond wrote, "Our Governer has Appointed Thursday Decr 4th 1862 for Thanksgiving Day so you see we are to have A thanksgiving whether we have any Government or Not."

★

IO

In 1862 the holidays came to northern Virginia with the snow-covered landscape looking a bit like home to the newly arrived lads from Vermont. Thanksgiving originated in New England as a feast held by the Pilgrim Fathers at Plymouth to give thanks for their safe arrival—and survival—in the New World. It would become a national holiday in November 1863, declared by President Lincoln, who designated the last Thursday in November the day of observance. But it had been for a very long time something of a local option; in Vermont, in 1862, Governor Holbrook issued a proclamation setting forth December 4 as the day of thanks. Soldiers' correspondence focused on how well their expectations were fulfilled.

That Thursday dawned at Camp Vermont with only two of the brigade's five units present. But the 12th and 16th regiments, which had been doing double picket duty, were cheered by the news that the 13th, 14th, and 15th were en route. The 12th planned to go all out in a Thanksgiving Day celebration. Private Benedict wrote to the *Free Press:* "It was emphatically a gay and festive time. The day was clear, air cool and bracing, sunshine bright and invigorating. The boys of our company made some fun over their Thanksgiving breakfast of hard tack and cold beans, but possessed their souls in patience in view of the forthcoming feast of fat things, for we had heard that our boxes from home were at Alexandria, and the wagons had gone for them."

Boxes from home and the day of discharge from service were two of the things for which the soldiers in the Second Vermont Brigade most longed. Pvt. Samuel Dana, in the 13th, wrote to his family in Warren soon after arriving in Virginia: "I got that box yesterday, and I tell you I had a good supper and breakfast. I had some sausage for supper and a piece of that bake meat for breakfast, and you better guess it tasted good. The sausage and meat got a little mouldy, but I can scrape it off. Everything else came all right except the mustard. The bottle got broke and all of it spilt. I am very thankful to all that put in stuff and will try and prove myself worthy of the regard that you have all shown me in your gifts. Those pies all came good and look very nice. I have not tasted of them yet and how nice those donuts are and how nice all of the stuff is in the box . . . that pop corn goes very well . . . I was sorry you didn't send me some tobacco but perhaps it wasn't convenient getting it in."

The day before the holiday, Roswell Farnham wrote to his wife, "The Burlington

Company has 3,800 lbs. of freight at the depot, all for Thanksgiving."

A soldier writing to the *Caledonian Record* in St. Johnsbury said, "Friends at home had forewarned us that we were not only remembered in their prayers and good wishes, but that our bodily wants also should not go unsupplied. As early as five o'clock in the morning, teams went to Alexandria to bring the vast stores supposed to be there in waiting . . . At ten o'clock the regiment was formed in front of Lt. Col. Farnham's quarters when, in accordance with the request of Gov. Holbrook, the proclamation was read by Chaplain Barstow."

Holbrook's message said, in part: "In obedience to custom and the universal sentiments of the people, I do therefore appoint Thursday, the 4th day of December, next, to be observed by the people of the state as a day of public prayer and praise and Thanksgiving . . . to lay aside the ordinary employments of life on that day, and to assemble at their usual places of public worship to render thanks to Almighty God for the fruitfulness of the year. It is a good thing to give thanks unto the Lord . . . Let it be our special prayer to Almighty God, that He will, in His good time, restore our beloved Republic, in peace and prosperity, in unity and power, and that therein the blessings of civil and religious liberty may be dispensed to mankind, to the end of time and . . . that He will hasten the promised time when there shall be 'Peace on Earth, Good Will Towards Men.' And though many of us, while gathered around the festive board or the domestic hearth, most inevitably observe the vacant chair, and direct our thoughts to him who is in the tented field, or lies in the soldier's grave, or sick or wounded is nursed by stronger hands, yet let our sadness be tempered by the thought of his manly and heroic purpose, to discharge the highest and last duty of the patriot to his country."

Writing to the *Freeman* in Montpelier, a soldier said, " . . . as that portion was listened to which referred to the vacant chair and those absent on the tented field a certain feeling came over us that they missed us at home."

His account continued: "The religious exercises closed by the regiment singing the familiar hymn, so full of patriotic inspiration, 'My country, 'tis of thee . . . ' Afterward Col. Blunt made some brief remarks, and invited the men to meet their officers on the 'Campus Martius' to the west of camp to spend a few hours in amusement."

Then came the time for feasting as the wagons from Alexandria drove into view. Alas, though, as George Benedict noted: "The teams arrived with but four of the forty big boxes expected, and the unwelcome news that the rest would not reach Alexandria till the next day. Most of the companies were in the same predicament. Co. I had a big box, and made a big dinner, setting the tables in the open air, to which they invited the field and staff officers. Two or three men of Company C received boxes, with as many roast turkeys, which they shared liberally with their comrades, so that a number of us had Thanksgiving fare, and feasted with good cheer and a thousand kind thoughts of the homes and friends we left behind us. We knew they were thinking of us at the same time. If each thought of affection and good will had had visible wings, what a cloud of messengers would have darkened the air between Vermont and Virginia that day!"

Private Irwin in the 12th didn't fare so well. "Well the day come," he said,

Vermonters cooking in camp, by Private Jackson

"and no boxes . . . so we had to make our Thanksgiving dinner on salt-mule and hard bread."

Benedict's letter continued: "At 2 o'clock, the regiment turned out on the parade ground. The colonel had procured a foot ball. Sides were arranged by the lieutenant colonel, and two or three royal games of foot ball—most manly of sports and closest in its mimicry of actual warfare—were played. The lieutenant colonel, chaplain and other officers, mingled in the crowd; captains took rough-and-tumble overthrows from privates; shins were barked and ankles sprained; but all was given and taken in good parts. Many joined in games of base ball; others formed rings and watched the friendly contests of the champion wrestlers of the different companies; others laughed at the meanderings of some of their comrades, blindfolded by the colonel and set to walk at a mark. It was a 'tall time' all around. Nor did it end with daylight. In the evening a floor of boards, laid upon the ground, furnished a ball room, of which the blue arch above was the canopy and the bright moon the chandelier. Company C turned out a violin, guitar and two flutes for an orchestra, some other companies furnished a violin; and a grand style Thanksgiving ball came off in style."

Another soldier in the 12th added, "Satin slippers, properly filled, would have been agreeable, but they were not there; but you see, we had a good Thanksgiving ball, nevertheless. Thus the day—old Thanksgiving Day—happily passed, tinged doubtless with many wishes for those at home."

One soldier still waiting for his food from home at the end of the day was Edmund Clark. "I guess you would have laughed to have seen me cooking my apple sause," he wrote to Mary. ". . . I cooked it on the coals until using my cup to stew them in. I did not burn it a bit & it was real good. When we get married we shall have more conveniences for doing such things."

Toward darkness, the 15th Vermont tramped in from picket duty along the Occoquan and Bull Run too tired for any festivities. The next day, December 5, the 13th and 14th regiments started for Camp Vermont. Capt. Joseph Boynton of Stowe and the 13th wrote to the *Morrisville News Citizen*, "We started at 10 o'clock AM; it beginning to rain and snow. At last I succeeded in getting them into a good [railroad] car. It continued to storm all day with a cold northwest wind . . . We came down on the cars to Alexandria; arrived there about three o'clock, PM, the storm unabated; got out of the cars, and, in the mud, started for our old camp. We had about two miles to march. It stormed so hard it wet my rubber coat through . . . Imagine yourself marching up a long hill, in the mud, ankle deep, with your feet cold and wet, in a bleak wind, then to think of going into the woods or rather brush, in a thick fog, with the snow loaded on to every branch so that the trees were white from top to bottom, without any shelter or any means of building a fire."

Private Benedict reported: "The Thirteenth and Fourteenth regiments came in from Union Mills . . . and marched into their deserted camps. They brought only shelter tents, and the prospect of camping down in the snow, with little food, no fuel, and scanty shelter, was a pretty black one for them, till our officers went over and offered the hospitalities of the Twelfth, which were gratefully accepted. The absence of some of our men on picket, left a good deal of vacant room in our tents, which were soon filled with wet and tired men of the regiments."

There wasn't room for everyone. As Captain Boynton recalled, "We ate our supper, which consisted of salt pork and bread . . . It cleared off and the wind went down at 12 o'clock, so we laid down to sleep; some slept, and some did not.—I slept . . . Our tents came the next day."

That day, December 6—with all five regiments back at Camp Vermont— wagons again pulled in from Alexandria, this time laden with boxes from home. The men of a company in the 12th, the old Saxtons River Light Infantry of the Vermont militia, feasted. A soldier in their ranks wrote to the *Bellows Falls Times:* "The tables were laid in our Co's street, and we all formed around for the feast. The Major, Sergeant Major, Chaplain, and several other officers of the regiment were present. After an appropriate prayer by the chaplain, all joined in the grand feast, amid good cheer and a thousand kind thoughts of homes and friends we had left in the old Green Mountain State. When the feast was over, the scriptures seemed to be fulfilled as of old. God bless the noble ladies of Saxtons River who furnished us this repast."

Many of the men of the 12th were on picket and had to wait for their food. "Our Thanksgiving boxes came yesterday," said Private Benedict, "after the regiment had gone on picket; and the few men left behind in camp have been sampling some of the more perishable articles, though booths of brush and picket fires almost extinguished by the snow, are hardly what one would choose for surroundings."

Back in camp, Thanksgiving went on and the officers of the 12th enjoyed a feast in the log hut of Maj. Rufus Kingsley. A menu, printed on brown scrap paper, included "Turkey, Mount Vernon Sauce; Fillet de Boeuf—a la smoke; Butter, Chittenden County; Pepper, a la contraband; pickles, a la confusion; Salt, ordinaire; Mince Pie and apple pie."

Private Irwin got his box on returning from a cold night on picket. He wrote to sister Ellen: "When we got back to camp thare the boxes were staring us in the face we pitched into them and each one took what belonged to him. I got butter, apples, tobacco, stockings, yarn Sugar all right."

Colonel Proctor saw to it that his men also enjoyed a Thanksgiving dinner. Pvt. Edwin Hall wrote home to Brookfield: "About Thanksgiving supper. The Quartermaster has sold over $100.00 worth of provisions and one thing and another. So the colonel took it and bought oysters for the Regt. There was a pint for every man—each one cooked his own and we 4 in our tent put them all together and we had all we could eat. It was the best meal I have ate since I came here. So you see the Colonel looks out for his boys."

Private Doubleday wrote to wife Asceneth: "You said you was not agoing to have any Thanksgiving, but would have it when I come. So we will, asceneth, let it be what time of the year it will, we will have it then . . . I don't want you to think I am homesick but I cant help thinking of you & the rest of the folks & of you pretty often."

In the 13th, Sergeant Palmer was on picket. "It is a bright, frosty morning," he wrote, "little crystals hanging from every limb. During the night, for several feet, ice gathered along the shores . . . Two or three are left at a post, and take turns keeping watch. They have as good a fire during the day as they choose to build, but a small one by night that cannot be seen far. It is Thanksgiving in our native state."

On December 6, Daniel Hammond wrote to his four soldier sons from West Windsor: "We passed off the Day as well as we could but finally on the whole it was rather lonesome we had A baked Chicken for Supper and had Enough left for Dinner Yesterday so you see that there is some lack of help compared with former years when it took 3 or 4 to make A Meal but so it is . . . the Horses and Cows are all in good comfortable quarters well Watered and fed . . . the hens on their roosts with their Roosters to Protect and care for them. the Guinea Pigs are in the Cellar the cats go where they are A mind to. Elwyn and Mark are in Bed. Lovina is getting the Potatoes for Breakfast your mother is mending a shirt for Mark. Dan is using his old Pen the same one that he has had for three years the house is Warm as summer and I wish you were all here to enjoy the comforts that we enjoy. It gives me disagreeable feelings to think that thousands are standing and Lying out of Doors this cold Bleak night, with no shelter to protect them save for the canopy of the Heavens."

Christmas seems to have been celebrated very quietly, the men in the ranks and the people back home having put their holiday energies into Thanksgiving. In the Second Vermont Brigade, Christmas observances varied among the regiments. "Our regiment spent Christmas in camp and no duty," said Private Sturtevant, of the 13th. "We thought of home and knew that many a stocking would not be found in its accustomed place, and the usual Christmas dinners and parties likely in many

The interior of one of the Vermonters' stockaded tents, probably Private Jackson's

homes would be omitted because of fathers and sons in camp . . . our cooks made extra efforts to have something nice for dinner . . . We had pork and beans that had been roasted and baked all night in a bed of coals hot for dinner, boiled rice with good sale molasses or muscavade sugar, old government Java coffee, nice hard tack (worms all shook out), sweet potatoes and corned beef, and all this cooked in good shape. We thought it a dinner fit for a king, and all were merry."

A soldier in the 16th, in a letter to Montpelier, wrote: "Today has been, if not a merry, a pleasant Christmas for the men of this regiment. Ordinary drill and labor had been suspended. The men had been called out for public worship, and the sermon was preached from Luke 2:14. We judge that 'Old Santa Claus' in his annual rounds does not visit the tented field. He must be too much of a coward to risk his life and treasures amid the perils of war. This is a barren place in which to spend a Christmas, but amid our destitutions we have Jesus for our present Savior, and those earthly blessings which the gospel freely offers."

Lyman Seeley, in the 13th, noted, "On Christmas day the Col. had all military parade dispensed with, and 2 PM our chaplain delivered an address."

Sergeant Palmer wrote: "In all the brigade there is no drilling. The chaplains preach to the various regiments. Then many visit the Chantilly battle field. A citizen points out the spot where the brave [Gen. Phil] Kearney fell; where the lines swayed to and fro. Here, side by side, are the graves of friend and foe. The enemy held the field. Their dead are buried decently; but shocking to say, only a few sods were thrown over ours, and frequently, feet, hands and skulls are sticking out, flesh still on. But we found men from the twelfth regiment covering those heroes that fought so bravely. We lose another of our soldiers. Oscar Reed dies suddenly of typhoid fever."

Private Benedict and comrades went all out for Christmas dinner. "We got some excellent oysters of the sutler, also some potatoes," Benedict wrote. "Two of the boys sent off to a clean, free-negro family, about a mile off, and got two quarts of milk, some hickory nuts, and some dried peaches. I officiated as cook, and, as all agreed, got up a capital dinner. I made as good an oyster soup as one often gets . . . The potatoes were boiled in a tin pan, and were as mealy as any I ever ate. We had, besides, good Vermont butter, boiled pork, good bread, and closed a luxurious meal with nuts, raisins and apples, and cocoa-nut cakes just sent from home."

Other soldiers observed Christmas on Sunday, December 28. One told the home folks: "Last Sabbath was a beautiful day. The weather was mild and pleasant so that the regiment were not uncomfortable in outdoor attendance upon public worship . . . The heavens above us were declaring the glory of God, the Firmament showing his handy work, the sun rejoicing in his strength, and the trees of the wood clapping their hands for joy . . . A whole regiment of men, quietly and attentively listening to the word of God, makes an interesting and impressive congregation."

But all was not peaceful in the Vermont camps. Heman Allen of Burlington, a member of Captain Lonergan's "Irish Company," recalled years later: "When Christmas came around the usual orders were issued to attend divine service. Knowing the feelings of his men, most of whom were Catholics, and while declaring afterwards the day might have been better observed under the circumstances by going to a non-Catholic service than by idling in camp, Captain Lonergan objected to being forced to go, and refused to turn out his company. For his breach of discipline captain Lonergan was placed under arrest and relieved of his sword. This occurrence, which attained much celebrity in camp at the time, ended in the honorable return of the sword, and in modification of regimental orders to the extent that in future attendance at church services was to be made voluntary."

Cpl. Edmund Clark wrote home, "There is a family about half a mile from here in a miserable old house not near as comfortable as one of our shanties. They are almost in a Starving condition. People in Vt can form no accurate idea of the AWFUL ravages of war upon the inhabitants. One of our corporals played with the fancy women in Washington . . . He has not been able to do duty for some weeks & has at last gone to the post hospital . . . It is shameful for a man to abuse himself in that fashion but thousands do."

The holiday brought out the men's melancholy. Corporal Williams wrote, "This is Christmas and my mind wanders back to that home made lonesome . . . I think of the many lives that are endangered, and hope that the time will come when peace, with its innumerable blessings, shall once more restore our country to happiness and prosperity."

Writing home on Christmas to Poultney in the language of his Welsh family, the other John Williams in the 14th said, "I was more homesick today than at any time since I enlisted in the army—thinking about home."

Back home, the men away were not forgotten. The *Rutland Herald* published a Christmas editorial that concluded, "Nearly three hundred thousand Vermonters, around the festive board in their peaceful homes, will remember with a fond pride, the brave men who are upholding the honor and fame of the State, and the existence of the nation, where the stern alarums of war affright the air."

★

*Brig. Gen. Edwin Stoughton, known as the boy general,
who for a time led the Second Vermont Brigade*

II

Between the holidays, the Second Vermont Brigade received an unwelcome present. Edwin Stoughton, with new and shiny stars on his uniform (though his appointment as brigadier was still awaiting confirmation by the US Senate), arrived to take command. His whereabouts since the brigade left Brattleboro are unclear, although Colonel Veazey wrote, "General Stoughton's lady love is dead and he has gone to New York where she died." Veazey added, as usual, an amorous sentiment: "My own sweet darling I do love you so much more than before we were married."

Joseph Spafford, in the 16th, observed, "Stoughton arrived here yesterday to take command of this brigade. I don't think any body would have felt bad if he had gone somewhere else."

Lieutenant Colonel Cummings noted, "The 'gallant' Brigadier has a great reputation in the army as a woman's man. He is probably the handsomest Brigadier in the army, or at least would be called so by the girls."

In Woodstock, the *Vermont Standard* declared, "We learn that Gen. Stoughton has arrived to take command of the brigade. This news is received with regret by all, not out of disrespect for Gen. Stoughton for he is undoubtedly an able officer, but Col. Blunt, who has been acting brigadier, has won the respect and esteem of every man in the brigade, and we had hoped he would be retained in that position."

The brigade had been spared the bloodbath 40 miles to the south at Fredericksburg, though the men heard the rumble of the guns. There, on December 13, the Army of the Potomac under Maj. Gen. Ambrose Burnside launched a series of futile attacks across open ground against a long line of low hills, held by Robert E. Lee's Army of Northern Virginia. Few soldiers even reached the rebel lines, as some 10,000 fell either dead or wounded. It was the worst Union defeat yet.

Burnside's mass movement to Fredericksburg naturally weakened Washington's outer defenses, so the Vermont Brigade was ordered to the vicinity of Fairfax Court House to take up picketing where the corps of Gen. Franz Sigel had been. "More moves on the big chess board of which states and counties are the squares and divisions and brigades the pieces," Private Benedict noted. "And as the older troops push to the front, the reserves, of which the Second Vermont Brigade is a portion, move up and occupy the more advanced positions of the lines around

Washington, vacated by our predecessors."

"Yesterday morning at break of day, the whole Vermont brigade bid farewell to Camp Vermont," wrote a soldier in the 13th regiment to the Morrisville newspaper. "We had to sling knapsacks and carry all out traps—sixty pounds weight. We marched 20 miles and got our fly tents pitched before dark. We were very tired, but all feel well this morning. Boys, just think, our loads were as heavy as a bushel of corn and we had to carry them twenty miles. The court house is an old dirty looking house. The village is about as large as Cambridge Centre; but not half as pleasant. It is a nasty, dirty place. The land in the vicinity is very good. The grass and weeds grow very high on the deserted plantations. We have seen grass as high as you could reach standing on tip-toe. You would have liked to see us on the march yesterday,—five thousands soldiers in uniform, with their glistening bayonets. Our regiment was in the rear, and when we passed over a hill, it was a splendid sight."

The Vermonters had come to an area scarred by the maneuvering of armies, not far from the battlefields of First and Second Manassas and Chantilly. As Lieutenant Colonel Cummings observed, "No fire, even if it should burn every house in our village of Brattleboro, could be half as desolating to the place as war has been to this part of Viriginia. Houses, cattle, fences and inhabitants nearly all gone—lands desolate running up to weeds and briars, and no encouragement for the future. The people here look dispirited, and ruined . . . Desolation is the word that most clearly conveys the idea, but that is hardly sufficiently emphatic."

One of General Stoughton's first acts was to appoint Charles Cummings provost marshal. The former editor wrote that his office was "a fine brick building, two stories high, erected as an office for the county and probate clerks . . . Until recently the will of George Washington was on file here but that and some of the more important papers have been removed to safety to Alexandria. But the office is full of papers going back two centuries or more. I use for my pillow one of these old volumes."

Back at Camp Vermont, George Benedict, who always seemed to miss long marches, and this time "was on special duty and did not accompany the column," wrote, "The Third Brigade of Casey's Division was already installed in the winter quarters built with much labor by the Vermont regiments. The quiet and discipline of the Vermont camps has disappeared. Muskets were popping promiscuously all around the camps; much petty thievery appeared to be on foot; and Mr. Mason, the gray headed 'neutral' who owns the manor, was praying for the return of the Vermont brigade. His fences were lowering with remarkable rapidity, the roofs of his out-houses had quite disappeared, and Colonel Grimshaw, commanding the brigade, had his headquarters in the front parlor of his mansion."

Meanwhile, out at Fairfax Court House, with the Vermonters now well into the Confederacy, a soldier in the Irish Company wrote of "the strange feeling of being in the enemy's country."

The Second Vermont Brigade's business was picketing; the 16th Vermont was first detailed to picket along Bull Run, while the other four regiments remained at Fairfax Court House. Lieutenant Spafford, in the 16th, wrote home:

Picket Reserve, Centreville, Va.
Dec. 13, 1862

This morning . . . came to Centreville where we are now stopping. The 16th is the only Regt. of the Brigade here . . . The others stopped at Fairfax Court House. We are to stay here and do picket duty for a week (half the Regt. out at a time) then we go back to Fairfax C.H. and another Regt. takes it, so you see our turn will come once in 5 weeks. In coming here we past a battlefield where we found plenty of bayonets, broken and burnt guns, dead horses and saw one man's head sticking out of the ground. Our picket line is out by the Bull Run battlefield.

Five days later, Spafford wrote: "You inquire what I have to do while on picket. I will explain as well as possible. It depends upon the nature of the ground and the nearness of the enemy how the pickets are posted. Ours have generally been two on a post and from five to ten rods apart; some other brigades meet the right & left of our line so they extend in that way for miles. Our brigade at Camp Vermont had a line of eight miles, at Bull Run a line about half as long. If there are 300 men go out at once they will be divided in three reliefs of 100 men each.

"Now, a Lieut. will take 50 of these men and post them on the right of the line beginning on the center and another Lieut. will post 50 on the left and relieve the men already on duty there. You see (in this case, sometimes they will take more men & sometimes less according to the length of the line) it would take six Lieuts each day, two to each relief. After posting the men they go back to the support, or reserve (where the other two reliefs are stationed) and stop there. The men remain eight hours on post then two Lieuts. take another 100 men (the 2d relief) & relieve

Vermont soldiers on abandoned Confederate earthworks overlooking Centreville, Virginia. Private Jackson is likely shown in the broad-brimmed hat, apparently sketching.

89

the men that were first posted. The Lieuts are SUPPOSED to visit that part of the line where their men are posted at least once after posting them before they are relieved, so as to see that they are doing their duty, not sleeping, etc."

Slowly, the bad news from Fredericksburg reached the Vermonters. On December 18, Spafford wrote to his sister, "We hear all sorts of rumors in regards to Fredericksburg. One day Burnside is all cut to pieces and retreating, the next Sigel has gone down with his forces & is fifteen miles beyond the city & driving the enemy before him. There is one report that does not change . . . Burnside has lost a great many men. I suppose our Old Brigade [First Vermont Brigade] is there. We could hear the cannonading."

Five days later, Spafford wrote, "We have got the HARDEST whipping at Fredericksburg that we have had since the war commenced . . . We have lost in killed and wounded at least 5 times more than the rebels have . . . I am disgusted with the way the war is carried on."

On December 19 Corporal Williams wrote, "We have just received full particulars on the bloody engagement at Fredericksburg by the army under Burnside. I hope it is not so bad as it is represented. Somebody is greatly responsible for the sacrifice of so many lives. I hope that the man will soon arise who is capable of leading our armies to victory."

Spafford told his sister: "We have lost one man from our company, S.E. Conner of Weathersfield. He was sick when we left Camp Vt., and was left there in the Hos . . . He was as fine a fellow as we had in the Co. Capt. Mason & Lieut Williams are both sick, theatened with a fever tho' Dr. Geo thinks they will come out of it all right in a day or two. You had better not mention this so that either of their wives may hear of it for they would only worry uselessly."

Sickness claimed Capt. Marvin White, a blacksmith from Enosburg, the first to enlist in the militia company that became Company G of the 13th Vermont. He died on December 13 at Camp Vermont, where Pvt. Ward Piper had been left behind to care for him. White had not lived up to expectations as company commander, though the men still liked him. A nurse who cared for White to the last said, "He impressed me as a man who had a very kind heart."

The previous day, an especially tragic death hit the 13th. In Brattleboro, just before the regiment departed, two young people from Bakersfield had been married, Miss Sarah Williams and Sgt. Edwin Reed. Private Sturtevant wrote, "Her brave young soldier boy husband she never saw again. He died at Camp Vermont on Dec. 12, 1862. There were other instances but none so sad."

Despite persistent rumors that the brigade might march again, the Vermonters prepared for a long winter around Fairfax Court House. "December 22 . . . Our tents are nearly all stockaded, and well prepared for winter," according to Corporal Williams. "The logs are cut of lengths depending upon the size of the tent to be stockaded, and are built after the fashion of log houses, the interstices being filled with mud or clay, for which the soil of Virginia is well adapted. The tent is then raised above this and fastened, so that the whole makes very comfortable quarters."

A soldier wrote to the *Freeman* in Montpelier of "the din of camp music in our ears." He added, "The greatest fault we have to find with this noise, is its

A picket standing guard on a fortified position overlooking Bull Run,
drawn by Jackson

endless clatter. It is heard by day, and rolls on in its restless beatings even at night. The stillness of midnight is little known here, for at these hours we listen to the hum of voices and tread of sentinels."

Another wrote to the *Bellows Falls Sentinel,* "It may seem very romantic, to those situated comfortably at home, to read of 'Dark columns of armed men, moving with steady and measured tread, at the silent midnight hour,' but the reality is not so romantic."

Still, soldier life had its lighter moments. A man in the 13th regiment remembered a certain private, John Greenwood from Colchester: "There were times when there was considerable confusion, noise, loud talk and some fighting in the Co., but Greenwood was never a participant, sometimes in the dead of night, when the turmoil began, and the captain appeared with the query, 'Who is making all the racket?' a dozen voices would reply, 'Greenwood.'"

And there was Pvt. Milo Gray, the son of a Waterbury preacher. A man in his company recalled, "One Sunday morning a party of us were on picket on Cub Run and it was proposed that we have religious services and he was selected to preach. He objected, but was compelled to do so . . . and preached a very good sermon, although his discourse consigned some of his hearers to a warm climate."

On December 19, Benedict penned an account of picketing near the Bull Run battlefield. "We started at 7:30 AM, with two days rations in our haversacks," he wrote, "and were marched briskly hither and thither over the Centreville turnpike, which has been so often filled with the columns of the Army of the Potomac, in advance or in retreat. The skeletons of the horses and mules, left to rot as they fell, were frequent ornaments of the highway, and the remains of knapsacks, bayonet sheaths, and here and there a broken musket, strewn along the road, told the story of strife and disaster in months and years gone by. Three hours brought us to the heights of Centreville, covered with forts, eight of which are in sight of this camp, connected by miles of rebel rifle pits which kept McClellan so long at bay during the impatient months of last winter. One of the famous 'Quaker' guns lies near our camp."

Benedict said his company marched three more miles, then was deployed "along the turbid stream of Cub Run, from a point near its junction with Bull Run, up to and beyond the ford and bridge where . . . opened the first battle of Bull Run, July 18th, 1861." Cub Run, he noted, "for the present is the boundary of Uncle Sam's absolute control."

He continued: "We took our posts in a flurry of snow at noon. The afternoon passed with little incident. At my station I had a solitary visitor, a gaunt and yellow [Virginian] who came to say that he was anxious to save the rails that he had left, around his cattle yard, and rather than have them burned he would draw some wood for the pickets—a suggestion that found favor with our boys. At our reserve station, in the old rebel artillery camp, some stir was occasioned by a colored individual, one of a family of free negroes who own a fine farm of 400 acres just across the Run, who came in to say a secesh soldier dressed in citizen's clothes, had just been at his house and made inquiries as to the number and position of our pickets. Lt. Wing at once started out with two or three men, saw the fellow making tracks for the woods, and gave chase. He gained the timber, however, and made good his escape.

"The night settled down clear and very cold. With darkness came orders to put out the picket fires or keep them smouldering without flame . . . The stream rippled away with constant murmur and the wind sighed and rustled through the trees; but there was little to hear till about midnight, when the reports of fire arms came from the direction of the cavalry vidette further out on the battlefield, two or three miles away, and shortly after a sound of the clatter of hoofs on the frozen ground. The sound died away and the night was still as before."

Benedict returned to the picket reserve to join his fellow soldiers around a fire in an abandoned Confederate hut. "Suddenly a hasty step is heard without," he wrote, "and one of the pickets puts in his head at the door to announce that men are moving on the opposite bank of the stream. While he is talking, bang goes a musket from our line to the left . . . We seize our pieces, and hurry down to the ford . . . hearing in a whisper from the three trusty men stationed there, that a small party of men had just come stealthily along the opposite bank, stopped at the ford, discussed in a low tone the expedience of crossing, and then, disturbed by the firing and stir down our line to the left, had hastily retreated . . . Dropping low, so as to get a sight against the star-lit horizon, we awaited developments."

All was quiet. "I returned to my sentry post," said Benedict; ". . . I saw the big dipper in the North tip up so that its contents, be they of water, or milk from the milky way, must have run out over the handle. I saw the triple-studded belt of

Orion pass across the sky. I saw two meteors shoot along the horizon, and that was all the shooting. I saw the old moon, wasted to a slender crescent, come up in the east. I saw the sun rise very red in the face at the thought that he had over-slept himself till half past seven, on such a glorious morning. I heard a song bird or two piping sweetly from the woods; but I neither saw nor heard any rebels."

The next day Benedict learned that the firing had been the work of two edgy pickets, who really had nothing to shoot at. And the men whispering on the far bank? It turned out that they were members of a Union cavalry patrol seeking a safe crossing to the Union lines. Eventually, they came in unharmed.

There was a rumor that the rebel cavalryman J.E.B. Stuart was in the vicinity and intended a raid, and, indeed, the enemy was on the prowl in the direction of the Second Vermont Brigade. On Christmas night, down in the camps of the Army of Northern Virginia near Fredericksburg, a certain Confederate cavalier in plumed battle hat was finalizing plans for a raid north behind Union lines.

★

PART III

Stuart and Mosby Ride

J.E.B. Stuart, who led Lee's cavalry on the Dumfries Raid.

12

Robert E. Lee's cavalry commander, Maj. Gen. J.E.B. Stuart, was fond of raids and rides. As the Army of the Potomac moved toward Richmond during the Peninsula Campaign, Stuart had ridden clear around it, reporting back to the Confederate high command with prisoners and valuable information. The exploit became an instant sensation throughout the Confederacy, and was widely reported in the North. Now, shortly after the bloody federal repulse at Fredericksburg, Stuart received just the kind of instructions he liked. On December 23, 1862, Lee issued the following order:

> General J.E.B. Stuart
> Commanding Cavalry
>
> General: You are desired to proceed with a portion of the cavalry across the Rappahannock, penetrate the enemy's rear, ascertain, if possible, his position and movements, and inflict upon him such damage as circumstances will permit.

On the morning after Christmas, bugles sounded in Stuart's camp near Fredericksburg, and in an hour his men were on the road. According to Stuart, he took with him that day some 1,400 men and crossed the Rappahannock River at Kelly's Ford. North of the river Stuart divided his column, sending a smaller detachment under Brig. Gen. Wade Hampton toward Occoquan, himself proceeding with the main body north to the federal supply base at Dumfries. But there, on the 27th, Stuart was met by a well-prepared Union garrison. After a brief fight, he was forced to turn away with losses. Hampton, meanwhile, was having little better luck up at Occoquan. The two columns united at Cole's Store, and Stuart gave some thought to turning back then and there. But on hearing that Burnside had sent troopers after him, on he came to Burke's Station, barely a dozen miles from Washington, where he displayed some of the flourish for which he has been long remembered. There he burst into the Union telegraph office, seized the operator, and put an operator of his own at the key. First, Stuart intercepted federal dispatches containing information on troop deployments being made to intercept his marauders. Then he sent a dispatch to Union Quartermaster Gen.

Montgomery Meigs at Washington complaining of the quality of federal army mules he had captured. Then he cut the wires and headed in the direction of Fairfax Court House.

From the beginning, it appears that Stuart's approach had been picked up and reported by the Yankees, and the fact that something was up seems to have been well known in the ranks of the Second Vermont Brigade. On December 26, Corporal Williams wrote, "A supply of ammunition has been sent to the regiment this morning. An attack is apprehend." The next day, he noted, "Firing is heard today in the direction of Union Mills, supposed to be an engagement with the enemy. There is a report that the rebel general Stuart is in this vicinity, and intends a raid here. The weather is quite comfortable."

Private Benedict wrote from the 12th Vermont's camp outside Fairfax Court House, "During the day on Sunday, rumors of a sharp engagement at Dumfries, twenty-five miles south of us, and the hurrying forward of troops to points threatened, reached us, and prepared us for a start. Just at night-fall came the command to fall in. Col. Blunt was absent at Alexandria, in attendance on a court marshall, and Lieut. Col. Farnham was in command, by whom we were marched hastily to Fairfax Court House."

Looking back after the war, George Benedict gave the following considered account of troop dispositions: "At nightfall on the 28th, Stuart's arrival at Burke's Station was announced, and the regiments were ordered to fall in. Colonel Veazey, with the Sixteenth, with a section of the Second Connecticut Battery, Captain J.W. Sterline, which was now attached to the brigade, was now sent to guard the army supplies there. The Twelfth, under Lieut. Col. Farnham . . . and the Thirteenth, Lieut. Col. Brown, Colonel Randall also being at Alexandria, were posted in some rifle pits, half a mile east of the village, running across the Alexandria Turnpike, by which Stuart was approaching, with four guns of the Connecticut Battery; and the Fourteenth, Colonel Nichols, was in reserve, a short distance to the rear."

The Second Vermont Brigade was obviously not about to be surprised, with a good share of its rifles and some supporting artillery sighted down the road by which Stuart's force was approaching. General Stoughton, who never lacked for bravery, was along the line, and he ordered two companies of the 12th forward to warn of the enemy's approach. Under the command of Capt. Ora Paul, of Pomfret, they moved along the road and then concealed themselves amid trees and bushes. It was now dark, though a bright moon was up, and Stoughton asked for volunteers to ride beyond the advanced companies to determine the rebels' position. Lts. George Hooker and William Shermerhorn, both of Stoughton's staff, volunteered, and off they rode through the main line of battle and past Captain Paul's men. On they went toward Burke's Station until they heard—on the moonlit roadway ahead—the command "Close up." The two lieutenants turned on a dime and hurried back to tell Stoughton that the rebels were coming.

Private Benedict wrote to the *Free Press,* "Col. Farnham rode along the line, giving the men their instructions. Major Kingsley added some words of caution and injunctions to fire low, and General Stoughton, riding up, said, 'You are to hold this entrenchment, my men. Keep cool, never flinch, and behave worthy of

Francis Voltaire Randall, commander of the 13th Vermont Regiment

the good name won for Vermont troops by the first brigade. File closers, do your duty, and if any man attempts to run, use the bayonets!' The captains, each in his own way, added encouragement . . . we waited hour after hour on the bright moonlit night."

During the long wait, the men of the 12th were startled to hear, from the north side of the road, a cheer from the ranks of the 13th Vermont that grew and rolled along their lines. "When the men became silent," Lt. Albert Clarke said, "the approach of the enemy over the frozen ground could be distinctly heard in the clear frosty air. Apparently they had reached the pike and were forming to charge from the east. A solitary horseman, having passed the Union picket, came dashing down the pike from that direction, paused a moment by Gen. Stoughton and then passed in rear of the Thirteenth. When the voice of Colonel Randall was heard the anxious men experienced relief and reassurance. He had heard of the raid and had ridden with all speed from Alexandria. It was only by strategy that he made his way through the foremost of the Confederates along the pike."

It was a moment that Colonel Randall's men would remember as long as they lived. Actually, Randall and Blunt had started together from Alexandria, 18 miles distant. But Randall had the faster horse and he reached the road on which the Confederates were approaching just as their advance guard came up. Apparently, in the darkness, Stuart's men mistook him for a fellow Confederate. By the time Blunt arrived, Stuart's full force was up and the Vermont colonel, seeing horsemen, veered off. He reached the brigade after Stuart had retreated.

James Hartwell, a private from Boston, Massachusetts, who had enlisted at Warren, recalled, "The boys of the 13th Regiment shouted themselves hoarse at the unexpected appearance of Col. Randall when we stood in line awaiting the expected charge from Stuart's Cavalry."

A soldier from Morrisville said of Randall's arrival, "Then the colonel rode along our lines and said; 'Boys, we have got lively work to attend to now, but let every man be firm, and stand his ground, and let every shot tell that you are marksmen.'" The soldier added, "I was surprised to see the coolness of the boys."

The tense night dragged toward midnight. Private Sturtevant recalled, "We heard the approach coming up the pike miles away and the magnitude of noise and clatter of hoof and rattle of sabre told us that the force was strong." Then Captain Paul's two companies spotted horsemen in the dim light. Benedict wrote, "Some scattered pistol shots; then shrill cheers as of a cavalry squadron on a charge; and then the flash and rattle of the first hostile volley fired by any portion of the Twelfth in this war. It was a splendid volley, too."

According to Sturtevant, "Captains Paul and Ormsbee greeted General Stuart's raiders with a simultaneous discharge of 100 Springfield rifles." Benedict said, "Both companies fired at once, and their guns went off like one piece . . . We heard the firing, and taking for the opening drops of a shower waited patiently for what should come next. Nothing came, however. All was still again. In half an hour camp fires began to show themselves about a mile in front, and our artillery was ordered to try its hand on them. Bang went the guns, under our noses, and whiz went the shells, but they drew no response. Capt. Ormsbee of Co. G—one of our best captains—with 30 men of his own and Company B marched over to the fires. They were found to be fires of brush built to deceive us."

In the 12th, Private Jackson reported, "We heard galloping, a hurrah! two or three shots then a volley—silence following—It was about a hundred rods from us and the flash of guns was plainly seen. We lay in breathless silence expecting the very next moment to see the enemy come dashing over the hill. We were ready for them, our pieces all aimed at the spot they would appear."

Lieutenant Colonel Farnham, commanding the 12th, was in a position to know. "Gen. Stoughton ordered some men to reconnoitre," he said. "A sergeant & a few men started from Co. G. of the 12th & the sergt. tied his handkerchief to his gun & walked boldly into the rebel camp. They asked him who he was & what he wanted—he told them he was a Union Soldier & wanted to know whether they were friends or foes—After conferring with their higher officers the sergt. was told that the Gen. would communicate with our forces in the morning—Stoughton concluded not to wait till morning but threw a few shells among them & they moved."

So Stuart had departed, in the night, behind simulated campfires. "A free negro, whose house was near by, informed Capt. O. that the rebels were under the command of Generals Fitzhugh Lee and Stuart, both of whom had been in his house an hour before," according to Benedict. "They had, he said, two brigades of cavalry, and some artillery, and had pushed on north. This news was taken to mean that they were making a circuit and would probably shortly attack from the north or west. We were accordingly double-quicked back to Fairfax Court House and were posted (I speak only of the Twelfth) on the brow of a hill, in good position to receive a charge of cavalry. Here we waited through the rest of the night. The moon set; the air grew cold; the ground froze under our feet; but we had nothing to do but to shiver and nod over our guns, till daylight. At sunrise we were glad to be marched back to camp, and to throw ourselves into our tents, where most of the men have slept through the day."

Stuart had swung north, all the way to Vienna. Then he turned west to Middleburg before riding south to Warrenton and back to safety at Culpepper. The Vermonters claimed that they had wounded eight rebels and killed three horses. William Doubleday, who had been left back at Fairfax Court House on guard, wrote, "The rebels gave an awful yell when 2 companies of the 12th fired into them. They wheeled their horses and left. It was about 11 o'clock. Our men killed one horse, one rebel hat & a sabre . . . I went to bed about 11 o'clock & slept so sound I did not hear the cannon . . . So you see that I was not so scared I could not sleep well."

In Stuart's report on the "expedition undertaken in late December, 1862," that history came to know as the Dumfries Raid, he spoke of the encounter with the Vermonters: "I had proceeded from Burke's Station toward the Little River Turnpike, where, halting the rest of the command, I advanced with Fitz Lee's brigade toward Fairfax Court House, with the view, if practicable, of surprising and capturing the place. On approaching, we were saluted with a heavy volley from the enemy's infantry, posted in their breastworks and in the woods near the road. Keeping up the appearance of attack, the rear of the column, turning to the right, continued to march by way of Vienna toward Frying Pan, near which latter point I halted about dawn and fed and rested some horses."

A soldier who was with Stuart, Lt. Col. W.R. Carter of the Third Virginia Cavalry, said, "Reaching the Little River Turnpike, the division turned toward Fairfax Court House, and on arriving within a mile of that place the enemy's infantry, in ambush, opened fire on the head of our column, fortunately killing only two horses and wounding one man very slightly. We made no reply to their fire, and only withdrew out of musket-range; whereupon the enemy, not knowing how to interpret it, and thinking it might be a party of their own men, sent a flag of truce to ask whether we were friends or foes. They were told that they would be answered in the morning. On this being reported back they began to shell the turnpike; but in the interim we had built camp-fires, as if about to encamp for the night, and had left, taking a cross-road toward Vienna."

Corporal Williams entered in his diary, "Gen. Stoughton had so disposed us that we should have cut the enemy to pieces if he had come up. Stuart has found out what we have got here, and that the Vermonters are ready for him." A day later, December 31, he added, "On the whole, I think it was an ingenious performance of Stuart. Great skill was displayed in entering our lines and passing out again, without being captured. The Generals in this department have been fairly outgeneraled."

Benedict, writing to Burlington, apologized for the number of words he devoted to the whole affair and added: "It has been an interesting experience and not without value in its effect upon the discipline of the brigade. It has added to the confidence of the men in their officers, from Gen. Stoughton on down."

Farnham believed that the Confederates intended to cause trouble because, on January 1, the Emancipation was to take effect. Many years later, the distinguished historian Douglas Southall Freeman, biographer of Lee, summed up the Dumfries Raid: "Stuart came back from his raid that first day of the month bringing with him about 200 prisoners and some plunder. He had stories of gallant encounters near Dumfries and around Occoquan to tell, but he had no definite news of the enemy's dispositions or plans."

Though the Dumfries Raid was something of a Confederate failure, it was not without its consequences. Within Stuart's ranks was a wiry horseman who impressed his commander with his nerve and military instinct. John Singleton Mosby wrote: "When we returned, Stuart let me stay behind a few days with six men to operate on the enemy's outposts. He was so satisfied with our success that he let me have fifteen men to return and begin my partisan life in northern Virginia—which closed the war. That was the origin of my battalion."

Mosby, who would become known as the Gray Ghost of the Confederacy, had gotten a look at the Vermonters' lines while on the Dumfries Raid. He would soon put that knowledge to good use.

On January 1, 1863, Capt. Henry A. Eaton of the 16th wrote from Fairfax Court House to his home in Rochester, "May the new year be a happy one. Oh, may the war be closed before the year closes. Marched at 8 AM for Centreville to do picket duty. Arrive at 11 AM. Take quarters in the church. Have as yet little or nothing to do. Play chess and euchre."

On New Year's Eve Private Wallace in the 15th wrote to his father in Barnet,

"I wish you a happy new year. We came in tonight from picket and we were glad to get back again to camp, but we find rather bad news in store for us for while we were absent three of our company have died [from disease] and it does seem so hard to have the boys die so fast."

Toward midnight on December 31, before turning in for the night, Private Williams made the final entry for 1862 in his diary, in Welsh. It translates to a considerable understatement concerning the year of the Peninsula Campaign, Second Bull Run, Antietam, the Preliminary Emancipation Proclamation, and Fredericksburg: "So ends the year 1862. Many events have taken place in it."

★

13

On the first day of the new year, 1863, the history of the nation and of the world changed as the Civil War officially became a struggle not only to reunite America but also to free slaves. On January 1, Abraham Lincoln's Emancipation Proclamation became law, declaring all slaves in the seceded states to be free. The immediate effect was to send thousands of escaped blacks into Union lines, seeking refuge and freedom. That day a Second Vermont Brigade soldier sent an unsigned letter to the *Caledonian Record*, reporting on an eight-mile march through the Confederate state of Virginia from Fairfax Court House to Bull Run. He also took note of Lincoln's decree:

"Here and there too are the remains of old camp grounds, and a few rails to remind one of where fences had been, greeted the eye, and occasionally peering round the corner of some house the black face of one or more of 'God's images, set in ebony,' served to bring to mind the cause of this unnatural and devilish rebellion. Thank God, that so far as a Presidential edict can accomplish it, this oppressed and downtrodden race are thenceforth and forever free in this state; so I sincerely trust that the strong right arm of our army may give reality to a scheme so eminently just and beneficient, and make the proclamation something more than a dead letter."

"This will be a memorable day for history to perpetuate," Corporal Williams noted in his diary on January 1, 1863, "as being the one on which the President's Emancipation Proclamation takes effect, which declares three or four millions of bondsmen to be free."

Wrote Pvt. Walcott Mead, of the 14th: "It is a most lovely day. I never saw the like at this season of the year. I have my washing out and drying nicely in the sun." That report came on January 2 from Fairfax Court House to a friend in the Champlain Valley town of Shoreham. Nine days later Mead wrote, "We had a good easy time since we returned from picket—all we do is to drill twice a day. We have things fixed up nice for the winter, good warm tents with a fireplace and bunks to sleep in. The last two nights, I have had my clothes off for the first time in six weeks."

The new year came in mild and fair, a pleasant change from the cold and snowy early winter in northern Virginia. General Stoughton took advantage of the weather and held drills almost daily.

"January 3. Another brigade drill today, and if our brigadier possesses the necessary qualifications for a General, then drinking and swearing are the chief requisites," noted Corporal Williams.

Sergeant Palmer reported, "The brigade head-quarters are established at the village, and for the past four days the regiments have taken turns in sending a hundred men to guard them. No little sensation has been produced by the arrest of several officers and privates, for not dressing, and washing, and stepping, and saluting, and other smaller things, just according to stern military rules . . . so we are under the eye of the General."

"We had a brigade drill yesterday afternoon of 5 regts under command of General Stoughton," William Doubleday reported home. "He is an awful rough man, but in my opinion he has not the least claim to manhood nor no one else who will use such language as he did yesterday to enlightened and civilized men. In making a movement the companies some of them did not take their places in front of their companies as they should. 'g-d d-mn it!' Said he, 'why don't you step out in front of your co's damn you.' Said he, 'you haven't all of you got brains enough to make a monkey.' Will our country & cause prosper with such men for our leaders? I had rather be at home than to be under control of such men." Doubleday added, "My cough is so much better that I call it about well. I cough some nights."

The previous winter, the First Vermont Brigade had been riddled by camp diseases, and hundreds died. The alarming sickness rate even provoked an investigation by the surgeon general. While no particular cause was found, it seems likely that the Vermont boys, fresh from small towns and isolated farms and far from dense populations where diseases thrived, had failed to build up many immunities. As the winter of 1862–63 progressed, more and more men in the Second Vermont Brigade were falling ill, though not at a rate that would ever rival the previous winter for their Vermont predecessors in the war zone.

Capt. John L. Yale, of the 13th Vermont, was the son of a church deacon in Williston. He had written to his family in November that "the filth which naturally accumulates around a camp is a great help to bring on disease." On December 29 he reported on the encounter with Stuart's cavalry. "Mother," he added, "you wanted to know if my socks was good yet. They have lasted first rate & with a little mending will do good service yet. I slept last night on the limber of a 14 pounder as comfortably as I ever did in our little room in Williston."

But within days, Yale was seriously ill with typhoid fever. Word quickly reached Williston, and Deacon Yale started south to do what he could for his son. A member of the Yale family wrote many years later: "The trip . . . was the first and only of his long life, and was attended with much more discomfort and anxiety than a trip abroad would be in later days . . . Reaching Washington he went to the Provost Marshall and made his wants known and was quickly informed that no passes were granted under ANY circumstances. John does not know what caused him to even THINK of going to the Secretary of War . . . At all events, John was dying and the pass he must have, so after much waiting and explaining, he presented himself before the Secretary of War [Edwin M. Stanton]. John remembers that father heard part of a conversation going on between some of the attending officers, while he waited to have his case discussed, to the effect that 'that man's face told its own story—so frank and honest, there could be no danger of his not being what he represented himself to be.'

"He received his pass, crossed the river and hired a negro to carry him to Fairfax, paying him before they started. It was nearly night and began to storm. Reaching Annandale, about half way, they were called by the picket to halt and show their pass. The soldier took the pass inside the tent and observed the name Yale. Coming out, he inquired, 'Is your name Yale?' 'Yes.' "Deacon Yale?' 'Yes.' 'Well,' said the soldier on picket, 'I am Sanford Marshall from Williston,' and shook him by the hand."

The trip to Fairfax Court House was completed. "John remembers the first time he noticed that father was there," the account continued, "but was so ill it occasioned no feeling of surprise . . . The time was long . . . They had, for several days, heard the crowing of a rooster in the early morning time, and it seemed to be not far away, so father thought one day perhaps one could be bought. He went down to the cook and inquired if it would be any way possible, and remarked that he would pay $2.00 for a chicken for John. The cook put on a knowing look and said he would see if any fowls could be found. The next day the broth appeared, and when father went down to pay for the chicken, the cook remarked, 'Oh! no, that's a present for the Capt.' They observed later that the cook 'confiscated' it, a perfectly legitimate transaction during the war . . . John went into the hospital the eleventh of January, and father brought him home the first week in March."

Always there were rumors that, somehow, the war might come to a quick end. Private Glover reported to his wife on January 16 "a touch of the jaundice." He added, "It is the talk here that they think the war will come to a close by spring and we all hope it will. The month will soon be gone. Every day that passes away brings me so much nearer home. Do not think of my changing toward you for that will never be while life lasts."

On January 18, according to Pvt. Lyman Seeley, "Sad news came to camp— it was the death of Hiram C. Wolcott. He was buried the next day with all the honors of the army, and 36 guns were fired at his grave. He is from Morristown, and leaves a wife, and one child to mourn his loss."

Colonel Randall, concerned by the growing sick lists, ordered his regiment to move its camp a half mile to cleaner, drier ground. Still, Edwin Palmer wrote, "In the afternoon there was a funeral. The soldier died last night at the village, and wished to be buried there, saying that his wife could not endure the sight of his dead body. The chaplain, musicians, his company, and such as choose to from the regiment, follow him to the grave. He is placed, before leaving the hospital, in a government coffin, made of boards painted black,—with the clothes on that he wore when alive. He is now laid in the ground four feet deep; twelve of his comrades fire their farewell shots; the chaplain speaks consoling words, offers a prayer to God and pronounces the benediction; and we turn away, not as when we came, with a slow and measured tread,—the drummers beating the dead march,—but with quicker steps, a livelier air,—Yankee Doodle."

He wrote, too, "The nights are growing colder; so two days are given us,

Pvt. Lyman Seeley, who wrote letters home
to the newspaper in Morrisville, Vermont
LIMOGE COLLECTION

Saturday and Monday, to put small stockades under our tents, and make them as warm as we can . . . Chestnut trees are slashed down, cut off the right length and split into slabs. A kind of a box, the bigness of the tent, three or four feet high, is formed out of these, the ends fitted together, the crevices, as usual, filled with mud. The tents are placed on these, and are much warmer than before."

Private Seeley, on picket, wrote to Morrisville of the countryside, "There is here a grist mill, all stripped; railroads, farm houses and other buildings; the fences all gone, and the land all grown up to grass and briars, from two to four feet high. The country is like a house where the woman is gone—nothing as it should be."

All was quiet on the picket lines. A steady supply of boxes arrived from Vermont, much to the soldiers' delight. John B. Fassett, looking back many years, wrote, "I can now almost hear the war songs that restored our drooping spirits and excited us on to war. The talented singers of Co. G when gathered in some comrade's tent would finish their concert with that song of all others, 'Home Sweet Home,' quickly brought to mind the dear ones we left behind up among the green hills and lovely valleys of our beloved state."

Capt. Henry Eaton of the 16th received a pass to visit Washington. He wrote in his diary, "Leave at 6 AM for Washington via F. Station & Alexandria. Visit House of Representatives when in session—Senate had adjourned. Was much pleased with the paintings & statues was highly pleased with a female statue, Goddess of Liberty."

A long-delayed payday came to the brigade on January 30, according to Lyman Seeley: "After supper the order came to have Co. E. report to the paymaster's quarters at the 12th regiment. There was not one lame or sick; and this is the first instance for a long time . . . The green backs is the best surgeons and made all well and ready for duty. After reaching our destination, we were called in alphabetical order, and marched into a tent and took the pay ($26.96), and went through the tent. At the other end stood the sutler to take his due."

William Doubleday wrote to Asceneth from Fairfax Station: "I sent you five dollars in my last letter . . . Tell the boys I send love to them. I am not sorry I enlisted when I did for I think there will be a draft by the first of Apr if not before. The government have got to have men to take our place & they will have to be raised before our time is out to have them ready. There is a report now that they agoing to make us stay three years from the time we come out here unless the war closes sooner. We don't see it that way exactly."

Private Benedict, another soldier on furlough, was called home to attend to some important family business. By the time he returned from Burlington, he had missed another march. On January 19, the Second Vermont Brigade again received orders to prepare to move. Down near Fredericksburg, Major General Burnside was again making preparations to cross the Rappahannock, and troops under Gen. Henry Slocum, stationed near the Vermonters, had been ordered south. Thus, the brigade was to replace those regular soldiers on a somewhat more advanced picket line.

"Our rations began to be cut down and we knew there was something in the wind," wrote Lyman Seeley. "The order came for marching at 8 o'clock AM (the 20th). The boys eat their supper and nearly finished their scanty allowance of bread, and packed their things. In the morning they finished their bread for breakfast. At the appointed time the drum beat, and the boys were all in line, stacked arms, and the colonel gave orders to strike their tents. The boys returned to their company, and all was done with haste, and the wood-work that they had made with so much care was set on fire, and into line again at the beat of the drum. The order for marching came, and the boys marched with firm step, with their knapsack, cartridge boxes with 40 rounds, canteens full of water, and empty haversacks. We marched 3 miles and halted to rest, then we marched by Fairfax Station. When a halt was again made, the boys began to feel around in their haversacks for crumbs. We halted 30 minutes, and then marched a mile to a rising piece of ground. The colonel gave orders to camp, and the ground was policed, and the tents set up for the night around the camp fire."

In chill winter rain, the entire brigade had been marched south to Fairfax Station, a large Union supply base. It was in such weather that Cpl. Gus Fisher, in the 13th regiment, was fond of saying, "Ain't you glad you enlisted." Surely they heard him that day.

The 14th, 15th, and 16th halted at the station, some men finding shelter in barracks abandoned by Slocum's troops. They would remain in that area for several weeks. The 12th and 13th marched seven more miles, to Wolf Run Shoals on Occoquan Creek. While the entire brigade had made a southward movement from Fairfax Court House, brigade commander Stoughton had chosen to maintain his

SCOTTS BLUFF NATIONAL MONUMENT

Jackson's view of a Vermont camp in a Virginia blizzard

headquarters there. He had comfortable housing in the village at the two-story brick home of Dr. William Presley Gunnell. The general had acquired a piano and added it to the house's furnishings. Stoughton had recently brought his mother and sister down from Vermont, and they were fond of entertaining. Outside, in a tent, a lady friend from Massachusetts, Miss Annie Jones, was in residence. Also, the general was keeping company with an attractive young lady in the village, Antonia Ford. Miss Ford, daughter of Edward Ford, a local merchant, was also acquainted with John Singleton Mosby and J.E.B. Stuart. Indeed, Stuart had given her an honorary appointment as an aide-de-camp. Whether Stoughton knew that fact or not, he now had several aides boarding at the Ford house.

Colonel Veazey wrote to Julia of an evening at Fairfax Court House, "The general was there with his mother and sisters, the parties were in a new building put up for commisary stores . . . I told one of these ladies after she had been waltzing with the general that I should like to see my wife doing that. I thought there might be a slight jar in our affections . . . She said her husband never wanted to dance with her but once in an evening."

At the Court House, the general was at least three miles from his outposts. On returning from leave, Private Benedict reported concern in the ranks that the brigadier might be "gobbled" by rebels if he weren't careful.

•   •   •

Some 20 miles south of Washington, two prominent streams, Bull Run and Occoquan Creek, form a natural defensive line against any force coming from the south. Bull Run meanders down from the Bull Run mountains west of the capital, and after winding and turning time and again flows into the wider Occoquan, which in turn flows to the Potomac. Camping at Wolf Run Shoals, a much-used Occoquan crossing on a north–south road, the 12th and 13th regiments were assigned to guard seven miles of streambank, from the Occoquan's mouth on the Potomac, west to Union Mills. South and west of Bull Run and the Occoquan, John Singleton Mosby and his raiders were steadily gaining recruits. Writing from Wolf Run Shoals, Lieutenant Colonel Farnham told Mary, "We are now at the front, that is there are no troops between us & the rebel forces."

Private Benedict, back after three weeks' leave, described the new encampment: "The Twelfth . . . has exchanged the broad stretches and open region of Fairfax Court House, for a rough and broken country, wooded with scrub oaks and second growth pines growing on worn out tobacco fields, and scantily peopled with scattered 'secech' farmers. Near us, several hundred feet below our camps, runs the Occoquan river, a muddy stream about as large as the Winooski. Across it, on the heights beyond, are earthworks thrown up by Beauregard's soldiers last winter, now untenanted. Our camp is on a knoll from which the men have cleared the pine trees. It is much narrower in its limits than our former fine camp near Fairfax, and it is less attractive in almost every particular. The men have had all they could do in digging rifle pits, picket duty, constructing corduroy roads,—of which they have made miles between this and Fairfax Station,—and the labor of clearing and making camp; and between the rain and snow and mud have had the roughest time they have as yet known."

He added, "There have been skirmishes between the cavalry outposts, sights of rebel patrols, and rumors of coming attack from rebel cavalry, enough to keep us somewhat on the alert; but the long roll has not sounded, nor has hostile shot been fired by us. Colonel Blunt has been practicing the men at target firing, and they are making sensible progress in the modern method of administering the 'blue pills' which are the only cure for rebellion."

In the 12th, Private Jackson was summoned to Colonel Blunt's tent and given a new job, that of regimental artist. "Finished a picture and commenced another from the sketch of Sallie Davis Ford," he noted, "and then took the first to the Colonel—praised them very much." A few days later, "Tomorrow will map the Bull Run and Occoquan from Union Mills to Sallie Davis Ford."

Private Sturtevant, in the 13th, noted, "Rewards were offered for such as showed best skill in hitting the bull's eye on the hill across the valley 300 yards and more away; a few succeeded and were excused from all duty for a week on account of their skill as marksmen."

In the 13th's new camp, Sergeant Palmer wrote: "At night I go over the camp. Each company has eight or ten fires between its row of tents. Here is a small one, where are four or five soldiers chatting; there is one that roars and lights up the woods for rods, its cone-like flames darting up ten feet and spreading as they curl among the spitting pine twigs and leaves. There is no war-whoop sounding out on the night air; no wild dance, or painted faces; but the scene really brings to mind the Indian stories of one's childhood. But no,—soon there are signs of civilization and of a fiercer war than of bows and arrows . . . and each man, armed with a rifle, has a copy of the New Testament."

Soon after the brigade moved, word came of another military failure to the south. Burnside's march up the Rappahannock, aimed at crossing and flanking Lee's army, had been defeated with scarcely a shot fired as the skies opened, the temperature climbed, and the luckless army became bogged down in deep mud. Within five days the Army of the Potomac was back in camp, never having gotten its bridges in place. It became known as The Mud March, something of a joke, and within days Lincoln replaced Burnside with Maj. Gen. Joseph Hooker.

The weather worsened. Walcott Mead reported from Fairfax Station on January 30, "We have at last all been captured, taken prisoner by one General Mud who with the combined forces of snow and rain have gained a complete and successful victory over the whole of the 2nd Vt. Brigade . . . There has been a great snow storm . . . it fell in the depth of 18 inches, pretty good for the sunny south."

January turned to February with continued snowstorms. "Writing to my kin sitting on a hard tack box," said Capt. Lucius H. Bostwick of Jericho. "The typhoid fever has raged a good deal in the Regiment recently and in many cases has proved fatal."

Still, Benedict reported the general health of the regiment as "good," though he noted that typhoid and pneumonia were taking an increasing toll. He put the total effective strength of the brigade at 3,901 men. Thus, since arriving at Brattleboro, nearly 1,000 men had been lost from the ranks. Among those on the sick rolls was Lt. Carmi Marsh, of the 13th Vermont. Marsh, from the northwestern Vermont town of Franklin, a wiry little fellow, had contracted typhus at Fairfax Court House, but made a quick recovery. However, he had insisted on following his regiment to Wolf Run Shoals, on a mule cart, and after his rainy trip he was again sick. The doctor now diagnosed him with meningitis, and his parents were sent for. On arrival they found him, in a tent, near death. They set out to find him better quarters, finally convincing a Mrs. Mary Wilcoxson, for a fee, to take him into her house near Wolf Run. Placing him in a bed close by a large fireplace, the outspokenly Confederate woman, who exhibited considerable nursing skills, slowly brought Marsh back to health.

A brigade hospital had been set up, called Green Mountain Hospital according to Pvt. Edwin Hall of the 15th, who described it this way: "The hospital is a large 2 story brick building standing on a little hill a quarter of a mile northeast of the Fairfax Village. It has a piazza on both sides and one on the second story. I should think it belonged to a rich man. There is 2 negro families left who do the washing for the hospital. It had just as good bed and as good care as I should at home. Each room is called a ward. There were four wards besides the attic . . . They have got 3 cooks so you see we had good victuals. About the surgeon, I have not much to say."

Private Welch, assigned to duty in the hospital, noted in his diary:

Tuesday—   Worked all night in getting the beds ready for the sick . . . It
             was necessary for me and two others to carry two corpses to

Mrs. Mary Wilcoxson, who cared for Carmi Marsh

	the ambulance wagon.
Wednesday—	Rainy and cold. I cut wood, cleaned inside the hospital and did errands for the doctor.
Thursday—	I was called up in the morning to get water for the cook, following I had to carry the body of a man who died to another ward, wash and dress him. Two of us worked on him. He belonged to the 15th Regiment.
Monday—	Called up in the morning to carry a man to the 'dead room' and to wash and dress him . . . Another man died about noon. Washed and dressed him.

Matters at home continued to concern Private Glover. "Tell John to get up wood enough to last through the summer," he wrote to his wife, "and I will help him in haying to pay him. Tell him to get up a good pile of it and I will pay him well for it and I want you to nurse up that smallest calf so he will make a mate for the other one . . . Have the straw all fed out so as to make the hogs go further. The oxen will do well enough on straw when they don't work. If there is any hay to spare let John have it if he needs it. Tell John I will help him enough to pay him for all the extra work he does."

In mid-February, Colonel Randall opened a school for sword instruction, requiring all sergeants in the 13th to attend. "This school furnished any amount of fun for the boys that watched the thrusts, strikes, plunges and guards and paries at each other with their little wooden swords," Private Sturtevant said.

The home of Mrs. Wilcoxson

Pvt. Samuel Dana wandered out of camp and reported on it in a February 21 letter home to Warren:

> Dear wife,
>
> I went off about 2 miles and came to a plantation and went to the house to see how things looked around there. The man came to the door and asked me to come in. I went in and sat down and had quite a chat, and they asked me to stay to dinner, which I gladly accepted. We had hoecake and bacon and butter cakes and apple pie and coffee with cream and sugar in it. I stayed until three o'clock and had a good time. Just before I came away the man told me to write to my lady that I had been to a rebel's house and took dinner and they didn't kill or hurt me. He said that he used to think if a Yankee got a chance they would murder or do anything else that was mean. He asked me to come again. Since then he has been in camp selling pies and biscuits.
>
> A nigger got drowned yesterday here. He was awatering a horse for one of the artillery officers, and the river was very high. The horse stepped off the bank shore where it was so steep the horse couldn't touch bottom and darky fell off and that was the end of him. Well, the drummer beats for the roll call and I will close. Write soon. Good night.

In a realignment of Federal forces, the Second Vermont Brigade and other troops guarding Washington were assigned to the 22nd Army Corps commanded by Maj. Gen. Samuel Heintzelman, a veteran of Bull Run, the Peninsula Campaign, and Antietam, where he had shown no special military genius. The brigade remained in Major General Casey's division.

Jabez Hammond wrote home on February 25, "Last night there was a lot of us out snowballing when there was a ball hit me in my right eye & nearly knocked me down. I have done nothing to day & as I write one eye is covered up with a handkerchief & the other one ought to be for as you might say I am blind in one eye & can't see very well out of the other one."

Private Benedict reported, "The spirits are good . . . and as I write, the music of a guitar and violin and well attuned manly voices, serenading the ladies whose presence in camp I have heretofore mentioned, reaches me on the evening air, and tells of light hearts and good cheer."

As February was coming to a close, the brigade saw increasingly ominous signs along the picket line. "The inhabitants of this region are all 'secesh,'" Benedict wrote in late February. "As wherever we have been in Virginia, the young and able bodied men are all gone. The old men are just quiet and civil enough in the presence of our soldiers to keep themselves from arrest; but render what aid and comfort they can give of any one, to the other side. The women are 'sesech' without exception; the little girls sing rebel songs, and the hoopless, dirty and illiterate young ladies . . . boast that their brothers and sweethearts are in the rebel army, and chuckle over the time coming, when the roads settle, when Stonewall Jackson will rout us out of here in a hurry. One or two skirmishes of the Michigan calvalry with White's rebel cavalry have occurred near us recently, in one of which our side lost fifteen men, and a cavalry picket was cut off but two days ago within three miles of our camp."

Lyman Seeley reported from Wolf Run Shoals, "The 12th is on the right of the 13th, and the Connecticut Battery is in front, secured by earth-works. It is impossible for a rebel force to cross the river, as all things are so planned as to rake the river in a cross fire."

Private Sturtevant recalled that on March 3, "Colonel [Percy] Wyndham, with quite a large body of cavalry, crossed Occoquan just above us at one of the fords on his way back to Fairfax Court House." Wyndham, an English adventurer serving in the Union army, had been on a failed mission to capture Mosby. Like General Stoughton, Wyndham made his headquarters at Fairfax Court House. Mosby did not like him at all.

★

14

Mention "Mosby's Confederacy" to the men of the Second Vermont Brigade in early March of 1863 and they probably would have responded with a puzzled look. Few if any of their letters written up to that time make mention of any "Mosby," though surely by then his name had been heard. Yet before many days passed that name would be on all their lips, and a substantial area south and west of Washington and out to the Blue Ridge Mountains would be known as Mosby's Confederacy. In the winter of 1862–63, beginning with some small raids in January, John Singleton Mosby began to stake claim to that territory. Starting after the Dumfries expedition, with 15 men and permission to operate independently given by J.E.B. Stuart, the Virginian was becoming a menace to Union soldiers on the outer lines of the national capital's defenses.

"He was thin, wiry and I should say about five feet nine or ten inches in height," according to one wartime description. "A slight stoop in the back was not ungraceful. His chin was carried well forward; his lips were thin, and wore a somewhat artificial smile; the eyes, under the brown felt hat, were keen, sparkling, and roved curiously from side to side. He wore a gray uniform, with no arms but two revolvers,—the sabre was no favorite with him. His voice was low, and a smile was often on his lips. He rarely sat still ten minutes."

In March 1863, Mosby, a native Virginian, was 29 years old, and two years earlier had given up a legal practice in Bristol, Virginia, to join the local cavalry. He had attended the University of Virginia, until he was briefly locked up for shooting a fellow student, and had become interested in the law during his trial. (He was acquitted.) He fought at First Bull Run (Manassas) and on the Peninsula, where, it was said, he had come up with the idea for Stuart's famed ride around McClellan's army. Later in the war, Mosby would lead as many as 240 men. His sector generally included Loudon and Fairfax Counties in Virginia, a gently rolling landscape of fields interspersed with woods, of small farms and little villages and meandering creeks called runs. His tactics would remain consistent—rallying his followers on short notice for quick strikes, then seeming to disappear into the woods and fields, or even the villages. He employed guerrilla tactics, and some of his men were but part-time soldiers, or men on leave from other units. Mosby became the greatest threat to Union troops in the north of Virginia.

A hero in the South, Mosby also became an object to his foes, not only of

John Singleton Mosby, the Gray Ghost of the Confederacy

fear, but also of wonder and respect. And in early March 1863, Capt. John S. Mosby became most interested in the goings-on at a certain Union-held village, Fairfax Court House. Though he certainly knew that Stoughton was there, he was focused on the presence of Colonel Wyndman, whom he despised.

"An English officer," Mosby wrote in his memoirs, "Colonel Percy Wyndham, a soldier of fortune who had been with Garibaldi in Italy, commanded the Cavalry brigade and had charge of the outposts. He was familiar with the old rules of the schools, but he soon learned that they were out of date, and his experience in war had not taught him how to counteract the forays and surprises that kept his men in the saddle all the time. The loss of sleep is irritating to anybody and, in his vexation at being struck by and striking at an invisible foe, he sent me a message calling me a horse thief. I did not deny it," Mosby continued, "but retorted that all the horses I had stolen had riders, and that the riders had sabres, carbines, and pistols. There was a new regiment in his brigade that was armed only with sabres and obsolete carbines. When we attacked them with revolvers, they were really defenseless. So I sent him word through a citizen that the men of that regiment were not worth capturing, that he must give them six-shooters."

One early-winter day a Union deserter, James Ames of the Fifth New York Cavalry, came to Mosby offering his services. They were readily accepted, though Mosby was for a time suspicious that Ames might be a double agent. But Ames soon proved to be reliable, and Mosby's men bestowed on him the nickname "Big Yankee." Ames told Mosby everything he knew about Yankee troops and their disposition in northern Virginia. "The account he gave me," said the captain, "of the distribution of troops and gaps in the picket lines coincided with what I knew." Mosby determined to strike at Fairfax Court House.

Meanwhile, the Vermonters were enjoying a break in the weather as March in Virginia came in like a lamb. Corporal Williams at Fairfax Station wrote in his diary, "March 5. Drilling this week six hours each day. The weather is very mild at present, and our camp still bears its usual quiet state."

Along the Occoquan, conditions were not as tranquil, as Private Sturtevant recalled: "The warm sun and south wind dried up the deep mud, but the weather was changeable . . . The usual stir on the picket line, the moving of cavalry in squads, the rumors of onward movements of the army, the firing on and capturing of videttes and infantry on the picket line, and the wild rumors in camp day and night led us to believe that we should soon be on the march to participate in some great battle. Battalion drill on the 3d, and then house cleaning in tents and camp every where, careful inspection of cook tents and sinks, our water supply, all places in and about camp, Surgeons Nichols and Crandall, and their assistants, giving directions here and there, as occasion demanded, to avoid an epidemic of fever in the approaching spring."

Lyman Seeley, at Wolf Run Shoals, reported, "Sometimes the pickets are aroused by the footsteps of horses, or the barking of dogs, which show that the guerrillas are ranging the country on the other side of the river."

Still, Private Hatch wrote to Lucina on March 5, "I went up to the battery to see them shoot their big guns at a target about one mile and a half off then we played ball a little while."

Corporal Williams made the following entries in his diary:

March 6. A rumor is afloat that old Stuart is again in this vicinity, and marching orders have been received. If this is the case, we shall doubtless have some fun.

March 7. The orders of yesterday have been countermanded and news has come that the programme is changed, and instead of an advance movement by Stuart, he has retreated across the Rappahannock with his whole force.

That same day, Hatch wrote, "It is all quiet on the Occoquon and Wolf Run I expect to be on picket to day but didn't happen. I shall be on tomorrow I hope it will be a good day don't you."

On March 8, Williams noted, "More wet weather, which makes it so muddy that there is no drilling." It was Sunday, and Hatch wrote, "I hope it is a pleasant day so that you can go to meeting. I should like very much to be there to get into the sleigh and go to meeting with you and hear Mr. Perkins once more but I guess the sleigh will be gone before I get home."

That day, Pvt. George Benedict at Wolf Run Shoals reported that his regiment had been in its present camp for seven weeks, "a longer stay in one spot than it has yet made." He added, "About a tenth of the regiment are off duty from measles, fever, and ailments of one sort or another."

Before crawling into his tent for the night of March 8, Private Dana finished a letter to his wife: "The Rebs act a little saucy over across the river occasionally, but if they want a flogging let them come in reach."

March 8 was a quiet day. But at nightfall that would change most dramatically; Mosby was on the prowl.

"On the evening of March 8, 1863," Mosby wrote, "in obedience to orders, twenty-nine men met me at Dover, in Loudoun County. None knew my objective point, but I told Ames after we started. I . . . got dinner that day with Colonel Chancellor, who lived near Dover. Just as I was about to mount my horse, as I was leaving, I said to him, 'I shall mount the stars to-night or sink lower than plummet ever sounded.'"

He continued: "The weather conditions favored my success. There was a melting snow on the ground, a mist, and, about dark, a drizzling rain. Our starting point was about twenty-five miles from Fairfax Court House. It was pitch dark when we got near the cavalry pickets at Chantilly—five or six miles from the Court House. At Centreville, three miles away on the Warrenton pike and seven miles from the Court House, were several thousand troops. Our problem was to pass between them and Wyndham's cavalry without giving the alarm. Ames knew where there was a break in the picket lines between Chantilly and Centreville, and he led us through without a vidette seeing us."

Mosby approached from the northeast along the Little River Turnpike. Nearing Chantilly, a little more than five miles out, the raiders left the road and swung south, passing easily—with Big Yankee's directions—between the campfires of federal cavalry. Riding cautiously through the soggy fields, they soon reached the Fairfax Station Road and swung north, now headed directly for Fairfax Court House.

"The plan had been to reach the Court House by midnight so as to get out of the lines before daybreak," Mosby noted, "but the column got broken in the dark and the two parts travelled around in a circle for an hour looking for each other. After we closed up, we started off and struck the pike between Centreville and the Court House. But we turned off into the woods when we got within two or three miles of the village, as Wyndham's cavalry camps were on the pike."

The wet weather of March 8 had washed out any possibility that General Stoughton would hold one of his beloved reviews. He may have enjoyed some piano music before he went to his bedroom, on the second floor of Dr. Gunnell's house; apparently there were some good times, since Mosby would report that he found empty wine bottles on the dining room table. But Stoughton slept soundly with rain on the roof that mild winter night, perhaps dreaming of his congressional confirmation, soon to make him a full-fledged brigadier general. He was, that night, the only commander of troops at sleepy Fairfax Court House. Colonel Wyndham had gone that evening to catch a train for Washington.

Stoughton, through his brief military career after graduating from West Point, had displayed a penchant for getting into trouble. In the winter of 1861–62, with the Vermont Brigade camped south of Washington at Camp Griffin, Stoughton had been summoned before a court-martial. He was charged with "disobedience of orders" for "visiting Washington City without a pass." It was his misfortune

Dr. Gunnell's house in Fairfax Court House,
where Stoughton was captured by Mosby

that the tribunal that heard his case was presided over by Brig. Gen. Winfield Scott Hancock, one of the better Union commanders of the Civil War and a man who brooked no foolishness. Though Stoughton made a fervent appeal for dismissal of charges, and Hancock lessened them, still there was the blemish on his record of "conduct to the prejudice of military discipline." Stoughton, however, was not reduced in rank, and subsequently led the Fourth Vermont capably on the Peninsula, displaying considerable bravery. But back home on leave, he had made that ill-advised speech in Bellows Falls suggesting that the army might march on Congress. And he had angered his men by unnecessary marching at Brattleboro, apparently for the purpose of showing off to the locals. Then he had caroused in Virginia, freely using profanity to the disgust of his men. And there were complaints that his punishments were far too harsh. Also, there were grumblings about his acquaintance with Virginians known to be strongly supportive of the rebellion. Now the biggest trouble of all was headed the young brigadier's way through a mild and murky Virginia winter night.

"We entered the village from the direction of the railroad station," Mosby recalled. "There were a few sentinels about the town, but it was so dark that they could not distinguish us from their own people. Squads were detailed to go around to the officers' quarters and to the stables for the horses. The court-house yard was the rendezvous where we all were to report. As our great desire was to capture Wyndham, Ames was sent with a party to the house in which we knew Wyndham had his quarters. Fortune was in Wyndham's favor that time . . . But Ames got his two staff officers, his horses, and his uniform."

Amos Whiting, a farmer from Calais in the 13th Vermont, was an orderly for General Stoughton. He remembered, "About half past two in the morning I was aroused by a troop of cavalry galloping by should say 25 or 30, I looked toward the telegraph operator's tent which was a few rods below on the other side of the street. The flap of the tent was thrown open and a gun set against it."

Whiting heard the rebels give the federal countersign, which was "Abercromby."

Pvt. Laforest Darling, in the 12th and from Westminster, stationed in the hospital at Fairfax Court House, wrote of "my own observation" to the *Bellows Falls Sentinel* in Stoughton's hometown: "I was aroused by the usual tramp of horses in the street. I arose from my cot, and looking out of the window saw about fifteen cavalrymen in front of the hospital . . . I supposed them to be relief guard, and thought no more about it, but kindled a fire and went out to the rear of the hospital, and again I saw troops come by. This time they were 25 in number. They rode up to the barn and stable where all of Gen. Stoughton's horses were kept. I saw them take all the horses. Meantime, I heard one of them say, 'Be quick.' I supposed then that there might be some rebels in the vicinity, and that our cavalry were getting horses ready for a start after them. As soon as the horses were out they proceeded to the General's house. I looked and saw no light there. I thought strange that there should be no light. I then went in and retired to rest again."

Mosby remembered: "When the squads were starting around to gather prisoners and horses, Joe Nelson brought me a soldier who said he was a guard at

General Stoughton's headquarters. Joe had also pulled the telegraph operator out of his tent; the wires had been cut. With five or six men I rode to the house, now the Episcopal rectory, where the commanding general was. We dismounted and knocked loudly at the door. Soon a window above was opened, and some one asked who was there. I answered, 'Fifth New York Cavalry with a dispatch for General Stoughton.' The door was opened and a staff officer, Lieutenant Prentiss, was before me. I took hold of his nightshirt, whispered my name in his ear, and told him to take me to General Stoughton's room. Resistance was useless, and he obeyed.

"A light was quickly struck," Mosby went on, "and on the bed we saw the general sleeping as the Turk when Marco Bozzaris waked him up. There was no time for ceremony, so I drew up the bedclothes, pulled up the general's shirt, and gave him a spank on his bare back, and told him to get up. As his staff officer was standing by me, Stoughton did not realize the situation and thought that somebody was taking a rude familiarity with him. He asked in an indignant tone what all this meant. I told him that he was my prisoner, and that he must get up quickly and dress.

"I then asked him if he had ever heard of 'Mosby,' and he said he had.

"'I am Mosby,' I said. 'Stuart's cavalry has possession of the Court House; be quick and dress.'"

According to Mosby, Stoughton asked whether Confederate cavalryman Fitz Lee was with him, for Lee had been a friend at West Point. Mosby then noted that while Stoughton was a brave soldier, he also had the reputation of "being something of a fop" and that the Vermonter took an inordinate amount of time dressing in front of a mirror.

Mosby's account continued, "Stoughton's horses and couriers were ready to go with us, when we came out with the general and his staff. When we reached the rendezvous at the courtyard, I found all the squads waiting for us with their prisoners and horses. There were three times as many prisoners as my men, and each was mounted and leading a horse. To deceive the enemy and baffle the pursuit, the cavalcade started off in one direction and, soon after it got out of town, turned in another. We flanked the cavalry camps, and soon were on the pike between them and Centreville. As there were several thousand troops in town, it was not thought possible that we would go that way to get out of the lines, so the cavalry, when it started in pursuit, went in an opposite direction. Lieutenant Preston and a good many prisoners who started with us escaped in the dark, and we lost a great many of the horses."

Mosby also took note of an incident that occurred while his men were riding out of the village. An upstairs window was raised and a gruff voice demanded to know what was taking place in the street below. Lt. Col. Robert Johnstone, of the Fifth New York Cavalry, had detected the enemy in the village. Mosby said his men laughed back, then several dismounted and entered the house. There they encountered Lieutenant Colonel Johnstone's wife defiantly confronting them in the hallway. By the time the Confederates barged past her, Johnstone, clad only in his nightshirt, had taken refuge under an outhouse. He avoided capture.

The route of escape was west by slightly southwest. "Our safety depended on our getting out of the Union lines by daybreak," Mosby said. "I called to [William] Hunter to come on and directed him to go forward at a trot and to hold Stoughton's bridle reins under all circumstances . . . We stopped frequently to listen for the hoofbeats of cavalry in pursuit, but no sounds could be heard save the hooting of owls. My heart beat higher with hope every minute."

A line of campfires was passed, and the way continued toward Centreville. Light was now distinctly showing in the eastern sky. At Centreville, the Union camps were silent and, Mosby said, distant sentinels paid the horsemen no mind.

"After we had passed the forts and reached Cub Run," said Mosby, "a new danger was before us. The stream was swift and booming from the melting snow . . . Without halting a moment I plunged into the stream, and my horse swam to the other bank. Stoughton followed and was next to me. As he came up the bank, shivering from his cold morning bath, he said, 'Captain, this is the first rough treatment I have to complain of.'"

Charles Barr, a private from Swanton, was on guard duty at Stoughton's headquarters and was captured along with the general. A comrade of his recalled years later that Barr said he had been put on a "raw boned, sharp backed shack of a mule without a saddle or blanket and a swim through the swift running stream of Cub Run." That fellow soldier remembered, "As soon as at a safe distance from our cavalry videttes and within his own lines . . . they were given the privilege of swearing not to take further part until exchanged and this alternative was preferable to bare back mule ride further, so accepted and started back toward camp."

Mosby's way of escape was down the Warrenton Turnpike, a highway already steeped in Civil War history. Along the pike Union regiments less than two years before had marched toward the battle of First Bull Run, and back along the pike they had retreated. Then, a year later, Stonewall Jackson had started the terrible battle of Second Bull Run by attacking a long Union column where the road gained the heights of Groveton. Now Mosby came to those once-bloody heights.

"We crossed Bull Run at Sudley Ford," Mosby said, "and were soon on the historic battlefield. From the heights of Groveton we could see that the road was clear to Centreville, and that there was no pursuit . . . The sun had just risen, and in the rapture of the moment I said to Slater, 'George, that is the sun of Austerlitz!' I knew I had drawn a prize in the lottery of life, and my emotion was natural and should be pardoned. I could not help but feel deep pity for Stoughton when he looked back at Centreville and saw that there was no chance of rescue. Without any fault of his own, Stoughton's career as a soldier was blasted."

The road led to Warrenton, where Mosby was pleasantly surprised that word of his exploit preceded him. "We found that the whole population had turned out and were giving my men an ovation," he wrote. Mosby said that Stoughton had breakfast with a local man named John Gregory Beckham. "The general had been a classmate of Beckham's son, now artillery officer," Mosby continued, "and had spent a vacation with him at his home. We soon remounted and moved on south . . . The next morning there was a cold rain, but after breakfast we started for General Fitz Lee's headquarters. When we arrived at our destination, we hitched our horses in the front yard and went into the house, where we found Fitz Lee writing at a table before a log fire. We were cold and wet . . . He was very polite to his old classmate and to the officers, but did not ask me to take a seat by the fire . . . So, bidding the prisoners good-bye and bowing to Fitz Lee, Hunter and I rode off in the rain to the telegraph office to send a report to Stuart, who had his headquarters at Fredericksburg."

Despite his acquaintance with young Lee, Stoughton was soon on his way farther south, to the infamous Libby Prison in Richmond. With this capture, Mosby had accomplished one of the great feats of the war. News of the brigade commander's "gobbling" by Mosby spread like wildfire through the ranks of the Second Vermont Brigade.

"The camp is humming with the news," Private Benedict wrote the next day, "but in the uncertainty as to how much is told of the attending circumstances is truth, I will not attempt to describe this very creditable (to the rebels) occurrence. I beg leave to say, however, that none of the disgrace of the affair belongs to the regiments of the brigade. General Stoughton was not taken from the midst of his command. The Vermont regiments nearest to the comfortable brick house which he occupied as his headquarters, were at Fairfax Station, four miles south of him, while the Twelfth and Thirteenth were a dozen miles away. The risk of exactly such an operation has been apparent even to the privates, and has been a matter of frequent remark among officers and men, for weeks past. How could they protect him as long as he kept his quarters at such a distance from them? Colonel Blunt has been assigned to the command of the brigade, and is removing his headquarters to Fairfax Station."

According to an unnamed member of the 13th Vermont, "There were some in our brigade that felt quite friendly toward Mosby for what he had done, believing General Stoughton's place could be filled without injury to the morale of the brigade and to the satisfaction of officers and privates alike."

★

Fairfax Court House, once a sleepy country crossroads where the legal business of a rural Virginia county was transacted, is now a congested and growing suburb of the ever-expanding Washington area. Finding parking space is a challenge. Yet remnants of the Civil War village where General Stoughton was "gobbled" survive, at its main intersection. The Gunnell house is now home to the offices of the Truro Episcopal Church. One sweltering summer day, the Rev. Paul Frey allowed exploration of the building, readily admitting me to his second-floor office, the bedroom from which Stoughton was carried off by Mosby. I ascended some rather steep stairs curving to the second floor, noting that both the stairs and the old banister creaked considerably and wondering whether they had done so under Mosby's tread. I found the bedroom to be a spacious and neat office, well lighted by two large front windows. The fireplace, with deep mantel, that once warmed the Vermont general is now only decorative. I sat rather a long time reconstructing the events of that long-ago night when "The Gray Ghost" slapped the bare buttocks of the boy general, on his way to destroying Stoughton's career and pulling off the

best-known escapade of his own storied career. On the third floor, in a
closet off a large bedroom, I found Civil War graffiti in the hand of some
New York soldiers. Back in the summer heat I walked a block to the old
wooden Moore House, where Big Yankee Ames had searched futilely for
Colonel Wyndham. And I walked to the old brick courthouse where
Colonel Cummings set up shop, once employing an old law book as a
pillow. Then I returned briefly to the Gunnell house, entering two large
and high-ceilinged downstairs rooms where Stoughton had once entertained. In the rear room I found, appropriately, a piano. On my way
out of the village, I noted that adjacent to the Gunnell house the Mosby
Apartments complex has recently been constructed.

Within the Manassas National Battlefield Park, the old Warrenton
Turnpike, now Route 29, is a fast and heavily traveled road. Take it south.
After passing the Stone House, the road climbs in a series of gentle rises.
These are the heights of Groveton, on the road along which Mosby rode
with his prisoner Stoughton. Look back for a view of where the white tents
of the Union camps once lay, toward which Stoughton looked that fateful morning, hoping, in vain, for some sign of pursuit.

15

The capture of Stoughton left the Second Vermont Brigade in a state of shock. With spring approaching and, presumably, the fighting about to resume, the nine-months Vermonters were suddenly without their controversial commander.

Private Williams summed up the episode the day after Stoughton's capture: "Monday, March 9, 1863. Very heartbreaking day here. At midnight 60 to 150 rebels came here unexpectedly and after capturing several guards, took several horses. Went into headquarters of General Stoughton and took him prisoner . . . The aides of the General escaped and Lieut. Col. Johnstone, 5th New York Cavalry escaped in his shirt and sent orders to the camp for the Regiment to pursue them with all haste. Three regiments of Cavalry pursued them but did not catch them according to the reports received today. The whole thing was attributed to the secech living in the village. They undoubtedly gave the information to the rebels and they came while the village was without soldiers. They accomplished it all without firing a shot and left at four o'clock in the morning. It must be said that they worked splendidly and slyly."

As he reported, considerable wrath descended on the residents of Fairfax Court House. The next day, Williams said, "The Provost Marshall gave orders last night to take all citizens of the village prisoners, and today nine of them were sent safely to Washington. No news of Gen. Stoughton today."

Many locals were arrested, though in the end none was proved to have had a part in helping Mosby. Much of the suspicion centered on Antonia Ford, and she and her father were shipped off to Capitol Prison in Washington, where she languished for several months. On release, Antonia went straight down to Richmond.

"The rebels bagged the old fellow in good shape," Pvt. Walcott Mead wrote to his parents in Shoreham.

As Jabez Hammond put it, "They say Stoughton's mother got a letter from him this morning stating that he was at Culpepper court house & should soon be exchanged & come back to his post may be so & may be woodchuck. I have to say that it [is] a little coolest thing that has ever happened in this war the capturing of a brigadier general and 13 armed men without a gun being fired upon either side is something that doesn't happen every day."

In the 16th Vermont, Capt. Elmer Keyes, a part-time schoolteacher in civilian life, wrote home to Reading on March 9, "The news came to our camp this morning about 8 o'clock but no one believed or entertained thought a moment, but it proved true . . . No one was to blame but himself. None of the Brigade was within 3 miles nor have they been since the middle of January. Not half of the Court House knew it until morning."

According to Pvt. John Wallace, "Some of the men whisper around that Stoughton is not loyal but I dislike to think him disloyal for if he had been we would have suspected the whole brigade."

Sgt. James Smith wrote to the folks in Chester on March 9, "Went to meeting this afternoon. Went to prayer meeting this evening. I am still speechless. Stoughton taken tonight." (It should be noted that news of the brigadier's capture had not left Smith wordless. He was suffering from laryngitis.)

There was a heightened sense of danger throughout the brigade. "There had been a party scouting among the rebs," wrote Pvt. Abraham Rowell of the 16th to his home folks in Andover. "We brought in forty hens and forty-three Niggers. We did not ask any of them to come into our lines . . . We have arrested most all the citizens round about. Most of them are nothing but bushwhackers— citizens daytimes, and the worst rebs at night. They are lying in the bushes ready to shoot our pickets. We are fired on every night either the infantry or the cavalry by those rogues."

Vermont newspapers were quick to comment on Stoughton's capture. "From the president down to the humblest private or civilian the capture of Vermont's Brigadier General has been received as a great joke," began the *Caledonian Record*'s editorial of March 20. "It seems almost heartless to make merry over an affair so expensive to the party most concerned, yet from all we can learn from private sources the capture was merited . . . It is further noted that he had ordered up a piano from Washington and a lady love from somewhere else . . . Although a man of fine military attainments, he was reckless, and his men said he was a hard drinker; and when under the influence his men said he was tyrannical and abusive. His men are not sorry that they are to have a CHANGE."

The capture was, not surprisingly, big news in the South. In the Confederate capital, the *Richmond Despatch* stated on March 16, "Most of the twenty-nine men captured, including Gen. Stoughton, an aristocratic specimen of Yankee manhood, with a profusion of gold lace on his coat, were surprised in bed . . . they were compelled to ride twenty-five miles on the bare backs of indifferent steeds surrounded by Confederate dragoons, over not the smoothest of road known."

The newspaper in Stoughton's hometown broke the news on March 13: "On Monday a telegraphic dispatch was received in this village by Hon. E.M. Stoughton announcing that his son, Gen. Stoughton, commanding the 2nd Vermont, has been taken prisoner by the rebels."

George Benedict later recounted this story: "Rev. George B. Spaulding of Vergennes, in a communication to the *N.Y. Times*, commenting on the capture of General Stoughton, said that his capture had been predicted in a letter from Fairfax Court House, written ten days before the event. General Stoughton's uncle, Hon. E.W. Stoughton of New York, took up the matter, avowed his disbelief in the existence of any such prediction, and offered to give $250 to the N.E. Soldiers Relief Association for the name and residence of any person who had received a letter containing such a prediction. These were furnished to Mr. Stoughton and he paid over the sum named."

•   •   •

A semblance of normalcy slowly returned to the Second Vermont Brigade, though with a heightened sense of justifiable alarm. Mosby was increasingly active on the perimeter of the regiments, with the support of a steady supply of Virginians willing to take a whack at the invaders.

On March 12, Henry White, a 19-year-old private in the 16th regiment from a hill farm in Bridgewater, wrote to his sister Mary, "We have been drilling very hard for a week past. Our Col. is evidently preparing us for active work. He has been drilling us in charge bayonet this week, designating some hill in the distance that he wanted us to take. He would order; charge, bayonet forward, double quick. Then with a yell we would go forward double quick over fences, across brooks, through underbrush, and often would not stop until sometime after the bugle sounded . . . This type of drilling is terribly hard, but yet it is interesting and I like it."

Private White added, "We have prayer meetings now every night and considerable interest has been manifested, quite a number have sought and found Christ precious and some have been reclaimed. I think I can say that I am enjoying the smiles of my Redeemer in goodly degree . . . I have tried to break off some bad habits and I know that I have succeeded. I am trying this month to read and commit to memory six verses of scripture daily . . . I am now learning the Sermon on the Mount . . . Time is so short now before I shall be called to speak in the name of Jesus."

George Benedict wrote to the *Free Press* on March 21. This time his letter came not from a private, but from an officer, Lieutenant Benedict. Soon after again assuming command of the brigade, Colonel Blunt commissioned his correspondent/private. Henceforth, Benedict would be attached to brigade headquarters, as an aid to the brigade commander.

"Colonel Blunt . . . has been making his presence felt at Fairfax Station in the right way," Benedict reported. "The quantity of quartermaster and commissary stores here is, of course, very large—and the position must be held at all hazards. It is now, I am happy to say, in a very much better condition than ever before. Rifle pits have been dug and breast-works by the mile thrown up by the men of the Fourteenth, Fifteenth and Sixteenth regiments, along the high ground surrounding the station on every side, from behind which we will be happy to meet any force likely to be sent against us."

Colonel Blunt's first order was to move brigade headquarters south from Fairfax Court House to Fairfax Station, close to and well protected by those strong new lines. Benedict continued, "The picket lines have also been closely looked after; the various departments of supply for the brigade have received attention; and the brigade and regimental hospitals have had the benefit of the colonel's occasional unannounced presence and quick eye for defects in management. One learns to value energy and attention to his business in a commanding officer, after seeing how the influence of such qualities is felt throughout down to the last private in the brigade."

He added, "How long the rebels will leave our infantry regiments unmolested, of course I cannot say, but the way in which our cavalry suffer of late, is a caution to all." Benedict noted that the First Vermont Cavalry, patrolling the countryside to the west, had clashed several times of late with Mosby. In one such encounter, Maj. William Wells of Waterbury and several of his cavalrymen were sent south to join Stoughton in Libby Prison.

Samuel Dana, in the 13th, wrote from Wolf Run Shoals on March 17, "We are having considerable trouble from the Rebs these days. They are firing on our pickets most every day. Saturday we was called out in a line of battle. Some rebel cavalry attacked our scouts and drove them in sight of our camp on the other side of the river."

Not all was serious business, however. Pvt. Edwin Hall reported from the 15th, "We had a snow fight last Tuesday with snowballs. The Col. took 5 Companies and the Lieut Col 5 Companies and went down where there was plenty of snow and had a regular battle. The Col lost his ground and retreated about 100 rods and finally out-flanked the Lieut Col when after a short time they came to a hand to hand fight and got all mixed up."

The winter persisted and the brigade's health declined. "Last Sunday afternoon & evening we had a very hard thunder Storm with some as heavy thunder & as sharp lightning as you Seldom hear or see," according to Jabez Hammond, recently promoted to corporal. "[Y]esterday . . . it was hail and Snow. yesterday it was very cold but to day it has been quite warm & the hail & snow has mostly disappeared. The typhoyed Pneumonia & typhoyed fever are both raging very

*Tents of Captain Lonergan's Company A of the 13th Vermont,
near Ford's barn at Wolf Run Shoals*

VERMONT HISTORICAL SOCIETY

Hospital tents of the 13th Vermont at Wolf Run Shoals in March 1863

high. there having seven died in our regiment within the last sixty two hours one of them was from our company."

Later he wrote, "Two men have died in Co. D since yesterday morning & one of them was buried in a pine grove near by. The procession was head by the band with muffled drums & at the grave three salutes were fired."

One death hit the 13th Vermont particularly hard. "We lost our Chaplain," Private Dana wrote home on April 25. "He died Tuesday night and was started for home this day. He had the jaundice. He was liked by the whole regiment." A collection was taken in the ranks for funds to embalm and ship home the chaplain's body. Joseph Sargent, of Williston, was the only Vermont chaplain to die in the Civil War. A bit later, Colonel Randall appointed his own brother, the Rev. Edward H. Randall, as Sargent's replacement. Thus four Randalls served in the 13th: the colonel, his two sons, and, briefly, the colonel's brother.

The long winter, the increased sickness, and boredom were taking a toll on the brigade's morale. The following notice appeared in St. Johnsbury's *Caledonian Record* in early March: "Roseme E. Bacon, 15th Regiment. Died March 5, 1863, by suicide, committed by reason of affectation of mind. Buried at St. Johnsbury Center."

Samuel Dana wrote, "We have lice big enough to carry a man off on their backs, and they will keep one awake playing but I never found one on me yet but probably will for they breed in the ground here."

In the 13th Regiment, men with bug problems sought the services of Pvt. Freeman Sunderland, 40, of Highgate, whose son George Sunderland, 17, served with him in Company K. Private Sturtevant said, "He did the washing for Company K and for many others in the regiment . . . He had some pretty difficult jobs, especially when woolen shirts and seams of trousers were alive with body lice and nits, as occasionally was the case with the careless . . . He would wash thoroughly then dash them back into boiling water, and then out into cold water as quick as possible, backward and forward a few times, was sure death as he said. This sudden change was as good as fire and completely killed the parasites."

During the last week in March there was a major repositioning of the brigade, prompted by the move of Major General Casey from the comforts of Washington to the area of operations of his men. Casey set up division headquarters at Centreville, bringing with him a sizable body of troops. The old tactician promptly moved the three Vermont regiments camped in and around Fairfax Court House south to strengthen defenses along the Occoquan and Bull Run. The 14th regiment joined the 12th and 13th at Wolf Run Shoals, while the 15th and 16th moved to Union Mills, upstream on Bull Run. Then on April 2, the 13th was moved five more miles downstream, opposite the village of Occoquan, setting up camp in a large field on the farm of a widow with the last name of Violet. The men promptly christened their new home "Camp Widow Violet."

Colonel Randall's 13th was ordered to guard the Occoquan River ferry at Occoquan Village, and several fords upstream to Davis's Ford, three miles from Wolf Run Shoals. There the regiment's right flank met the left flank of that portion of the Occoquan bank held by Colonel Nichols's 14th and by the 12th, again commanded by Lieutenant Colonel Farnham. The responsibility of those two regiments was the Occoquan upstream beyond the confluence of Bull Run, then along Bull Run to Yates's Ford two miles below Union Mills. From there, Proctor's 15th and Veazey's 16th held the left bank of Bull Run past Union Mills to Blackburn's Ford, on the edge of the old Bull Run battlefield. The Second Vermont Brigade now had some 20 miles of river and run to picket.

While the 12th remained in its long-held position, Lieutenant Colonel Farnham ordered that its camp be relocated for health reasons. Corporal Hammond told his father: "Well we went to work and cleaned up our ground & our company had put their tents all up when Lieut Col. Farnham (who has good deel more red tape than he has brains about him) said that we must turn around. So that every company had to move. our Co. from one end of camp to the other. Yesterday morning we commenced moving our [tent] stockade. that done we moved our tents from the old camp. had to fetch them on our back. got our tent up just time enough to get it up before night. today we have been to work a putting in our bunks and mudding up the cracks in the stockade & to speak plain I have had the guts ache all day."

Pvt. Unite Keith, of Cambridge, wrote to the Morrisville paper of a lieutenant's encounter with a local man of whom he asked directions to Wolf Run Shoals:

"'It's a right smart walk I reckon—a heap sight further than I want to walk.'

"'But, how far is it?'

"'Wall, it is about three halloos and a long walk beyond.'

"'But my friend, you do not measure distance as I do; how far is three halloos?'

"'Oh, I reckon it is as far as you can hear a man halloo at three times.'"

Pvt. Fayette Potter, in the 13th, was well known to his fellow soldiers for his ability to bark and bay like a hound. One evening, while some of his friends were playing euchre, Potter stuck his head in the tent door and howled. "Go long hound and catch a coon," said one of the men. "Potter started at once, gave a jump and a howl, and at full bay run down the company street and down the

VERMONT HISTORICAL SOCIETY

Camp of the 12th Vermont at Wolf Run Shoals in March 1863

company lines, and from thence to the woods a short distance off; as luck would have it, he had no more than struck the woods than he run across a coon, and running it down caught it, and started on the run again for camp. It was not twenty minutes from the time he started from the tent, before he was there again with the coon; you can well imagine what a shouting there was in camp for a time."

Hammond wrote on March 18, "the affair at the courthouse . . . cost Stoughton his commission as general which by the way he had never received the president sent his name to the Senate to be confirmed but before they acted upon it he was taken prisoner & the president withdrew his nomination. At least that is the report."

The report was accurate. Lincoln, always having problems with generals, did not take Stoughton's capture lightly. Instead of blaming the rebels, he blamed his aspiring young brigadier. Lincoln withdrew Stoughton's confirmation from the Senate, hastening to add, "I don't care so much for brigadiers; I can make them. But horses and mules cost money."

Colonel Veazey wrote to Julia of liking his regiment's new camp: "We moved to Union Mills, 6 or 8 miles from the old camp at the extremity of the Rail Road . . . We are in a beautiful locality & have a fine camping ground. I wish my own darling wife was here in the tent tonight." He also reported, "One of my men got back that was taken with General Stoughton. He gives a dismal account of things in Richmond. Says they came into the prison & gave 5 dollars of Confed. money for one of ours."

Perhaps Stoughton's only supporter in the entire brigade was Lieutenant Colonel Cummings, who had been appointed provost marshal back at Fairfax Court House. Whether Cummings was vocal about his feelings within the brigade is questionable, but he vented them to his wife: "I see by the newspapers that the recent capture of General Stoughton is the all absorbing topic of conversation and criticism, and that it provokes all sorts of comment. I was pained to see copied from the *New York Times* a gross charge of dalliance with a woman of easy virtue—a Miss Ford—and this assigned as reason for his remaining away from the immediate command and his consequent capture—made against him. The family of Mr. Ford was one of the most respectable in the place, and the reputation of Miss Ford—whom I knew but was barely acquainted with, was as fair and unspotted as that of any lady in Virginia. Although the general made his quarters at that house about a month, he could have seen but little of her as he boarded in his mess and his apartments were taken care of by an old negro wench. His mother and sister occupied the same apartments but took their meals with him at his quarters in a house a square distant. Gen. S. is a handome man, is young and fond of female society, but he never had the reputation nor does any officer in this Brigade believe him capable of 'conduct unbecoming an officer and a gentleman.'"

Cummings wrote, too, "I regret that there should be so much bitterness manifested toward him by city press and such petty spite and small, low sort of malignity at home. He was a good tactician, and disciplinarian and did much in these respects for the Brigade."

Stoughton languished several weeks in Libby Prison. When released, he was in poor health. He came home to Vermont for a time, then returned to Washington in an attempt to gain a new military assignment. According to Lieutenant Colonel Cummings, he sought the command of the First Vermont Brigade. He was unsuccessful. He then moved to New York City, where he entered the law practice of his uncle, E.W. Stoughton.

A soldier in the 13th Vermont wrote later that Stoughton was once heard to say that he wished he had been killed leading his regiment at Antietam, rather than suffer the humiliation of Fairfax Court House.

Gradually the stir over the brigadier's capture subsided, and soldier letters spoke more of the weather than the absent commander. "About the 10th of April the weather became more settled," according to Lieutenant Benedict. The Virginia winter, one of the hardest on record, had finally broken. Corporal Williams wrote from the banks of the Occoquan: "April 12. The weather is again very fine this morning, and the brass band has been giving us some of its most beautiful pieces. I am getting tired of so much music, and long for the time to come, when reveille and tattoo shall no longer disturb my rest, when I can go to church, breakfast, dinner and supper, without being drummed there. I wish there was more fighting and less display of 'red tape.' The roads are getting very dry and dusty."

Said Sergeant Palmer, "'We have a pleasant day on picket; a plenty to eat of soft bread, fresh beef, sugar and coffee. The air is filled with song of birds by day, and the ceaseless peeping of frogs by night."

★

16

In early January, while General Stoughton was still living the good life at Fairfax Station, Colonel Veazey wrote to Julia: "Mrs. [Redfield] Proctor is here, has been for several days, also Mrs. Blunt & two other ladies in the 12th . . . I love you my sweet angel." And later: "My quarters are excellent . . . Only want a wife to complete my household . . . Saw Mrs. Blunt to day. She has been kiting around here all winter but is going home tomorrow. Looks as tho she would have to hurry to get home in season to be confined. What a place for a woman in her condition. The ladies like camp life very much. Some of their husbands look as tho they had seen hard times . . . Never had so comfortable quarters before. Have two tents floored and a splendid bed, perfectly warm the coldest nights . . . Fire place between the two tents."

Veazey's strong hints that his wife should visit him in camp were interrupted in February when he hastened home to New Hampshire after a telegram brought news of his mother's death. On returning, he resumed his entreaties, but only succeeded in convincing the pregnant and strong-minded Julia to make a brief visit to Washington, where he joined her for a weekend, two days he found disappointing (in that they did not rival the Brattleboro farewell).

During the winter of 1862–63, several officers' wives took up residence with their husbands in the camps of the Second Vermont Brigade. Some stayed several months. Among them was Mary Farnham, the wife of Lieutenant Colonel Farnham, who counted 11 visiting wives. Little is known about their lives with the army, though several soldiers mentioned that officers' spouses helped care for the sick. But some of the letters sent home by Mary Farnham to her family in Bradford survive, as does a diary she kept while with the armies, both providing a rare woman's view of life in a Civil War army camp.

She was born Mary Elizabeth Johnson, on January 19, 1828, one of seven children of a former captain of the Bath, New Hampshire, militia, Ezekiel Johnson, and his wife, Nancy (Rogers) Johnson. Mary grew up in Bradford, and in 1849 journeyed north to Durham, in the Province of Quebec, to marry schoolteacher Roswell Farnham, a graduate of Bradford Academy and, the previous spring, the University of Vermont. After a year in Canada, the couple moved just south of the border, to Franklin, Vermont, where they both taught school. They then returned to their hometown, and in 1854 took over operation of Bradford Academy. Roswell served as principal and teacher; the school record book lists Mary as

No.   Head-Quarters Probisional Brigades,

Washington, 16 Dec 1862.

Guards will pass

The Ambulance &
... and Mrs Blunt & Mrs Farnham
and Wagons, Ambulances, Detachment across "Long

Bridge," to *Camp of 12 Vt. Vol.*
Fairfax C. House Va

By order of General Casey:

Assist. Adjt. General.

A pass allowing Mrs. Blunt and Mrs. Farnham to travel from
Washington to the 12th Vermont's camp

"preceptress," offering instruction in "piano forte, penciling and watercolor."

Their first child, Cyrus, born in 1859, lived only a month. (After the war, Mary would bear three more children, all healthy, whom she and Roswell christened Charles, Florence, and William.) In 1859 Roswell, who had been studying law, was elected state's attorney of Orange County. He held that post until the spring of 1861, when he enlisted in the First Vermont Regiment. At the end of three months' service in Virginia, he returned to Bradford, continuing his duties as county prosecutor. Then he was back in the military, this time as second in command of the 12th. Upon his return to Virginia, Roswell began urging Mary to join him in camp. But she took her time. "Oct. 29: As soon as we get settled, if we ever do, I shall have you with me," he wrote.

On November 14: "Had you not better go up and see Mrs. Blunt & make arrangements about coming out here?"

On November 30: "Write in your next letter the day you expect to come out here."

Finally, on December 3, "I want to know if you are REALLY COMING NEXT WEEK. My house is in good comfortable condition."

Mary Farnham proceeded south in early December, stopping on the way to visit friends in Boston. Then she spent a few days in Washington. The day before

Christmas, she wrote to her brother Henry Johnson in Bradford that she and Roswell were boarding with a Mrs. Whiley at Fairfax Court House, who seems to have taken delight in frightening her Yankee guests. "We came here one week ago tomorrow," Mary wrote. "We are very near the rebels and our army may be attacked any day. But rebels treat women well, and there are three of us Northern ladies here so I should have company, and we could SKEDADDLE in haste . . . Mrs. Whiley with whom we board has seen three thousand Cavalry all armed, their sabres glistening in the sun, passing in front of this house at a time, their horses tongues all out and the men screaming with a horrid yell . . . I hope there will be no trouble here this winter, but I do expect it."

She continued: "Sunday morning I went out with John Whiley a little boy to see if there was a Rabbit in his trap. But nary rabbit did we find. But the day before we caught one and brought it home alive. We had it for breakfast . . . You never saw such briers as they have here the ground is covered with low blackberry bushes, and Bramberry, which grows as high as your head bright green stalk. Tis awful to go through I assure you. There is among briers a kind of grass which they call hens grass. The boys gather it to make their beds of. It looks like oats growing. The soil is as red as brick in most places.

"Nelson Rogers has been over to see me today . . . He is building a log cabin for Col. Farnham and Col. Blunt is having one built for the second time this winter. I do hope they will not be obliged to move again, if they do, I hope it will be towards Washington . . . In the hospital I did not find but one man that I knew. There was no one from Bradford. There was a good many sick with coughs and jaundice . . .

"Mrs. Blunt Mrs. Stearns and myself were invited up to Camp to dine to-day. We had chickens potatoes Pickels Bread butter coffee and some jelly Aunt Lucy Jane sent Ros. Mr. Peach is the cook, and he does first rate . . . Ros is looking very well. I dread to have the 12th go on picket again. It is so dangerous. And they suffer so with cold."

Roswell wrote to his sister Laura on December 31, just after the Dumfries Raid, "Mary is still boarding at Mr. Whiley's . . . I went over to see Mary and took breakfast with her. She and Mrs. Blunt had not slept much—The firing had caused them a great deal of anxiety. Mary thinks she is seeing enough of war."

On January 19, Mary moved to her husband's quarters at Wolf Run Shoals. The next morning was her first in an army camp and she wrote in the diary, "When I opened my cabin door such a splendid scene I never beheld before. Twenty fires were burning, 600 or more men were hurrying about . . . Beyond glowed the blood red tint of morning."

On January 27, Mary wrote to brother Henry from Wolf Run Shoals, mentioning their brother Ezekiel, who was serving in the 10th Vermont Regiment. "All the boys are having pies, apples, cake, cheese, apple sauce, chickens, etc.," she said. "You cannot tell how they gladden their eyes, and all these things remind me of my brother Zeke and how he would like a box of the like. Now I want you to get some of these articles and box them up and direct to Ezekiel's Captn's care for your brother E. I know grandma, Mary, Uncle Thomas and Mother will put in a slice of brown bread. Now you just see to this when you go home.

They all will do this for Zeke who is the sole representative of the family in the 10th Regt . . .

"I came to Wolf Creek Shoals yesterday. It is near where the Wolf Run empties into the Occoquan River . . . You cannot have the least idea of the travelling out here. The mud is just the color of brick pounded up, and the wheels go nearly up to the hub in many places. We had to walk the horse most of the way. The driver would make nothing of going over stumps of trees a foot high . . . I only held on for dear life for fear I should DROP out behind the ambulance. I was a little tired as well as Mrs. Blunt, Mrs. Ormsbee, Mrs. Stearns, the ladies who came with me. But I only exclaimed This is splendid! So much better than I expected! So we kept up one anothers spirits till we arrived in camp and then I had to go to a Secech house with Mrs. Stearns and stay the night. I felt rather home sick for the FIRST TIME since I left home, for I do not like the looks of the people . . . Bushwhackers are all around. I shall not dare ride so far from Camp, as I did at Fairfax . . . am now accommodated in Camp where I shall remain a while if the Rebs do not shell us out, for they are but a little distance off."

Roswell wrote to Bradford on February 1: "Since we have been here we have had only army blankets for bed clothes & Mary thinks they are rather ROUGH. Our bed tick is only wide enough for one & we have to piece it out . . . Mary came from Mr. Whiley's last Monday, & the first night she stayed at a Mr. Davis',

Mary and Roswell Farnham, on horseback, in the 12th Vermont's camp. Colonel Blunt leans against the tree, and Major Kingsley stands with hands behind his back.

Bradford Historical Society

Col. Roswell Farnham after the war,
as governor of Vermont

who lives about a mile from here. The family is strong 'secech' and Mary says
that the woman barely spoke to her. Since Monday night she has stayed with me.
She eats in 'our mess.'"

A diary entry on February 3 tells of a visit to a tent in which an enlisted
man's wife and children were living. The husband and father was Pvt. Charles
Dyer, of Rutland, a musician with the 12th. "Mrs. Blunt and I called on Mrs.
Dyer, a private's wife," Mary wrote. "We found her in a little hut with two children, one two years old and FOUR MONTHS, she having been in Virginia two
months. I should think she was about twenty years of age. She was in a stockaded
tent on the ground, but said they were to have a floor and cupboard and table.
She was busy when we went in, her children looking very dirty and the little babe
in a new kind of cradle, a CRACKER BOX . . . She is a simple Irish woman, used
to all kinds of hardship, and I think the children will be used to the same . . . She
said that she could do my washing in a few days."

On February 8, Mary wrote in her diary, "There has been company in camp
for two days past quarter master Bronson's wife, she is not of my sort, so I don't
put myself out too much to entertain her. She is rather too fond of married men
. . . So poor Mrs. Blunt has had her all to herself rather more she wanted I reckon.
Mrs. Dyer our wash woman has been sick and my washing is not done . . . Mr.
Benedict has been in this evening, I like him very much.'"

On February 17, Mary wrote to Laura of a trip to Washington: "Ros invited

Lieut. Benedict (for he is Lieut now, has been promoted lately) to accompany us. I was glad to have him go as he is well acquainted with some of the members of the House and has been in Washington a number of times. We were obliged to go to the station in an Ambulance as both of Col. Farnham's horses are sick with the horse distemper. It was snowing hard when we started and the mud up to the axletree half the way and the driver would stop and take a drink out of every canteen he met . . . I should judge they contained whiskey by the way he took us over logs and everything that lay in his path. I was obliged to keep hold on to a strap or rail of the Ambulance to keep myself on the seat. But at last I was tired of holding on and thought I would sit up independent. I had hardly got my independence established before I was thrown up a foot and landed in the bottom of the carriage at Mr. Benedict's feet!! I could not help myself for some time, Mr. B & Ros tugging with all their might to raise me. I never was so mad when Ros said, Well, you cut a PRETTY figure! I was VERY WELL AWARE OF IT. I told them I hoped they would both find themselves in the same situation . . . I watched them both the rest of the way, and I think Ros did get just a little taste of the floor once but it was when he was looking the other way and he hurried himself up. I never saw anything like it."

The Farnhams arrived in Washington the next day, and secured a room that Mary complained was "four flights up." Then they were off to see the Capitol, where Mary—the teacher of watercolor and penciling—indulged her love of art. "We ascended two long flights to reach the building," she wrote. "OH I WAS SO TIRED. The first room of any importance we went into was the old House of Representatives. I thought the walls were beautifully ornamented before I saw the NEW house. There were some fine statues in this room. One that I liked best was the conquored Indian. He sits there with folded arms, and his head bowed in grief at the loss of his country. I think it was executed by Crawford. There were quite a number of his statues. One thing about the room struck me as very beautiful. The massive pillars in this room were brought from Italy. They look as though they were inlaid with pearl. The marble is of such beautiful color. We went round in the galleries a while then went into the House of Representatives. The room is beautifully ornamented, but the Representatives are anything but representatives of dignity and order. All they did was keep the Pages, little boys of ten and twelve years old, running for them . . . Then we went into the Senate. Salusbury of Delaware was holding forth at the top of his voice. Then Collamer and Foot of Vermont spoke and Sumner . . . We saw some fine paintings by Church and one by Leutze."

The Farnhams had dinner at The National, where Mary found herself in the presence of Washington society ladies and Gens. Benjamin F. Butler and Edwin Stoughton. "The ladies were dressed in the height of fashion," she observed. "They dress more like summer here than they do north. Gen. Butler [sat] at one of the tables. Butler's head is mostly behind his ears . . . Our Gen. Stoughton was there. He is a young man of twenty four years. He is now very attentive to Miss Hale of Bath, Senator Hale's daughter . . . They were out in the hall walking a long time after dinner. She is older than he and rather plain looking although said to be a fine girl. I guess they are quite in love as the Gen. spends most of his time there. His sister came out to Washington the day before I left and came out to Fairfax yesterday. Miss Hale is coming out while Miss Stoughton is at Fairfax. I invited the Gen. to bring his sister over here, but it is too horrid travelling. She is coming over to Mrs. Bronson's. She is going to have a dance in her tent. Her tent is sixteen feet square and quite spacious!! This Mrs. Bronson is quite a character. She rides any horse she can get, and with all the officers that ask her. And they are not a FEW. For she will ask them if they do not her. I was sick the second day in Washington and did not leave the house . . . There are eleven ladies, married ladies in the vicinity from the north. I do not know many of them as I have not been well for a week or two and there is no way to go only on horseback, and it has been quite unfortunate to have both horses sick at a time."

Mary wrote to her father, Captain Johnson, on February 26, from Wolf Run Shoals: "I am quite well now . . . We are very comfortable in our stockaded tents and warm as one need be . . . This is a wild life to lead here in the woods but it is different from what I ever lived before and I have enjoyed myself exceedingly well. Time has passed rapidly for I cannot realize I have been here nearly three months. I find people can live with few conveniences, and not any of the elegancies of life. We have two chairs, a table, a bedstead with the bark on for furniture. And I would not have more if I could. There is no need of dressing up here. Two dresses is all I use . . . This noon we had rather an extra dinner. Turkey, beef, Sardines, Pudding, besides a couple of quail which are a new kind of bird to me. They look like young turkeys running about on the ground. They are very good to eat but it takes a good many for dinner. The boys generally well, a few sick in their quarters . . . There are but a few women here in this country. What are left are all secesh and look as black as night at you, but can do no harm as long as the Union Army is here. They all wear log-cabins for bonnets and go without hoops. The low whites are dirty and lazy. And some of the better class are not much neater for they have always depended upon negroes to do their work. As Mrs. Ford near here said she never knew how a meal of victuals was cooked until one year ago, and now she is obliged to do her OWN WORK. I cannot help pitying some of them, but they voted for this war and they must suffer the consequence. This Regt. has had a comparatively easy time, but they have got to see war in earnest I fear before long. I do wish I could be here or in Washington until Ros goes home. But probably shall not, for it is known that this Regt. may move forward. I intend to remain a while longer if I can."

Henry Johnson, Mary's brother, received a letter written at Wolf Run Shoals on February 28 that touched on some criticism being voiced about wives tenting with their soldier husbands. "Henry I do think you ought not to have excited my curiosity by telling me I ought to be home," Mary wrote, "and not give me any reason for your saying so. I have not done anything I am ashamed of, or that other ladies have not done before me. Even Generals wives stay in camp with their husbands, and now there are ten or twelve ladies in this Brigade living in Camp. As for expenses I live much cheaper than I can board with Uncle Dan or with any of my friends in Boston, so I cannot divine the reason."

Mary then discussed a letter she had received from Zeke in the 10th Regiment, and mused on spending a few days in New York City on the way home to Bradford. Then she returned to the subject of women in camp. "Now Henry I want you to answer my questions I have asked you Particularly for I shall not be so apt to write often if you do not tell me WHY I OUGHT TO COME HOME AND WHO MADE THE REMARK! Ros wishes to know."

In the March 9 entry in her diary, she noted the capture of General Stoughton: "The general has been taken and carried to Richmond . . . So he chose to be where he could have a piano and good shelter."

On March 10, Roswell wrote to sister Laura, "Enclosed you will find a couple of pictures. The ambrotypes you can keep till we come home. You will probably recognize Mary & myself . . . Col. Blunt stands leaning his shoulder against the tree in the center. Maj. Kingsley has his hands behind his back."

Two days later, Mary noted in her diary: "I called on the sick today and may I never see such a sad sight again. Some 20 laying side by side and burning up with fever. Poor sufferers away from home and friends and have to die alone. I found but two whom I knew . . . Then I visited the convalescent tent. It looked dark and gloomy, but the boys looked cheerful."

Another entry reads: "Yesterday I visited quite a number of soliders in their quarters who were sick and made gruel and coffee for them . . . There are so many sick. Our battles are in the hospital . . . Col. Blunt made a stir in the Hospital about it being so dirty . . . So the surgeon has ordered the floors to be washed."

Another letter went to Henry on March 19, in which Mary mentioned the March 17 battle at Kelly's Ford, to the south along the Rappahannock River. That clash between Union cavalry under Brig. Gen. William Averell and Confederate horsemen under Brig. Gen. Fitz Lee saw Union cavalry, for the first time, hold their own against their southern counterparts. "Col. F thinks I have been here so long," she wrote, "he shall be lonely to have me leave. So I keep staying a day longer . . . the rebel patrols come very near us. The pickets two nights ago were fired into a short distance from here. Also some five were taken a week ago nearly. Two days ago we heard the cannonading at Kelly's Ford when our cavalry crossed over and they had an engagement, of which I presume you have seen an account. The firing was quite rapid for some time. I think they kept it up five hours. We knew by the sound that it was an engagement. The men fought with their Sabres, but the cannonading was kept up to protect them while crossing the river which is quite wide there and only one could ford at a time. We have not heard the number killed only our men drove them back.

"This is one of the worst and most unhealthy places we have been in," she continued. "Nine men have died in two weeks, and three in one twelve hours. Stevens, Dr. Henry Dickey, C.C. Carpenter have died in the Bradford Co. And some twenty more are off duty . . . I tell you, Henry, it is war here indeed in these Hospitals. They are not sick but a short time some of them. Surgeon Conn thinks it is bad water. I do not allow myself to drink much of anything.

"Friday morning: I have had one pleasant ride this week over to Woodyard's Ford, where the Pennsylvanians are stationed. It was over a very muddy rough road. We were obliged to hold back the pines so to keep them from brushing us off our horses . . . We went down the steepest hills and then at the bottom would be a brook to wade through. My horse always will stop in the middle of every stream, so I have to whip him through."

That is the last letter Mary sent from Virginia, or it is the last that survives.

Mary Farnham late in life
BRADFORD HISTORICAL SOCIETY

On April 12, Roswell Farnham wrote to Bradford from Wolf Run Shoals: "We have had three pleasant days in camp and the ladies have enjoyed themselves finely . . . Yesterday they all attended Guard Mounting, Picket Guard Mounting, rode down to see the battery practice, & then to see our Regt. drill! Mrs. Nichols was just getting ready to go down to the 13th about nine miles below here when the order came for us to be prepared to move—the whole brigade. The ladies of course thought that we should have a fight at once. They all cried of course. Arrangements were made to take them to the Station and fortunately they had a train just ready to start for Alexandria . . . The Adjutant, Vaughn, went to see them off."

Mary went to Alexandria, then to Washington, where she visited brother Zeke, who was on a pass from the 10th Vermont. (On July 9, 1864, he would be shot in the head at the Battle of the Monocacy. He survived, and even returned to duty.) She also had a VIP caller while there, as Roswell noted in a letter sent April 23: "Your welcome letter written just before you left Washington is received . . . You saw what Genl Stannard was when he called on you. He is just the same at all times."

Then she traveled to Boston, visiting friends in nearby Charlestown. On May 6, Roswell wrote to her, "I have not heard a word . . . It seems a long time since you ran away and left me." Mary went to Quincy, Massachusetts, and Roswell wrote on May 10, "I feel lonesome when I think of you and miss you very much . . . Laura does not know where you are. You ought to have written her." The next day he added, "When you finish your visit you had better go to Bradford. I want you to be there some time before I get there so as to make things a little more comfortable."

But it was late May before Mary returned home, after several more anxious letters had reached Bradford from the colonel. She set his mind at ease with a message that prompted this response on June 10: "Your kind note of June 5 was received tonight . . . How much good your kind and gentle letter did me in response to my foolish letter, that I almost feared would offend you. I am so glad to hear from you & I will try & be as good & pure as your true love deserves."

That love would last four more decades.

Most of the wives who took up residence with the Second Vermont Brigade in the winter of 1862–63 seem to have been the spouses of officers, with at least two exceptions. One was the Irish wife, mother, and washerwoman, Mrs. Dyer. Private Sturtevant, after the war, recalled that James Kingsley, a private from Swanton in the 13th, also welcomed his wife to Virginia. "He was short and slight, too puny for soldier business," Sturtevant wrote, "and yet he was tough and endured army life much better than many who seemed better fitted for it. He was much attached to his wife and she undoubtedly was lonesome when left behind in Vermont . . . She arrived some time in November and joined her husband while we were in Camp Vermont. That made it a little inconvenient for her husband, for three others occupied a small A tent by themselves and no sleeping room for more. Kingsley hustled around, went and saw Colonel Randall who was always kind and thoughtful, and very courteous to the ladies, and taking into consideration the circumstances, at once ordered a special tent for Kingsley and his wife . . . It was number four down the company street on the left at Camp Wolf Run Shoals. Kingsley now lived happy and contented and so was his wife . . .

"Mrs. Kingsley seemed to enjoy the outdoor life," Sturtevant went on, "and for a time had the proud distinction of being the only woman in camp . . . Kingsley was annoyed because of the boyish capers invented to make fun and bother him, all innocent fun, nothing more. Kingsley got permission from the captain to do guard duty in the camp and not go out on the picket line, that his wife might not be left alone, but that was entirely unnecessary, for there was never the slightest danger of any of Company K boys planning an elopement with her. Some said James was jealous, I could never believe it, yet it might have been so. Mrs. Kingsley remained and moved with us to our next camp, Widow Violet . . . When there appeared some prospect of a spring campaign, Comrade Kingsley was alarmed and was advised to let his wife go to Washington, or home to Vermont, and about the first day of June she left for Washington, and from there home to Vermont. Comrade Kingsley was very lonesome for a while, but soon was all right and did good duty for the rest of the time."

★

 Much of the area of northern Virginia where the Second Vermont Brigade camped in the winter of 1862–63—once farm country dotted with small villages—is now an expansive suburb of Washington, gobbling up more and more of the once rural landscape. Finding the places the Vermonters described in their letters and diaries is a challenge at best, requiring map-reading and urban driving skills. At worst, the places are lost and gone forever.

There are exceptions, of course. A narrow parkland stretches along the north banks of the Occoquan and Bull Run, from Fountainhead Park near Occoquan to Bull Run Park at Manassas. This ribbon of greenery encompasses much of the land that the Second Vermont Brigade was charged with picketing during the winter of 1862–63. A 17½-mile trail runs its length, and thus you can walk the river bluffs and ravines where the Vermonters, a century and a third ago, stood guard.

One winter day I drove from Occoquan west on Prince William Parkway along the heavily developed southern bank. Then I turned north on Route 612. Crossing Bull Run just below its confluence with the Occoquan, I stopped at Bull Run Marina. Along the bluff overlooking the stream, I found traces of earthworks, surely thrown up by Vermonters. At the entrance to the marina, closed in winter, I met John Stevenson, who works there. The marina is owned and operated by nearby George Mason University, he told me, and canoes may be rented to explore the historic streams. Or you can set out along the park trail, upstream or downstream, to explore the broken woodland once occupied by the Vermonters. Stevenson drove me a few miles north to a studies center the university owns in the parkland. We walked a rough trail a mile to the confluence of Pope's Head Creek and Bull Run. Across the stream lay the tracks of the Orange and Alexandria Railroad. In the woods were foundations of a long-ago settlement. We were standing, Stevenson explained, at Union Mills. (It was at Union Mills that the Vermonters assembled to begin their long march to Gettysburg.)

One fall day, guided by Civil War historian Edwin Bearss, I walked a narrow and rough jeep track to the shore of the Occoquan River, now dammed and much wider than it once was. Here at Wolf Run Shoals we gazed to the wooded bluffs on the far side that once held Confederate earthworks. It was impossible to determine where the Vermont campground had been located. Bearss noted that J.E.B. Stuart and his Confederate cavalry had crossed the river there, on their way to Gettysburg, and rode up the road we had just walked down. The woods are still thick with pine and the landscape rises and falls as described by the Vermonters. But NO TRESPASSING signs warn against exploration, and though earthworks are reported to abound in the woods, I decided against seeking them out.

Fairfax Court House offers a cluster of antebellum houses, already mentioned. And at Fairfax Station there are two churches the Vermonters would have known, one in which Clara Barton tended to wounded soldiers. At the village of Occoquan, which marked the eastern end of the Vermont picket line, many Civil War–era buildings still stand on what was once the Confederate side of the river.

At Alexandria, I was unable to locate Camp Vermont. But on a hilltop amid a maze of city streets, I discovered a remnant of Fort Lyon, which the Vermonters reluctantly helped construct. Just off Route 1 in Alexandria, along James Drive, I came on Fort Lyon Court, a narrow curving roadway lined by modest houses. They stand on what was the main bastion. If you look closely, along the southern side of James Drive you'll see a low mound of earth, once part of one of the fort's bombproof shelters. That is all that survives. But it is clear from the glimpses between buildings that the view from those Alexandria Heights is as magnificent as the Vermonters described, looking far north to Washington and south toward Mount Vernon.

Also in Alexandria, just off Route 395 south, take Seminary Road east and follow signs to Fort Ward. This massive ridgetop fort with earthen ramparts more than 500 yards long is a contemporary of Fort Lyon; it is beautifully preserved and looks much as Fort Lyon must have. And visit lovely Mount Vernon, Washington's home—in much better shape than when the Vermont soldiers were there. Go as a tourist, as they did, and gaze upon that wonderful symbol of freedom, the key to the Bastille, presented by Lafayette to Washington.

PART IV

Stannard Takes Command

Brig. Gen. George Stannard, who led the Second Vermont Brigade into battle

17

Late in Mary Farnham's stay with the Second Vermont Brigade, a new commander arrived in camp. "General Stannard has made his appearance among us, and fixed his headquarters at Union Mills," said a soldier in the 16th Vermont. "We are much pleased with his appearance, and judge that he will make himself one among us, cheerfully sharing the toils and perils of the soldier's life. The General quarters with us, will be protected with the best defense that our men are able to supply in the hour of peril."

A soldier in the 13th wrote to the *Vermont Standard*, "On Sunday we were favored with a visit from our new Brig. Gen. G.J. Stannard. We were marched in review on Monday and had a battalion drill, together with the seventh Michigan cavalry, who had encamped nearby. After forming into a square we were highly complimented by our General in a neat little speech. The boys seem to like him, and claim he looks more like a fighting man than our ex-General."

"Our new brigade commander is here," said Sgt. George Hagar in the 12th, "every one seems glad to have him. He is a very different man from Stoughton. He is plainly dressed wearing his old uniform with new shoulder straps. Drunkard officers have little mercy at his hands."

Pvt. Edwin Hall wrote to Brookfield, "We have got another general—but not a Stoughton he is just the opposite. You would take him for a private, if he had not any shoulder straps on. His name is G.J. Stannard."

The new brigade commander, George Jerrison Stannard, arrived on April 20, and Colonel Blunt once again resumed command of the 12th regiment. "This is good news," wrote Lieutenant Colonel Cummings, defender of General Stoughton, "we have been sadly in want of a general since Col. Blunt has been in command. The colonel is not up to Veazey or Proctor by a long chalk."

Despite that opinion, Stannard appears to have paid Blunt a considerable compliment in doing little to change operations in the Second Vermont Brigade.

Stannard, 45, balding and with a short beard, clear eyed, a bit under six feet with a trim athletic build, was already a veteran when he arrived at his new command. When the war began he was one of the first of all Vermonters to offer his services, leaving at home a wife and four children. He served as lieutenant colonel of the Second Vermont Regiment, was on the firing line at First Bull Run, and went through the battles of the Peninsula Campaign, along the way gaining a reputation as an officer fearless under fire. Then he accepted command of the

Ninth Vermont Regiment, and as Lee moved north in September 1862, he found his regiment in the bottleneck at Harpers Ferry, part of a 12,000-man force under the incompetent command of Col. Dixon S. Miles. With the approach of Stonewall Jackson, and with cannonballs raining in, Miles decided to surrender, virtually without a fight. Stannard protested vigorously that he would shoot his way out but was overruled, and his regiment was captured and paroled. Much to the chagrin of its men and commander, the Ninth Vermont spent several unpleasant winter months at Camp Douglas in Chicago, guarding Confederate prisoners, themselves virtual prisoners until exchanged. Now the farm boy from Georgia, Vermont, who grew up to manage a foundry in nearby St. Albans, was a brigadier general.

Stannard assumed command of an outfit that was much on edge, for on April 10 the regiments had received orders to stand in readiness for more active duty. A-tents and officers' baggage had been sent to Alexandria, sick men were moved to hospitals in and around Washington, marching rations and extra ammunition were dispensed. Meanwhile, near Fredericksburg, General Hooker was preparing the Army of the Potomac for another strike across the Rappahannock, as the spring sunshine made the Virginia roads fit for march. In a few days, the Vermonters' alert passed. Camp life returned to normal. Both to relieve boredom and to supplement diets, many soldiers ranged beyond camp on what they called foraging expeditions. Pigs and chickens were the favored quarry, much to the displeasure of their owners. A private in the 13th recalled that Pvt. Francis Jangraw, an 18-year-old Montpelier lad, was an excellent forager: "One day on picket an old sow with ten nice pigs came near his post, his love for baked pig got the better of him, and he gave chase. He stuck his bayonet through a pig but the squealing brought the old sow to the rescue. With his gun over his shoulder, the pig squealing on the bayonet and the enraged sow in hot pursuit, Frank made pretty fast time for a rail fence. The pig wriggled off the bayonet, the old sow took a piece out of the seat of his pants and he picked up his gun, looked after the retreating pigs and simply remarked, 'That was a mighty close shave.'"

Pvt. William Lawson, 21, from East Montpelier and nicknamed Ed, went in search of poultry in the vicinity of Union Mills. "Geese were scarce—and shy," a fellow soldier recalled. "Somehow Ed discovered a small flock in a farm yard, but as the owner was friendly to the Union cause, orders had been given not to molest them. 'But if I should be passing and one of these geese should chase me into camp, no harm would come of me?' 'Certainly not,' said Captain Coburn . . . Late that afternoon Ed bethought himself of the days when he caught bullfrogs in Sodom Pond, and having a fish hook he secured it to the end of a small but exceedingly stout fish line, and baiting the hook with a colonel of corn, he cast it among the flock of geese. An instant later a big white gander had swallowed the hook. Just as Ed started to leave the premises . . . the good woman of the house appeared upon the scene shouting, 'Don't be afraid of that old gander young man; he always chases strangers out of the yard but he won't bite you.' That evening the goose that chased Ed Lawson into camp was served 'a la Virginia.'"

Pvt. Edward Freeman, of Colchester, remembered, "Down the River Occoquan near the village . . . had a great time there fishing and playing ball and pitching horseshoes, etc. We were now and then around the farmers' houses stealing

A Civil War–era lithograph showing Union soldiers foraging in Virginia

chickens and drinking milk and had a great time with the girls. I had a fine little girl by the name of Violet and came pretty near marrying her."

According to Pvt. Fenimore Shepard, "Comrade Woodcock came into camp one day, with a pig under his arm. Colonel Randall saw him and called him to account and asked him if he had forgotten the order about shooting pigs, and he said no, but this was no pig, but a rabbit. The colonel said, 'No fooling, and you may report to headquarters immediately.' The result was that the colonel had some of that rabbit for dinner the next day."

Pvt. Caleb Nash in the 13th said, "While in camp on the Occoquan a Virginia citizen complained to Colonel Randall about his men milking his cows." Randall denied it because, according to Nash, the colonel said the regiment was "composed entirely of theology students."

But civilian complaints about thievery increased, and finally Randall took action. An elderly man came to the camp of the 13th to charge that a soldier with the number 13 on his cap had stolen his last two chickens. The colonel said he could not believe it was any of his men; more likely someone from the 12th Vermont was the culprit. The man could look around camp, if he chose, but Randall reminded him that there were standing orders against such thievery. A soldier remembered: "In one of the company streets in front of a tent they saw feathers. The old gentleman identified the man and the chickens, and both were taken to the Colonel's tent. He at once flew into a rage greater apparently than that of the old gentleman, ordered the man placed with his back to a tree, and a gun strap passed around binding him tight to the tree; he had the long roll beat, and as the men assembled, he walked up and down, pulling his long moustache, he addressed them to this effect: 'You see this miserable rascal—been caught stealing chickens. You knew I issued an order forbidding such things, and when I issue an order I want it obeyed. Now take notice, if any of you steal any more chickens from this respectable and loyal gentleman, and use insulting and disrespectful language to him, and leave the feathers in front of your tent, I'll have you hung up by the thumbs, I will.'"

The soldier said that the men were much more careful about their chicken stealing thereafter.

The 14th Vermont certainly was not immune from thievery, gaining the nickname the Stealing 14th. The regimental chaplain, William Smart, claimed that the men had once stolen a brick church. And the 14th took pride in the fact that one of its men had swiped a quart of liquor from General Stoughton's saddlebag.

The Vermonters continued to see the effects of the Emancipation Proclamation. A soldier writing to the *Green Mountain Freeman* from the 16th said, "During the night our camp, for the first time in Dixie, echoed the music of crying children. Such a sound must come to the soldier's ear with the stirring memories of home. This was occasioned by the presence of a large family of contrabands, who were brought in on the cars from the section of Warrenton. Men, women, and children made up the company, who were anxiously seeking food and freedom within our lines."

Several days later, the soldier wrote, "The negroes tell the truth. Some scouts recently rode up to a man's house, who claimed to be a Unionist but did not wish to take the oath. While the others entered the house, one of the party rode around to the quarters occupied by the negroes and asked them if their master was a Union man? 'He be Union day times,' was the reply, 'but nights he be sesech and goes with the guerrillas.'"

J.B. Chamberlin in the 13th wrote from Wolf Run Shoals, "The rebs made a raide in here thursday about 8 o clock in the morning . . . took 12 mules 4 horses & 7 men . . . They took them off about 30 miles & parolled them sent them back they got here this morning." Apparently it was the work of Mosby's men, and among the spoils was some baggage that belonged to the commander of the 13th Vermont.

Pvt. Mark Day in the 13th recalled, "This raised the wrath of the old fighting Colonel Randall and he vowed he would have as many horses from the rebels as they taken from us. He called for a hundred volunteers, ordered them to make a raid into the enemy's country and not to return until we had the necessary number of horses."

The raid brought in as many stolen horses as Mosby had seized, and Private Day described one seizure from a man found plowing his fields: "After passing the time of day to make it easy to approach him, I asked him to loan his horses to ride into the country, which we knew he would not do. He replied, 'No I am late getting in my wheat and besides you will not bring them back' . . . I then handed my gun to my comrade telling him to watch Johnny while I took the harness from the horses, threw it upon the ground, climbed upon the fine bay mare and my comrade took the other horse. We bade goodbye to our friend Johnny as we rode away—leaving

Men of the 12th Vermont outside their stockaded tents at Wolf Run Shoals

him still hanging on to the lines and damning the Yankees from away back." So a Virginia man faced the planting season without his pair of workhorses.

Sergeant Palmer noted: "I called at a citizen's house to get a meal of victuals. The old man was killing his hogs, and scalded them by putting hot stones into the tub of water . . . I soon observe that the owner is not in the best of humor for some reason, when he turns up his red face and stares at me with his bloodshot eyes: 'Buy,' he mutters, 'soldiers buy? They've stole all I've got that they could carry away—them devils that followed Dan Sickles—my potatoes, my turkies, and most all my cattle. I never had any niggers; don't want them; but if soldiers should come into your country and steal your goods, wouldn't you fight? By the Gods, wouldn't you fight?'"

Private Sturtevant said, "The hitherto most upright and best of fellows as soon as they left home and became soldiers seemed to think their relations and obligations were entirely changed, and were entitled to do those things that would not have been even thought of at home . . . all the little foraging expeditions for hens, pigs, potatoes (sweet and Irish) honey, milking cows, etc."

Wheelock Veazey wrote as spring came that he had been given "a black reb puppy" that he named Jefferson Davis. "He sleeps on my feet nights & when it is real cold towards morning he creeps up to get under the blanket."

A week later he told Julia, "I should not dare send Jeff home. He is a blood hound and is getting savage."

"Whiskey rations (a rare thing with us) were dealt out to the soldiers last night," according to Palmer. "The army regulations say: 'One gill of whisky is allowed daily, in case of excessive fatigue and exposure' . . . Occasionally one gets so much he is noisy, and somewhat irregular in his actions. This morning one is drunk, and in for fighting. He speaks contemptuously to his lieutenant; strikes the corporal of the guard; pays no attention to the officer of the day; it takes four or five to manage him and get him in the guard-house, and he bites one of them quite badly. But he is not abused. He strikes them; but they do not return it, only hold him as well as they can. As soon as his hands are tied behind him, he gives up in despair, and the poor fellow cries like a child."

There was more trouble on the picket lines. "An orderly came up from the Ferry 1 mile and $^1/_2$ from our camp and said our pickets were attacked by a large force of cavalry and infantry," Samuel Dana wrote in mid-April, "but we had no trouble, only being kept awake."

According to Edwin Palmer: "A cavalry man is standing on his beat, when he imagines that he sees a rebel. Now he fires his pistol four times, and thinks the enemy returning the shots. The horse is scared, turns, and gallops towards the reserve, throwing off the more frightened rider. Instantly the pickets are out, for they lie down with equipments on, and the guns by their sides, running for the rifle pits. As they meet him, no cap on: 'What's the matter? Are you shot?' quickly asks Capt. Blake. 'No, no—they've shot my horse under me. For God's sake don't let 'em across.' By this time all are convinced that the coward is more alarmed than hurt; but the posts above and below have heard the reports, and pass the signal up and down the winding river, by discharging their rifles. Soon all is quiet, the soldiers in their bough-houses, save those on the beats possibly peering more sharply through the darkness."

Walcott Mead told the folks in Shoreham, "There was four of our boys sent out on picket last night and were fired on by a party of twelve rebels. They returned the fire with affect . . . all returned safely."

Three days later Mead wrote from Camp Widow Violet that the name of the camp had been changed to Camp Carusi. Dana explained, "The Col. is famous for naming camps after his favorite women." (Old maps show a home in the area owned by a family named Carusi.)

Generally things were quiet; as Sergeant Palmer put it, "Indeed, a soldier's life may be likened to a stream, to-day, calm and placid as the blue heavens; to-morrow, swolen beyond its banks . . . You seen a thousand faces together, none looking just alike, yet so near, it might even tax the painter's genius to point out each difference. So are many quiet days in camp, one very like the other."

Boredom put the men of the 13th to work on a theater, as Pvt. Henry Meigs recalled: "Two or three hundred of us set to work, some digging a trench around a piece of ground about thirty by forty feet, others cutting down the white oaks and splitting them in half; others carrying them in and standing them close together in the trench which was then refilled, and the cracks were then plastered with mud and made tight. A door was put in and the whole covered with flies from wall tents; benches were put in, a platform built and in a couple of days the theatre was ready for occupancy . . .

"Some time after completion, however, a couple of boys coming into camp about 10 PM, were surprised to see that it was occupied. The lights inside showing through the canvas roof clearly indicated that at least there was something doing. They tried the door and found it fastened on the inside. After knocking, it was opened by a man with a drawn sword who asked what they wanted; replying that they wanted to come in, they were refused admission and ordered away. Protesting that they had helped build the theatre and had a right to enter, an officer appeared from the interior, who hastily inquired by what right they were out of camp at that hour, and ordered them to return to their quarters forthwith . . . Inquiries were started next day, however, which resulted in showing that this was not a theatre or intended for a theatre . . . Some of the officers and older men were members of the Masonic fraternity, and having a dispensation from the Grand Lodge of Vermont to organize a lodge, had gotten up the theatre story to get the boys, most of them under twenty-one years of age, and therefore ineligible to join the Masonic order, to build them a lodge room . . . It was a clear case of bunco."

Trouble erupted in the 13th Vermont, again involving the spirited Irish Company and its feisty Captain Lonergan. It happened after the second and third in command of the regiment, Lt. Col. Andrew Brown, of Montpelier, and Maj. Lawrence Clark, of Highgate, resigned their commissions. Lieutenant Colonel Brown quit to accept a federal appointment in Vermont. The reason for Clark's leaving is unclear. Capt. William Munson, of Colchester, was promptly promoted to lieutenant colonel and made second in command of the regiment. Captain Boynton was promoted to major and replaced Major Clark. Captain Lonergan, being the senior captain in the regiment, seethed, feeling he should have been made lieutenant colonel.

"One day when Colonel Randall was absent and Munson was otherwise engaged," recalled Lt. Albert Clarke, "Boynton was designated in command of the regiment. Nothing out of the ordinary occurred until the line was formed for dress parade, and then Captain Lonergan asserted what he considered his right and undertook to displace Boynton as regimental commander. Standing near together, both issued orders—the customary dress parade orders—which were partly obeyed until they became so conflicting that company commanders did not know what to do, and then Boynton ordered the parade dismissed. Some of the companies promptly marched to quarters, and there being only a minority left, Captain Lonergan wisely concluded to transfer the controversy from the field to brigade headquarters."

The Irish captain had been voted down by the majority of the men following Boynton's orders. According to Clarke, "General Stannard came to investigate . . . but did not deem it necessary to subject anybody to discipline."

In early May, Pvt. George Barnett came down with the measles: "I was asked by the Capt to go if I liked to a farm house, which I did, and have been here ever since . . . I am about two miles from camp in a very nice large 2 story brick house on a plantation containing nearly three thousand acres. I do not have anything to do at all except to cast my eyes over the place to see that everything is right," he wrote home to Newbury, "if soldiers come along here my business is to keep them from molesting the property; they have not troubled me hardly any yet. The white folks here which are strong Sececionists consists of an old lady who with her 2

Private Jackson sketched soldiers demolishing a Virginia house,
probably for firewood.

sons, one in the rebel army and the other somewhere, own the place; and another
family, a man woman and two children that came here some time ago to live; they
are also 6 or 8 darkeys including children, that have not run away. They treat me
first rate. I eat with the rest of the family and live well, and when night comes I
has as good a bed to sleep in as I should have at home."

Ralph Sturtevant recalled that a private in the 13th, John Brough from
Morristown, was fond of visiting local homes. "John was a great hand to visit the
houses near by our camp," remembered Sturtevant, "to see the people, but never
made only a single visit to a house that did not contain some fair and blushing
damsel, and his diary kept by him gives names and ages of fair maidens near by
every camp we had. His musical talents were a passport into the cabins and man-
sions in the neighborhood of our several camps. John played the fiddle and the
colored boys and girls the banjo and bones and some . . . who were occasionally
invited by John to go with him remember still the stamp of feet and clap of hands
and animated dance; all were delighted. It was fun to see the colored boys and
girls as their bodies from head to foot kept time to the music."

Wheelock Veazey wrote to Julia on May Day, "Have you been maying today? The country is getting to look beautiful here. The hills are looking green,
fruit trees are in bloom & spring though late is upon us in all its beauty. How
soon nature obliterates the traces of war."

Charles Cummings reported: "We have a musical choir in the regiment that
does much to cheer us . . . To add to the enchantment of this climate and location
not more than 20 rods to the rear of my tent a dozen whip-o-wills make music all
night long. As I write I hear these distinctly, although the drums are beating tattoo.

If this country could be settled by good New England people it would be almost a paradise . . . Tomorrow morning we have a couple of fine fresh Potomac shad for breakfast. We have had them several times within two weeks."

Sergeant Palmer wrote, "The warm sun is shining on the fresh, green earth . . . the little birds are singing their sweet matins; and one can scarce believe that war, mad furious and desolating war, is in the land."

Private Hatch wrote to his Lucina, "I don't know what the matter with my under shirts it is growing yellow. I guess they want boiling . . . It was a cool night and I wanted to cuddle up so I thought to get my hand on your skinny bosom but come to find out it was Sant Whitney and I backed out very quick. It was mean, want it?"

Cummings added, "A conondrum has been circulating in camp, 'Why is the 2nd Brigade like an unborn babe?' which is answered, 'Because it is in for nine months unless sooner discharged.'"

Though life was comparatively easy in the Vermont camps, General Hooker was setting the Army of the Potomac in motion along the Rappahannock, beginning the fighting in the east in the third summer of the war. He was marching upriver, bound for a crossing that would bring him to a country crossroads called Chancellorsville. Soon the big guns spoke, echoing out along the Occoquan and Bull Run.

★

18

On May 3, 1863, Sergeant Palmer wrote home to Waitsfield: "MY DEAR FATHER AND MOTHER;—You will have heard of the great battle now going on near Fredericksburg, before this shall reach you. It is a still, Sabbath morning; not a cloud in the sky; and all nature clad in the freshness and beauty of spring. Since daylight we have heard the roar of the cannon growing heavier and heavier, till now it almost shakes the solid rocks on which I am writing."

On May 5, Colonel Veazey wrote to Julia, "Hooker began to fight . . . We can hear continuous cannonading. What I would give to be with him. I sometimes think fortune is against me in this military business."

Corporal Hammond wrote to his father on May 9: "They have had a ripping battle at Fredericksburg but we aren't called on, only we have been under marching orders for a week, but the Col. says today we shan't march at present."

Two days later Lieutenant Colonel Cummings reported, "Hooker's attempt, like those of his predecessors, is a failure. It does seem as if the Army of the Potomac was fated to ill success."

The Chancellorsville campaign, another great Union failure, set in motion a chain of events that would change the course of the war. The Second Vermont Brigade was first affected on May 2, when the 12th regiment was sent to Warrenton Junction, 20 miles to the west, to guard the Orange and Alexandria Railroad. The regiment marched to Union Mills, where it boarded an outbound train. Two companies were dropped off at Catlett's Station, while the rest of the regiment went seven miles farther, going into camp three miles beyond Warrenton Junction. The men had hardly reached their new location when Mosby's raiders appeared. Three pickets were promptly captured (though quickly paroled), and Mosby bore down on Warrenton Junction, where he clashed with Union cavalry. After a brisk fight, reinforcements arrived, and the Gray Ghost was forced to make a hasty retreat, suffering a number of casualties.

A day later, Lieutenant Benedict took a train from brigade headquarters to the scene, reporting early in his journey, "The country from Bristow on to Warrenton Junction and beyond, is a fine, open and comparatively level region, in strong contrast to the barren hills along the Occoquan." On arrival he found "A body of cavalry, in blue uniforms of Uncle Sam's boys, held the Junction, and the bodies of a dozen dead horses strewn around the solitary house at the station

Railroad bridge at Union Mills, guarded by the Second Vermont Brigade and drawn by Private Jackson

told of a sharp skirmish on that spot. Springing from the train, I had hardly taken twenty steps before I came upon the body of a dead rebel, stretched stark and cold, face upward, in coat of rusty brown and pantaloons of butternut. They showed me papers taken from his pockets, showing him to be one Templeman, a well known scout and spy of Mosby's command. Passing on to the house I found lying around it seventeen wounded 'butternuts' of all ages, from boys of sixteen to shaggy and grizzled men of fifty years. They lay in their blood, with wounds as yet undressed, for the skirmish ended but a little while before we arrived, some with gaping sabre cuts, some with terrible bullet wounds through face, body or limbs. Four or five rebel prisoners, unhurt, stood by, with downcast faces, but willing to answer civil questions. Close by, covered decently with a blanket, lay the body of a Union cavalry man, shot in cold blood after he had surrendered and given up his arms, by a long haired young rebel, who had received his reward for the dastardly act and lay near his victim, with a bullet wound in his stomach. The floor of the house was strewn with wounded men, among them Major Steele of the First Virginia, mortally wounded, and two of Mosby's officers. Their wounds had just been dressed and the surgeon began to give attention to the wounded rebels outside."

Pvt. Amos Whiting of Calais, in the 13th, said, "There were 20 wounded ones lying around the house. They were the first wounded men I had seen and I wished I was at home."

Benedict went on to the camp of his old regiment: "I found the men considerably stirred up by the events of the morning," he said, "which took place so near under their noses, and feeling as if they were pretty well out into the enemy's country."

157

On May 7, the 12th Vermont was moved deeper into enemy territory, to the north bank of the Rappahannock River, where a railroad bridge, now badly damaged, once carried the Orange and Alexandria line across the water. The 15th Vermont was turned out of its camps along Bull Run and dispatched in support, camping four miles north, at Bealton. Benedict wrote, "The camps were pleasant, the region healthful, and the health of the two regiments was much benefitted by the change. They were twenty miles from any infantry supports; the Confederate pickets were in sight across the Rappahannock; Confederate scouting parties were frequently seen."

Roswell Farnham wrote to Mary from "Rappahannock Bridge, Va." on May 10: "We are more pleasantly situated here than we have ever been before. This is the most splendid country I ever saw. From the door of my tent I can see miles of beautiful rolling country in a high state of cultivation. The planters don't look much like the inhabitants about Wolf Run Shoals. We are beginning to have delightful weather and the men are not as sick as they were . . . Hooker is back this side of the river and he has NOT succeeded."

On May 11 he added: "Today has been the warmest day of the season. It is like summer. I heard a piano this afternoon for the first time since I heard you play. It was at a Mr. Bowen's. His daughter played. She is secesh to the back bone, if a lady may be supposed to have so vulgar a thing. Her last tune was entitled 'Run, Yankees, Run, or Jackson will catch you.'" (She surely did not yet know that Jackson, wounded at Chancellorsville, had died the previous day.)

Pvt. Joel Glover, farmer and devoted husband, had written in late April to his wife in Topsham: "I had a bad cold and lame back but it has got well . . . Tell Willy and Emily to take good care of the others." A few days later he added: "I hope you will make a good lot of sugar this spring for I want a good lot when I get home. We expect to get home in June. Write often as you can there is nothing does a soldier so much good as letters from home. Don't worry one mite more for I am all right."

It was Glover's last letter. He died on May 13 of disease and his body was taken to Alexandria for burial. It never returned home.

The soldiering went on along the long Second Brigade front. On May 16, Farnham summed up the disposition of the brigade: "The 13th is still at Occoquan, the 14th at [Wolf Run] Shoals, the 15th $2^1/_2$ miles above us, at Bealton, the 16th at Union Mills. We are stretched out fifty miles. Genl. Stannard makes his headquarters at the Mills."

Private Irwin told his family, "The rebs made their appearance on the other side of the river—there could not be less than a Regt. of them. they advanced their pickets to the river and they began to throw up rifle pits. we watched them all the afternoon and they watched us. there is a RR bridge across the river . . . and our men guard this end and they the other end. they talked all night with our men and said if we would not fire on them they would not on us. they offered to exchange some whiskey for coffee with us but our Colonel would not allow us to go over . . . in the morning we had to leave we come back to Bristow's Station."

On May 16, Roswell Farnham reported from Rappahannock Bridge, "We don't have very much to do. Either I or the Col. look over the picket line every

*Vermont soldiers at Wolf Run Shoals, as pictured by Brattleboro
photographer George Houghton*

day . . . I struck off straight across the country thro' fields & woods to a Mrs.
Bogues, a widow lady . . . where there was an ice house filled. We got a drink of
ice water & iced currant wine & returned. This PM I have been reading *David
Copperfield.*"

On May 18, with rebel strength obviously building across the Rappahannock,
veteran cavalry under George Stoneman arrived to guard the riverbank. The 12th
and 15th regiments were promptly withdrawn, the 15th returning to Union Mills
and picket duty along the Occoquan. The 12th moved back along the Orange and
Alexandria Railroad, patrolling the line from Catlett's Station to Bristow Station.

Lieutenant Colonel Farnham wrote on the evening of May 18 from Bristow:
"We have a good camping ground . . . Mr. Peach has his quarters in an old house,
with the sides torn off so that the wind has a free circulation. The plastering is
ornamented with various charcoal sketches, in which the different aspects of female loveliness are displayed in as great a variety of postures as the imagination of
the different artists were able to conceive, relieved with a few male figures, that
to say the least, are not modest in their intercourse with the charcoal beauties."

Back at Wolf Run Shoals, Corporal Williams noted on May 22, "In consequence of the weather being so extremely warm, we have only two and one-half
hours' drill per day, which is mainly in the bayonet exercise. Picketing is getting
somewhat tedious—requiring two-thirds of the regiment to perform it, and thereby

159

giving only two days out of seven for rest."

But in the 13th, Pvt. Abraham Benjamin, a Richford man, "fished the Occoquan for herring, shiners and pumpkin seed."

Word had been joyously received in the camps that General Grant had succeeded in bringing the great Confederate bastion of Vicksburg, on the Mississippi River, under siege. Lieutenant Colonel Cummings wrote from Union Mills, "Hurrah for U.S. Grant! He is the big man of this war . . . how gloriously he is succeeding for he must get Vicksburg and lots of prisoners."

One spring day, Pvt. William Backus, from Bridgewater, had a narrow escape. "He was scouting around south of the Occoquan," a friend related, "when he stopped at a house and got into conversation with a fair Rebel who did not hesitate to avow her principles. The siege of Vicksburg was then in progress and she said very confidently, 'Grant can never take Vicksburg.' Backus was a great lover of poetry and before he came away he borrowed a book of Tom Moore's poetry. Rumors were circulating in camp that the 13th was about to march, so Backus thought it would be dishonorable not to return that borrowed book and started out with it. When he had nearly reached the house, he saw all at once a squad of rebel cavalry, who also saw him and gave chase. He sprang over the fence, leaving the book on it as he went and took to the woods. The rebels fired at him and followed a short distance but he struck swampy land and [they] gave up the chase. After a time he came out on the banks of the Occoquan where it widens out toward the Potomac. How to cross was a puzzle but he found an old barn from which he pried a large door and constructed a rude craft and paddled himself across."

Colonel Veazey wrote on May 23, "We had a temperance lecture last night from a perfect old fool, but we had a good time, had some singing & the band played."

Despite the warm weather, sickness lingered. On May 21, a soldier in the 16th wrote to the *Freeman:* "Our company has again met with a serious loss. On Saturday, at three o'clock in the afternoon, Sergeant Charles McKnight, of Calais, Vermont, breathed his last, having been sick for over two weeks with typhoid fever. At about the same hour, we lost Seth Moore, drummer, of Co. H, by typhoid fever . . . Sgt. McKnight is a deep, and never to be forgotten, loss to our company. He was taken sick in quarters, but was soon removed to a private house near our camp, where every attention was bestowed on him by his brother soldiers in the company. Night and day we watched by his side, and at intervals when delirium came on, he would speak of home and wish to be there."

From Camp Carusi on May 31 Corporal Hammond wrote, "We sent little Ben Reed home yesterday boxed up, and I am afraid we shall have another to send before long, Dave Stahl of Moretown but I wish he might get well."

Private Sturtevant remembered the death of Sgt. Orloff Whitney as being especially sad: "He was prostrated with typhoid fever in camp Widow Violet on the Occoquan, Virginia, and removed to Alexandria, Va., and placed in a hospital where the next day in an unguarded moment on account of negligence of nurse, as his comrades believe, and while in a raging fever, without knowing what he did jumped through an open window, and died in a few hours."

The 15th and 16th regiments were reviewed on May 26. That evening General Stannard sent a message to the two units that concluded, "Gen. Abercrombie speaks in high terms of the review and inspection, especially of the manner in which both regiments passed through the manual of arms, and noticed with pleasure the attention that has been paid to drill and discipline by both officers and men."

Yet the Vermonters were in for a shock. In mid-May John Mosby wrote to J.E.B. Stuart asking for a "mountain howitzer" for use against railroad trains. The request was granted and Mosby attacked the Orange and Alexandria, just south of Catlett's Station, on May 30. His target was a southbound supply train that had stopped at Union Mills to pick up a 25-man detail from the 15th Vermont, commanded by Lt. Elden L. Hartshorn, of Lunenberg.

"A train was destroyed by the rebels yesterday between Bristow and Catletts," Sgt. George Hagar reported. ". . . They had two small field pieces, with which they put a ball into the boiler of the Locomotive before it had come to a stop. They had taken up a rail to make sure of stopping the train. The Lieut. commanding the guard on the train ordered his men to look out for themselves instead of showing fight. He had fifty men with him and he could have kept them from the train until some of our cavalry reached him if he had showed fight. The sergeant wanted to rally the men and pitch into them. The lieutenant is under arrrest. One of the guard fired contrary to orders taking deliberate aim and killing his man. The guard was from the 15th Regt. Col. Blunt has gone out with 200 men to clear the tracks of the ruins of the train."

Pvt. Nelson Rogers, in the 12th, wrote on May 31: "They had pulled the spikes out the length of one rail and then made something fast to the rail and took the end up into the bushes and just as the Engine was coming up they pulled the rail so as to run the train off the tracks, and then they fired into it with two pieces of artillery; putting one shot through the boiler. Chaplain Barstow was on the Engine but he made good time and we haven't seen him since."

"It was my misfortune to be on the train the 30th of May," Pvt. Amos Whiting of the 13th recalled. "At or near Catlett's Station Mosby derailed the train; a young lad, I do not remember his name, had a supply of sutler's goods to sell the boys. We both jumped at the same time, but he broke his leg but crawled into the bushes and escaped being captured."

Also on the train was Pvt. John Wallace, who wrote, "We were under Lieut. Hartshorn and were outnumbered eight to one besides the artillery they had to help them. I fired at them from the top of the cars just before I got off but after we were on the ground the bushes were so thick we could not see them, while they were firing grape and canister at us. I was displeased with the Lieut. for marching us off, but I do not think we could have saved the train."

Union cavalry gave chase and entered into a running battle with Mosby and his howitzer. As a result, Lieutenant Colonel Farnham reported a few days later, "The Vermont Cavalry boys took their piece of artillery from them & on Sunday passed thro' our camp with it."

In a letter to Mary, Farnham noted that charges were considered against Lieutenant Hartshorn. On June 8 he wrote, "I am still employed upon court of inquiry into the conduct of Lieut Hartshorn, who had command of the guard

Vermont troops and the blockhouse protecting Catlett's Station,
drawn by Private Jackson

of the train that was burned the other day."

On June 10 he wrote, "We got thro' with the examination of witnesses in the case of Lieut. Hartshorn but have not made our report yet. Yesterday we went over to the hospital to take the testimony of that little red cheeked boy . . . who jumped off a car & broke his leg. He laid right there in sight of the rebels when they came to the train & set it afire." Hartshorn was acquitted of any dereliction of duty.

The 12th Vermont was withdrawn June 1 to Union Mills. The 16th took its place, for a two-week stay. Joseph Spafford wrote to Weathersfield from Bristow Station: "There have been quite a number of houses destroyed and burned down . . . Back two, three & four miles from the railroad we find now and then a family trying to stick by the old place & tough it through. At almost every place we find pretty girls, which I notice is generally the greatest safeguard they can have for their chickens, pigs, etc., etc. This is a very fine country; from Manassas Junction through to Warrenton Junction is so straight we can see almost from one place to the other as we stand on the RR here. There is an old wind mill here, I think about 50 ft. high; through the daytime we keep a look out stationed on top with a spy glass and he informs us if he sees cavalry coming at any time & we fall in and wait to find out if it is ours or rebs."

In mid-June the 15th replaced the 16th along the railroad. Meanwhile, the 12th and 15th remained along the Occoquan. "On picket," Sergeant Palmer wrote. "The night is really splendid. The blue bay of Occoquan, many feet below us, gives back the shining moon and stars, the air not uncomfortably hot, and just wind enough to stir the luxuriant foliage of oaks near our post. Then there is the noise of the river to the right of us, (here it empties itself into the bay,) dashing against huge rocks; of the whipoorwill, singing its own name, by turns, all night, and often imitated by the soldiers; and of yelping curs, and now and then, loud baying, barking blood-hounds, disturbed in their kennels."

Upstream, Pvt. Hall, in the 15th, wrote from Fairfax Station on May 3, "Our Co is on picket duty here at Headquarters doing the guard duty at the station. I am first relief and have to walk before the Genl. and salute the officers when they cross the beat and look out that the Genl. don't 'skedaddle' or get gobbled up. The tents are open during the day so I can see all that is going on. He has got his wife with him and she is a beauty—now I tell you. She is about the only white woman I have seen since I left Washington last Oct—and I don't know but that is what makes her so handsome in my estimation. I have 'presented arms' to her twice and am going to every time I have a chance. The Genl. is about 35 years old and his wife about 30. He don't look so 'gay and festive' as Stoughton used to with a plume in his cap and a shawl crossed over his shoulders, parading the streets of Fairfax with a—well, I won't say what—but she proved a foe instead of a friend. Gen. G.J. wears, when he isn't 'on his military,' a black slouched hat and a blouse with a silver star on each shoulder. If it were not for that you would not know him from a Capt. or a Lieut. Anyway, he is a plain man and a good General."

On June 2, from Union Mills, Farnham wrote, "In the evening I rode with Col. Blunt down to Wolf Run Shoals by moonlight. We were gone only about three hours. When we came back we found that the boys had cleaned out the sutler. They tore down his tent, drank his beer & eat his nuts and fruits."

He added on June 8, "Camp life is about the same from day to day—The same amount of discomfort, which at first was very well for its novelty, is getting to be a little boreus. Fly bites, mosquito bites, flea bites, spider bites, bug bites & wood ticks are not very poetical & are certainly for me the cause of a great deal of discomfort. My left hand is swollen with fly bites & itches very uncomfortably."

All was quiet in camp. Pvt. Walcott Mead in the 14th got a pass from Wolf Run Shoals and visited Mount Vernon. "For scenery the best I ever saw," he said. "Leaf from a tree set out from Washington's own hand." (The leaf survives, folded in his letter, preserved at the Vermont Historical Society.)

At the Shoals, Pvt. Charles Mead wrote to his brother, "I took my revolver and went hunting. Ed Baldwin was with me—we killed a rabbit a partridge and a chipmunk. We could not carry our game to camp as it is contrary to orders to fire off guns here only when on drill or in battle. There is talk among the officers that there will be a grand review of this Brigade in Brattleboro Vt. the 10th of July. Now if you want to see the best looking five regiments in the U. States you had better be there."

On a day in early June, a group of officers from the 12th, 13th, and 16th regiments toured the Bull Run battlefield, scene of two major battles. The tour leader was Colonel Randall, who had fought at First Bull Run, and in the party were Colonels Blunt and Farnham, Major Kingsley, Lieutenant Benedict, and others. Benedict reported to the *Free Press:* "The ruins of the Henry House, around which the battle raged and in which a woman was killed, were near us. The rose bushes still grow in the rank grass which covers what was once the door-yard or flower-garden, and blossom as freely as if the storm of battle had never swept over them . . . Guided by Col. Randall we saw where the fighting opened on the right and centre; where the Second Vermont, then a regiment a month old, first went into action . . . Many of the dead who fell in both the battles of Bull Run were not buried in graves but simply covered with earth as they lay, and skulls and bones frequently protrude from the little mounds . . . There are no head-boards to mark the graves, and the grass grows thick over them. We passed by Dogan's house, still standing though unoccupied; we saw, of course, 'the stone house' window-less and deserted and marked by cannon shot; and we took our homeward way by the turnpike, fording Bull Run at the famous stone bridge, now a bridge no longer.

"On the battle-ground," he continued, "I saw not a trace of rifle-pit or earth-work of any description, and the fighting must have been in the main open standing-up work. The ground is almost covered in one or two spots with skel-etons of horses. Its surface is ridged with graves, and strewn with cartridge boxes, remnants of uniforms and knapsacks, and here and there a rusty bayonet or unexploded shell. Many of the marks of the conflict are doubtless hidden by grass, which grows probably thicker than before on soil enriched by blood and bones of fallen patriots and rebels. It is now entirely uncultivated and deserted; but several of the farms around and near it are in a pretty good state of cultivation for Vir-ginia, and in time, no doubt, the plough-share will be driven over its slopes, through grave and cannon rut, and all traces of the great battles will become obliterated."

Farnham told Mary, "I saw one man with both feet sticking out with his stockings still on. He lay upon his face, with the soles of his feet up . . . We found a large number from whom the rain had washed the earth, & skulls & feet lay bare to the weather. One man fell upon his face and was covered with earth in that position . . . I saw one bony hand thrust out from beneath the scanty cover-ing still in the coatsleeve. Dr. Nichols, cut a brass plate such as soldiers wear (U.S.) from a waist belt, still around a man's body. The Adj't opened a cartridge box which was fastened to a body in its grave . . . I picked up a bullet from the top of a grave where the woolen shirt of the occupant was exposed to the air. Not a mark of any kind indicated who had given up his life for his country in hundreds of instances on that fatal field . . . Life is of small account in the army."

The battlefield tour put Farnham in a somber mood, and several days later he wrote, "How soon the dead are forgotten. At home they are forgotten soon enough, even with every effort to preserve their memory, but here in war men die & they are buried where they fell and no one remembers them. There is a grave just back of my tent, not ten feet from it. No one knows who it is. There is no head board,— nothing of the kind, just two stakes stuck into the ground, one at each end."

Colonel Veazey reported from the 16th's new post at Bristow Station on June 5, "Everybody is having a joyous time. We play ball, pitch quoits, play Euchre, have foot races, ride horseback, drink whiskey, eat and sleep . . . No set of fellows ever had a better time, except some of us want our wives."

Cummings told his wife in a letter written on June 9, sent from Catlett's Station, "Within a week we have had two divisions of cavalry, [John] Buford's and [Alfred] Pleasanton's, in camp within a mile of us, but yesterday they both left for the Rappahannock. There is some movement in the wind but what it is I do not know. Either Lee or Hooker or both are moving. Our camp has been saturated with rumors of all sorts."

On June 10, Farnham wrote from Union Mills, "Tattoo has just been beaten— and a train is now coming in that has been expected for several hours from Rappahannock with prisoners. Stuart was intending to make a raid & Genl. Pleasanton crossed over at Beverly's Ford, where we were a few days ago, and attacked Stuart before he left camp yesterday. The fighting lasted almost or quite all yesterday. Cavalry and artillery with very little infantry. A long train of cars went past here last night with the wounded . . . The fighting was in sight of our old camp at the Rappahannock R.R. Bridge."

Farnham, from a considerable distance, was writing of the Battle of Brandy Station, the largest cavalry clash of the war. It had, indeed, been a battle between Union cavalry under Alfred Pleasanton and Confederate horsemen commanded by J.E.B. Stuart. The series of daylong clashes, some in the classic cavalry saber-swinging mode, had not been decisive. But one clear result was that Pleasanton had discovered beyond the shadow of a doubt that Robert E. Lee's Army of Northern Virginia was on the move, to the west and, likely, well to the north.

By June 15, Cummings and the 16th were back at Union Mills, Colonel Proctor's 15th having taken their place farther along the railroad. "Our picket line on Bull Run," Cummings stated, "seven miles long, has been strengthened by trees felled into the river forming an abatis almost impenetrable . . . Lee is without a doubt an abler general than any other in either army. He is evidently bound to do something striking, something that shall arouse the drooping spirits of the Confederacy, strike consternation into the North and help advance the recognition of the Confederacy by foreign powers. I should like to see a little field service before returning . . . If we have an engagement I shall be green and awkward, but I shall try to do my duty, as cooly and as faithfully as I can."

In the 15th, "Tip" Turner wrote to sister Addie on June 15, "If there has got to be a battle any where about here I almost wanted to be in it. I don't know that I should feel scard & run the first fire. I cant tell till I try. I should feel rather green to go home & have to say that I never fired a gun at a reb."

In the Virginia encampments of the Second Vermont Brigade, there was a sense of electricity building in the air, much like the anticipation of an afternoon shower coming over the mountains toward a Vermont hayfield. First come the thunderheads, then the distant rumble, then the lightning and the crash and roll accompanying the downpour. The approaching storm was being sensed far and wide. In St. Johnsbury, on June 4, with the disaster of Chancellorsville still in the headlines, Charles Fairbanks, just returned from Europe, reported to the townsfolk in a speech he called "The American Conflict As Seen from the European Point of View."

At the close of a lengthy address, Fairbanks concluded: "I believe the day of our deliverance is not far distant. Let us take counsel of Hope rather than of doubt. The darkness of our night is beginning to be dispelled, and Hope sits smiling in the dawn of a new day."

★

Southwest from Manassas, the railroad still follows the nearly straight course that prompted one Vermont soldier—accustomed to the wandering hill-country courses of Vermont railways—to remark that you could practically see from station to station. Route 28 from Manassas closely parallels the railroad line. The landscape, though undergoing development, is still for the most part open farm country. Just south of Manassas is Bristow Station, where the Vermonters camped. A cluster of houses where a narrow highway crosses the tracks, the village was the scene of a vicious battle in mid-October 1863, well after the Second Vermont Brigade had gone home.

Just east of Route 28, south of Bristow, lie the little railroad villages of Catlett's Station and Bealton, both known to the Vermonters. In or near each hamlet, a Civil War—era building or two remains. Indeed, at Catlett's the station survives, enveloped by a new building. To travel out along the railroad is to gain a steadily increasing appreciation for the isolation the Vermonters felt farther and farther from the relative safety of their main lines. You are also struck by the sheer length of the line entrusted to the nine-months soldiers, all the way from Occoquan to the Rappahannock River.

Just before the Rappahannock a sign points east to the village of Remington, known at the time of the war as Rappahannock Station. Just south of the village, a country road crosses the Rappahannock and there is a narrow dirt turnout on the eastern side of the road. Park there and walk no more than 200 yards along the riverbank and its almost junglelike growth to the railroad bridge, at the site of the wartime structure. This southern bank of the river was occupied by Confederates; the Vermont troops held the northern bank. Here they faced each other with an understanding that they would hold their fire, a hint of the kind of trust that eventually allowed the country to bind up its wounds. As at Bristow, a hard battle would be fought at Rappahannock Station months after the Vermonters went away.

South of the Rappahannock is the village of Brandy Station. To the west is Fleetwood Hill and the woods and fields that were the scene of the biggest cavalry battle of the Civil War. While the Vermonters did not fight there, they heard the firing. After a long preservation effort, the Brandy Station battlefield has been saved and should one day soon become one of the largest of all Civil War battlefield parks.

The Manassas battlefield, which the Vermont officers toured, has long been preserved as a national battlefield park. An island of serenity amid a sea of development, the park preserves the Dogan house, stone house, stone bridge, and other battle landmarks the Vermonters saw. And atop Henry House Hill is the reconstructed house of the widow Judith Henry, killed in her bed by cannon fire. Her grave is still in the dooryard, and she lies between a son and a daughter, in a carefully tended little plot in the quiet of a landscape once shot-torn and bloody, but now a national shrine.

19

The season of war was now upon the bloodied northern Virginia countryside. The June 9 cavalry battle at Brandy Station set the Army of the Potomac into motion from its camps down toward Fredericksburg, in an attempt to stay abreast of the Army of Northern Virginia. Lee had actually put advance elements of his army on the march as early as June 3, and Hooker, after some delay, was trying to keep pace, under orders to stay between the Confederates and Washington. There was much excitement in the camps of the Second Vermont Brigade.

"Hooker is moving his whole army in this direction," Roswell Farnham told Mary on June 15. "A portion is crossing at Wolf Run & a portion at Occoquan. Two corps go up the Potomac and west through in this vicinity. The sky is filled with clouds of dust in the direction of Manassas as I write. I have just looked out my tent to see a train of pack mules passing through our camps . . . there are several batteries at the Shoals, but no infantry has crossed there yet. We are in the midst of great movements evidently. What it all means no one knows, but everyone has an opinion about it. It is reported that Lee has passed or is passing into the Shenandoah Valley for Maryland or Penn."

The same day, Sergeant Palmer noted, "All day artillery, teams and now and then a regiment, have been going to the rear . . . Gen. Hooker and his staff passed about three o'clock."

"Hooker's army is on the move and a strong one it is to me," wrote Private Barnett on June 18. "The eleventh Corps reached Centreville last night, four miles above here; the fifth, sixth and twelfth corps will get here tonight, they are just across the river from here now, the First and Second are at Wolf Run Shoals now, with one hundred and eighty pieces of artillery; the rest of Hooker's army reached Aldie last night and a large force of cavalry passed through here yesterday on the way to Centreville; a long train of baggage wagons has passed through here today on the Centreville Road; large clouds of dust can be seen in the direction of Manassas indicating troops passing . . . there will be severe fighting somewhere soon."

On June 19, Farnham wrote, "It was a great mistake enlisting men for NINE months. Just as our brigade is in the best fighting condition it is to be discharged & sent home. I suppose you are glad of it, but it will have a bad influence on the war."

He reported on June 21, "Today we are going again to post the pickets. We shall have to work hard now all the time. We are the front of every thing except cavalry scouts. Yesterday there was a fight up at Aldie & so down to Thorough-fare Gap, between cavalry & artillery. We heard the firing all day. I am sitting under a tree, horses saddled and waggons loaded—all ready."

In the midst of it all, on June 20, Samuel Dana reported, "I wrote you about going to see the old brigade . . . I found them encamped in some fine weeds (or laying rather) for they had no tents up."

The First Vermont Brigade—known affectionately as the Old Brigade—had indeed been by, marching with the Sixth Corps to the north and west, and had camped near the other Vermont Brigade. "I got there about three o'clock in the morning," said Corporal Hammond. "Jim Heraman was the first man I saw. He was on guard, standing by a fire. He lit a candle and went down into the weeds with me. There the boys laid around so we had to be careful not to step onto them. We found Foster, and I tell you it was hard work to wake him up as well as the rest of them. I pulled him out of his nest and when he saw who it was you better guess he was wide awake. Wallis is well and Harris Stoddorold and all the boys that I knew . . . You tell Mr. Chase that I never saw John look strong in my life as he does now and tell Mr. Bettis that Lew is tough and rugged. But the boys in the old brigade have gone through everything but death, still their grit is good . . . The Twelfth Reg. leaves for home next Friday, and a captain in Gen. Abercrombie's staff that inspected us yesterday said the 13th would start one week from next Monday."

Dana had been watching the passing of other regiments: "It looks hard," he said, "to see clothing thrown away as it is all along where the army has moved along. Overcoats, dress coats, blankets, and some of them threw everything they had got."

Private Barnett wrote to his family in Newbury on June 21, "The 1st Vermont Brigade is in, and the boys had a chance to see their friends in it . . . I suffered a great deal with my tooth aching last night and this morning I had it pulled out. Cherries are ripe here and very nice."

At headquarters, 16th regiment, Colonel Veazey's mind was as much on impending events at home as it was on war developments in Virginia. He wrote to Julia, eight months pregnant, from Bristow on June 9, "Do you think I could hold you now? It is a splendid time for fighting now. We stand a poor chance of seeing any as our time is near out. I shall not have many honors to bring back to you this time."

Two days later he wrote, hoping for a son, "How long before he makes his appearance? I want the glad tidings from the East that a son is born. Will the morning stars seize together and the elements clap their hands for joy? . . . Wish I could win some great glory this month to make it doubly memorable. It might make a great impression on the young stranger."

By June 16, Veazey had begun to think that his chance for glory was improving. "Two great events will soon happen," he wrote home. "A great battle is to be fought and a great advent is to be made into the world."

The Second Vermont Brigade was, by mid-June, posted back along Bull Run and the Occoquan, with two exceptions. The 15th was to the west on Broad Run at Bristow Station, and four companies of the 15th were still on duty seven miles out along the Orange and Alexandria Railroad at Catlett's Station, under the command of Lt. Col. William W. Grout, a 26-year-old lawyer from Barton. The movement of the armies in recent days had brought to Grout's camp a large number of escaped slaves, seeking refuge in what they hoped to be a permanent army camp. On June 23, a cavalry officer in the command of Brig. Gen. John Buford arrived and informed Grout that he was to withdraw. The four companies had been moved to Catlett's by train, and thus had a considerable amount of baggage that needed transporting. With no train available, Grout's men put a set of wheels from a wrecked train back on the tracks and hastily built a small railway car. A rope was attached to the front, baggage and a black woman with a day-old baby were put on board, and the men of the 15th started up the Orange and Alexandria, taking turns pulling. With them went several hundred former slaves, bound for freedom. At nightfall they all joined the rest of the 15th at Bristow.

Back along the Occoquan, a soldier in the 16th wrote to the *Freeman,* "One day last week a smart looking young negro of twenty two passed by our camp and, as usual, a crowd gathered around him to hear his story. We learned that he left his master three weeks before, and was now serving the Colonel of the First Vermont in the capacity of hostler—a position which he seemed to like much. He was now after his wife. He had twenty miles to go, having formerly lived in Middleburg. As guerrillas frequently appear in the vicinity, he feared he might be taken and sold south; but a day or two after we saw him coming down the railroad accompanied by the object of his visit . . . she hid in the bushes till he came; then by travelling all night they succeeded in eluding the search of their master."

In the 14th, Corporal Williams noted, "There have been numerous rumors afloat concerning the movement of the rebel army; but it is evidently a fact that Gen. Lee is advancing up the Shenandoah Valley. Heavy firing is heard today in the direction of Thoroughfare Gap. The regiments of this brigade have not changed positions lately. The general impression is, now, that the second brigade will have a chance to be tried in battle . . . The First Brigade has won a name which the State, as well as themselves, may well be proud; and although we have been called by some, 'nine monthlings, hatched on two-hundred-dollar-bounty eggs,' we understand the use of the bayonet, and if we ever have a chance to meet the foe we shall not falter."

On June 20, Williams wrote, "Another member of Company B, by the name Caleb Fisk, died last night. What greater sacrifice can a man make for his country, than to give his life. To the memory of him, and all others who sacrifice their lives for their country, should be raised monuments which, like the pyramids of Egypt, shall stand to be gazed upon by future generations."

On June 23, Sergeant Palmer wrote to his sister: "These changing whirls have not yet caught us. Last night we received orders to be ready to march; but we have seen no signs of it during the day, and we may—but I must change the tone of my letter at once, for an orderly has just come from headquarters to tell us that the whole brigade is to march in the morning. This monotonous drama is ended, and the next will close with the battle-field. May God shield the soldiers, and give them victory."

That same day, according to Lieutenant Benedict at brigade headquarters,

"General Stannard was notified that his brigade has been attached to the First Corps of the Army of the Potomac; that he was to hold his line till all the rest of the army has passed on; and then he was to follow the column to the north, and report to General Reynolds, commanding the First Corps."

The veteran First Corps, heavily bloodied at Antietam and Fredericksburg, was under the command of Maj. Gen. John Fulton Reynolds, one of the most respected soldiers in the Union armies. A Pennsylvania native, the 42-year-old West Pointer was a veteran of the Mexican War and had led troops through the Peninsula Campaign and in most of the subsequent major battles of the Army of the Potomac. He had recently been offered command of that army, though he declined. Now Reynolds was marching his corps toward Maryland, having just received the news that the nine-months Second Vermont Brigade had strengthened his forces. The veteran regiments of the First Corps were to move, however, before the Vermonters took up the march. Stannard's brigade would get a late start.

First, the brigade had to be assembled. On June 24, orders went to the five regiments to meet at Union Mills, along the route of march of the Army of the Potomac. The next morning, the 12th had a short tramp to the rendezvous, from Wolf Run Shoals to Union Mills. Lieutenant Colonel Farnham wrote to Mary, "We left the Shoals at seven o'clk and reached the Mills before ten . . . We left nothing behind on the picket line."

In the 14th, Corporal Williams noted, "We now belong to the Army of the Potomac . . . The line was formed in heavy marching order at seven o'clock, each man being supplied with three days rations in his haversack . . . We arrived at Union Mills at the appointed hour."

The 13th marched in from its camp out along the Occoquan, and Ralph Sturtevant remembered that as preparations were made, there was a sudden realization that the regiment was considerably reduced in strength from the 953 men that had mustered in at Brattleboro. In fact, subtracting those who had been discharged for various health reasons, men in hospital, those who had died, the few men who had deserted, and those under arrest, 760 men were present for duty. And that number included, he noted, "cooks who acted as guards to wagon trains, drum corps, ambulance detail and hospital corps." If there was to be fighting done, there would be far fewer than the 4,898 men who had reported to the Second Vermont Brigade at Brattleboro.

Indeed, General Stannard on June 20 listed the strengths of his five regiments:

—12th, 700
—13th, 719
—14th, 729
—15th, 621
—16th, 735

Thus, according to Stannard, five days before the march began the total number of officers and men in the ranks stood at 3,504. Still, it was a big brigade for the summer of 1863; the veteran units of the Army of the Potomac had suffered greater losses. Ralph Sturtevant said, "The most of our regiment had prepared for a long

*Maj. Gen. John Reynolds led the First Corps, including the
Second Vermont Brigade, to Gettysburg.*

march and discarded everything that we could get along without, experience having taught us that guns, forty rounds of cartridges, haversacks stuffed with rations, with canteen and shelter tent, rubber blanket, an extra shirt and pair of socks, letter paper, testaments that had been given us before we left home, needles, thread, etc., etc., tucked away in our knapsacks would be quite enough to carry. Some of the homesick and anxious hoped that our destination when we started on the march would be Washington, and therefore they packed their knapsacks full, loaded themselves down with overcoats, woolen blankets, extra pairs of shoes." The aim was not personal comfort, but to bring home as many souvenirs as possible.

Sturtevant reported: "We took the road leading to Fairfax Station and after a few miles took a road running nearly parallel with the Occoquan River leading direct to Union Mills . . . We arrived at Union Mills about two o'clock in the afternoon where we found the 12th, 14th, 15th and 16th regiments awaiting our arrival. We halted about an hour for a little rest and to complete a few preliminaries . . . General Stannard was anxious to comply with General Reynolds request to join the First Corps as soon as possible."

It might have been surmised that a march was imminent a couple of days previously when Lieutenant Benedict was suddenly ordered to Washington; again he was not present at the start of a long tramp. But he set the stage for it. "Our men . . . were not inured to marching," he wrote. "Some were poorly shod, for in view of the speedy termination of their service they had not been allowed to exchange old shoes for new; but they marched well. With sore and bleeding feet, in some cases barefooted, they pushed along." On the day the brigade assembled, June 24, to the north and west, most of Robert E. Lee's Army of Northern Virginia had already entered Union territory, with many divisions as far north as Pennsylvania.

On June 24, the recently promoted Corporal Doubleday penned the following letter:

> Dear wife,
>
> Well, Asceneth we have got orders to march in the morning. We are to start at 7 and be at Union Mills by 11. Where we are to go from there, we are not allowed to know. Some say we are going to Harpers Ferry, some to Maryland, but we shall not know until we get to our stopping place. I think we shall go where we shall see rebs and perhaps some fighting, but I don't calculate to get killed now just before our time is out. I put an overcoat in a box to send home today . . . I was in hopes we should not have to move until after I got another letter from you, but I may get yours just as soon as I should here.
>
> I am afraid I shall hear some bad news from home when I get a letter from you if there is anything in dreams. I dreamed that you and I stood up with a couple to be married last night. I hope I shall hear that Freddy is better and the rest of you are well. The boys are all wide awake for a fight here. I can't say that I really want to be in one but I don't dread it much. If we do

get into one I shall try to do my duty. If I should get killed perhaps it would be as well for you. You would draw a pension of $8 a month and have a chance to get a younger and better husband. Kiss the boys for me, from Willie down to little Fred. Hoping I shall be spared to meet you all again in a few weeks. I wish you good night from your ever loving Husband,

Wm.O.D.

★

PART V

Into Battle

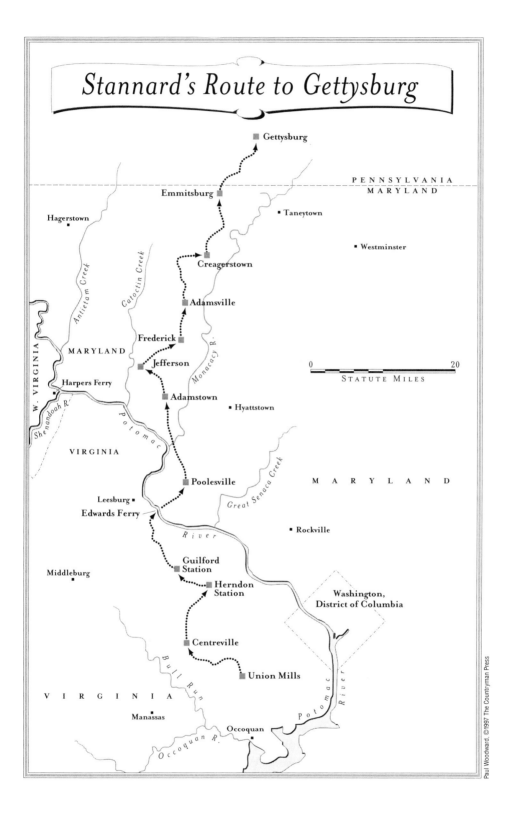

Stannard's Route to Gettysburg

■ Gettysburg

PENNSYLVANIA
MARYLAND

Emmitsburg ■

■ Taneytown

Hagerstown
■

■ Westminster

Catoctin Creek

Creagerstown ■

Antietam Creek

■ Adamsville

MARYLAND

Frederick ■

Monocacy R.

Jefferson ■

W. VIRGINIA

Harpers Ferry
■

Adamstown ■

Shenandoah R.

■ Hyattstown

Potomac

VIRGINIA

0   20
STATUTE MILES

Poolesville ■

Great Seneca Creek

MARYLAND

Leesburg ■
Edwards Ferry

River

■ Rockville

Middleburg
■

Guilford
Station ■

Herndon
Station ■

Washington,
District of Columbia

Centreville ■

Bull Run

■ Union Mills

VIRGINIA

Potomac River

Manassas
■

Occoquan ■

Occoquan R.

20

According to Cpl. John Williams, who was there, the long march that would end at Gettysburg began for the Second Vermont Brigade, assembled at Union Mills in the rain, at 3 PM on June 25. Though some of his regiments had already been on the road several hours that day, General Stannard did not wish to waste any time.

"On leaving Union Mills," Private Sturtevant recalled, "we travelled for about two miles almost due north and then bore off to the left in a direct line to Centreville, leaving Fairfax Court House far to our right, crossed the Alexandria and Warrenton Turnpike at Centreville just before sundown, taking the road that led to Chantilly and westerly to Gum Springs, and there finding a suitable place for camp grounds, a mile or so beyond, went into camp for the night having travelled (the 13th Regiment) nearly 25 miles and nearly all the way from Union Mills in the rain and mud, and some of us were thoroughly tired and willing to lie down for rest and sleep, though wet, hungry, and tired."

Corporal Williams, in the 14th, noted, "Arrived at Centreville about five o'clock in the afternoon, and encamped in the form of a hollow square, two miles beyond, for the night, making about fourteen miles we had marched during the day. It rains quite hard to-night."

That night, General Stannard entered in his diary, "All the regiments did well. Came in closed up in good shape."

Lieutenant Colonel Farnham dashed off a letter to Mary: "For a while at least there was nothing to prevent the Rebels coming into our rear as we marched from the Shoals. What we should have done if they had made a strong dash with cavalry into our rear is more than I can say . . . Our time is still going on and these moves cannot stop time's passing. The 4th of July shall come soon and I shall soon be at home." (J.E.B. Stuart's cavalry crossed the Occoquan at Wolf Run Shoals the afternoon of June 25.)

Of the next morning, Private Sturtevant said, "It had poured down rain all night and nearly all were wet through to the skin, and some of the boys appeared and talked as if they felt ugly, but it mattered not, breakfast must be prepared in haste for we were to be on the march at six o'clock, and at the bugle call we were all ready to fall in. We were a little slow in moving on the morning of the 26th for the rain during the night made the condition of the roads bad . . . We directed our course this day toward Edwards Ferry where the army had crossed and were crossing the Potomac on pontoon bridges and reached Herndon Station on the pike from Alexandria to Leesburgh and here camped for the night."

Sturtevant said the brigade passed the village of Aldie that day, where Union cavalry had clashed with J.E.B. Stuart's horsemen several days before. He noted that the brigade proceeded in that area "cautiously," slowing its pace.

Sturtevant's description of the march was written many years later. He and other men in the ranks generally had little time, or were too tired, for daily letter or diary writing. Pvt. Myron Clark, however, noted that night, "Start again but got only to Herndon Station on the Hampshire & Loudon R.R.—not very hard marching."

Stannard assessed the day in his journal: "Had to wait for Howe & Newton's divisions of the 6th Army Corps to pass, and our march was very slow, and in many places the road was bad and were much detained in consequence thereof."

On the next day, June 27, Private Clark wrote, "March at daylight. It has been a little rainy since we began to march but on the whole a fine time. Came in sight of the Potomac at one o'clock. We cross about two hours after on pontoons— go by the camp of the 1st VT. Brigade. Saw Ward Hurlburt again. We are in Maryland now. I hope that I will see Virginia no more. Went two or three miles further and camped. Cloudy and cool."

But the pace began to tell on some men slogging along the muddy roads in the summer heat of northern Virginia and western Maryland. Lieutenant Colonel Farnham's nightly letter to Mary, sent from "between Edwards Ferry and Poolesville, Md.," said, "Our men are marching bravely but they have a hard time. Overcoats, blankets &c. cover our route . . . My dinner consisted of hard tack & a piece of ham broiled on a stick. We some expect a fight in this vicinity. If our brigade goes in they will not disgrace the state."

The way was now almost due north, beyond the Potomac River and into the green hills of Maryland. Pvt. Calvin Richardson, from Vershire, said, "I had been sick in camp with the mumps and was in bad shape when I started. My old army shoes got filled with mud and gravel and my feet were sore and blistered long before we reached Edwards Ferry, where we crossed on a pontoon bridge into Maryland."

In crossing the wide river, the Vermonters were passing from rebel to Union territory. "We now had reached Maryland where the inhabitants were generally loyal and appeared more prosperous," Sturtevant wrote. "Their fields were cultivated and everything indicated thrift and prosperity . . . On the Virginia side we were not able to buy or beg a canteen of milk or a loaf of soft bread, pie, hoe cake or anything that could satisfy our hunger. We were glad to cross over, as some said, into the promised land . . . for we were anxious for a change having been for some days confined to boiled pork, salt beef, hard tack and a little coffee. We found a mile or more after crossing Edwards Ferry, a convenient and suitable place for camping and were glad to lie down and rest. Some of our regiment had already fallen behind not being able to endure the heat, rain and marching. We had now marched sixty miles in three days."

As the brigade moved north, the hot and tired soldiers spotted cherry trees laden with ripe fruit. Sgt. George Scott, of Bakersfield and the 13th, recalled,

"The brigade halted one mid-day and some of the boys climbed some cherry trees near by. General Stannard sent an orderly to command them to return to the ranks, but they told him he was nothing but a private and he might go back to headquarters. Then the General sent one of his staff officers, who ordered them to get down. They obeyed, but as soon as his back was turned they climbed back. Then the general went himself and that was effectual."

One of the men in the trees was Pvt. Lewis Hix, who later remarked of Stannard, "I like the old General: he don't take on any airs, he isn't above speaking to a private."

Sergeant Scott then asked, "Has he ever had anything to say to you?"

"Maybe I can't repeat it all, for it kind of took my breath away, but I remember this much, 'God damn your eyes, get out of those cherry trees,' and I didn't wait to hear any more."

The brigade was now approaching Frederick, Maryland, not far from the old Antietam battlefield. On Sunday, June 28, the start of the march was delayed until 8 AM. "Our boys are pretty well used up," wrote Lieutenant Colonel Farnham. "Folks at home don't know anything about marching. The men must keep up no matter what they suffer, unless they have a certificate from the surgeon that they are unable to march & then they are taken into the ambulance. If they fall out without such a certificate, the provost guards, who march in the rear, arrest them & they are punished as stragglers. So you see that many weary, footsore boys have to keep up when they feel as tho' they could hardly move one foot before the other . . . Knapsacks have disgorged their contents today."

The brigade waded the Monocacy River near its mouth, and John Lonergan entered the river on his horse. Farnham described the scene: "Capt. Lonergan's horse got bemired in the Monocacy & the captain in dismounting got completely covered with mud. Of course he was the laughing stock of the whole brigade as he lay foundering & attempting to get out. The horse was finally got out alive."

On reaching the shore, according to Private Sturtevant, Lonergan said, "Too much liquid on the outside, and not enough on the inside, or it would not have happened."

Farnham wrote, "Those who have horses all take turns with those who need rest. I have walked half the way & someone has ridden. A great many of the men have picked up stray horses & they are loaded with sick boys and knapsacks."

Men in the 15th long remembered that their commander, Colonel Proctor, walked most of the way, allowing tired men to use his horse, Old Charlie. Henry Dudley said that Proctor came along and offered a ride "when I was tired out." Proctor asked, "Dudley do you think you could hit a half a sheet of paper at 60 rods tonight?" Dudley replied, as he mounted Proctor's horse, "I don't know colonel, but I could try."

Private Sturtevant said, "Our noonday halt of an hour was over, we were now refreshed and pushing on as fast as possible for Frederick City, Maryland, where General Hooker had established his headquarters. We reached Adamstown late in the afternoon and every girl young and old was out to greet and cheer and in every way to express loyalty to the Stars and Stripes . . . Beautiful young ladies with flags in hand lined the streets, some with their hearts in their hands, and as a good looking

Green Mountain boy came along lovingly extended their hands . . . We had seen nothing like it since we left Springfield, Mass., on our way to Washington. Some of the boys were given bouquets and pressing invitations to return after the war was over. Love at first sight had captured not a few. This quite enthusiastic and loyal greeting cheered our hearts and rested our weary legs and gave us new courage for the rest of the march. We passed through Adamstown and bivouacked for the night about two miles beyond, having marched twenty miles or more during the day. The weather had become hot and sultry, rain and sunshine nearly every day, and the road was full of small sharp pebble stones and many of the boys had become footsore with blistered feet and were well nigh exhausted, but only a few of our brigade had fallen out."

One sight that helped cheer the men was the sight of the 14th's commander, Colonel Nichols, on horseback in the company of his pet hen. According to Pvt. Fenimore Shepard, of Fair Haven, who later became brigade historian, the hen faithfully provided the colonel with one egg a day.

Private Jackson wrote, "Passed around Sugar Loaf Mt. through Licksville and encamped three miles out of Adamstown. The many bright, handsome faces we saw in those towns made us think of home."

That night Lieutenant Colonel Farnham apologized to Mary for the shortness of his letter, "as I am very tired." But he did inform her that a woman was along on the march: "Do you remember hearing that a Mrs. Capt. Williams came into camp of the 13th about the time they went down to Occoquan? Well, she came with the Regt. all the way from Occoquan to the place where we crossed the R.R. at Adam's town, two miles back of here. She must have had a hard time for she has ridden about seventy miles in four days."

Before he slept the night of the 28th, Myron Clark wrote in his diary: "Fine weather for marching and we improved it too. Hard."

According to Sturtevant, "News of devastation and fighting to the north of us ran through the camp . . . It was said that there were Confederate troops to the west, north and east of us and not far away, and no one was able to guess when and where we should meet them."

When darkness fell, General Stannard noted, "The men were much wearied. Some part of the day it was quite warm."

The march was taking its toll. After all, the men of Stannard's brigade had been soldiers for less than a year and were unused to long treks. Now they were expected to keep pace with a veteran corps. But remarkably, they were gaining on the rest of General Reynolds's units.

The next morning, June 29, according to Sturtevant, ". . . we took up line of march at seven o'clock." General Stannard had issued issued two orders aimed at speeding the pace. First, all officers' baggage was to be removed from wagons and burned, to lighten the tasks of the horses and make room for exhausted men. Second, no soldier was to leave the ranks to procure water while on the march. Sturtevant said, "This order, under the circumstances, seemed cruel, because of the weather 90 degrees in the shade and marching from dawn to sunset at our utmost speed stopping only at mid-day to rest and to eat a sandwich of hard tack and boiled pork."

Dr. Lucretius Ross, assistant surgeon in the 14th, recalled, "It was a hot forenoon, roads dusty, men dry and thirsty, the column passed a fine well, the temptation was too much for some, forty or fifty men were at the well when the Major appeared on the scene, looking up stragglers; I was waiting my turn. 'Surgeon!' demanded the major, 'What company are these men from?' After looking over the crowd I replied, 'From every company in the regiment.' Instantly his horse was turned toward the head of the column and I thought I heard swear words in the warm air."

Many years later Lt. Albert Clarke, who left a law practice in Montpelier to enlist, remembered, "Sometimes we marched for hours after the last drop of water had been drawn from the canteens. Many of the men became fevered and the sufferings of others were so intense that they fell out and crawled to some muddy pool to lave their cracking lips. Shortly before reaching Frederick, Maryland, we halted for a brief rest in sight of a well." Clarke noted that General Stannard had placed a guard by the well, fearing that the men would break ranks. "More than one captain," Clarke said, "went to him and sought permission to fill one canteen for the worst suffering men, but in vain. Hearing this and being deeply moved by a few pitiable cases in our own company, Lieutenant Stephen F. Brown of Company K handed his sword to a private, loaded himself with canteens . . . filled them and returned to his company and was soon arrested and obliged to give up his sword."

Lieutenant Brown wrote, "As they marched, men fainted and fell! Some with ghastly upturned faces as if dead. Others struggled convulsively in the dust! They had no helper! We were ordered to leave them in the road where they fell. I looked on the suffering men as martyrs of liberty, each bearing his cross from Gethsemane to his Golgotha, there to offer himself up to the good of others. Assisted by Oliver Parazo . . . I took the canteens of our exhausted comrades towards a well, beside which was a mounted cavalryman with drawn sabre, who, upon our approach, announced that he was a safeguard, and that we could get no water there."

Brown said he told the man he intended to get water, by whatever means necessary, and gave the man his name, rank, company, and regiment. "We filled our canteens from the well that would have supplied the brigade," Brown wrote, "and returned to our company. Capt. Blake immediately informed me that General Stannard had sent for my sword, and that I must consider myself under arrest. I remarked that my men should have water just the same while I was with them. My tent-mate . . . carried a camp hatchet in his knapsack. This I borrowed and carried instead of my sword, and proceeded as if nothing had happened."

According to Brown, Stannard soon eased the water restriction. "We were never, afterward, hindered from getting water," he said.

"At about twelve o'clock were passing through Frederick," Sturtevant reported. ". . . The clouds seemed to open and the rain fell fast as we reached the city . . . along the line of march on both sides of the street we saw fluttering in the breeze the Stars and Stripes and many a fair hand waved her white handkerchief as a token of friendship and expression of loyalty; and whenever we saw these evidences of welcome and encouragement hearty cheers from our ranks rang out along the line . . . While we were marching through Frederick City, rumor of a

Stephen Brown, of the 13th Vermont, en route to war

change of commanders of the Army of the Potomac reached us and was at once the sole topic of discussion . . . It was said that General Meade was to succeed General Hooker."

Lieutenant Benedict spent the previous night in Frederick, having ridden to overtake the brigade. He had missed the beginning of the march because, he wrote, "I was sent to Washington . . . by General Stannard, on special duty." After finding a room for the night in Frederick, the next morning, "I met Charles Carleton Coffin of the *Boston Journal* and *N.Y. Times,* who directed me to the headquarters of the army, just outside the city. Thither I hurried in a drizzling rain to find Col. Edward R. Platt, of General Hooker's staff, who, being a Vermonter I thought would know where I could find the Second Vermont Brigade. As I reached headquarters, I met General Hooker with several officers of his staff, riding away. As he returned my salute, I noticed the expression on his striking features, and said to myself: 'Something is going wrong with Hooker; he is not happy.' Later I learned that he had been relieved; had just turned over command to General Meade, and was taking his final departure from army headquarters."

Hooker had offered his resignation, which Lincoln accepted readily. Thus the Army of the Potomac had a new commander in the midst of what might be the war's decisive campaign. George Meade had been elevated from command of the Fifth Corps, and on June 28 he took charge of the massive army marching straight for the border of his home state, Pennsylvania. Hooker went south, away from the gathering storm, and soldiers in the Second Brigade saw him that morning, riding with his staff down their long line of march. "He looked downcast and sad," Private Sturtevant recalled.

Winding northward through gentle farm country, with the long ridge of South Mountain on the western horizon stretching away north and south as far as the eye could see, the regiment camped near the hamlet of Creagerstown, 12 miles north of Frederick. "Nearly all were exhausted and hungry," Sturtevant said, as the men in the five regiments faced another evening meal of hard crackers. In the evening local residents came into camp, offering food. "The price was high, but the food was the very best," said Sturtevant. "The great loaves of wheat bread and large fat cherry pies hot and steaming from the outdoor oven we deemed cheap at any price and quickly exchanged our greenbacks for bread, pies and milk bantering not a word as to price. I paid one dollar a loaf for bread and fifty cents a piece for cherry pies. We were hungry and cared not for money . . . We freely parted with our greenbacks and script and the thrifty Marylanders as freely parted with their pies, cakes and bread, butter, cheese and milk and their pockets were filled with money and our stomachs with food we bought and both were satisfied. I did not learn of any pilfering by any of the boys of our brigade while passing through Maryland."

Lieutenant Colonel Farnham sent two brief letters on Monday, June 29. The first, written at Frederick at 1 PM, said, "There are several corps here, all mixed up & we shall stop an hour or two and then on again. I don't know where we shall turn up, but, as the boys say, they can't keep us but about four days more. Nobody knows where Lee is, or where we are going."

That evening he wrote, "We are still on the march. This is our fifth day. I

*Capt. John Lonergan, who commanded Company A—
the Irish Company—of the 13th Vermont*
VERMONT HISTORICAL SOCIETY

am very tired & the men are almost tired to death . . . It has rained today & is very muddy. Twenty thousand men have passed over these roads within a few hours and they are tread into mortar. We have a long march tomorrow, as we are expected to reach Gettysburg, Pa. Where we shall be discharged I dont know."

Sergeant Palmer wrote that night, "Some of the soldiers' feet are in bad condition. I saw one round blister an inch in diameter on the bottom of the heel. 'Can't go far tomorrow,' said many a boy."

On the 29th, General Stannard's faith in his nine-months brigade wavered. He wrote in his journal, " . . . many of the men fell out . . . I think whiskey the cause. They marched until this time first rate. They count their time by days. Consequently they do not have any heart in the work. Officers as little as men."

The entire Army of the Potomac was on the move toward southern Pennsylvania, over a large portion of which the Army of Northern Virginia now ranged. But on learning that Meade's forces were north of the Potomac, Lee began to concentrate his forces. One Confederate brigade headed toward Gettysburg, a country college town of 3,500 people located 10 miles north of the Maryland state line. These Confederates were in search of shoes, approaching Gettysburg from the west on one of nine roads leading into town. The brigade was about to run into Union cavalry, and the resulting fight would bring blue and gray forces rushing in on those roads. The greatest battle of the Civil War was about to take place, with Meade bringing some 90,000 soldiers to the fray to confront Lee and his 70,000. Meanwhile, the Second Vermont Brigade was steadily gaining on the other units of the corps to which they had been assigned, John Reynolds's First Corps. That corps comprised some 8,500 men, before the addition of the Vermonters. With Stannard's men, its strength rose to some 10,500.

The next morning, tired and footsore, the brigade began the most punishing day of the march. "A number of men fell out yesterday & today it is hard marching & if we don't get rest I'll fall out tomorrow for I cannot stand it," said Myron Clark.

According to Private Sturtevant, "The 30th of June was . . . the hottest day's march thus far on our journey . . . We were, as it seemed, marching faster and faster each day; the regiment in the rear often had to double quick in order to keep up. The roads were now full of cavalry, artillery, infantry, ammunition trains, ambulances and frequently bunched and parked in such a manner as to impede our onward march, making our officers mad and progress slow and disgreeable. We reached Mechanicstown late in the afternoon and bivouacked for the night just south of Pennsylvania state line."

Henry Sparks, a private in the 13th, had just about had it. "The Quartermaster saw my condition," the Stowe man recalled, "and said, 'Pile on to the wagon when tired; march when you can.'" Alternately walking and riding, he kept on, and many of the country fellows stood the ordeal remarkably well. Another 13th soldier wrote of Pvt. Eli Hoag of Franklin, a farmhand and woodsman in civilian life: "There was not a man in the regiment that carried on his shoulders so full and heavy a knapsack. He hid things away of no value in his knapsack that he found around camp, or elsewhere, and when we started on the long march the last of June he had with him besides what was inside, on top . . . two woolen blankets, one winter overcoat, one rubber blanket, and these he carried to the end while many who started with woolen blankets and overcoats threw them away."

Said Sergeant Palmer: "The march this afternoon has been exceedingly hard. Two soldiers are left in houses on the way. At one time, near evening, as we had been exerting every chord for near two hours, splashing, splashing through the mud, faster, faster every moment, 'it seems,' said an old soldier, whose lips had never uttered a complaint before, 'it seems as though the General meant to kill the whole of us.'"

Pvt. James Wilson, 20, from Warren, was keeping the pace. A friend said, to lift his spirits, "Our time will soon be out and we shall go home." According to Pvt. Edward Fisk, of Waitsfield, Wilson replied, "I shall never go home alive. We shall have a fight and I shall be killed."

Stannard reported that night, "The men marched well and the road clear. Just before we reached Emmitsburg, the men fell out badly, in consequence of exhaustion. Was ordered to guard train for 1st Corps which was parked at the former place. Was in camp at 7:30, men very much exhausted, but they all came but two after a time. 6th day of continual marching. Roads very muddy and rained considerable every day. Marched 17 miles."

Lieutenant Colonel Farnham wrote to Mary at midnight, "Our boys are much better today than I supposed they would be. The roads are very muddy. It has commenced raining again. We have passed thro' a splendid country in Maryland. It looks like New England."

Up ahead in Gettysburg, Union cavalry under John Buford were on high alert, lookouts posted to the north and west of town expecting the approach of Confederates the next morning.

Ranging well ahead of the corps that night was Lieutenant Benedict: "I was sent forward by General Stannard with a report to General John Reynolds, commanding the First Corps. To reach his headquarters involved a ride of ten miles in the strong current of the Army of the Potomac, moving north. The march of an army of a hundred thousand men is an imposing spectacle, though the uniforms be dusty and the marchers footsore. All the roads and avenues throughout a wide stretch of country were thronged with artillery and army wagons; the newly-made but already hard-trodden pathways along the roadsides were filled with troops; the very landscape seemed to move with the movement of armed men. It was after sundown when I reached the head of the column of the corps, then halted for the night. I found General Reynolds at a little country tavern, about five miles from Gettysburg. He was resting from the fatigue of the day, his tall form stretched at full length upon a wooden settle. He received my report without rising, and scarcely raising his head from his arms, folded under it, made some inquiries in regard to the strength of the Vermont Brigade, sent back a message to General Stannard, and remarked that he was glad to have the brigade join the corps, for he thought all the men they could get might be needed before many hours. When I returned to the brigade, bivouacking near Emmitsburg, the word was running through the ranks that 30,000 rebs were in Cashtown, Pa., twelve miles away . . . The armies were converging."

Back at Emmitsburg, according to Sturtevant, the Vermonters "slept the sleep of the weary and awoke at dawn of day refreshed and ready to take up the line of march at the bugle call and push forward." As they stirred, well out of hearing to the north, Buford's pickets were exchanging fire with advance elements of Lee's army, moving toward Gettysburg from the west along the Chambersburg Pike through an early-morning mist. The dawn skirmish was about to become a major battle that would grow through the day. As the first light touched South Mountain, John Reynolds was out in front of his First Corps, making hard for Gettysburg, where he had received word that Buford was hard pressed.

"The morning rumor in the brigade," wrote Sturtevant, "was that General Stannard's Aide Benedict had brought an urgent message from General Reynolds to General Stannard to hasten forward his brigade, for likely in a few hours his corps would be engaged and he would need every soldier in his command. The morning of July 1 was cloudy and gloomy, all was commotion and confusion and the vast army all about was moving forward in the direction of Gettysburg, cavalry, artillery, infantry, a grand and impossing spectacle . . . Every road was filled with a moving mass of soldiers occupying every available avenue, path and field over which an army could march . . . Everything seemed to be on the move, the forest, cattle-dotted meadowlands, fields of waving grain . . . the clouds above and the land beneath apparently all moving in the same direction, was indeed a most ravishing and beautiful sight. An army of 100,000 equipped, arrayed for battle and on the march surpassed in grandeur and sublimnity all other spectacles ever witnessed by man. We, the 2nd Vt. Brigade, impatiently waited at Emmitsburg for a chance to take up our line of march."

Myron Clark wrote that morning, "Thought we were to lie still to day but about 8 we had orders to march. I washed myself, changed my shirt, threw away my old one so it makes my load only a Rubber & Fly tent & pr. socks, but it is enough."

Said Private Jackson, "About 11 AM passed over Mason & Dixon under a drenching rain storm and more than ankle deep in water."

About an hour along, according to Benedict, "Stannard received orders to leave two regiments to guard the corps trains, and to follow . . . with the rest of his brigade. The Twelfth and Fifteenth Regiments were accordingly directed to remain with the trains, and the other three regiments moved forward to the north. The forenoon was misty and rainy, but later the sun came out, and during the afternoon the heat was oppressive."

The Second Vermont Brigade had lost two-fifths of its strength, with the commands of Colonels Proctor and Blunt left to guard supply wagons. However, later in the day, along came brash Maj. Gen. Daniel Sickles, commander of the Third Corps. Sickles remembered, "On my way [to Gettysburg] I discovered Stannard's Vermont Brigade guarding a wagon-train. This was a duty those splendid soldiers did not much relish, so I took the responsibility of ordering them to join my command. You can hardly imagine their joy when they found they were going to join in the battle. They gave a rousing cheer."

Maj. Gen. Daniel Sickles, who ordered the 15th Vermont to Gettysburg

Sickles's memory, two decades after the battle, was rather inaccurate. He had, of course, come on just two of the brigade's five regiments. Lieutenant Benedict later corrected the account: "He inquired what brigade it was, and under what orders it was acting, and remarking that one of two such large regiments was enough to guard the train, directed Colonel Blunt to leave the smaller of the two with the wagons, and to have the other follow the division (Birney's) of his corps, then passing at a hurried pace. 'Let your men,' he said, 'drive up all the stragglers, and bayonet any man that refuses to go forward.'"

After a quick count, which the men disputed, the 15th Vermont was declared the larger regiment. Thus the 12th Vermont lost its chance to reach the battlefield.

Up ahead, the 13th, 14th, and 16th regiments pressed on. "The first news that the great battle we were expecting had begun reached us about noon on Wednesday, July 1," Benedict noted, "when a courier, spurring a tired horse, met General Stannard riding at the head of his brigade, eight or nine miles south of Gettysburg, with word from General Doubleday that a big fight was in progress at Gettysburg; that General Reynolds had been killed and he had succeeded to command of the First corps; that the corps and cavalry were fighting a large part of the rebel army and having hard work to hold their ground, and that Stannard must hasten forward as fast as possible."

Sturtevant wrote: "General Stannard at once passed the information down the line and gave orders to move as fast as possible and keep the ranks well closed up. We had been marching thus far during the day at our very best and yet we tried to move faster and faster observing General Stannard's anxious face as he rode up and down to converse with the Colonels and see if we were doing our best . . . General Doubleday's aid wheeled about his tired horse and returned in all haste over the road he had come to report the approach of General Stannard. We took up the march . . . and moved on over hill and through valley often in mud over our shoes faster than before until within about four miles of Gettysburg, as we reached an elevated tableland with open country to the north, we heard for the first time booming cannon way to the front of us which announced that artillery was actively engaged and a battle was raging . . . As the sound of cannon rolled down the valley and broke on our waiting ears the brigade involuntarily and suddenly halted and eagerly listened . . . We gazed inquiringly into each other's faces but spoke not a word."

Palmer said, "Suddenly, at four, the smoke, like a vast, dark, snow-drifting cloud, rolls up before us from the field of Gettysburgh."

General Stannard put the time that his men first heard firing at 3 PM, noting, "The men brightened up and marched in the very best of order."

According to Benedict, "The sound put life into the men, and there was no lagging after that. As we neared Gettysburg we began to see groups of excited inhabitants, most of them women, gathered wherever there was an outlook toward the field . . . The smoke of the battle was now mounting high over the field, and the 'sultry thunder' of artillery, rolling continuously and heavily, filled the air."

Palmer saw a woman by the roadside waving her arms and shouting, "Go-ahead boys, the rebels are off there."

Marching well back in the brigade was Pvt. Ira Smith, in the 13th, allowed to keep his own pace because he had been sick. He recalled, "[T]he boys began to throw away their cartridges and the night before reaching Gettysburg the boys of some regiments in front of us must have thrown away nearly all they had left and they were scattered along the ground. About the middle of the afternoon I succeeded in running onto General Stannard. I saluted and told him what I had noticed and, pointing toward Gettysburg where we could see smoke and hear cannonading, I told him 'we are in sad shape to meet the rebs.' Then a smart aide asked to see my cartridge box. I lifted the flap and it was full. The general very soon called a halt and ordered up ammunition and all cartridge boxes were filled."

Observing the passing of the army toward Gettysburg, from the porch of a roadside house, was Lt. Frank Kenfield of the 13th. Ill and with eyes almost closed from swelling, he had been left behind as the long march began. But soon, having partially recovered, Kenfield headed north on horseback, cutting cross-country, to overtake the army. Now in sound of firing, he looked for Stannard's brigade in the long column. Finally, he inquired for its whereabouts of none other than Major General Sickles, who told him the brigade was just back down the road. He had somehow gotten ahead of them. According to Sturtevant, when Kenfield reached his fellow Vermonters, his regimental commander, Colonel Randall, exclaimed, "Good God, Kenfield, where did you come from?"

Sturtevant continued: "We approached Gettysburg on the south by way of Marsh Run and crossing Willoughby Run to the Emmitsburg road southwest of Little Round Top and marched along this route until we came up with General Buford's cavalry; then crossed the valley and ascending Cemetery Ridge moving north near to the old cemetery . . . We met wounded on their way to the rear for surgical care and attention."

The Vermonters approached along a dangerous route, swinging west from the Emmitsburg Road toward enemy lines. They eventually turned back east and came upon the battlefield in the area of the soon-to-be-famous Peach Orchard. Up on Cemetery Ridge was Capt. Charles Horton, in a New York brigade of the 12th Corps. "Skirmishers were posted well to the front and preparations made for entrenching," he said, "when the head of a column appeared on our front and left. This was, I think, between six and seven PM. It was at first supposed to be the enemy, and came near being fired upon by the batteries, but was soon discovered to be the Vermont Brigade of Reynolds's corps."

Benedict added: "About sundown, as the brigade reached the outskirts of the field, I was again sent forward to report its arrival to the division commander and was thus the first man of the brigade to reach the actual battle ground. The artillery firing had ceased, but carbines were cracking on the plain as I rode across it. Passing inside of a skirmish line of dismounted cavalry I took my way to a low hill, which seemed to be the center of operations. Batteries were in position on the brow of the hill and troops forming along its top. They were what was left of the Eleventh corps, after its retreat through the village, rallying on a new line to meet an anticipated attack from the enemy, then apparently forming for an assault, at the foot of the hill. I rode up to a colonel who was directing the disposition of a line of battle. A white handkerchief was wound around his neck, through

Lt. Frank Kenfield chased Stannard's brigade to Gettysburg.

the folds of which blood was oozing from a wound in his throat. He directed me to where he thought I could find a portion of the First corps, and I found Gen. Rowley, commanding the Third division of the corps, stretched on the ground by a little white house. He was asleep, overcome by fatigue, or something, and his aides would not wake him. They told me to guide the brigade to that point."

Sturtevant reported: "Lt. Benedict returned with orders to join our corps on Cemetery Ridge. The sun was still shining just above the hills and mountains as we hastened forward to position guided by Benedict of Stannard's staff . . . We finally reached a position just at the close of day exhausted, completely worn out with seven long days of marching, especially the hurried march to reach the battlefield on July 1st, and we were told to lie down on our arms as we were, with straps and belts on and gun in hand ready for immediate action, for we were liable to be attacked at any moment. It was apparent as we reached this position that orders and commanders were considerably mixed up for on our arrival no one seemed to know just where we belonged or what to do with us. We were moved about from place to place."

Finally, well into the evening, the three regiments of Stannard's brigade lay down to rest. Albert Clarke recalled, "Stannard's brigade was stationed back of Buford's cavalry, near the copse of trees . . . where it remained over night." (That copse, or clump, of trees was about to receive worldwide fame.) The ever-faithful letter writer Colonel Veazey got off a note to Julia that night: "I am well, expect to be at home in a few days. Am too busy to write more." It was Veazey's first letter home in more than a week—testimony to the strain of the march.

Stannard noted in his diary, "The day's fight was over when we arrived and our corps had fought most of the day . . . Was in position at 7:30 o'clock. Men are much wearied, but feeling well."

There was one order of business that had to be attended to before the soldiers could enjoy a night's rest. An officer in the 13th approached General Stannard and was able to convince him to remove Lieutenant Brown from arrest. But his sword could not be located.

Back along the road, in the 12th Vermont, Edmund Clark likely spoke for the brigade when he wrote to his sister, "A more weary, tired and footsore crowd I think never lived. No use in trying to describe the march, but it was the most fearful thing I ever done in my life."

The 12th, left behind north of Emmitsburg, had then been ordered back south, to guard trains near Westminster, Maryland, some 20 miles distant. Farnham, reflecting on it all, wrote, "Most of them have blistered feet & I saw one man today whose feet were purple over two thirds of the bottom from the bloods settling. We marched eight days in succession & marched twenty three & a half the last day . . . It rained every day but one . . . The roads were very muddy & the men's shoes gave out entirely in some instances. Many of the men went barefoot & some tied up their feet in strips or rags, or went in their stocking feet till their stockings dropped off. Still not withstanding all that hardship we had but few stragglers. In repeated instances have I seen men who could barely limp along, refuse to ride or allow any one to take their guns. They had not been helped & they were determined to put it thro' alone."

Pvt. Edwin Hall, in the 15th, reported: "We got started at dark for the battlefield and reached the Brig. there at 11 PM. We were drawn up in line of battle and rested until next morning." Despite that account, it appears that the 15th did not actually join the other Vermont regiments until the following morning, sleeping somewhere near them in the darkness.

The long march to Gettysburg was over.

★

It is still possible to follow much of the Vermonters' route—some 130 miles—to Gettysburg, and the journey should begin on the north bank of the Potomac. (The unregulated development in northern Virginia makes the task all but impossible south of the river.)

From Washington, take River Road until it becomes a narrow country lane, ending at Edwards Ferry on the banks of the Potomac. This shaded boat launch in a riverside parkland is the site of the long pontoon bridge that carried most of the Army of the Potomac from Virginia to Maryland. Upon crossing the river, the army quickly passed over a lock of the Chesapeake and Ohio Canal, which is preserved. Once a small village stood at Edwards Ferry, and the white-brick canal house survives, as do the red-brick walls of a general store. The Vermonters would have seen both structures.

Follow country lanes north to Poolesville and try to imagine them choked with soldiers, the long line of blue-clad marchers rising and falling with the rolling landscape. Along Poolesville's main street are many buildings that witnessed the army's passing. Proceed north through Beallsville and Dickerson, turning left on Mouth of the Monocacy Road. At its end follow the sign that says AQUEDUCT and come upon a park where the Monocacy empties into the Potomac. A great arched stone aqueduct carries the old canal across the Monocacy. Walk out on the structure for a fine view of the river's mouth, where Captain Lonergan was dunked.

Proceed north to Adamstown, noting that the rocky summit of Sugarloaf to the east dominates the landscape. It was used by both armies as a lookout. On the sultry day that I first saw Adamstown, flags hung from many of the prewar houses, as if saluting the return of a Vermonter. Along the shaded main street the Second Brigade was cheered on its hot and tired way by flag-waving ladies.

North of the village, proceed northwest and uphill to Jefferson and pick up Route 340, which quickly joins with Route 15. Follow 15 into Frederick, through which the Vermonters marched and where many Civil War–era buildings still stand. Take Route 15 north from Frederick and exit onto Old Frederick Road, which generally follows the Second Vermont Brigade's line of march. Creagerstown, near where they camped and bought food, is a small ridgetop village that can be missed without the aid of a map.

Traveling north, the road moves closer to long Catoctin Mountain to the west. Pass through a covered bridge in a quiet valley and, just to the north, bustling Route 15 blocks the way. Turn east and do a U-turn as quickly as possible, returning to Old Frederick Road, and drive through Emmitsburg, filled with wartime structures.

North of the town, follow Old Gettysburg Road on what was the final leg of the Vermonters' long march. This is the Emmitsburg Road of wartime fame. It was in the vicinity of Marsh Creek, where an iron historic marker notes that the First Corps was headquartered before the battle, that the 12th and 15th regiments were detailed to guard wagons. Just north of Marsh Creek, the road climbs and then levels, the likely site of the "tableland" one Vermonter described where the Vermonters first heard the "sultry thunder" of Gettysburg. Approaching the battlefield, their route of march veered west, coming back toward the Union line in the vicinity of the Peach Orchard on the Gettysburg battlefield.

On entering the great battlefield park, Big Round Top and Little Round Top are seen to the east. North of them you can distinguish Cemetery Ridge by its long line of prominent monuments, including the solitary figure of George Stannard, sword in hand.

21

The night of July 1 found Stannard's Vermonters in the midst of the gathering Union army at Gettysburg. In the darkness, the exhausted soldiers may not have had much attention to pay to their surroundings. Still, it must have been obvious that they had stepped into a huge struggle that gave every sign of growing larger.

"The tired men stretched themselves upon their arms in a wheat field, and sank into the deep and reckless sleep of the weary soldier," Lieutenant Benedict reported. But before sleep was allowed, "Immediate command of the brigade was at once claimed by the commanders of the First, Third and Twelfth corps, and under contradictory orders from one and another, the brigade was marched and countermarched to and fro for an hour, to the immense disgust of the men who had had enough marching . . . It was finally placed on the right of Birney's division of the Third Corps, and the men stayed their stomachs on hard bread in their haversacks and sank to sleep upon their arms." Lieutenant Benedict summed up the first day at Gettysburg: "It had been a hard fought day."

The Vermont brigade, however, had missed savage fighting by arriving on the field toward evening. General Lee's forces had rolled in powerfully, meeting stubborn resistance from John Buford's dismounted cavalrymen, who fought bravely to the west of Gettysburg. Then General Reynolds's First Corps had come up, and the general soon took a fatal bullet. But the Confederate onslaught was too much, and the Union forces grudgingly gave ground. The addition of the Eleventh Corps helped little, and by late afternoon the Confederates were driving the Union forces through the streets of Gettysburg. Finally, Maj. Gen. Winfield Scott Hancock took command and rallied the Union forces on East Cemetery Hill. An attack ordered on the hill by Lee, late in the day, never materialized. At the close of the fighting the bloodied Union troops had been forced to retreat, but into a strong defensive position that was gaining strength hourly with the arrival of new units, including the Second Vermont Brigade. By morning the line resembled a great fishhook, curving from Culp's Hill to Cemetery Hill, then wending south along Cemetery Ridge to rocky and prominent Little Round Top. The Vermonters, in the First Corps now commanded by Maj. Gen. Abner Doubleday, were slightly behind the center of the line, apparently on the eastern slope of Cemetery Ridge and not far from the Clump of Trees.

Most of the Vermonters got a few hours' sleep. But as Benedict noted, some were sent forward: "A picket detail of 200 men of the Sixteenth, under Major [William] Rounds, brigade field officer of the day, was posted out in front, relieving Buford's cavalry. Colonel Veazey accompanied Major Rounds to the picket line, and with some difficulty, darkness having fallen on the field."

Veazey said, "Cavalry had done the skirmishing before dark until we relieved them. We posted the line across the pike that extended along from the village of G nearly parallel to our line of battle. With some difficulty we connected right and left with pickets of other corps."

Nor was there sleep for brigade commander Stannard. According to Benedict: "General [Henry] Slocum appointed Stannard general field officer of the day, or night rather, for the left wing of the army; and while his men slept their general watched the front and rode the lines in the moonlight. There, on the left of Cemetery Hill, at three o'clock in the morning, he met the vigilant commander of the army, who, having arrived at midnight, was satisfying himself by personal observation in regard to the disposition of the troops."

General Meade was on the field. In the shuffling of command that occurred with the continuing arrival of high-ranking officers, the First Corps division to which the Vermonters were assigned was turned over to Major General Doubleday. Over him, named by Meade to command the entire corps, was Maj. Gen. John Newton, a 40-year-old Virginia native and West Point graduate.

As the sun rose through a morning haze that promised midday heat, the Vermonters had a partial view of the growing spectacle. "The day . . . opened

HOWARD COFFIN

The Taneytown Road, which the Vermonters used as they moved to Cemetery Ridge, with the Leister house, Meade's headquarters, on the left

without firing, save now and then a shot from the pickets, but we saw considerable moving of the troops on our side behind the low ridge which concealed us from the enemy, and doubtless the same process was going on, on their side, unseen by us," said Ralph Sturtevant. "The batteries alone on the crests of the ridges menaced each other, like grim bulldogs, in silence."

The men on picket returned about sunrise. It was still early morning when, much to the surprise of everyone, the 15th Vermont joined the other Second Brigade regiments, in time for breakfast. In the night four wagons had wheeled up to the brigade, brought in from Rock Creek without anyone's official permission by the brigade's Acting Quartermaster Gen. Charles Field. Aware that the men's rations were nearly depleted, Field bravely made a night drive with his wagons filled with hard bread, pork, and coffee. He approached the battlefield by the Emmitsburg Road, which led through the dangerous area between the two armies and, eventually, into Confederate-controlled Gettysburg. But pickets from the Third Corps intercepted the little caravan and turned it to the right, or east, toward friendly lines. "We got up and made our coffee and roasted our meat as if nothing was going on," wrote Private Hall, in the 15th, "and then we got into line and waited for orders."

Benedict noted, "As the troops poured in and lines extended and batteries multiplied, the Vermonters of the Second Brigade awoke to the full realization of the fact that they were in the centre of the vast field of what might be the decisive battle of the war." Sometime early in the morning, Stannard's brigade was moved several hundred yards. Benedict said, "[T]he brigade joined Doubleday's division to which it belonged, which was lying in the rear of Cemetery Hill, a little east of the Taneytown Road." So the Vermonters were now in a wheat field across the road from, and perhaps 250 yards north of, the little white cottage of the widow Lydia Leister, now General Meade's headquarters.

About noon, instructions came for the 15th to return to its originally assigned duties of guarding wagons. "By order of Gen. Doubleday the Regt. was again sent to guard the train, then parked at Rock Creek Church about 2¹/₂ miles from the field," wrote Colonel Proctor, "where we remained the most of the afternoon." Stannard protested the order to higher authorities, saying that he could well use another regiment. The appeal fell on deaf ears. The 15th left the battlefield marching south along Cemetery Ridge, passing the base of Little Round Top and swinging east through the notch between that hill and Big Round Top. The regiment was off the battlefield for good. Proctor said, "The train having been divided, two companies were left with the ammunition and the remainder were ordered back to Westminster, Md., with the train which place we reached about noon July 3d."

From Westminster, Lieutenant Colonel Farnham in the 12th wrote to Mary, "All the wagon trains of the whole army are here. They cover acres of ground. There are from four to six hundred for each Corps. There are also large quantities of cattle here . . . One wagon near us exploded. It did no damage except the loss of the wagon. The old darkey who was driving came up with his eyes sticking out, but when one of the boys asked him if he was scared, he said, 'Dis darkey aint skeered no how.' He stopped and unhitched his mules after running the burning wagon out of the road."

Farnham's regiment had marched 23 more miles to reach Westminster. On arrival, Farnham said, "the men were so tired out that they laid down on the ground & went to sleep without stopping to put up tents."

Back at Gettysburg, the men of the 13th, 14th, and 16th regiments were getting some badly needed rest as the day warmed and morning gave way to afternoon. "General Stannard was notified that he was in command of the infantry supports of batteries upon the hill, and would be held responsible for their safety," said Lieutenant Benedict. "Our batteries were planted, not actually upon the graves, but close to them within the cemetery—such are the necessities of war." Stannard was thus spending a good deal of his time up along the crest of Cemetery Hill with the guns. He found that where the Taneytown Road crossed the hill on its way into the village of Gettysburg, there was an especially good view of the field. Save for an occasional shot from a picket or sharpshooter, all seemed remarkably quiet for a field on which two great armies were assembled. "Our regiments lay behind the hill through the forenoon, men lounging on the grass," said Benedict.

But off to the west, well behind Seminary Ridge, screened from the view of Meade's forces, Confederates were on the move toward the southern end of the Union line, preparing an all-out assault on Meade's left flank. Previously, General Sickles had advanced his Third Corps from Cemetery Ridge to some high ground he felt to be more defensible out along the Emmitsburg Road. The great bulge, or salient, he thus created in the Union line would be directly in the path of the building onslaught.

Benedict wrote, "About three o'clock . . . the ball opened with the whizzing of shell around our ears. The first thrown exploded over the Thirteenth regiment, and two or three men of it were wounded by fragments." Among those hit was Capt. Merritt Williams. "The shell that wounded him exploded above, in front, and a little to the right of him," according to Cpl. J.W. Hitchcock. "A small fragment entered the right breast, taking a downward and backward course to the liver."

Private Sturtevant recalled, "Lt. Albert Clarke of his company gave him brandy as he opened his eyes and feebly said, 'I am shot and feel as if my last hour had come.'" Williams would linger 11 painful weeks before that hour finally came.

The same shell exploded near Pvt. Alfred Olmstead, of Essex, and Private Slater, a musician who had just traded his fife for a rifle. Both men would be partially deaf the rest of their lives. "The shells fell like hail about us," wrote Private Williams.

Just before the barrage, Walcott Mead and a comrade had gone with a batch of canteens in search of water. Finding grazing cows, Mead proceeded to milk "the gentler one." Then a shell came screaming over Cemetery Hill and buried itself in the muddy field, throwing up a great fountain of slop, covering cows and men. Mead's cow did not flinch; Mead finished what he'd started, returning to the 14th on a dead run with the fresh milk.

Benedict said, "There was a sudden scattering to the rear of ambulances, orderlies, and all whose duties did not hold them to the spot." Albert Clarke: "Colonel Randall . . . upbraided the fugitives . . . citing to them, veterans though they were, the steadiness of the Vermonters, many of whom had never been under fire before."

Atop Cemetery Hill, General Stannard sent orders for his regiments to move closer under the hill, and this was promptly done, giving the brigade considerably more protection. Benedict was with Stannard at the time and he reported that the spot where they stood "was much exposed, not only to the enemy's artillery, but to his sharpshooters on the skirmish line to the front, whose bullets hummed by with unpleasant frequency. General Stannard was at one time whirled off his feet by the explosion of a shell which burst almost in the group of himself and his staff; but none were hurt, though a fragment of the shell cut a button on the breast of Lieutenant Prentiss."

As the shelling continued, Stannard was notified that a gap had developed in the picket line along the Emmitsburg Road. He immediately ordered a company from the 16th Vermont to fill it. Colonel Veazey sent forward Company B, commanded by Capt. Robert Arms. Stannard told Capt. Asa Foster of his staff to go with the company and see that it was positioned properly. "The company moved down under partial cover of Bryan's House," said Benedict, "and thence to the Emmitsburg road in front, and had barely time to get protection in a ditch by the road side when a volley from a body of the enemy whistled over them. By this time Captain Foster fell with musket balls through both legs, and was taken to the rear. Captain Arms deployed his company and advanced some distance beyond the road, connecting with the picket line on the right. There was some picket skirmishing here during the afternoon, in which two men of the company were seriously wounded."

Early in the cannonade Stannard had sent five companies—D, E, F, H, and K of the 13th, under the command of Lt. Col. William Munson—to support a battery near the crest of Cemetery Hill, thus halving Randall's command. Private Sturtevant described the position of those companies just to the right of where the Taneytown Road crossed the crest of the hill. The men, he said, lay down and found what shelter they could while nearby Generals Stannard and Doubleday "did not seem to pay any attention to the bursting shells or bullets that whizzed about them" and "sought the most elevated position, climbed up and stood on top of the wall with their field glasses."

Behind Cemetery Hill, the Vermonters stayed low and endured the barrage. The firing quieted and the day grew hotter as the afternoon progressed. About 4 PM, a mighty roar of battle erupted to the south. Cannon thundered, muskets rattled, and the Vermonters saw smoke rise just west of the Round Tops. The big Confederate attack, directed by James Longstreet under firm orders from Lee, had begun.

The fighting rolled steadily north, growing in intensity to a deafening fury. Soon Joshua Chamberlain's Maine troops, and others, were waging a desperate battle to save Little Round Top, the vital southern anchor of the Union line. Vicious fighting developed around rocky Devil's Den. It came on north, like a great wave striking a beach on the oblique, up the valley of Plum Run and on to the Peach Orchard and Wheat Field, where Sickles's advanced and exposed regiments took and gave a terrible pounding. Soon Sickles was down with a wound that would cost him a leg, as his corps was driven in retreat back to Cemetery Ridge. General Meade shifted troops to his left to meet the rebel onslaught.

On Cemetery Hill with a good view of it all, Sturtevant recalled, "We could distinctly see (except when too much smoke) as well as hear the continuous roar of cannon, the rattle of musketry and the yell and cheer as the lines swayed to and fro, as one side charged and then the other. While intensely watching the fighting in this direction, endeavoring to ascertain whether we were being driven back, our attention was called to the fact that a nearby battery had for some reason suspended firing; only two or three gunners stood beside their guns steadily gazing across the valley . . . Lieutenant Stephen Brown . . . saw the forlorn situation and hastened to them to ascertain the trouble, and after a brief interview came running back and reported to Captain [George] Blake and suggested assistance and asked to take some of the boys and go up and help them fire the guns of that battery."

Brown said he found the artillerymen "standing with folded arms beside their silent guns with powder-begrimed faces so blackened by smoke and dust of battle that the lines caused by sweat streaming down their faces enabled [me] to discern that they were white men."

Brown learned from the two surviving cannoneers that the battery had exhausted its ammunition. Upon asking where a resupply might be found, he was told, "Down the hill behind our guns." Brown then asked why the rounds were not nearer the guns. If nearer, one man said, the Confederate cannonade would likely explode them. The two artillerymen also claimed that they were under orders not to leave the guns, though Brown rather thought the fact that more shells were landing near the caissons than near the guns was a factor in their refusal to budge.

Captain Blake agreed that something should be done and gave Brown permission to take Pvts. Henry Meigs, Smith Decker, Daniel Manahan, and James Hagan with him. They helped pull a dead gunner off one of the pieces, and promptly ran for ammunition. "The ground was literally being ploughed with shell and sown with shot," Brown said later. "There was no single instance in which earth was not hurled against [me] by the enemy's missiles while [we] crossed and re-crossed the ridge."

Soldiers cheered as they watched Brown and his volunteers, exposed to the deadly fire, bring part of a devastated Union battery back into action. "Some carried shells from the caisson . . . and the others . . . assisted them in firing their guns," Sturtevant said. Of the privates who worked with him, Brown much later said that "each was serene as if walking with God," but the passage of years may have muted the experience considerably.

The battery was firing again, and soon other artillerymen came to relieve the Vermonters. Sturtevant wrote, "Lieutenant Brown and his boys returned to our position safe and sound with powder-smoked hands and faces. Some had holes and rents in the clothing they wore."

The afternoon lengthened as the battle moved closer. Stannard noted, "About 6:30 the fighting was immense." The Confederates were now pushing for the center of the Union line on Cemetery Ridge, just south and east along the crest from the Vermonters. As the sun went down toward South Mountain, Major General Hancock ordered the First Minnesota Regiment forward in a desperate attempt to slow the

*Maj. Gen. Winfield Scott Hancock, who ordered
the 13th Vermont to recapture cannon*

assault. In a matter of minutes, that regiment lost 215 of its 262 men engaged, the highest casualty percentage sustained by any Union regiment in the war.

Private Sturtevant: "About seven in the afternoon we could see that our lines way to our left were being slowly driven in though every inch of ground was desperately held until overwhelmed . . . We saw regiments and brigades hastily moving from our right wing and double quick across the field to the support of our battle lines . . . and the numbers and haste indicated a desperate need of immediate help to prevent Longstreet breaking through and possibly capturing Cemetery Ridge and Hill."

The Union line on the ridge broke, not far south of the Clump of Trees. Cpl. Joseph Hitchcock in the 13th, 21 years old, from Bakersfield, recalled, "While we were in reserve back of Cemetery Hill a vigorous attack was made in front. What a ghastly sight as wounded men and horses trooped over the ridge seeking shelter; men with arms or legs disabled, pierced in the head, the face, the bodies or extremities stained with blood, hobbling along supported by comrades, or alone. Horses covered with blood, wounds and gashes of head, body or legs; limping, some of them on three feet, the fourth gone or dangling in the air."

General Meade was at the Leister house when informed of the crisis by Capt. John C. Tidball. "If you need troops," Tidball advised, "I saw a fine body of Vermonters a short distance from here, belonging to the First Corps, who are available." Meade replied that he should tell General Newton to send in troops of the First Corps, then mounted his horse and rode toward the summit of the ridge.

"The nearing of musketry firing to our left indicated the spot," said Benedict, "above the din, the yell with which the rebels charge. There was scarce time to think what it meant, when orders came for our brigade to hurry to the left, where the lines were being borne back by the enemy."

General Newton told Major General Doubleday to move his division from behind Cemetery Hill over Cemetery Ridge and into the gap. Doubleday rode toward his division and found Colonel Randall on his gray horse, ready for action. According to Sgt. George Scott, the following exchange transpired:

"'Colonel what regiment do you command?'

"'The Thirteenth Vermont, Sir,' said Randall.

"'Where is General Stannard?'

"Randall replied pointing to a clump of oaks some 70 rods away.

"He then said, 'Colonel, will your regiment fight?'

"'I believe they will sir,' said Randall.

"'Have you ever been in a battle Colonel?'

"'I personally have been in most of the engagements of the Army of the Potomac since the war began, but my regiment being a new organization has seen but little fighting, but I have unbounded confidence in them.'

"The officer then said, 'I am General Doubleday. Introduce me to your regiment.'"

Doubleday spoke: "Men of Vermont: the troops of your state have done nobly well on the battlefields of this war. The praises of the old Vermont Brigade are on every lip. We expect you to sustain the honor of your state."

Scott said the men responded "with three cheers."

The Vermonters hurried into line and Randall gave the order to move forward at the double quick. General Stannard was still on Cemetery Hill, having just learned of the orders to move his brigade. "When I arrived the whole were moving," Stannard said, ". . . three regiments in the brigade amounting to about 1,800 men." The route led south along the Taneytown Road a short distance, then into the fields sloping toward the crest of Cemetery Ridge.

Lt. Col. George Meade was with his father, the commander of the Army of the Potomac. General Meade's view of the battlefield certainly confirmed his worst fears; there was, indeed, a gap near the Union center on the ridge. Advancing toward it was a sizable body of troops, Georgians under Brig. Gen. Ambrose Wright, better known as "Rans."

Young Meade recalled of his father, "As the general rode up toward the line the firing was very sharp, both of artillery and of infantry. Between the left of Gibbon and some troops further to the left, there seemed to be a vacant space in the lines, and apparently no organized body of troops there. Many of our men were scattered about, coming back. Directly in front of the general a line of the enemy could be seen advancing in the open between our ridge and the Emmitsburg pike . . . They seemed to be making straight for where we were. The general at once took in the situation. He once or twice looked anxiously in the direction whence Newton should come, and then rode slowly forward . . . Just as we were making up our minds for the worst, someone shouted, 'There they come, general.'

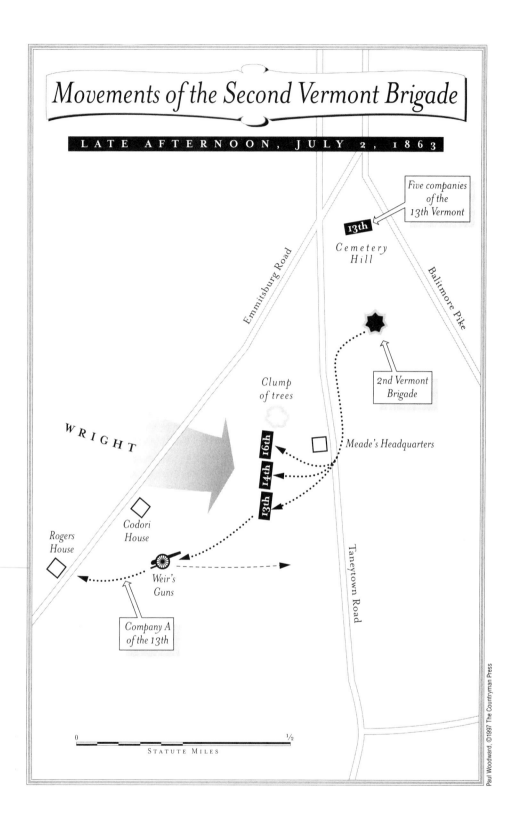

Movements of the Second Vermont Brigade

LATE AFTERNOON, JULY 2, 1863

Five companies
of the
13th Vermont

13th

Cemetery
Hill

Emmitsburg Road

Baltimore Pike

2nd Vermont
Brigade

Clump
of trees

16th
14th
13th

WRIGHT

Meade's Headquarters

Codori
House

Rogers
House

Weir's
Guns

Taneytown Road

Company A
of the 13th

0   ½
STATUTE MILES

Paul Woodward. ©1997 The Countryman Press

"Looking around," young Meade continued, "we saw a column of infantry come swinging down the Taneytown Road from the direction of Cemetery Hill, in close column of divisions, at a sharp double-quick, flags flying, arms at right shoulder, officers steadying their men with sharp commands. They came on as if on review . . . Newton came up ahead of the column and General Meade rode to meet him. They had a few hurried words; the head of the column wheeled to the right and moved up to the line of battle . . . Someone about this time rode up to General Meade and remarked at one time it looked 'pretty desperate.' 'Yes, but it is all right now, it is all right now' . . . I have always understood that at the head of the column was Stannard's Vermont Brigade."

Lieutenant Colonel Meade later said that he wished "I could command the power of description, so that I could give it as I saw it then." Up on Cemetery Hill, Private Sturtevant—with those five companies of the 13th—took it all in and later did his best: "Among those we noticed, that passed in our immediate rear into the Taneytown Road just south of our then position was the Second Vermont Brigade with Colonel Randall of the 13th in the lead, moving rapidly down the road, passing General Meade's headquarters into the field beyond, up over the ridge in the direction of our left center that appeared from our observation to be in great danger. We . . . recognized our colonel by the familiar colored horse he rode. It was a pretty sight, flags fluttering in the breeze, bayonets glistening in the setting sun as they passed. We saw them disappear down the hill into the valley in the direction where only a few moments before we heard the Rebel yell."

The moment was perhaps not fully appreciated until some 13 decades later when distinguished Gettysburg historian Harry Pfanz wrote: "The scene . . . must be beyond the imagination of twentieth-century man . . . There was the ever-present bitter smoke that blanketed the area, blurring and obscuring features that ought to have been clearly seen. It was evening and the sun was setting behind South Mountain to the west in the attackers' rear, adding its reddish glow to the flashes of rifles and cannons. There was the ear-splitting boom and barking from nearby artillery, duller thumping by the Confederate guns in the distance, and a roar produced by thousands of muskets near and far . . . There were individual and mass federal cheers, as in a stadium, competing with high-pitched, distant Rebel yells and screams of wounded horses. There was all of this and more."

Francis Clark, a Bridgewater lad in the 16th Vermont, recalled that the sun had set as he advanced onto Cemetery Ridge. In reality, it may have been too early for the sun to be down, but the smoke perhaps made it seem so. "The summer twilight was fast deepening," he said. "Back of us our artillery raged like an angry fiend . . . Through the gathering darkness and the clouds of smoke the lurid sheets of flame leaped forth in uninterrupted flashes from the enemy's guns. At this moment a scene was presented indescribably grand, surpassingly sublime . . . The idea of personal danger seemed entirely swallowed up. One might be in 50 pitched battles and not behold a spectacle to equal it, the array of men . . . the gathering darkness."

Some of Wright's brave Georgians—1,000 strong when they began their advance—had even approached the crest of Cemetery Ridge. But Union units on

Lt. Charles Randall,
son of the 13th Vermont's commander

both flanks responded well, and by the time the Vermonters came up, the Confederates were giving ground toward the Emmitsburg Road. Yet there was much work to be done, with a yawning gap still in the Union line on the ridge. The Vermonters crested the ridge with Randall on horseback leading his five companies. Close behind was the 14th Vermont, and then the 16th. Orders came immediately from General Meade for the Vermonters to deploy in battle line along the ridge crest. "We moved forward through the middle of the fire to the front," according to Private Williams.

Then came the 16th, filing in to the 14th's right. As Colonel Veazey's regiment came on the crest, it deployed near some Second Corps artillery, under fire from Confederate batteries near the Emmitsburg Road. "When we came up to the batteries on the crest I saw no supports whatever with them," Veazey said later. "The smoke obstructed the view, but little could be seen. Here we encountered a furious cannonade." One shell burst along the deploying line of Veazey's regiment, killing Sgt. Moses Baldwin and Pvt. Sylvanus Winship and knocking down others.

The always aggressive General Hancock encountered Colonel Randall, who was out ahead of his regiment on the ridge. According to Sgt. George Scott, "General Hancock had been endeavoring to rally the supports of [Lt. Gulian Weir's Fifth US] battery, now in danger of capture by a regiment of Wright's brigade. Weir's horse had been shot and the lieutenant was stunned by a spent ball. The gunners had abandoned three of his guns." Hancock pointed to the cannon, far out in the smoke toward the Codori house along the Emmitsburg Road: "[Hancock] said, 'Colonel where is your regiment?'

"'Close at hand,' said Randall.

"'Good,' said Hancock, 'the enemy are pressing me hard—they have captured that battery yonder and are dragging it from the field. Can you retake it?'

"'I can, and damn quick too, if you will let me.'

"At that moment they both observed a rebel brigade deploying from the woods on the left and making for the guns.

"'Dare you take the chance, Colonel?' said Hancock.

"'I do, sir,' said Randall.

"'Then go in.'"

Though Meade had told the Vermonters to stay atop the ridge, nobody was going to countermand any order given by Hancock the Superb. They went forward.

Just as the charge began, Pvt. Edward Fisk, of Waitsfield, was hit in the knee by a spent shell. Though the wound was painful, he limped along and did his best through the rest of the battle. A fragment of the same shell also hit Pvt. Lester Dow, from Duxbury, in the foot, taking him out of action.

Down the long, easy slope of Cemetery Ridge went Randall's five companies, no more than 350 men. Randall, on his big gray, led the charge with Captain Lonergan's Company A, and he had not gone far when his mount was struck in the neck by a piece of exploding shell. The animal fell, pinning the colonel to the ground. Pvt. Henry Sparks, from Morrisville, was the first to reach him. "Damn them," he heard the colonel growl. "They did not get me that time." Sergeant Scott heard Randall shout, "Go on boys, go on. I'll be at your head as soon as I get out of this damned saddle." Other soldiers joined Sparks in rolling the horse off their commander. In so doing, Private Sparks suffered a rupture. Randall's son Charles, a lieutenant though only 16, saw his father go down and requested permission of his company commander to go to his aid. He returned quickly. "He is all right," he reported, "it was only his horse."

Lt. Albert Clarke saw Randall run forward "hatless but with sword in hand." Scott said, "In a moment he was up on his feet, running, with a limp, around his regiment to the front. Swinging his sword in the air, he cried, 'Come on, boys. I'm all right.'"

A fragment of the shell that struck Randall's horse also hit 18-year-old Pvt. Albert Chase, of Middlesex, in the temple. His friends at first thought him dead, but he soon began to crawl and they helped him to the rear. He would suffer from headaches for 20 years, until a running sore developed where he had been hit; he then died within days.

Suddenly Pvt. Major Smith was down. A comrade recalled, "He nearly doubled up and, turning to Lieutenant Clarke, he said, 'I'm killed. My bowels are all coming out.' The officer pulled his hands from his stomach and saw that there was no blood but that his belt clasp was doubled up like a fist . . . His belt plate had saved his life."

Sergeant Scott said, "The Confederates were surrounding our guns and dragging them off the field. After advancing . . . to within 10 rods of the guns, we halted. Volunteers were called for to retake the guns . . . Perhaps because I could run faster than those who followed me, I was more than a rod in advance . . . I reached the first gun. Others followed and we dragged it to the rear . . . The enemy did not await us. They abandoned the guns and fled."

Said Lieutenant Benedict, "The Georgians were driven from the guns; the cannoneers withdrew two of them, and four were passed to the rear by hand, by the men of the Thirteenth."

General Hancock saw it all: "The guns were drawn from somewhat higher ground to the front, by my direction, by a Vermont regiment, under fire."

There was a pause while the recaptured cannon were brought back to safety. It was a struggle, but one of the haulers was Pvt. John McMahon, brigade wrestling champion. Lt. Albert Clarke joined in and McMahon, after the guns were inside Union lines, shook his hand. "By thunder, lieutenant," he said, "you ought to be a brigadier general."

During the process Clarke heard a veteran soldier from another unit ask, "What troops be you fellers?" The reply came in unison, "Green Mountain Boys."

"Well," the soldier said, "I thought you must be green, or you'd never gone in there."

Back down in the valley of Plum Run, Colonel Randall was still full of fight. Benedict described the situation: "They did not stop there, however, but pushed on to the Emmitsburg Road, stepping over some Confederates who were lying in the ditches, on the way, one of whom rose and fired at Major Boynton's back after he had passed him." Several Vermonters took aim at the wounded rebel, but Boynton told them not to shoot and the man was taken prisoner.

Rifle fire now hit the Vermonters from the vicinity of a house south along the Emmitsburg Road. Randall turned to Captain Lonergan and his Irish Company: "That house is full of sharpshooters, take your company and capture them." Cpl. Eli Marsh heard him say, "Boys, those fellows are firing at us. We will drive those damned rebels out of those buildings or kill them—about face charge."

Lonergan remembered, "Near the door I saw an officer with a rifle in his hands and called for his surrender, demanded and received his sword and shouted, 'Come out here, every confound one of you.' My order was obeyed instantly, for the Confederates came tumbling out until we had a large number of prisoners. Each man laid down his gun, until I had a considerably larger number of men as prisoners than I had in my entire company."

Henry Stevens, a private from Enosburg, recalled, "As we charged the rebels, about fifty of them stopped under cover of a house and barn. As we came to the buildings they ran for the woods a little way back. The colonel said, 'Halt!' without effect. Then he very emphatically said, 'God damn you boys stop that running.' They stopped, threw down their guns and came back prisoners."

What the Vermonters had attacked was the Peter Rogers house, fronting on the west—the Confederate—side of the Emmitsburg Road. The number of prisoners taken isn't clear; some men spoke of 50 and others of 80. Randall reported 200, but he had a tendency to overstate.

On Cemetery Ridge, General Stannard had caught up with his brigade. "I was at this time much annoyed at not knowing where he [Randall] was," Stannard recalled, "and sent every way to find him, and was much pleased when he reported his condition."

"An aide to General Stannard rode down to see what we were up to," Sergeant Scott reported. "Our colonel was not the most modest man in the world, and, as the aide approached, said, 'Captain, report to the general what we have done. We have captured four guns, taken two from the enemy, driven them half a mile and captured 200 prisoners. Tell him we propose resting on our arms until he acknowledges our achievements.'"

Certainly, the number of prisoners claimed by Randall was an exaggeration. And the claim of seizing two rebel cannon was untrue. So far as is known, General Lee lost no cannon at Gettysburg. The truth may lie in the recollection of Pvt. Rufus Farr of Company A: "Colonel Randall, after we secured [Weir's] cannon, sent Captain Coburn with his company to take what appeared to be a battery, but turned out to be caissons that had been blown up by our guns."

The Vermonters were dangerously far to the front, and Randall soon thought the better of holding his advanced position until receiving confirmation of his regiment's exploits. Sergeant Scott: "Our colonel soon discovered a movement on the part of the enemy to flank and capture us, and, preferring to lose his laurels to imprisonment in Libby prison, he led us back to our lines. As we approached our troops, the soldiers who had witnessed our achievement gave us cheer after cheer for the gallant nine months' boys in their first engagement."

Joining in the cheering were the five companies of the 13th Vermont that had been posted on Cemetery Hill. They had returned while Colonel Randall and their comrades were recapturing cannon and attacking the Rogers house. The 13th remained united through the remainder of the battle.

In the gathering darkness, the Confederates launched determined attacks to the north, in the area of Culp's Hill and Cemetery Hill. Like their assaults on the Union left and center of the afternoon and evening, these attacks on the right also failed. The Vermonters must have heard the late racket, but made no mention of it. Clearly they were tired, and as the stars appeared, sleep came fast. "They slept the sleep of the tired soldier, and heeded little what was going on around them," said George Benedict. The Vermonters stayed where they had filled the Union gap, on the forward slope of Cemetery Ridge, in the front line.

Benedict wrote, "After nightfall of Thursday Colonel Veazey was detailed as division field-officer of the day, and taking the Sixteenth Vermont Regiment and a detail from the brigade on his right, posted a picket line along the front, from the right of Codori's house on the Emmitsburg Road through the low ground to the left, till it joined the picket line of the Fifth Corps. Three companies were deployed on the picket line, and the remainder of the regiment lay as picket reserve."

"It was," said Veazey, "the saddest night on picket that I ever passed. The line ran across the field that had been fought over the day before, and the dead and wounded of the two armies, lying side by side, thickly strewed the ground. The mingled imprecations and prayers of the wounded, and supplications for help, were heart-rending. The stretcher bearers of both armies were allowed to pass back and forth through the picket lines, but scores of wounded men died around us in the gloom, before anyone could bring relief or receive their dying messages."

This gun marks the position of the recaptured Weir's cannon on Cemetery Ridge.

Francis Clark recalled, "There soon was a lull, for darkness, like a gentle spirit, interposed, and put an end to the carnage. We descended nearly to a ravine or depression which served as a dividing line, between the swells or elevations upon which each army had respectively posted its artillery . . . Here we halted. About 9 o'clock we were marched still farther to the front and posted as picket guard, or line of skirmishers." He continued, "Here and there the moon revealed, amid the trampled grain, prostrate forms, whom no long roll, or reveille, could rouse again. The air was tremulous with a sound, low and almost indescribable, resembling a far-off and just audible moaning of a forest of pines. It was the groaning of the wounded swelling up from field and wood and blending for miles in one low inarticulate moan . . . After a fruitless search for water I wrapped myself in my blanket and, with the wounded on either side, lay down to sleep. With up-turned face to the mild majesty of the Queen of the Night as she looked down so calmly upon us, and with flitting thoughts of home, and friends, and other times, breathing a prayer, I fell asleep."

Along Cemetery Ridge, James Hartwell, a private in the 13th said, "[t]he firing had ceased for the day and nothing was heard save the groans and prayers of the wounded and dying. I espied a short distance from where I was standing four women on their bended knees with bandages and cooling drinks, doing all in their power to lessen the pain and prolong the lives of those who had fallen. God bless them for they passed none by, not knowing or caring where they were born, at what altar they knelt, or whether they were clad in blue or gray . . . Upon inquiring I learned that they were called Sisters of Mercy."

Benedict reported: "During the night word was brought by a prisoner to Colonel Nichols that General [William] Barksdale, of Mississippi, lay mortally wounded on the field in front of his line. Colonel Nichols at once sent out a detail under Sergeant [Henry] Vaughan . . . who brought him in on a stetcher and took him to a small temporary hospital in the rear. His last message, 'Tell my wife I fought like a man and will die like one,' was delivered to Sergeant Vaughan . . . His body, with ball-hole through the breast, and legs bandaged and bloody from gun-shots through both of them, lay in the rear of the position of the Vermont Brigade . . . and was temporarily interred upon the spot."

Nichols recalled years later: "He was so badly wounded that he wanted to be brought in on a stretcher. I then sent back to the battery hospital and borrowed a stretcher and sent out 8 instead of 4 men with Sergt. V. (Barksdale weighed 240 pounds.) When the men took him from the ground one of the men picked up his hat and glove and handed to him but he said he did not want them and gave them to the man that picked them up and the man brought them to me. I have them now."

One stretcher bearer, Pvt. David Parker of the 14th, cradled Barksdale's head and spoon-fed him coffee. The general lingered past midnight, dying on July 3.

"As the moon was rising," Benedict recalled, "I rode out upon the field in front of our lines. My horse started aside at every rod from the bodies of dead men or horses; and wounded men, Union soldiers and rebels in about equal proportions, were making their way slowly within the lines . . . General Stannard, anticipating harder fighting on the morrow, wanted more cartridges for his men, and sent me to find the division ammunition train . . . I spent the rest of the night in search of these wagons, zig-zagging around the field wherever I saw a camp fire or light. I stopped at a dozen Pennsylvania barns, looking more like large factory buildings than our New England barns."

He described the horrors: "Each of them was a field hospital; its floor covered with mutilated soldiers, and surgeons busy at the lantern-lighted operating tables. By the door of one of them was a ghastly pile of amputated arms and legs, and around each of them lay multitides of wounded men, covering the ground by the acre, wrapped in their blankets and waiting their turn under the knife. I was stopped hundreds of times by wounded men, sometimes accompanied by a comrade but often wandering alone, to be asked in faint tones the way to the hospital of their division, till the accumulated sense of bloodshed and suffering of the day had become absolutely appalling. It seemed to me as if every square yard of the ground, for many square miles, must have its blood stain."

Benedict's search proved futile, and on his return—not long before dawn— he had a close call. "The moon, now setting, had become obscured, and, lacking its guiding light and following a road which I supposed to be that over which I went to Rock Creek Church, but which was really, as I learned afterward, the Baltimore pike, I found myself toward morning passing under a tall arch, beyond which stood two field pieces in the roadway. Everything was still around," he remembered, "but as I rode between the guns, a form rose beside them, and a voice asked where I was going. The arch was the entrance to the cemetery; and the rebel lines were near by at the base of the hill. I had completely lost my way, and but for the warning of the artillery man I should now be on my way to Libby prison."

Private Sturtevant was out on the battlefield that night, with Sgt. James Halloway, looking for wounded Vermonters. The pair went all the way to the Emmitsburg Road and stopped at the Rogers house, where, Sturtevant said, the house and outbuildings "were crowded with wounded, some dead, and others in the last struggle of life side by side and most of them in the Rebel army." They continued on west of the road until a Union picket stopped them, whispering, "Better go no further in that direction, for Johnny Rebs are only a few rods away." On turning back, they came upon a wounded Confederate.

"It was a young man not more than twenty-two," Sturtevant said, ". . . belonged to a Georgia regiment, declared his home was in Georgia, said he had father and mother and brothers and sisters and a happy home, that he had been in battle before but none so terrible. He had been shot through both legs above the knees . . . His pressing request was to be taken from the field, for he said, 'The battle is not over, there will be awful fighting here tomorrow and I do not want to be run over and crushed to death by horses feet and cannon wheels.' We made a stretcher out of our shelter tent and tried to carry him, but he could not endure the pain in that position. Then, we, one on each side attempted to carry him in an upright position, but his wounds were serious and he could not stand the pain, and at his request we moved him a little ways where the dead were not so thick, made him as comfortable as possible and cheered him with the hope that an ambulance would find and take him to our hospital for surgical care before morning."

The second day of fighting at Gettysburg had ended. Still the Army of the Potomac held its formidable fishhook line, from Round Top to Culp's Hill. More reinforcements were coming in, among them the Sixth Corps, including the First Vermont Brigade. Lee had severely tested the Union right and left; in the morning he would have a go at the right again, then try to smash the center. Near that center the Second Vermont Brigade—tested for the first time in battle—slept the night of July 2–3. The men were down on the edge of the low ground toward the foot of Cemetery Ridge, and they may have felt rather vulnerable, there in the front line. Even in the darkness they could make out the outline of the Codori house and barns, and the battered Rogers house near the Emmitsburg Road. In the ranks of the 13th was 19-year-old Pvt. Jude Newcity, who had helped recapture Weir's cannon. On the march to Gettysburg he had repeatedly said that the only thing needed to end the war was one great battle, and it was coming soon. Now he felt he was helping to win that battle, and before going to sleep, he was heard to say of the morrow, "We shall win the day and then for home."

★

At Gettysburg today, the little white farmhouse of the widow Leister, which was appropriated by General Meade for his headquarters, still stands along the Taneytown Road. Across it, and somewhat north, is a two-story postwar house now used for office space by the National Park Service. The field behind it and in front of the huge Gettysburg National Tower is where Stannard's brigade waited to go into action on July 2. As artillery fire came in, Stannard moved his brigade closer to the shelter of Cemetery Hill. New graves added to the expanding cemetery now fill that area. The National Tower, a private enterprise, whose ugly modern steel framework mars the Gettysburg battlefield, has stood for nearly 30 years despite lengthy efforts by preservationists to bring it down. It surely stands on land once occupied by the Second Vermont Brigade.

Most of the scores of monuments that stand along northern Cemetery Ridge honor the deeds of the battle's third day. But just to the front of the Clump of Trees is a marker honoring the attack of Wright's Georgians, who may well have penetrated deeper into Union territory than the storied charge of the next day. It is a good place to ponder how close the Confederates came to victory at Gettysburg, not only on the ridge, but also at Culp's Hill, Little Round Top, and Cemetery Hill. Shelby Foote, writing from the Confederate geographical perspective in his Civil War narrative, said that the Georgians "crested the ridge and stood poised there, silhouetted against the eastern sky for one brief fall of time as they pierced the enemy center."

The Codori house and barns still stand along the Emmitsburg Road and just south, across the road, a marker denotes the site of the Rogers house.

Robert E. Lee, Confederate commander

22

For Stannard's Vermonters, Friday, July 3, began with cannon fire well before dawn, a fitting start to what would be a long and bloody day. "I reached brigade headquarters as day was breaking," Lieutenant Benedict said, "and as the cannonade of Friday morning began, a shell struck near my feet as I dismounted. A minute later another broke the leg of an orderly's horse ten feet away. Still another took off the hoof of another horse, close by." Private Williams noted in his diary, "The rebel batteries opened fire on us at five o'clock in the morning." Benedict wrote, "The artillery fire was quite sharp for a while in the morning from the rebel batteries opposite us, but died away in an hour or so. It was perhaps intended to divert attention while the enemy was preparing a desperate attack upon our extreme right."

The fire was coming from a rebel battery on Seminary Ridge commanded by William T. Poague in Isaac Trimble's division. Private Sturtevant recalled, "The reveille that awoke us on the early morning . . . was the martial music of General Longstreet's booming cannon now pointed along the low ridge that he gained the afternoon before. We could plainly see the flash of powder and puff of smoke and then hear the horrid crash of exploding shell as they passed over or fell among us."

Myron Clark was in the ranks of the 14th, the 21-year-old keeper of a diary who had written late in the long march, "I'll fall out tomorrow for I cannot stand it." But the next day he had washed and changed his shirt and made it to Gettysburg. Sometime early July 2 he wrote, "Picket skirmishing this AM. Some artillery." The next entry is in another hand. "July 3, 1863—Early in the morning, about 4 o'clock, the Batteries commenced firing & CLARK WAS KILLED at nearly the first fire by a solid 12 lb. shot taking off all the back part of his head, killing him instantly. He was a good boy and soldier. The whole Co. mourns his loss & Especially his Capt. Such are the fortunes of war and they are deplorable."

The shell that killed Clark had blown up a caisson, wounding several other members of the 14th. To the front of the 14th and 13th regiments was a very shallow ravine, running north–south, that appeared to more and more of the soldiers a better natural defensive position than the low stone wall behind which they lay. But there was a problem: The ravine, filled with brush and boulders, was well to the front of the main Union line on Cemetery Ridge, and if the Vermonters were to take advantage of it, they would be considerably isolated.

The explosion of the caisson that killed Private Clark convinced Stannard that the place should be used. According to Benedict, "Gen. Stannard adjusted a little the position of our regiments. The Sixteenth was on the skirmish line in front. The Fourteenth was moved forward several rods to a line where some scattered trees and brush afforded partial cover. The Thirteenth was placed to the right and a little to the rear of the Fourteenth. No troops were in front of us."

Since the depression led away from the Union lines as it ran south, the 14th was now a bit closer to the enemy than was the 13th. To the left of the 14th, and a few yards farther front, was the group of men that made up the 16th's reserve. Near the Emmitsburg Road, the majority of Colonel Veazey's boys had been under some fire from first light.

"At quarter before 4 AM . . . the enemy sent down a line of skirmishers against my picket line, and the skirmishing continued more or less all the forenoon, my line was reinforced by a dozen sharp shooters," Veazey said. According to Lt. Francis Clark, "Not a rebel could show his head without the compliment of a bullet. They were particular in showing the same deference to us."

The cannon fire lasted less than an hour. "The shell from the enemy and from our own guns passing over our heads screeching as they passed," Sturtevant recalled. ". . . The pieces of exploded shell that fell and struck the damp ground all around inclining the boys to move a few inches this way or that way and flatten out and hug the ground . . . but we were becoming used to it and remained pretty quiet and carried on conversation without lifting heads or hands . . . The cannon on our left and front stopped as suddenly as they commenced, and then we eagerly watched for the expected advance and charge, but no solid lines of gray appeared and only the increased firing on the picket line."

Benedict reported, "About six o'clock the musketry firing became tremendous about a mile to our right. We could see nothing of it but the white smoke rising above the tree tops; but the volleys rolled for six hours. The sound did not recede or advance, and we inferred that each side held its ground."

The Vermonters were hearing the strong Confederate assault on the far Union right, against Culp's Hill. "During the forenoon," said Colonel Veazey, "the great battle on the right was fought, which created a good deal of alarm as it seemed to be directly in our rear, by reason of the turn in our line." The nearly morning-long fight on Culp's Hill ended with Confederate repulse.

Sometime that morning, a Minnesota soldier passed Stannard's men. "The Vermont Brigade consisted of full regiments in new uniforms," he remembered, "and was therefore noticeable in contrast with the thinned regiments, in dusty garments, of the Second Corps."

General Stannard and his staff were just to the rear of his advanced regiments. "During the forenoon the Confederate sharp-shooters discovered from the movements of staff officers to and fro around General Stannard that a general officer was closer to the front at that point than any other, and began to pay especial attention to him," said Benedict. "After a ball had passed through his coat and another cut a piece from the rim of his hat, he thought it was time to return these favors, and a dozen United States sharp-shooters, under a tall sergeant, were sent down in front."

Stannard made no mention of the close call, noting only, "The weather was extremely hot through the day, and some men nearly fainted from the effects of the heat . . . I had to move some portions of my command to shelter them from the rays of the sun."

With the end of the assault on Culp's Hill, "almost absolute quiet prevailed along the lines," Benedict wrote. Around midmorning, according to Sturtevant, "Lt. Albert Clarke in the 13th saw that a nearby rail fence might be readily converted into a low breastwork and placed considerably in advance . . . Clarke called Colonel Randall's attention to it, and obtaining his consent called for volunteers to go out and do the work of building a breastwork with the fence rails." Randall, in turn, broached the idea to Stannard, who, according to Capt. Aro Slayton, said, "That's right, colonel go ahead, go ahead." Sturtevant added, "Sgt. George Scott was the first to volunteer and then others followed until some twenty or more of our regiment . . . charged the rail fence, carried the rails . . . in advance and further down the slope and laid up a temporary bulwark of rails perhaps two feet high parallel to the battle line then occupied by the 13th regiment."

Lieutenant Clarke wrote that the rails were placed "45 yards in front of the regiment . . . Though there was a sharp fire of sharpshooters . . . not one was injured." Pvt. Sumner Warner remembered, "We did a good job and quickly, too, for the bullets . . . made us hurry. A bullet hit a rail being carried on the shoulder of Fernando Willett that brought him to the ground, rail and all, but it did him no harm."

Sometime in the morning, Colonel Randall approached Pvt. Ziba McAllister and told him to take his two horses to the rear. "If anything happens to me," he said, "you see that Jim gets home all right, for this is going to be a hot fight and I do not know what will happen." McAllister said he also took the colonel's young drummer boy son—and the horses—far to the rear near the Baltimore Pike.

The quiet continued toward noon, and the day grew very hot. "A detail buried some of the dead, so as to lessen the stench, and they also escaped unharmed," according to Albert Clarke.

On July 2, according to Pvt. Cornelius Palmer, "Some of us had noticed three or four cows traveling from the direction of the Codori farm buildings . . . During the forenoon of July 3 we were getting short of water and recalling the incident of the cows, the farmer boys knew they were going for water, and it was decided by five or six of us that one of our number should take the canteens and all and try to find the spring. We 'drew cuts' and as usual [I] drew the short straw."

Palmer had enlisted in place of his brother, Simeon, and was known in the regiment by his brother's name. Palmer recalled that he "strung the canteens across [my] shoulders . . . and soon located the spring by reason of a bunch of boys from other commands being there ahead . . . We found a square box sunk in the ground, and the water entering the box through a hole in the bottom. So many boys with canteens were there that they were in turn scooping the water up from the bottom of the box as fast as it ran in. We could get about a teacupful at each scrape . . . this made it mighty slow work for eight or ten of us to fill six or eight canteens apiece. Soon after arriving at the spring a rifle ball struck in the mud at our feet, and it was then said that a rebel sharp-shooter had wounded a comrade at the spring a few minutes before. I had secured about one canteen of water, and

George Meade, Union commander at Gettysburg

calculating the time between shots, I left the spring just before the third shot was due. When I was about three or four rods away I heard the boys again yell at the third shot. On my return to the company and passing in the rear of the batteries, I came on a sharp-shooter. I recall his heavy gun was resting on a frame, and a telescope extending over his rifle barrel. I told him of my experience at the spring. He had learned of one of the boys being hit, and said he had been trying for an hour to locate the Johnnie, and thought he had him and pointed to a tree standing away down on the opposite slope nearly as far down as the Cadori house. He said he had seen puffs of smoke come out of the tree top three or four times, and he was trying to get his glass on him. Nothing more was said and I returned to my comrades, with just about water enough for each one short drink."

Private Sturtevant wrote, "Our lines were continuously menaced by sharp shooters, and we moved but little in an upright position unless required. The burning heat demanded water to quench our thirst and one at a time would volunteer to go a few rods to the left of our then position to a spring for water taking as many canteens as he could carry and then crawl along on the ground dragging the canteens after him to the spring, wait his turn and flat on the ground fill his canteens and in like manner return, all the while exposed to the shell and bullets that filled the air."

One veteran seeker of water, Lt. Stephen Brown, again risked his life, as he seemed so eager to do at Gettysburg. Sturvevant described his trip for water: "Brown . . . deliberately walked to the spring loaded with empty canteens, filled them and returned in safety, but only once, and then advised the others not to try it and they did not, for quite a number (from other regiments) had been killed procuring water at that spring . . . The most of us suffered the pangs of thirst rather

216

than be targets for those fellows behind stones and fences and buildings and in tree tops with their telescope rifles watching an opportunity to shoot anything within range."

Gilman Foster recalled, "As I belonged to the drum corps I had not gun, but was offered a pistol, which I declined fearing it might 'go off' accidentally. I went to a spring to get water for Co. B, but before reaching them my canteens would be empty, as I could not resist the call of the wounded rebels, whom I had to pass before reaching my company, but necessity on the part of our boys soon compelled me to turn a deaf ear to the gray, and take water to our boys, and the most thirsty of all was Colonel Randall." The colonel took a long drink and ordered Foster to the rear.

"I found in the rear of our line a house which had been vacated," Foster continued, "and in the pantry some flour, so I mixed some of it with water, put the dough on my plate and baked it over a small fire which I had built, and when done I ate it and pronounced it equal to my mother's cream cake. I repeated the operation, and took my product to the boys and they agreed with me that it was the best cake they ever ate."

Sturtevant described the Vermonters' position: "Our location in the afternoon was about one-third of a mile south of Cemetery Hill between the Taneytown and Emmitsburg Roads, almost at the foot of the west slope of Cemetery Ridge some two hundred yards from its crest . . . On our immediate right and in the same front line were Generals Alexander S. Webb, Norman J. Hall's brigades of General John Gibbon's division, Hancock's corps and Thomas A. Smith's brigade of General Alexander Haye's division, Hancock's corps, and in rear supporting were Graham Ward and DeTrobriand's brigades of the Third corps, and at the left and front of our brigade was an open field for considerable distance. Our nearest supports on the left was McGilvery's reserve artillery which was well up the slope to our left and rear, advantageously situated to send death and destruction into the ranks of any charging columns that might cross the open field before them from any direction with a raking fire of shell, grape and canister. The left flank of Stannard's brigade was well down on the low flat ground of Plum Run behind thick copse that lined its banks."

Noon passed, and all was quiet save for the sharpshooters. "The stillness through the middle of the day was almost painful," said Wheelock Veazey. Suddenly, a man in the 13th, Pvt. Edward Gorman, began to roll on the ground, moaning and crying out. Sturtevant said he was found to be suffering "cramps and awful pains in the bowels." Pvt. Hardy Ladue, a muscular 20-year-old blacksmith from the Canadian border town of Alburg, reported the matter to the company commander. Sturtevant noted: "Hardy pointed to an ambulance twenty rods to the rear and Captain Blake said, 'Take him to that ambulance as quick as possible and return, for we are liable to be called on to charge at any minute.' I saw Hardy deliver comrade Gorman to the ambulance and my attention was then called to a caisson that exploded." That was the last that anyone in the 13th saw of Hardy on July 3.

The lull continued, and Ralph Sturtevant was surprised by the sudden appearance at his side of his cousin Cpl. Wesley Sturtevant, of the 14th. "He said, 'I shall never see home and dear friends again, something tells me I shall be slain in this battle, and I cannot drive away the awful thought. I have come to tell you and request that you tell father and mother, brothers and sisters and dear friends for me good-by.'" Sturtevant's cousin asked to be buried in his hometown of Weybridge, saying: "I am sure that my life will end on this field." Alarmed, Sturtevant "in every way endeavored to dispell the awful thoughts that held and controlled him, but to no purpose." All the while he recalled that the mother of his cousin had long been a firm believer in the prophetic power of dreams.

"My efforts were all in vain," wrote Sturtevant. "With deep emotion he extended his hand and said 'Good-by' and deliberately walked back to his regiment nearby paying no heed to the deadly missiles . . . Before my cousin reached his regiment, which was in sight and not two hundred yards away, two signal guns in quick succession from General Longstreet's artillery broke the awful silence that had for an hour or more hovered over the entire field." General Stannard noted, "The enemy opened on us in the fiercest possible manner."

Lieutenant Benedict remembered that the signal guns fired at "ten minutes past one o'clock." He said, "An instant later the air was literally FILLED with flying missiles." Sturtevant wrote that "150 cannon in battery along Seminary Ridge as far as we could see were belching forth their deadly storm of solid shot and shrapnel shell against our left center battle lines and in another moment almost simultaneously from Round Top to Cemetery Hill one hundred cannon or more of the Union side replied, and a blazing stream of fire from hill top to hill top and along the valley, accompanied with a deafening roar, signaled back . . . We of the front battle lines lay flat on the ground."

The Confederate artillery, massed to the front of Seminary Ridge, had opened on the Union positions at a range of less than a mile. General Lee was attempting to silence the cannon protecting the Union center—the point of his pending attack—and also to weaken the infantry positioned there. From Cemetery Ridge, Union guns replied.

Benedict added: "It was converging fire which came upon the Union lines at every angle, from direct point-blank at which [canister] was served with effect, to an enfilading fire from a battery of Whitworth guns far to the right, which sent their six-sided bolts screaming by, parallel to the lines, from a distance of over two miles. Shells whizzed and popped and fluttered on every side; spherical case shot exploded overhead, and rained showers of iron bullets; solid shot tore the ground into furrows, and [canister] hurtled in an iron storm against the low breast-works of rails."

Sgt. George Scott recalled, "All the hellish energy which modern ingenuity could invent was now engaged . . . Solid shot, grape, canister, spherical case, elongated shell, whizzing, whirling, shrieking, moaning, booming, bursting over our heads . . . Our men lie low; they get behind trees, stones, knolls, stone walls, breast-works—anything to give them a partial protection."

As the first shots slammed in, Pvt. Silas Mozier, 19, from the northern Vermont town of Sheldon, lit out. "While the shot and shell filled the air," Sturtevant wrote, "Mozier watched his opportunity and started on the run for the rear, throwing down his gun and other accoutrements as he ran. We saw him disappear over the ridge out of sight. Some of Company K and others who saw him run sang out, 'Shoot the damn coward; see him run, shoot him.'"

Mozier survived, though unbeknownst to him he was running into the worst of the shelling. As the shells rained in, the Vermonters began to realize that most were landing well to the rear. The Confederates had aimed too high. "All lay motionless, heads to the front and faces to the ground," Benedict said. "Though most of the shells went over us, occasionally a man would be struck. The wounded men invariably received the injuries without outcry, and lay and bled quietly in their places."

Louis Barttro, a native of Quebec who had enlisted in Richmond, wrote: "A piece of iron about two inches thick and ten inches long was seen coming towards us, the ends striking the ground now and then. Just as I was going to call to the boys to look out, the iron struck William Crosby in the forehead. He was lying on the ground near George Fenwick, where he raised his head just in time to be hit by the iron, Fenwick at the time saying, 'Oh! My God, Willie, are you hurt?' When he saw the blood come from the wound, Fenwick took his handkerchief and put it on the wound, and saying, 'lie down Willie, lie down.'" Crosby survived.

A shell burst over Company G in the 13th, and several of the prone men were wounded. Another shell plowed into the earth close to a sergeant in the same company. "A boy's curiosity led him to dig it up with his bayonet," George Scott wrote. Then, he added, the sergeant fell asleep. Indeed, many of the Vermonters were falling asleep. Colonel Veazey remembered, "The effect of this cannonade on my men was the most astonishing thing I ever witnessed in any battle. Many of them, I think a majority, FELL ASLEEP, and it was with the greatest effort only that I could keep awake myself."

Scott said, "We hardly dared rise on our elbows, even, for just above our heads raged a tempest of orchestral death. Shot and shell struck, rent and tore the bank just back of us . . . On that hot and sultry day we were exposed to the full glare of the sun. Many overcome with heat . . ."

Through it all, General Stannard walked the lines of his prostrate men. "The general and his staff alone stood erect or passed up and down the lines, and kept a close watch to the front for the first indication of the expected charge," wrote Benedict. "Of course our batteries were not silent. They fired rapidly and well, but the enemy seemed to fire two guns to our one. Suddenly with a loud explosion a caisson of a battery just to our left blew up, struck by a solid shot. The smoke rolled up in a tall column, from under which the frightened horses, one or two minus a leg, dashed wildly to the rear. The rebels on the crest cheered to the sound, and poured in their shot still faster. Ten minutes later a whole battery seemed to blow up to our right. For a moment there was a scene of great confusion around it; but a fresh battery dashed up in its place, and our fire reopened with fresh vigor from the spot. A minute afterwards a rebel caisson opposite us exploded, and it was our turn to cheer."

Out on the picket line, deafeningly close to the Confederate cannon, Veazey's men stayed low. "Our shells were timed to burst just above us and then passing on to work the greater destruction in the Rebel ranks," Lt. Albert Clarke recalled.

Lt. Albert Clarke of the 13th Vermont
LIMOGE COLLECTION

"The Rebel shells, on the contrary, burst on reaching us and swept over and around us in iron showers. As our position was low, the greater portion passed over us. Not a very pleasant sensation possesses one when observing a large piece of iron strike off a limb of a tree or bury itself near knowing that it is just as likely to strike where you may be . . . Some hugged the ground almost in delirium, others were apparently unconcerned."

Charles Cummings, on the picket line and thinking of his hometown, Brattleboro, said, "Their guns were served with a precision I never thought possible. A great tree around whose base we were lying, as big as one of the oaks in Judge Kellogg's yard, was so cut up that not a single branch, nothing but the stump remained."

Back in the 13th, Pvt. Loomis Bentley was hit "by a grape shot which passed through his left arm breaking both bones," a comrade said. Pvt. Fred Gale, famed in the regiment as a singer, was nearby when a shell fragment tore off the leg of Pvt. Calvin Seaver. Gale wrapped a cord tightly around the stump and Seaver survived.

Pvt. William March was hit while lying low. Pvt. J.H. Lyon said, "He was wounded in both legs below the knees by cannon shot. He unaided placed tourniquets above the wounds and was carried off the field to a large barn used for a hospital. There he died in an hour."

"For two awful long hours this unparalleled artillery fight raged without advantage to either side," Private Sturtevant recalled. But gradually the men noticed that the Union fire was slackening, though Confederate shells continued to rain in. Said Pvt. Edward Fisk, in the 13th, "Dexter Parker received a very painful wound from a piece of shell which cut through one of his hands and he was in such agony that Corporal O.G. Miles and James Wilson started to help him to the rear, one on each side. They had only gone a short distance when a shell struck in a pile of stones and burst. All three fell to the ground and it was found that a small piece of shell had pierced Wilson's heart, killing him instantly . . . Miles had splinters of stone driven into his back."

As a lull came, Pvt. Walcott Mead in the 14th glanced up and saw a rabbit hop out of some bushes to their front. "A soldier cheered, 'Go it old Molly Cotten Tail, now's your chance.' There being no break in the line, bunnie presently hopped over the soldiers and sped to the rear and safety."

All the Union batteries then ceased fire, saving their ammunition to meet the expected assault. The Confederate cannon also fell silent. Pvt. Albert Mead looked around, checking on his buddies; eventually he saw Pvt. Albert Walker, who had found a straw hat on the field and wore it as he lay low during the shelling. He heard the Bridport lad say as the shells whined overhead, "Boys do you know what those bullets are saying? They say, 'Walker next, Walker next.'" Suddenly Walker was silent, a bullet in his brain.

In the 14th Vermont, Pvt. Edwin Pierce, from the mountain hamlet of North Shrewsbury, turned to speak to his best buddy, Pvt. Billy Cairns of Middletown Springs. The two men had taken cover behind some stones during the cannonade. Cairns did not reply. He, too, had died without a sound.

"After the cannonade," Sergeant Scott recalled, "a general rode along the line and said, 'The Rebels are forming for a charge. Prepare to meet them.'"

★

23

Pvt. Sturtevant remembered the advance of the long Confederate lines from Seminary Ridge toward Cemetary Ridge: "The dread spell of silence suddenly gave way to excitement and activity, from Cemetery Hill to Round Top and like the rush of a mighty wind the word came down the lines, 'See they are coming' . . . Where all was still and motionless before was now animated, with excitement and hurrying to and fro on every part of the field. Hurried orders came from commanders, and almost at the same moment the officers and the rank and file were told of the approaching charge . . . it could be seen only by those on Cemetery Hill and Round Top . . . We saw them first as they reached the crest of Seminary Ridge a full half mile away, at first horse and rider, then glistening bayonets and then flags and banners waving and fluttering in the sultry air could be seen."

Lee's men came in view of the Vermonters upon cresting a rise well to the front of Seminary Ridge, a rise Sturtevant mistook for the ridge itself. What history would remember as Pickett's Charge was approaching that hot afternoon of July 3, 1863.

"The assaulting forces were formed in two main lines, having a front of about 1,000 yards, with supports in the rear extending beyond the flanks of the front lines," Lt. G.G. Benedict reported. "The ground selected for the movement was the only portion of the field over which so many men could have rushed in line. It was the broad stretch of meadow extending to the southwest of the village of Gettysburg, perhaps a mile and a half in length, and varying from a half mile to a mile in width between the confronting ridges. It sloped gently for most of the distance, from the crests occupied by Lee's batteries, for half the way across, and then rose with a gentle incline to the crest of Cemetery Ridge."

In a last, desperate attempt to win a decisive victory in the North, General Lee launched a massive frontal attack against the center of General Meade's line. The target was the now shot-torn Clump of Trees on the crest of Cemetery Ridge, north of where the Second Vermont Brigade lay in the most advanced of all positions along the Union line. The soldiers who were there believed that from 15,000 to 17,500 troops were advancing across the shallow valley, though some later estimates have suggested a slightly lower figure. Nevertheless, it was a formidable wave of armed men as it moved resolutely from west to east, the battle flags of the Confederacy to the front.

HOWARD COFFIN

A Confederate bugler, in bronze, sounds the advance toward Cemetery Ridge.

"Suddenly a battery opened on Cemetery Hill with a deafening roar," said Sturtevant, "and sent [shells] hurtling across the valley into the approaching columns . . . that warned them that all of our guns had not been silenced by their hundred and fifty guns during the early hours of the afternoon, but on they come regardless of exploding shells."

On Cemetery Ridge that day was Lt. Frank Haskell, born and raised in Tunbridge, Vermont, but now serving with the Sixth Wisconsin Infantry. Destined to play a major role in bringing troops into position to confront Pickett, Haskell was about to become one of the true heroes of Gettysburg. "[T]he enemy is advancing. Every eye could see his legions, an overwhelming resistless tide of an ocean of armed men sweeping upon us!" he wrote. "Regiment after regiment, and brigade after brigade . . . the red flags wave, their horsemen gallop up and down; the arms of 18,000 men, barrel and bayonet, gleam in the sun, a sloping forest of flashing steel. Right on they move, as with one soul, in perfect order, without impediment of ditch, or wall or stream, over ridge and slope, through orchard, and meadow, and cornfield, magnificent, grim, irresistible."

Well to the front, Colonel Veazey's pickets felt most vulnerable. Lt. Francis Clark was on their line, in a low spot with a poor view of the unfolding drama: "The heavy cannonade was kept up about two hours when the enemy was observed advancing in force. Capt. Eaton, whose coolness and bravery was every-

223

Pickett's Charge hitting the Union lines

where remarked, ascertained this by climbing a tree . . . He passed along the line the generally cautionary order to be ready to fall back a few yards to an open place, there to form and move upon the reserve companies of the regiment." Colonel Veazey said, "My pickets held the enemy's skirmish line until their main line of battle came upon us when we gradually drew in on the reserve."

Company B of the 16th was north of the Codori house and was separated from the regiment's other pickets. It withdrew toward the Clump of Trees and would fight there.

"The advance of Pickett's veterans was magnificently steady," Benedict reported. "Preceded by their skirmishers the long gray lines came down the slope at quick step. As the Confederate skirmishers struck the skirmishers of the 16th Vermont, the latter fell back to the main body of the regiment." Lieutenant Clark described the 16th's retreat as coming "in the very nick of time." Veazey's skirmishers came back to the front of Cemetery Ridge to join the regiment's reserve. The regiment was aligned to the left of the 14th and slightly to the rear, "with not a bush to cover us," according to Francis Clark.

In the 13th Vermont, Colonel Randall, with General Stannard concurring, had determined to move his men even closer to the front. Pvt. Louis Barttro recalled: "The order was given to go where there were a few rails laid along for protection . . . John Johnson was hit in the hip by a piece of shell that was buzz-

HOWARD COFFIN COLLECTION

ing in the air, but did not cut the flesh as it struck on the flat side of the shell . . . M.P. Scullin who was standing with me was hit on the instep by a ball, which since his foot has had to be amputated. After Crosby was hit I advanced a few yards ahead of him to the rails."

Scott observed, "[T]he 13th Vermont formed in line, in the ravine, then at once marched out of it, over the ridge in front of it to an efficient breastwork of rails." Sturtevant may have more accurately described the advance: "The boys of the 13th crawled carefully along the ground to the rail fence line . . . a helter, skelter zig-zag crouching crawl and run each taking his own way to reach the rail breastwork as best he could. The stone and bushes and rails and smoke on the way obscured our way so no one was killed making this change . . . Some of the boys were a little frightened and others slightly wounded and all as soon as they reached the rail breastworks flattened out."

Lt. Albert Clarke reported, "No sooner had we become prostrate than a volley passed over our heads which must have nearly annihilated us had we been standing."

By then, Colonel Nichols had also moved the 14th forward, up from the shallow ravine to the low crest in its front. Nichols wrote, "Lt. Hooker [George Hooker of Stannard's staff] communicated the order to me 'to form my line of battle on a little rise of ground in front of the position then held, to wait till they

225

Union troops move to counter the Confederate assault.

were close upon us and give them one volley and the bayonet.'

"'How close do you mean Lieutenant?' said I. 'Three or four rods,' he re-plied. I ordered the regiment to creep forward to the position indicated."

Benedict recalled, "Preceded by their skirmishers, the long gray lines came on at common time, till they reached the lowest ground half way across the open interval, when the Vermont regiments . . . were ordered up in line by Gen. Stannard." Sturtevant remembered, "On they come regardless of exploding shells hurled against them, turning not to the right or left climbing the fences and walls, quickly reached the Emmitsburg Road, passed on both sides of the Cadora House [sic] and other buildings in that locality making momentary openings in their lines as they passed."

226

Along the right of the 13th's line, in the Irish Company, John Lonergan's dear friend Lt. John Sinnott worried that his men were rising up, some standing, to see what was building to the front. Pvt. Heman Allen heard him say, "Boys, lie down or you'll surely be hit." Then Sinnott collapsed, a piece of shell having slammed into his forehead. He died instantly; his friends found in his pocket a message, written July 1, bidding farewell to his fiancée in Rutland.

Lt. Eli Peck, in the 13th, noted, "Our men . . . sought to return the fire, but Lieutenant Clarke commanded us to hold our fire until we received an order. This annoyed us, for resting our rifles on the rails, we secured perfect aim."

"On they came regardless of the carnage among them," Ralph Sturtevant remembered, "nearer and nearer, until horse and rider, officer and private, standards and banners waving in the lead were plainly seen, and almost within musket range, the right wing now face to face with Stannard's brigade. Down the line of the 13th comes the order from company to company, 'Steady boys, hold your position, don't fire until the word is given, keep cool, lie low till the order is given to fire.'"

According to Benedict, "The enemy's right at this time appeared to be aiming squarely at the position of the Fourteenth regiment, and an order was sent to Colonel Nichols, by General Stannard, to hold fire till the enemy was close upon him, then to give him a volley, and after that the bayonet."

Colonel Nichols was concerned about just how to obey his precise orders to fire one volley and then charge with fixed bayonets when the rebels were three or four rods distant. He recalled, "At the rate the enemy were coming at the time . . . as soon as I could get the regiment up and properly aligned to make a charge they would be as near as the General intended by his order. I accordingly ordered the regiment up and to my utter surprise the instant it was up the enemy moved by the left flank."

Benedict noted: "At the instant that the regiment rose, the enemy's lines changed direction and marched by the flank to the north across its front by some sixty rods."

The right flank of the advancing columns suddenly changed direction, turning north and marching not toward Stannard's men, but passing before them. The Confederates were concentrating the mass of their attack toward the Clump of Trees to the north. "It was a terribly costly move for the enemy. The Fourteenth regiment . . . at once opened fire and continued it with very great effect," Benedict wrote.

As the regiments rose, they moved forward a few steps, first the 14th to the crest that sheltered the ravine in which they had lain, then the 13th up to their rail breastwork.

"My first impulse was to charge," Colonel Nichols noted, "but a moment's reflection concerned me that a charge at that distance, which I then estimated at 45 rods, was not what the General contemplated in his order, that it would leave the battery unsupported and be likely to get my line in disorder by making a charge on the run at that distance and the additional distance they would gain before we could reach them, and as they were moving by the flank I knew that a sudden fire would cut them up and create confusion. These reasons settled my purpose in an instant. I sprang to the rear of the regiment and opened fire by battalion and continued it by file. Its effect was better than I had anticipated. It decimated their ranks and threw them into utter confusion."

The 14th opened first. In the 13th the commands were, "Make ready, take good aim, fire low," said Private Sturtevant. "Then like an electric flash, came down the line the order from Colonel Randall quickly repeated by every officer in the line 'Fire.' Up rose the Green Mountain Boys . . . as if by magic taking deliberate aim and with a simultaneous flash and roar fired into the compact ranks."

Benedict said, "The Thirteenth . . . joined its fire with that of the Fourteenth, with equal effect, and a long line of Confederate dead soon marked the line of their march across the front of the Vermont brigade." The 16th joined in as the Confederates swung to the north, Veazey's men, as Benedict said, "firing obliquely into the enemys' lines." (Veazey's men must have had to fire carefully, with their comrades to the front.)

Years after the war, Colonel Nichols assessed those significant moments: "I do not believe when the enemy began that charge," he said, "they supposed my regiment had remained all day in position . . . under such a fire as had been poured in upon them. The 16th, i.e. the reserve, was concealed in the belt of bushes on the left. The 13th was massed among the trees and rocks to the right mainly out of sight of the enemy, so that when they began the charge, I have no doubt they supposed there were no troops between them and the battery and I shall always believe it was the sudden appearance of the 14th Regt. which induced the commander of that Rebel Brigade to attempt a flank movement in the face of the enemy and in this instance fatal—for I know it was commenced just the instant the colors of the 14th rose and the men sprang to their feet." (Despite Nichols' claim, it appears the Confederates veered north by pure coincidence at the moment when the 14th rose to fire.)

"The men had a short range and deadly aim," Albert Clarke observed, "and as the smoke lifted it was seen that they had done fearful execution. The fire was vigorously returned, but with little loss, and meanwhile the enemy continued to move to the [Vermonters'] right until the front of the Thirteenth was uncovered."

Sturtevant "saw at every volley the grey uniforms fall quick and fast and the front line hesitated, moved slowly, and melted again." The attack was piling in toward the Clump of Trees and The Angle—a spot just to the north where a stone wall, behind which Union troops held position, made a sudden jog.

"With a wild yell which rose above the sound of cannon and musketry, the enemy now came in upon the charge," Benedict reported. "The Second Corps met them in front with a destructive musketry fire, and the batteries on the slope, firing grape and canister, opened cruel gaps in the serried lines. But still they came on."

Sturtevant saw "Pickett's massing of columns and verging on his left and our right opened a clear field in front of Stannard's brigade."

Suddenly, to the Vermonters' front, an opportunity such as military commanders can but dream of had presented itself: The Confederate right flank was totally unprotected.

Benedict was beside Stannard. "The opportunity for a flank attack had been

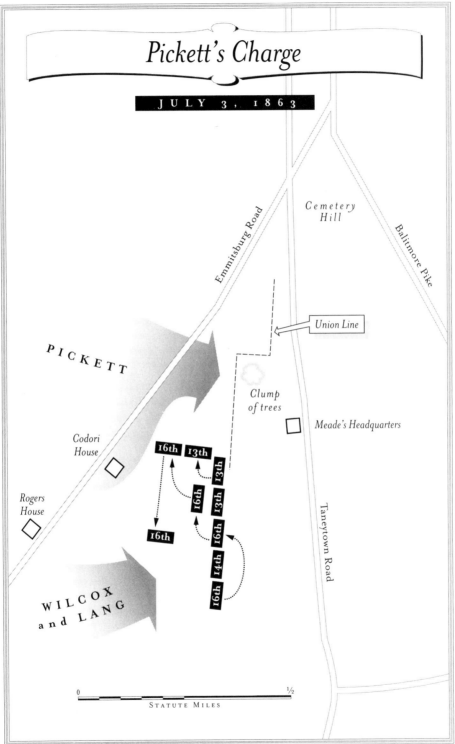

Pickett's Charge

JULY 3, 1863

Cemetery Hill

Baltimore Pike

Emmitsburg Road

Union Line

PICKETT

Clump of trees

Meade's Headquarters

Codori House

16th   13th

13th

Rogers House

16th   13th

16th   13th

16th

16th

14th

16th

WILCOX and LANG

Taneytown Road

0   ½
STATUTE MILES

HOWARD COFFIN PHOTO

Knoll on which Hancock and Stannard were wounded

noticed by Stannard . . . Without hesitation he ordered the Thirteenth and Sixteenth regiments out upon the enemy's flank. The Thirteenth moved first." Albert
Clarke added: "General Stannard then directed the regiment to advance to the
right and form a line at right angles with its present position. The din was so great
that Col. Randall could not make his orders understood, so he rushed along his
line from left to right shouting." Clarke heard, "By the right flank, double quick,
follow me."

As muscular, 200-pound Pvt. Benjamin Wright rose to obey the command,
he was shot through the body. "As we passed him when we changed front,"
Cpl. William Holden said, "he raised on his knees and while the air was full of
shot and shell he bade us good by and many of us shook his hand as we passed
him . . . He died that night."

Pvt. Alanson Nye, the farmboy son of a former state legislator from Plainfield,
was shot in the leg as he rose to join the advance: "When I found myself unable
to get along, and looking down, saw my boot leg torn to pieces, then I lay down
behind the breastworks . . . and from there fired four rounds. Two generals rode
up, and one of them asked me why I was not with my regiment, I replied, 'I am
wounded, General, but I mean to do what I can here.'" Nye kept shooting.

Pvt. John Hanlin, another native Irishman in Captain Lonergan's company,
recalled that "a rifle ball passed through my jaw. I did not pay much attention to
it at the time, but blood filled my mouth and run out pretty fast."

As the Confederate attack pressed in, higher up on Cemetery Ridge, the
idea that the Vermonters could make an effective attack on the Confederate flank

also occurred to Gen. Winfield Scott Hancock, who later said, "I directed Colonel [sic] Stannard to send two regiments of his Vermont Brigade, First Corps, to a point which would strike the enemy on his right flank." Hancock spurred his horse, riding in the direction of the Vermonters. Benedict wrote years later, "No general officer or mounted man had come to Stannard, or so far as is known to his brigade, after Pickett's charge commenced, nor had any order to move upon the enemy's flank been received by Stannard, previous the time when General Hancock rode to his side." Hancock reined in near Stannard, and the two began a shouted conversaton. "Hancock . . . wanted to know what I was going to do," Stannard remembered. "When I told him, he said it would leave a gap in our line of battle for a column on the right of Pickett to force its way into and break our line of battle. I assured him I could resume my position in the regular line of battle before a support to Pickett on his right could advance, as there was none in sight. Hancock still insisted I was making a great mistake."

Then Hancock was wounded. As Benedict remembered, "He was caught, as he sank from his horse, by Lieutenants Hooker and Benedict, of Stannard's staff, and the bleeding from his wound—a singular and very severe one from the joint entrance, at the upper part of the thigh, of a minie ball and a twisted iron nail, carried from his saddle-bow, through which the bullet first passed, into his body—was stopped by their hands." Later Hancock jokingly said, "The enemy must have been short of ammunition, as I was shot with a tenpenny nail."

To the front, the first company to hear Randall relay Stannard's command to move was Captain Lonergan's Company A, the Irish Company, on the right end of the regimental line. That company led the 13th to the right "at double quick . . . about 100 yards" toward the massed Confederates, according to Sturtevant.

"'Change front, forward on first company,' Colonel Randall repeated this order to Captain Lonergan and sent it along the line," Sturtevant reported. "Captain Lonergan on receiving the order halted his company . . . placed First Sergeant James B. Scully in position and quickly swung his company around into position, and thus each company was brought forward facing the right flank of General Pickett's advancing heroes." Randall later said that Company A's position, at the pivot of the brigade's great right-hand wheel, "was the most trying of all, being at a stand-still while the other companies were in motion."

It was a maneuver practiced many times on the parade ground. Company A swung on Sergeant Scully's hinge 90 degrees to the right until it squarely faced the Confederate flank. The other companies each swung out just 45 degrees, then marched directly forward until they extended the line of battle anchored on Company A and Sergeant Scully.

"The regiment swung out squarely on Pickett's flank," said Lieutenant Benedict. But there were problems. Sgt. George Scott, in the 13th, wrote that he saw that "as Randall was bringing the companies of the regiment upon the new line, the right of his regiment was suddenly thrown into confusion by an interference in the command on the part of a drunken aide, who gave orders to Company A to move back upon the line. He wanted to know of Randall what in Hell he was forming a new line for. Randall replied if he had any orders from General

Stannard, he hoped he would give them to him as colonel of the regiment, and not interfere with the command; but the line was soon and handsomely formed."

Benedict indicated that he played an important role in launching the flank attack: "Under a fire opened from the enemy's rear lines the extreme left of the regiment seemed to falter for a moment; but the men who were hanging back were faced into line by one of Stannard's aides who had taken to Randall the order to change front and had staid to see the movement accomplished." Sergeant Scott recalled: "A body of rebels get into a clump of bushes in front of us and poured into our ranks a murderous fire . . . Our men are dropping all along our lines. Our gallant little Sergeant-Major Smith came up to me, spatted his hands, and exclaimed, 'Scott, aren't we giving them hell?' In a moment he fell dead, shot through with a cannon ball." By then the entire 13th was in formation. According to Benedict, "A line of fire ran down the front of the regiment as it opened at half pistol range on the crowding mass in front."

Drummer boy Gilman Foster, a schoolteacher from Moretown, was tending to the wounds of Lt. Frank Kenfield. Foster recalled, "He said, 'We are giving it to 'em,' His coat sleeve was covered with blood and brains of the sergeant major."

Pvt. John Lyon remembered that as the 13th advanced, Sgt. Julius Densmore, one of the best-liked men in the regiment, "fell forward on his face." Lyon "saw Lieutenant Hibbard raise him sufficiently to see who had fallen and heard him say 'poor Jule' as we passed on." Densmore's skull was "shattered" and he died a few days later.

Stannard also ordered Colonel Veazey's 16th to join Randall's men in the flank attack. Benedict said: "Veazey thereupon drew out from his position, passing behind the 14th, (which had been edging to the north) and the regiment, after moving by the flank to the right for some fifty rods, made an oblique change of front and moved up to the left of the Thirteenth and opened fire." The Vermont line facing the rebel flank was now building to some 900 men, firing almost point-blank into the Confederates, and extending well out toward the Codori farm buildings "to within a few rods of the Emmitsburg Road," according to Sturtevant.

Though the Vermonters surprised the Confederates, they also caused a sharp response, as more and more rebels turned south to fire in self-defense. Despite that fire, the Vermonters' line began to advance north even before it had been fully extended. "The front of the two regiments was hardly a dozen rods from the enemy's flank, and they advanced while firing, so that the distance was considerably lessened," Benedict reported. "At this short range the Thirteenth fired 10 or 12 rounds, and the Sixteenth perhaps half that number, into a mass of men on which every bullet took effect, and many doubtless found two or three victims. The effect upon the Confederate mass was instantaneous. Its progress ceased."

While the Vermonters attacked the Confederates from the south, to the north around The Angle and Clump of Trees vicious and sometimes hand-to-hand combat raged as the Confederates sought to penetrate the Union line. Farther north, other Union troops—the Eighth Ohio and 126th New York regiments—moved along the far (left) flank of the attacking rebels, delivering a fire not unlike the Vermonters'.

With two of his regiments now devastating the Confederate attackers, Stannard was ready to order a third, the 14th Vermont, to join in the flank assault. "I intended at first to place my whole command in the same position," he said, "but saw the rebels forming in line of battle on my left again. I ordered Colonel Nichols to remain on the original line to protect that." A growing threat on the Vermonters' left would soon have to be dealt with.

"The havoc wrought on Pickett's right was dreadful, and his men huddled to the left," said Lt. Albert Clarke, "but the Confederates continued to load, fire, concentrate and advance. Great sheets of fitful flame and smoke flashed in front of the lines, standards waved and fell and were again uplifted, the artillery of both sides tore through the ranks wherever they could aim past or over their own men, and the whizz of bullets, the cracking of rifles, the din of cannon, the encouraging shouts of officers, the cheers of Yankees, and the 'rebel yell' all blended in a fury indescribable. Already the lines were so near together that the blanched faces of the men could be distinctly seen. Every motion was quick. Every man exerted himself to the utmost . . . Men fell like leaves before the autumn blast, but others took their places."

Capt. H.T. Owen, of the Ninth Virginia, was in Pickett's advance and felt the fury of the Vermonters' attack: "We were about 400 yards from the foot of Cemetery Hill," he said, "when off to the right, there appeared in the open field a line of men at right angles with our own—a long, dark mass, dressed in blue and coming down at a 'double quick,' upon the unprotected right flank of Pickett's men, with their muskets upon the 'right shoulder shift,' their battle flags dancing and fluttering in the breeze created by their own rapid motion, and their burnished bayonets glistening above their heads like forest twigs covered with sheets of sparkling ice when shaken by a blast. Garnett [Brig. Gen. Richard Garnett] galloped along the line saying, 'Faster, men! Faster!' and the front line broke forward into a double quick, and rushed toward the stone wall, where forty cannon were belching forth grape and canister twice and thrice a minute. A hundred yards from the stone wall the flanking party on the right, coming down on a heavy run, halted suddenly within fifty yards, and poured a deadly storm of musket balls into Pickett's men. Under this terrible cross-fire the men reeled and staggered between falling comrades, and the right came pressing down upon the centre, crowding the companies into confustion. But all knew the purpose to carry the heights in front, and the mingled mass, from fifteen to thirty deep, rushed toward the stone wall, while a few hundred men, without orders, faced to the right and fought the flanking party there, although fifty to one, and for a time held them at bay. Muskets were crossed, as some men faced to the right and others to the front, and the fighting was terrific, far beyond all experience, even of Pickett's men.'"

Confederate artillery commander Col. E. Porter Alexander saw it all: "When Pickett's division appeared on the slope of Cemetery Hill," he recalled, "a considerable force of the enemy were thrown out, attacking his unprotected right flank. Meanwhile, too, several batteries were firing on him very heavily. We opened on these troops and batteries with the best we had in the shop and appeared to do them considerable damage; but, meanwhile, Pickett's division just seemed to melt away in the blue musketry smoke which now covered the hill."

General Stannard wrote, "The heavens were completely filled with missiles of death, of all kinds of descriptions, that ever was invented to be projected from the cannon's mouth."

Back up toward Cemetery Ridge, General Hancock was bleeding badly. Sturtevant recalled that Sgt. Sidney Morey, a store clerk from Swanton, went in hurried search of a tourniquet, and seeing another Swanton lad, Pvt. Clark Butterfield, yelled, "'Butterfield, give me your tourniquette' . . . Returning with it on the run . . . it was applied, hoping to stop the flow of blood, but the wound was so near the body it was of little avail, and other means were adopted." Minutes later a shell exploded near Butterfield and his hand was painfully burned.

Tall Pvt. Augustus Shontell was advancing with the 13th when a shell took away his bayonet. According to company commander Capt. Orcas Wilder, "Shontell whirled around two or three times but finally stopped and called out, 'Captain, they have shot my bayonet off, so I can't charge.'

"'You can shoot, can't you?'

"'Yes, I can shoot.'

"'Well, get back into the ranks and let them have it as fast as you can.'"

Twenty-year-old Pvt. Albert Walston, a Richmond farmer, said he was "knocked down three times by the bursting shells near me in our flank movement . . . but was not seriously injured."

Pvt. Winslow Blanchard, a musician and the smallest man in his regiment, was, according to a fellow soldier, "Struck on his cross belt and ended over without drawing blood. The shock rattled him and he screamed and ran and was not seen until the fight was over."

According to Sgt. George Scott, Pvt. John Coombs, a Richmond farm boy, was hit as "a bullet passed through the left arm into the side, struck a rib and glanced out, removing a nipple." He survived.

Sergeant Scott remembered big and bearded Pvt. Joseph Warner and how a shell fragment struck his cartridge box as the Vermonters advanced against Pickett: "The impact threw him to the ground and as he rolled over Lieutenant Clarke said, 'Try to get up, Warner, I guess you are not hurt.' Warner felt of his right hip and coming to his feet replied, 'Wal, I vow, I guess I ain't, but I've lost my cartridge box.' He soon obtained one, however, from a man who had fallen, and was loading his rifle when a bullet passed across the front of his legs midway above the knees, cutting the flesh about one-half its size. He dropped his rifle, placed his hands over the wounds, and in that stooping attitude loped to the rear, without objection. After getting out of range he examined his injuries and, finding they were only slight, returned to the front explaining he would rather be with the boys than looking out for himself."

Not so fortunate was popular little Jude Newcity, who had said the previous night, "We shall win the day and then for home." While driving in on Pickett's flank, the 19-year-old farm boy fell dead. Down and dying, too, was Pvt. James Wilson, who on the long march to Gettysburg had said, "I shall never go home alive."

When Sergeant Marble, carrying the flag of the 13th Vermont, was wounded and the flag fell to the ground, Colonel Randall was there to raise it, handing it to Cpl. Theodore Stow, a Woodbury man. Though six members of the color guard were shot that July 3, Stow kept the colors high through the remainder of the battle.

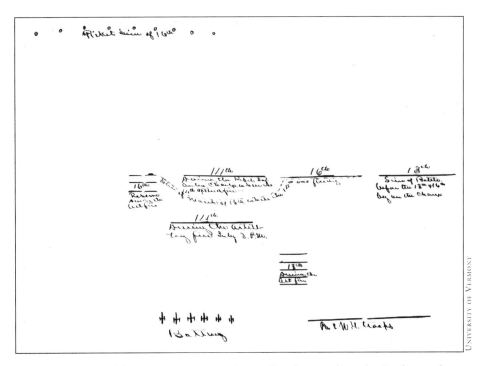

Colonel Nichols's map of movements immediately preceding the flank attack

A lad from a Cabot farm, Pvt. Freeman Wilson, recalled, "I apprehended death during the battle, and was, I think, a little timid . . . I tried to do my duty and I received a wound that might have been fatal had I been a trifle taller . . . no more serious than a brief sleep and the loss of some blood."

Capt. Aro Slayton, once a sawmill operator in Calais, also was lucky. A bullet took away his hat rim, then minutes later—as he stooped to pick up a knife—a shell slammed past where his head had been, killing and wounding several men beyond.

As the Vermonters continued to advance, Pvt. P.O. Harris in the 16th stumbled upon the battle flag of the Eighth Virginia Regiment, lying next to its wounded color bearer. He picked it up and brought it back within the Union lines. Said Lt. Francis Clark, "Two stands of colors with 'Williamsburg' and 'Fair Oaks' were our trophies."

The loss of their flags was a sure sign that the Confederates were defeated. Benedict reported, "For a few moments the gray lines crowded together, falling meanwhile like wheat before a reaper; then breaking into a disorderly mob, they fled in all directions . . . Their dead and wounded and small arms by thousands strewed the ground over which they charged."

According to Sergeant Scott, "Mortals could not stand such a fire longer . . . regiments had been annihilated. To retreat over that field of slaughter would be madness. They threw down their arms and surrendered."

"The Confederates began to throw down their rifles and wave their hands

James Scully, the pivot of the flank attack
UNIVERSITY OF VERMONT

in token of surrender," Lt. Albert Clarke remembered.

"Graybacks are throwing down their arms, running into our lines, some crying, 'Don't fire, don't fire,'" wrote Palmer.

Sergeant Scott reported: "As the air was thick and hissing shot, Lieutenant Clarke ordered the prisoners to lie down, which they were very glad to do. One of our men said to him, 'You are treating the enemy better than you treat us.' Clarke replied that was true, but that 'we are at work and their work is over.'"

Pvt. Edward Freeman said, "My comrade shot a rebel right in the head because he would not give up his gun."

Maj. Nathaniel B. Hall, of Bennington, in the 13th, wrote of "the beastly man who fired at the rebs as they were coming in after throwing down their arms . . . His dastardly act excited me as nothing did in my army life." Colonel Randall now stepped to the front of his men. According to Clarke: "Randall ordered his men to cease firing but the order was not heard. Breaking through the line to the front and turning his back to the enemy, he waved his sword and hat and shouted his order until it was understood. Then though still under fire from the enemy and from the Union line above and from our batteries, he moved rapidly among the yielding host, directing them into his lines."

"What share of the 3,500 prisoners taken at this time actually surrendered to the Vermont regiments cannot be stated," said Benedict. "Colonel Randall states that large numbers of the enemy came in to the rear of his regiment for shelter, and that he had more prisoners to take care of than there were men in his com-

236

mand. One body of about 250 were sent to the rear in charge of two companies of the Thirteenth. As the left of the Sixteenth extended beyond the rear line of the enemy, it undoubtedly prevented the retreat of a large number of them, and many surrendered to the Sixteenth." He continued: "Lieutenant Spafford with a squad of men brought in a number of Confederates who were scattered among the trees of the orchard near Codori's house; and still larger numbers threw down their arms to the Union front."

Sturtevant recalled: "The crouching rose up and all the living including the slightly wounded hurriedly and anxiously passed through our ranks to the rear turning over their guns, pistols and sabres as they passed."

Pickett's Charge was broken. Up at The Angle and the Clump of Trees the gallant Confederate penetration of the Union lines had been brutally stopped. Out in the thick of the Vermonters' attack was Lieutenant Brown, still armed with a hatchet. Sturtevant was nearby: "One of General Pickett's lieutenants approached and was about to pass as a prisoner within our lines, Lieutenant Brown demanded his sword. The officer in gray hesitated, saw the upraised hatchet as it glistened in the sun and then quickly unbuckled his belt and passed belt, sword and scabbard and pistol to Lieutenant Brown, said not a word and passed on. Lieutenant Brown buckled on the belt, dropped the hatchet and took the sword and thereafter carried it."

As the Confederates surrendered, Captain Lonergan hurried back up the slope to his dear friend John Sinnott. "I lay by his side when wounded that terrible day," said Lonergan. "I tied his head with my kerchief and dropt a tear on his aching brow. He could not speak, he was senseless! His eyes were closed by the enemies' guns. My eyes burned with tears for his relatives and friends . . . his father, mother, sisters, brothers, three thousand miles away, the exile dies in a foreign land in defense of Ireland's hope, the starry flag. For nearly a year we marched together, we ate together, we prayed together, we fought together!"

General Longstreet witnessed the defeat he had feared. "When the smoke cleared away, Pickett's division was gone—nearly two-thirds of his men lay dead on the field. Mortal man could not have stood that fire," he said.

"Pickett's charge had failed, " Benedict wrote, "but the work on the left centre was not yet ended." The movement of troops that Stannard had seen, causing him to keep the 14th facing front, was the beginning advance of Alabama and Florida troops commanded by Brig. Gen. Cadmus Wilcox and Col. David Long. Those support troops, come too late to aid the defeated Pickett, were nonetheless advancing toward the 14th Vermont. Colonel Veazey moved his 16th to meet the new oncoming threat. "While engaged in the flank movement to the right," he wrote, "I observed another force of the enemy charging down at double quick away to the left, and apparently aiming toward the position we held before making this flank attack to the right . . . I immediately conceived that I should change front obliquely to the left and charge the left flank of the new line when it came within striking distance, just as we had charged the right of Pickett's division."

Having successfully executed the complex maneuver of swinging his regiment out 45 degrees to meet an attack to the right, Veazey was now preparing to swing his men 90 degrees—a full about-face—and move against an attack to his rear.

"I therefore at once called to the men to fall in," Veazey recalled, "as they were broken into squads, gathering up prisoners, and had started or were about starting on the new movement when I received an order from General Stannard to double quick back to our original position. [Stannard had just sent orders to both the 13th and 16th to come in from the field and resume the lines they had held before the charge.] Just then I came upon General Stannard and explained my plan of a charge. He at first opposed it, on the ground that it would be rash and too much to ask of men to go alone so far to the front against so large a force; but he soon yielded and said, 'Go ahead.' At that moment the enemy had reached the bottom of the basin, their left flank being not more than thirty or forty rods distant, and they were crouched behind the low bushes and rocks which afforded some shelter from the artillery and infantry fire in front."

Wilcox's and Lang's men were taking fire from the Union lines to the front—most especially from Colonel Nichols's 14th Vermont—and they were returning it. Bushes to the front were now "twitching" with the passage of bullets, according to Walcott Mead. Among those who fell dead was Sergeant Vaughan, who the day before had listened to the dying words of the Confederate General Barksdale.

Veazey wrote: "The ground from our position toward the enemy was fairly smooth and a little descending; and upon receiving the order to charge the men cheered and rushed forward at a run without firing a shot. They quickly struck the rebel flank and followed it until the whole line had disappeared. The movement was so sudden and rapid that the enemy could not change front to oppose us."

Many years later, eminent Gettysburg historian Edwin Coddington wrote of Wilcox's and Lang's charge, "The situation became unbearable when the 16th Vermont, having just completed its work of destruction of Pickett's lines, turned about, re-formed, and charged the left flank of Perry's brigade, taking most of the 2nd Florida as prisoners . . . If Wilcox had been ordered to follow more closely on Pickett's heels, he might have turned the flanking attack of the Vermonters into a bloody shambles."

Up on Cemetery Ridge, Maj. Gen. Abner Doubleday, witnessing the second Vermont flank attack, shouted, "Glory to God. Glory to God. See the Vermonters go at it!" In the ranks of the 14th Vermont another Doubleday, William—recently promoted from private to corporal—was down and bleeding badly. A Confederate bullet had shattered his left leg; comrades carried him to a field hospital.

"A great many prisoners were taken," Veazey wrote, "but I cannot tell the number, as they were sent to the rear without a guard, as I had no men to spare for that purpose, and none were needed as the prisoners were quite willing to get within the shelter of our lines and away from the exposure to which they were subjected as well as ourselves from the rebel artillery, which followed us with merciless vigor . . . We took two stands of regimental colors and another standard from which the flag had been torn. This was the last effort of the infantry of the enemy."

He continued: "Our forty rounds of ammunition were mostly used up, but this was done mainly before our first flank movement to the right, and while making it. In the second flank movement but few shots were fired and those were after we struck the enemy . . . We were also very much enveloped in smoke of the battle and thus obscured from view. I failed to see a single man falter in the least

The Vermonters' flank attack
LIMOGE COLLECTION

throughout the battle. They made the changes of front first to the right and then to the left with almost the precision of a parade, and as though the fire upon them was from the blank cartridges in a sham fight."

At some point, Companies A, F, D, and I of the 14th, led by Lt. Col. Charles Rose, were detached and ordered by Nichols to join Veazey's attackers. According to Nichols, though, "The charge was made and the rebel brigade captured before Col. Veazey sent for help though it is true that four companies went down and assisted in bringing in prisoners."

As casualties mounted among the Vermonters, even their leader was hit. Lt. G.G. Benedict described the action: "During the last shower of [canister] and shell, with which the enemy strove to cover Wilcox's approach, General Stannard was wounded in the leg by an iron shrapnel ball, which passed down for three inches into the muscles of the inside of the thigh. I was not at Gen. Stannard's side when he was wounded, having been sent by him a little before with an order to Lt. Col. Rose commanding the detachment of the Fourteenth Vermont which supported the Sixteenth in its charge on Wilcox's brigade. The men of the battalion had just been ordered to cease firing, when I reached their line, the enemy in their immediate front having thrown down their arms. One or two men, in their excitement, paid no heed to the order and kept on firing till collared by Major Hall."

Though the fighting had about ended, Confederate shells still came in. Following Stannard's orders, the regiments began to move toward their original positions. Sturtevant was near Cpl. William Church, a farm boy from Highgate. "A hostile shell hit him and burst," recalled Sturtevant, "causing almost instant

UNION COUNTERTHRUST
July 3, 1863

From this position green troops of Vermont struck the flank of Pickett's division even as its front ranks were locked in savage struggle at the Angle. This action helped turn the Confederate high tide.

HOWARD COFFIN

The marker showing where the Vermonters' advance ended.
The Clump of Trees is in the background.

death. Among all the bodies that I had seen on this gory field, his was the most horribly mangled."

That shell, he added, also wounded Pvt. James Hogaboom and Pvt. Clark Butterfield, and others slightly: "The shelling that the 13th received when returning to position was accurate and destructive, and it was miraculous that not more were killed or wounded," said Sturtevant.

Lieutenant Brown, withdrawing up Cemetery Ridge with captured sword in hand, saw a member of his company lying badly wounded. Brown ran to the man and was applying a tourniquet when a Confederate shell burst nearby. The concussion knocked Brown briefly unconscious, and when he attempted to rise he was so dizzy that he had to be helped to the rear.

As the battle closed, Company B rejoined the 16th Vermont. Veazey said they "did not rejoin the regiment during the battle, but did good service and lost several men." They had fought somewhere near the Clump of Trees, supporting a battery.

Private Sturtevant, before moving back up the ridge, looked about the area where Pickett's Charge had been broken: "If there was any spot on that great field of battle that approximated more nearly than any other the maelstrom of destruction, this was the place. They lay one upon the other clutched in death, side by side. The dead, dying and horribly wounded, some had on blue, but nearly all wore the gray, for on a few square rods one could hardly step so thickly lay the dead."

Lt. Albert Clarke was among those detailed to take prisoners beyond Cemetery Ridge. Years later, at a gathering of veterans in Boston, he heard a former Maine artilleryman say that after Pickett's Charge had apparently been stopped, "[w]e saw a body of Confederates . . . surge out of the smoke and move toward the Baltimore Pike. Then we thought the opportunity had come, but looking through the glass we saw a thin line of blue surrounding the column of gray and realized that the men were prisoners being conducted to the rear." Clarke rose and thanked the man. "I was in command of the column," Clarke told him

General Stannard remained with his troops. "His wound was very painful till a surgeon came [which was not for an hour] and removed the ball," Benedict said, "but, though urged to do so by his aides and others, he refused to leave the field. He remained in front with his men till his command was relieved from duty in the front line, till his wounded had been removed and arrangements made for burying the dead; when, having done all that could have been asked of a man whole in flesh . . . he sank fainting to the ground." The general was carried to a field hospital in a barn to the rear.

Before he lost consciousness, Stannard had given command of the brigade to Colonel Randall. "He remarked," said Sergeant Scott, "with eyes suffused with tears, 'I leave the boys with you Colonel, you know what they can do; take good care of them.'"

Sturtevant observed that "quite a few of the boys brought from the field pistols, sabres and guns and other mementos recovered in the charge or scattered over the field . . . We reached the position from which we started the charge about six o'clock some little time before the sun disappeared below the distant moun-

Stephen Brown and George Stannard, in bronze, on Cemetery Ridge

tains. The battle of the day was evidently over, nothing to indicate its renewal. General Longstreet's batteries on our left still held their positions and continued firing principally in the direction of the position occupied by General Stannard's brigade as if seeking revenge for their discomfiture and destruction of General Pickett's command that had proceeded from that locality. We were now again flat on the ground and having become quite familiar with the crack of gun and screech of exploding shell carefully watched the enemy and the direction of his firing to guard against needless exposure . . . We heard the roar of musketry and the booming of cannon in front of Little Round Top, and the charge and crash of arms when General Elon Farnsworth led his brigade in which was the 1st Vermont Cavalry . . . This occurred about seven PM.'"

Well after Pickett's Charge had been repulsed, the Second Vermont Brigade was still under sporadic fire. "Soon another puff of smoke and flash of fire and then a shell struck the ground only a few feet to our rear," wrote Sturtevant, "passing between two large boulders and there exploding, killing and wounding quite a number who had what appeared to be a well protected position. The gunners were directing their fire at the heap of rocks and bushes to our rear . . . our heads were safe, but our legs were in danger if any more shells came from that battery. I was on the side where the shells had passed so near and was becoming nervous and suggested to Captain Blake to swing his legs around to the right that I might do the same . . . We both moved and placed our bodies on an angle with the firing of the guns and before we were fairly straightened out on the ground in our changed position, we saw a puff of smoke and flash of powder then a crash against the ground and a shell plowed along the ground which only a minute before was occupied by our legs. It covered us with dirt as it passed exploding a few feet to our rear.

"As soon as it was dark enough so there was no danger from sharp shooters," he went on, "we begun to look up the casualties in our regiment during the battle . . . the thought flashed through my mind what of my cousin Corporal Wesley Sturtevant . . . I wondered now if his premonitions of death had proven a reality. I could not wait and hastened to the 14th to ascertain if dead or alive. Just before reaching his company I met some of his tentmates that were then on their way to find me. They took me only a few steps further and there on the ground as he fell was the mangled body of my cousin W.C. Sturtevant having been shot through the breast by a solid shot or shell. His comrades told me that he fell just as the regiment rose to take part in the advance against General Pickett's charge."

Also lifeless on the bloody field was Pvt. Charles Mead of the 14th Vermont, who had written to his brother in Hinesburg in January, "We think we shall appreciate living at home if we ever get there, as I presume most of us will."

Pvt. Henry White, from Bridgewater, was also killed. Back at Camp Vermont he had promised his family that he would learn a verse of Scripture a day.

That night in Westminster, Maryland, Roswell Farnham, with the 12th regiment—still guarding wagon trains—wrote to Mary, "There has been a terrible battle at Gettysburg in Pa. about twenty five miles from here. We have not heard the result. We have been in no fight . . . There is a rumor here that Genl. Stannard is killed but I think there can be no truth to it. It is the general opinion here that the rebs are whipped."

Private Williams wrote at nightfall, "We killed many, took colors and captured hundreds of prisoners. Lieut. Bosworth was badly wounded. Merling was killed. Lieut. Hamilton mortally wounded and many others killed and wounded. It was a fierce battle. In the evening we were released from the front and came to the rear to sleep. It was a great victory."

Francis Clark recalled: "The cannonade languished and at last nothing but the occasional musketry of the skirmishers could be heard. The Battle of Gettysburg had been fought and won."

Sturtevant reported: "It was long after dark when orders came to move back to the reserve lines for refreshment and sleep. We were given a position directly back and over the crest near the Taneytown pike in an apple orchard and near a large barn and told we could lie down and sleep. Rations did not come, but sleep did, and though now we were very hungry and thirsty every one laid down where he was and soon were sleeping the sleep of the victorious. The lightning flashed, the thunder roared and the rain poured down and drenched us, and still we slept on until morning . . . It was the first night's sound sleep we had had since we broke camp on the Occoquan nine days before."

The final grim count found 47 men of the Second Vermont Brigade killed at Gettysburg; 24 others soon died of wounds. A total of 236 more Vermonters had been wounded and others would die after returning home. Many would bear the physical and mental scars of battle the rest of their lives.

★

Along Cemetery Ridge today, a 55-foot column topped by a 10-foot statue of General Stannard honors the Second Vermont Brigade. Nearby, a statue of Lieutenant Brown—his famed hatchet at his feet—honors the 13th Vermont, and close by stand stone monuments to the 14th and the 16th regiments. Those monuments can be somewhat misleading in locating the ground on which the Vermonters fought. The monuments are close together, and cover but a small portion of the original line formed by the three Vermont regiments.

Over the years, the ground on which the Vermonters fought has been considerably disturbed. A trolley line, now long abandoned, was cut through the landscape, and Hancock Avenue, along which the Vermont monuments stand, was constructed. Indeed, two decades after the battle, General Hancock observed that "the historic swale and trees lining it have long since disappeared." Gettysburg historian Kathy Georg Harrison, who has meticulously studied the terrain, wrote that "avenue construction in that area and War Department monument policies are both to blame for the errors in location and interpretation . . . It is apparent from the maps and descriptions of not only Vermonters, but other eyewitnesses and participants, that the position of the Vermont Brigade extended further south and was somewhat westward than is presently indicated by the monuments to the 13th, 14th and 16th Vermont."

It appears that the tall Stannard statue stands near the right of the 13th Vermont's position before that regiment began the flank movement. Three small markers note first, second, and third positions of the 13th during Pickett's Charge. The first marks their place, along the main Union line, during the night of July 2–3. The second, in the pasture across Hancock Avenue, apparently lies on the line of their rail breastwork. The third, well to the north in low ground south and west of the Clump of Trees, marks the point of their farthest advance toward the Confederate flank. The stone markers were placed by veterans of the regiment and seem to be properly located. Despite the altered landscape, a visitor to-day can envision where all the Vermont regiments fought. Just south of the Stannard statue, Hancock Avenue makes a jog to the east. From that point a somewhat marshy area, through which runs a ragged line of boulders and trees, courses off south and slightly west. This is probably what remains of the shallow ravine in which the 14th took shelter during the cannonade. Out in the field in front of the Stannard statue is a small marker, on a rocky knoll, denoting the spot where Hancock was wounded. A map drawn by Benedict soon after the battle clearly notes that the 13th and 14th Vermont lines met at that point. Apparently the portion of the ravine in which the 13th kept low was filled in during the building of Hancock Avenue.

The entire Vermont position is best seen by walking west several hundred yards into the pasture south of the Codori farm. As you cross the field, the low crest behind which Veazey's sharpshooters were stationed seems to be visible. Their line ran from the Emmitsburg Road north of the Codori house to a point a short distance south of the house, then slanted across the field toward Round Top. From out in the field, look back toward the Vermont monuments, then turn your gaze a few degrees south toward the line of trees and rocks in the pasture. A low crest becomes obvious to the front of the Pennsylvania monument. That seems to be a remnant of the terrain feature behind which the 14th rose to fire. And to the south of that point—even into the trees around the beginnings of Plum Run—the line of the 16th, lengthened by the return of its pickets, likely extended. The Vermont position appears most isolated to the front of the main Union position, denoted by the line of monuments erected along Cemetery Ridge. Also, the Vermont position seems a bit distant from the point of attack of Pickett's Charge. But recall that the Vermonters moved north as they fought, inexorably closing on the Confederates. It is interesting to retrace the route of Pickett's Charge, from Seminary to Cemetery Ridge. Putting yourself in the position of the Confederates, the Vermont positions seem much closer.

One summer evening, as darkness descended on the battlefield, I sat in the woods on Seminary Ridge near the Lee monument, about where Longstreet must have watched the great charge. A rise of ground to the front blocked from view all of the big Vermont monument but the figure of Stannard. There stood the general, sword in hand, as if with feet upon Cemetery Ridge itself. There he was, one citizen soldier who in a brief moment of golden opportunity had seen the grand chance and, in seizing it, brought his nine-months brigade into the history of his nation. I looked that way a long time, until the stars appeared. Still Stannard stood against the night, truly larger than life, forever determined that the Union should not fail because of anything left undone by his nine-months Vermont boys.

PART VI

Aftermath

24

The gruesome aftermath of the battle burned in the Vermonters' accounts.

"On the 4th of July I helped bury some of our dead. This was a sad duty but had to be done . . . In many places the dead and seriously wounded lay side by side, some wore gray, but the larger part in that part of the field had on the blue. The bloated corpses and stench and moans of despair and pleadings to be taken off the field were awful to bear," wrote Cpl. Eli Marsh.

Rain fell hard on the bloody fields of Gettysburg. "The farm houses and barns for miles around were converted into hospitals, yet they were insufficient to contain the wounded," said Sgt. George Scott. "On the 4th of July, a rainy day, thousands lay in the open air exposed to the pelting of the storm."

The two great armies faced each other throughout the day across the shallow valley between Seminary and Cemetery Ridges, filled with the wreckage of war. The Vermonters helped with the formidable, depressing task of burial. Yet all was not somber. Cpl. Mark Day, 24, from Essex, recalled, "The fourth the different bands of music came out and played patriotic airs to celebrate our victory; some of the bands had dwindled down to two or three men." Walcott Mead added: "In the pouring rain, band after band, of regimental musicians, gathered, the dead of both armies on every hand, playing the national airs and hymns, until a great volume of music and thanksgiving rose from the field."

Private Sturtevant wrote: "The morning of the 4th of July was dark and the rain fell as if the clouds had burst and though there was running water on the ground and sheets of water falling fast upon us, many still slept on till awakened by the occasional shell that came over screeching and cracking in the air just above us. While but little attention was now paid to the bursting shell or the sharp shooter's deadly bullets that hissed as they passed, all were soon up and astir to learn the news and look for the promised hard tack and coffee. There was plenty of water in every little hole, rivulet and brook with which we quenched our thirst and filled our canteens . . . Aides were flying over the field from headquarters to headquarters," he remembered, "officers attended with their quite numerous staff and were passing to and fro, the musical notes of the calls of the artillery and cavalry from Round Top to Culp's Hill resounded on the morning air. Ambulances rapidly moving out on the field and slowly and carefully returning laden with precious anguishing lives on their way to the many field hospitals, that the dangerously and mortally wounded might have immediate attention. Squads of soldiers armed with mattock and spade slowly and silently marched out on the field where strewn with the dead, to cover over, in shallow trenches, all that remained of the immortal heroes that had fallen in battle . . . Officers praised their commands and the rank and file heartily cheered in response . . . The Stars and Stripes heartily waved from every regiment and battery on hill and in valley . . .

"It was nine o'clock in the forenoon of July 4th," he continued, "when we saw loaded wagons approaching on the Taneytown Road and they brought us rations which were quickly distributed and all now had a royal feast of hard tack and rain water . . . During the forenoon details from the several companies were made up to go in search for and bring in and bury those of our brigade who had fallen in battle."

Sturtevant went on to describe the scene: "The dead lay scattered over the field where they fell and the black and bloated condition of the corpses made it difficult to recognize in all cases an intimate comrade, and no one was removed until fully identified . . . Those of the 13th were buried near the position now occupied by us on a slight elevation, near a stone wall at the south end of an apple orchard near us. We buried them as they were, without removing their clothing, covering them over with their blankets, for shrouds and coffins, and then sacredly and carefully filling the graves with mother earth. Each grave . . . was rudely marked with inscription of name of company and regiment and date of death, carved on a cartridge box cover or pieces of board from hard tack boxes that their remains might be found . . . [I] was with the squad that brought from the field and buried Cpl. Wesley C. Sturtevant of Company E, 14th regiment. The temporary monument that marked his grave was a cartridge box cover on which I carefully cut with my jack knife, name, company, regiment and date of death . . . The rest of the day was spent in writing letters home to relatives and anxious friends and talking over the incidents of the battle . . . Each was sure he had killed an officer, and a dozen or more of the enemy."

Corporal Williams found "the dead in piles and heaps, horses and riders mingling in the same mass. In one trench dug by the rebels I saw seventeen officers, and a number of other trenches were filled with the rebel dead but remained uncovered."

That morning, Cpl. Joseph Hitchcock, shot in the thigh as Pickett's Charge swept in, finally made it to a hospital. "A light rain fell sometime in the night," he said. "Spreading my rubber blanket over me, folded over my shoulder during the battle, I 'let it rain.' It rained again before noon the next day. I asked help to reach the barn nearby, for I could not walk, and took the only vacant place, by the open door, beside a wounded rebel soldier. A bullet had entered his mouth. He could not articulate a word plainly. His mouth, chin and flowing beard were covered with clotted blood. Wounded, blood-stained men filled the barn floor and covered the ground outside." Hitchcock survived, though the bullet remained in his leg for years.

Wrote Sturtevant, "General Lee's batteries still in position on the crest of Seminary Ridge were a significant warning that though defeated, the army was not demoralized and routed and were waiting and expecting to be attacked . . . If all the regiments were as thoroughly worn out and faint with hunger as the 13th Vermont . . . then it is certain it would have been madness to have assumed the aggressive on the morning of July 4th . . . We fixed up our cotton tents as best we could, but the wind and rain during the afternoon and night of July 4th was so severe and furnished us but little protection."

Private Williams wrote, "July 4, 1863—We were assembled to receive the commendation of Major General Doubleday to us as a brigade . . . for standing so bravely in the face of the fire of the enemy yesterday and for turning the fight to victory . . . Some skirmishing and every sign that the rebels were skedaddling. We slept on the damp earth in the rain."

Some 25 miles southeast, at Westminster, Maryland, on July 4, Lieutenant Colonel Farnham wrote to Mary, ". . . news that the Vt. Brigade was engaged in the fight—the 13th 14th & 16th. They fought hard and well. The Adjt. brought back an order for our regt. to go home immediately." The night of July 5, the 12th boarded a train bound for Baltimore filled with Confederate prisoners over which the Vermonters stood guard. The first regiment of the Second Vermont Brigade to head home was on the first leg of its journey.

On the morning of Sunday, July 5, Private Sturtevant said, "A cool breeze came from the west, and the morning sun soon dried our clothes . . . Rumors were rife that the whole army would soon be on the move to intercept General Lee before he could cross the Potomac. While there was much to justify the rumors afloat, the army remained in position during the 5th of July, except cavalry that

Confederate prisoners being led away from Cemetery Ridge.

was pressing forward."

As most of the Army of the Potomac held its positions, General Lee's Army of Northern Virginia had gone, in the night, beginning its long and agonizing retreat.

That day, the wounded General Stannard noted that he "was comfortable, but very lame and sore and made up my mind in forenoon to get some place and stay a few days, in afternoon made up my mind to go east; and concluded to start, as I could not keep along with my command, and came about four miles and staid at farm house. Was very tired."

Lieutenant Benedict rode again over the battlefield and reported to the *Free Press*, "In the open ground in front of our lines on the centre and left, multitudes of the dead of both armies still lay unburied, though strong burial parties had been at work for twenty-four hours. They had died from every conceivable form of mutilation and shot-wound. Most of them lay on their backs, with clothes commonly thrown open in front, perhaps by the man himself in his dying agony . . . The faces, as a general rule, had turned black—not a purplish discoloration, such as I had imagined in reading of the 'blackened corpses' so often mentioned in descriptions of battle-grounds, but a deep bluish BLACK, giving to a corpse with black hair the appearance of a negro, and to one with light or red hair a strange and revolting aspect . . . As late as Sunday noon, wounded men were still being brought into the field hospitals, some of whom had lain on the field since Thursday.

"On Sunday night," he continued, "after midnight, as I lay asleep, face up to the sky, on the field, a man shook me by the shoulder. It was an orderly with a led horse, who came with a message from General Stannard, directing me to join him at the farm house several miles away to which he had been carried. The night was pitch dark, and how we made out to thread the lines of sleeping soldiers and find our way to the house, I cannot understand; but we did before daylight. Next day I took him, in an ambulance, to Westminster, a twenty-seven mile ride, and we spent that night in a freight car, one of a train of fifty or more cars, which were filled with wounded officers. Most of them were wholly unattended and groaned the night away on the bare floors . . . I left the general in Baltimore, while I went to Washington to obtain transportation for him to Vermont, whither I accompanied him later."

Lieutenant Benedict's term of service had ended, just a few days later than that of his old regiment. He wrote as he departed for Washington, "The Second Vermont Brigade is now disbanded."

Four of the brigade's five regiments remained on active duty, however, though their enlistments were fast running out. Ralph Sturtevant noted: "Those of our regiment who were counted after the battle as missing (most of them) came straggling in after the fighting was over . . . Quite a number of these fell out on the last day's march to Gettyburg overcome with heat and fatigue and faint because of thirst and hunger, and some when we first heard the roar of cannon were suddenly stricken with symptoms of cannon fever, and could not march any further in the direction of the battlefield."

Among those who appeared was Pvt. Hardy Ladue. When last seen, during the cannonade that preceded Pickett's Charge, he was helping Private Gorman, beset with severe stomach cramps, to the rear. He claimed that in the fury of the shell bursts, he could not find his way back to his regiment. He was severely chided for the explanation by his disbelieving fellow soldiers. "Well, I would rather be a live coward than a dead hero," Ladue replied.

On Monday, July 6, Capt. Elmer Keyes of the 16th wrote to his wife, at home in Reading:

> My ever dear Lettie:
>
> This is probably the most welcome message you have ever received from me. I have time to write but a few words. This is the first opportunity I have had. I have been engaged nearly all the time for the past few days in one of the worst battles this continent ever knew. We are all well except Floyd, who went to the hospital this morn. None of us were hurt in the battle but Floyd is all tired out, but think he will be all right when he gets rested. 2 of my company were killed and 7 wounded. A spent-ball struck me, knocking me down but I got right up again madder than ever. E.T. Davis of Felchville was killed. OH SUCH SCENES SUCH SCENES. I cannot write now but will if ever I get the time. I am sitting on the battle field now and there is a man here who says he will try and get this to some P.O. He is waiting, I must close. We have suffered for want of food on the long march and the fight. I haven't had a mite of clothing on me night or day except my blouse and pants for three days and nights and slept right in the mud without tent or a sign of anything. We lived on excitement for two days certain for I didn't eat more than two or three hard tacks all the time. We won a great victory and are now following the enemy. I counted 115 dead rebels today on a piece of ground four rods square. The troops have all left, except the Vt. Brigade. We are burying the Rebs now and shall leave as soon as we get done. Our Reg't won the admirations of all for its gallantry, having captured 3 stands of colors and lots of prisoners. I will write again as soon as I can possibly get time.
>
> FROM YOUR LOVING HUSBAND,
ELMER

The third day after the battle ended, the Second Vermont Brigade joined General Meade's belated pursuit of General Lee's defeated army, making its way southward toward the Potomac river crossings and the safety of Virginia. Sturtevant reported: "A general move of the army commenced on the morning of the 6th of July in hot pursuit, and our brigade now commanded by Colonel Randall took up the line of march across the field where we had our most desperate fighting . . . during the last hours of the day of July 3rd."

In the march was Private Palmer, who had been fired at by a sharpshooter as he went for water on July 2. He had sought the help of a Union marksman who had seen puffs of smoke coming from a tree near the Codori house. It was now four days later. "I, in passing," Palmer said, "looked over to the tree and there at its foot lay a great six foot Confederate, all in a bunch, and seemingly just as he had fallen out of the tree. A few feet from him lay his big smooth bore muzzle loading rifle, with barrel about as long as its owner. The rifle ball had pierced his forehead just over one eye and apparently had gone directly through his head. We struck the Emmitsburg Pike followed the crest along which Longstreet's artillery had been located . . . and then westerly through the fields and over Willoughby and Marsh Run to the same road that had brought us to Gettysburg on the 1st of July, reaching Emmitsburg about mid-day and halted for dinner where we bivouacked for the night."

Private Williams wrote, "Monday, July 6, 1863—Moving after the enemy . . . rested in the woods through the night. Started four o'clock in the morning and marched until two in the afternoon. We were placed as the rear guard of the corps. A hard march on very dirty roads and across the mountain. A heavy rain came on and we had to stay all night in the woods."

According to Sturtevant, "Our line of march this day was south down the Monocacy valley over the same roads that we hurried north on the week before and then west over the Catoctin mountain on our way to Middletown, Maryland . . . The march over the mountain was a hard one, and part of the time in rain. We must have marched thirty miles this day before stopping for the night, and some were not able to keep up and did not reach camp until morning. It was the longest march made by us on this campaign . . . It was long after dark when our regiment received orders to halt for the night . . . That night was hot and the rain warm, and some who lay in shallow hollows were awakened by a flood of water that came down the mountains dashing and tumbling."

Moving ahead of the rest of the Vermont Brigade was the 15th regiment, still attached to the First Corps wagon train.

The next day, July 8, the sky cleared and the sun shone by midmorning. "It was nine o'clock before we started on the march down the steep mountain road, and as we hastened we were as happy, gay and musical as boys could be," said Sturtevant. "We soon reached the beautiful little village of Middletown . . . from many a window and house top waved the stars and stripes we had volunteered to defend. The porches and front yards and houses were crowded with beautiful women who greeted us on every hand with waving handkerchiefs and banners, enticing smiles, patriotic songs and hearty cheers. These gaily dressed girls reminded us of those over the mountain in Adamstown.

"We marched through the village," he remembered, "and a mile or two beyond into an open meadow field commanded by a beautiful and extensive view of the country for miles around. The Catoctin and South Mountains loomed up to the east and west and to the north and south, as far as the eye could see were cultivated fields and farm buildings . . . [we] were ordered to rest and prepare for dinner. The valley seemed filled with troops on the move and we were informed that the Sixth corps was nearby. Many of the men received permission to walk to the camps of the First Vermont Brigade, and there found friends and relatives. The Old Brigade had missed the fighting at Gettysburg, having been held in reserve behind the Round Tops."

"Hucksters from Middletown village passed through our camp with well filled baskets of luscious berries and cherries, pies and cakes," Sturtevant added,

"... but only few could buy because our green backs and scrip were pretty much spent on the march to Gettysburg ... The rumor of being detached was soon verified by Colonel Randall who came riding in among his regiment, having turned over command of the brigade to Colonel Veazey of the 16th regiment ... The boys of the old brigade ardently expressed high hopes that they too would soon be marching home."

But nearly two long years would pass before the Old Brigade went marching home. Among the battles that lay on its long road to Vermont were The Wilderness, Spotsylvania Court House, Cold Harbor, Petersburg, Winchester, Cedar Creek, and, finally, the pursuit of Lee toward Appomatox.

"All must remember how happy we were that last evening in camp," said Sturtevant, "how the army songs rang out with unusual spirit and emotion, with what zeal and feeling the whole regiment sang 'John Brown's body is marching on.'" The 13th Vermont's term of service thus came to a close outside a little town in western Maryland in a green valley between long ridges, a place that surely reminded the lads of home.

The next day the regiment was marching at 7 AM. "It was a lovely morning," Sturtevant recalled, "and the hills and mountains that held the valley and the thousands of soldiers moving westward over the mountains towards Sharpsburg and Boonsboro and where the army of Northern Virginia were held at bay by the high waters of the Potomac ... made an inspiring and attractive sight." Lee's army had come to rest at Williamsport and Falling Waters, Maryland, its retreat blocked by the Potomac risen to near flood stage due to the recent days of rain. The Army of the Potomac, with the 14th, 15th, and 16th Vermont Regiments, was on the move to destroy Lee before he could bridge the river and make good his escape to Virginia. But the 13th Vermont was marching east toward Frederick, Monocacy Junction, and the long train that would take them out of the war.

The 13th watched the Old Brigade pass, on its way toward where fighting was sure to occur. Then it marched up into the mountains, east from Middletown, reaching the crest about noon, when it halted to rest and eat. According to Sturtevant, the men were aware of being near Harpers Ferry, where John Brown had been seized after his failed attempt to start a slave uprising in 1859. "It was no wonder," said Sturtevant, "that when the order came to fall in the boys all along the line involuntarily commenced to sing the familiar lines 'John Brown's body lies mouldering in the grave,' as it seemed to me with more fervor and emotion than ever before."

As the 13th approached Frederick late in the afternoon, Sturtevant said, "[P]erhaps a mile outside, a rumor run through the regiment that the same sweet singer that sang patriotic songs in our camp while at East Capitol Hill, Washington, D.C., and who sang a piece ... which ended in the chorus 'From many a spire in Richmond,' had been convicted as a spy and was now hanging by the neck to a tree nearby ... Quite a number went to see ... We found a man dressed in citizen's clothes on the ground, a rope around his neck ... His size and general looks justified the claim that he was the same man ... We hastened away from the gruesome sight, overtook our regiment before it reached the city."

Wrote Capt. Orcas Wilder, in the 13th: "As we turned our faces homeward, marching over the mountain to Middletown, Maryland, I found myself too sick to keep up with the company and Dr. Nichols induced me to ride in the ambulance . . . We soon came to a small house and entering found it contained two rooms, one below and one above, with a bed in the lower room, of which we took possession without question. We were too tired to remove our boots. Here we spent the night but not alone for soon the house was filled from top to bottom with other soldiers."

But most of the regiment kept on, now moving through Frederick, where, in Sturtevant's words, "[t]he whole city was out to see and greet us . . . Quite a number of the boys stopped to make love to the girls they could not pass by." At evening they reached Monocacy Junction, where Colonel Randall complained loudly about the dirty and dilapidated freight cars that waited for his heroes of Gettysburg. Better cars were soon brought to the station. "We sat our guns up in the corners and made seats of our knapsacks, those that had any, and we were on our way to Baltimore soon after dark," said Sturtevant.

That evening, at "Camp Lincoln, Brattleboro," Cpl. Jabez Hammond in the 12th wrote to his father for the first time since June 22, ". . . a few lines to let you know that we are all alive & once more in the good old green mountain State. we are in hopes to be able to get home by Saturday night if everything works to suit."

The 13th arrived at Ellicott City, Maryland, well into the night. There was a delay, and the Vermonters were allowed to detrain. Morning came, and shops opened. "The little money we had was soon spent," said Sturtevant, "but we came out of the bath houses and barber shops so changed in appearance that even our tentmates hardly recognized each other. It was a relief to be rid of dirty tattered garments as well as body lice."

The Second Vermont Brigade, now under Colonel Veazey, was down to the 14th, 15th, and 16th regiments, with the 15th still detached and accompanying the wagons. The night of July 9, Capt. Henry F. Dix, commander of Company F in the 16th, wrote from "Fox Gap, South Mountain" to his father in Wilmington—his first letter since the march to Gettysburg began. "I have had no chance to write till now," he said. ". . . I arrived here last night about nine o'clock with 39 men am nearly worn out. We hear many rumors about the Rebs moving in great force near this place. We have thrown up something of a breastwork here and are guarding a pass in the mountains. We may move into battle at any moment and we may remain here a week . . . Many of the clothes worn by the men of my Co . . . are perforated with bullet holes. The boys are pretty well used up. They did some glorious fighting . . . I will close. I have much to do."

Private Williams wrote: "Friday, July 10—Started early through Boonsboro, rested a while. We were moved as a command into the wood to support a battery opposite Hagerstown. Worked hard as soon as we reached there raising breastworks of wood and dirt around the wood." Up ahead, the Old Brigade approached Lee's outer defenses, at Funkstown, Maryland, and the men of the Second Brigade heard the sound of heavy firing.

On the next day the brigade moved toward Funkstown. Wrote Williams:

"Pleasant country with many fruitful fields. Raised breastworks in the evening."

That day, July 11, Maj. Gen. Robert C. Schenk, with headquarters in Baltimore, saw the 13th Vermont and fired off a telegram to Secretary of War Edwin Stanton: "I am astounded. Here is a fine regiment, Thirteenth Vermont, 663 strong, just arrived from Middletown, from the very presence of the enemy, on their way home because their nine-months' term expired on the 9th. Can nothing be done to stop this? This regiment is of General Newton's corps. I suppose I must give them transportation, but I cannot help denouncing them."

That same day the "fine regiment" boarded a train in Baltimore and up the tracks in Philadelphia an excellent meal was provided, according to Sturtevant. "The first women of the city waited upon us at the tables with sympathetic hearts and earnest solicitations made inquiry as to our health and our part at Gettysburg . . . The Thirteenth Vermont was the first that passed through their city that was in the fight at Gettysburg."

On Sunday, July 12, back in the war zone, Private Williams wrote, "We as a corps, moved forward with the 6th and 11th corps through Funkstown and Hagerstown. It was a very hot day. In the afternoon we had a very heavy thunderstorm. Camped through the night in a wheatfield. Skirmishing near us." That day the 15th marched in to join their comrades. "From Westminster the Regiment went with the train via Frederick City and South Mountain, toward Hagerstown," said Lt. Col. William Grout, "and rejoined the brigade in front of Funkstown."

The diminished brigade remained in position with, as Williams noted, "[t]housands of soldiers arriving here from all directions." Sometime during that Monday, July 13, Lieutenant Colonel Grout, brigade field officer of the day, took a picket detail of 150 men from the 16th toward Lee's defenses around Williamsport. Shots were briefly exchanged with Confederate pickets, the last rounds fired in anger by the Second Vermont Brigade. Two Vermonters were wounded. That night, under cover of darkness, with the Potomac falling steadily in the drier weather, the Army of Northern Virginia crossed to Virginia, living to fight another day.

By then, the 13th Vermont was also back at Brattleboro. The regiment went from Philadelphia to Jersey City, then by steamboat to New Haven, where, on July 13, it boarded a train bound up the Connecticut Valley for Vermont. "Our home coming had been announced in the newspapers," Sturtevant recalled, "and every hamlet, village and city we passed through were out in great numbers waving handkerchiefs and flags and with smiles and cheers enthusiastically welcomed us on our way home. Some of the boys claimed they saw the same girls they had made love to when we passed through on our way to join the army . . . We reached Springfield, Mass., about eight o'clock between sundown and darkness, and here as before we made quite a stop. The wheels had hardly ceased to turn before the cars were filled with loyal citizens, lovely girls with baskets of ham sandwiches, pies and cakes, and pails with hot coffee . . .

"It was a continuous ovation from New Haven to Brattleboro," he went on. ". . . We reached Brattleboro, Vt., just before midnight and to our great surprise the whole town seemed to be at the depot . . . Governor Holbrook and

Adjutant General Washburn and Colonel Blunt with the 12th regiment were out and with torches and music and banners gave us a royal welcome, and escorted us to Camp Lincoln to the music 'Home Sweet Home,' 'Yankee Doodle Dandy,' etc. and after the reception were assigned to the same barracks we occupied when waiting to be mustered in as soldiers the October previous . . . Not a word of complaint now made because only bare boards for beds."

Back in Maryland, Private Williams reported on July 14, "Foggy and hot. In the afternoon we moved forward through the woods and fields and on the pike between us and Williamsport." On July 15, he noted, "A very hard march and hundreds fell out," as the way led toward Harpers Ferry. Cpl. John Williams wrote, "Passed Antietam battle ground at two o'clock in the afternoon, and saw the burial ground wherein repose peacefully the remains of those honored heroes who fell on that bloody field."

On July 16, the three regiments crossed South Mountain via Crampton's Gap and bivouacked at Petersville, Maryland, near Berlin. "Friday, July 17—Rained hard all day," said Private Williams. "I am sick and full of cold."

On Saturday, July 18, he wrote, "Orders to move at four in the morning, but orders came to discharge us as a brigade of the First Corps. The corps went on and crossed the Potomac at Berlin. We moved there and rested near. The whole army crossing to Virginia. A busy crossing. The bank of the river full of army suppliers."

What was left of the Second Vermont Brigade watched the rest of the army cross the Potomac, then turned back to Berlin, where they boarded a train of boxcars. "We boarded the cars as three regiments and started for Baltimore at four o'clock in the afternoon," said Private Williams. "Arrived there at half past twelve at night. Slept in the depot."

On July 19, they reached Baltimore and took a train to Philadelphia, where they received the usual warm reception. The regiments reached Perth Amboy and took a steamer for New York City, a city torn by draft riots. Private Williams wrote: "In the afternoon, we were assembled and asked by the colonel to remain in New York for a week to defend the city. The matter was twice put to a vote and the majority was against it each time." Corporal Williams said, "The men of the 14th being greatly fatigued and exhausted by the late campaign, and having faithfully served out the term of service required, was too anxious to get home to comply with the request." At 9 PM the 14th boarded a boat for New Haven.

Several hours officially remained in the terms of service of the 15th and 16th, and Colonels Proctor and Veazey did not put the matter of riot policing to any vote. Much to the chagrin of the men in the ranks, the regiments were encamped on The Battery. Meantime, the two old friends rounded up a group of fellow officers and proceeded to the Union League Club for a grand evening.

While they wined and dined, the 14th Vermont continued on toward Brattleboro. "Reached Springfield at ten o'clock," said Private Williams. "Had plenty of food there free. A bridge had been burned twenty-six miles from Brattleboro. We got off the cars and walked across it to the other side. Heavy rain all day. Passenger cars started at half past four for Brattleboro, arriving there at six o'clock. A brass band led us to the camp ground and we stayed for the night in the barracks."

Two days later, with other troops having arrived in New York, the 15th and 16th regiments were released from duty there. On July 23, after the same heroes' welcome along the Connecticut Valley, the regiments chugged into Brattleboro. The Second Vermont Brigade was home from the Civil War.

★

25

While General Stannard's brigade marched from northern Virginia to Gettysburg, fought at Gettysburg, and then pursued General Lee, the flow of letters from the tired soldiers virtually stopped. Thus an oppressive silence settled on their loved ones in Vermont—while at the same time the local papers were delivering ominous, though slightly delayed, accounts of military events in western Maryland and southern Pennsylvania, making it clear that a great military crisis was building.

The *Green Mountain Freeman* had reported on June 25, 1863, "There is no longer any doubt the rebels are in strong force on this side of the Potomac and marching into Pennsylvania." The *Burlington Free Press* noted, "The rebels are now advancing with serious intent on Harrisburg."

THE REBELS ARE WITHIN 4 MILES OF CARLISLE, said a *Rutland Daily Herald* headline on June 26.

"The news of our military affairs in Maryland is quite threatening and gloomy," wrote William Hoyt of St. Albans in his diary on June 27. That same day the *Freeman* stated, "There is no longer any doubt that another great battle will be fought, in Maryland, probably, in Pennsylvania, possibly."

Still, life went on. Hoyt wrote, "Attended the Democratic State Convention . . . a large gathering at Montpelier, gathered upon the grass between the State House and the Pavilion [hotel], where a stand had been erected to listen to an address by Hon. James Brooks, of the U.S. 'Express.'"

On her farm in Starksboro, high on the western slope of the Green Mountains, Sidney Bushnell, described by a family member as "wife, mother, logger, farmer," went on with a strenuous life made even more so by the absence of those at war. In her diary, she noted:

> June 23, Tuesday. Laid foundations and put sills on.
> June 24, Wednesday. Finished framing and raised.
> June 25, Thursday. Tied up hop vines and cultivated the same.
> June 26, Friday. Cultivated hops.
> June 27, Saturday. Very hot—hoed hops.
> June 28, Sunday. Warm. Robinson preached.
> June 29, Monday. Warm and dry, commenced hoeing potatoes.
> June 30, Tuesday. Warm and dry, finished hoeing potatoes.

July 1, Wednesday. Warm and dry. Went to Bristol and got a grindstone.
July 2, Thursday. Warm and dry, drawed load of shingles.
July 3, Friday. Made grind stone frame. Drawed load of bricks.

Though momentous events that would shape the history of the world were taking place 500 miles to the south and west, the busy life on a Vermont upland farm obscured their importance.

As June turned to July, a hot spell settled on the state. Some members of the family of Pvt. Charles Mead, of Hinesburg, treated themselves to a hotel atop Vermont's highest mountain, Mansfield, to escape the valley heat. "From the elevated position I now occupy I look down upon my friends, less favored, with pity," wrote an aunt. The last the family had heard from Charles was a letter sent June 23 from Wolf Run Shoals: "There has been considerable fighting near us— but we have been so fortunate so far as to keep out of it. My pen is very poor and as I have no more to write I will bring this miserable scrawl to a close."

Life went on as usual for Mary Tucker in Vergennes, as her diary makes clear:

June 25. Spent the forenoon in the old cemetery seeding and cutting grass. Been delightful.

June 27. Warm, but bright and pleasant. Bell returned famished from school. We had some fine strawberries of her picking for tea.

Sgt. George Scott, of the 13th Vermont
LIMOGE COLLECTION

260

June 28. An exceptionally warm day. We all attended meeting this forenoon . . . preached from Acts 2-38. This evening attended an excellent prayer
meeting. Delightful with a brilliant moonlight.

June 30. I arose at 4 o'clock cooked breakfast for the family and got
the week's ironing done. Forenoon in the garden. This evening was brilliantly
beautiful.

July l. I got up at 5 o'clock and baked jelly and cup cakes before breakfast.

July 3. The heat has been excessive . . . Our flower garden looks beautiful. We were favored with an excellent shower in the afternoon . . . A battle
is in progress today in Pennsylvania.

In Woodstock on June 26, the second day of the Second Vermont Brigade's
long march, the weekly *Standard* reported that "Ellis, Britton & Eaton of Springfield
are building a fine shop for the manufacture of baby carriages." The paper also stated,
"We are requested to remind those who subscribed to the soldier's bounty fund
last year that the boys will be home in a few days and will want their money." The
editor advised, "The time of the Twelfth Regiment will expire on the 4th of July,
soon after which time the men will repair to their homes. We would suggest that
some appropriate reception be given the Woodstock Light Infantry on the occasion of their arrival at home . . . Let the matter be taken in hand at once."

The *Standard* also reported that "S.W. Benjamin and G.H. Wells of Woodbury
had 18 sheep killed on the 15th inst." And it advised that all those interested in
seeing a demonstration of the new "Hubbard's Improved Mower" should appear
at the Ovid Thompson farm, near the fairground, on July 2. With more and more
men at war, sales of mowing machines were increasing throughout Vermont. In
Burlington, the *Free Press* reported that "Mr. Thorpe agent for Hubbard's mower
has given to the Ladies Relief Society of this place, for the benefit of the sick and
wounded soldiers, the prize of $25 which his machine took at the trial at Essex
Junction on Saturday."

The Woodstock Marble Works was advertising "Peace Prices for War Monuments," explaining that since its proprietor was expecting soon to be leaving for
the military, all headstones would be sold at prewar rates. J.N. Murdock & Sons
was offering coffin plates "constantly on hand and for sale . . . worth 75 cents to
5$, with inscription." A Boston firm, Palmer's Artificial Leg, was offering, through
the *Standard,* "the justly and widely celebrated Artificial Leg which just received
the Great Prize Medal in Europe."

On June 28, in the Champlain Valley town of Shoreham, the mother of Pvt.
Samuel Northrup of the 14th Vermont wrote to her son: "Father has hired Solomon Duma to work one month haying his time commences tomorrow he worked
here Friday and Saturday by the day $.87 a day . . . The weather was quite warm
yesterday. We nearly roasted in church. The beas have swarmed again. We expect
to have some honey when you get home."

Private Northrup's sister added a note to the letter. "Mother, and aunt Ruth
are sitting by the table in the sitting room picking over strawberries. Father has
not got back from Richville. Bert is out milking. Maria is upstairs putting Ralph
to bed. The two [hired] men Frank and Sol are up on the long shed doing some

thing (I don't know what) to the roof. And your humble servant is sitting by the desk in mother's room scribbling for dear life to her soldier brother. Don't you think we are all occupied?"

On July 3, in Woodstock, the *Standard* reported, "The *Bellows Falls Times* suggests Col. [Lewis] Grant, who has long and credibly commanded the 1st Vermont Brigade, as a desirable candidate for governor. For heaven's sake do let us, when we find a good officer, keep him in the field." And that day—the day after Pickett's Charge—the paper reported, "Lee's entire army has advanced into Maryland and Pennsylvania and is ravaging the country and stripping it of all supplies . . . We hope General Meade is equal to the situation." It also printed a dispatch received just before going to press dateline NEW YORK, JULY 1: "A heavy engagement since 9 this AM has been going on . . . I regret to say that Maj. Gen. Reynolds has been killed."

The *Standard* also ran a notice that "Mr. T.P. Collins who made the nitrous oxide entertainments exceedingly popular during the last year proposes to give one on Tuesday evening next July 7. LAUGHING GAS."

In St. Johnsbury, William Herrick, an employee of the Fairbanks manufacturing company, followed closely the war news. Herrick was especially interested; he had served, as a musician, with the Old Brigade through the Peninsula Campaign. A mainstay of the St. Johnsbury band, he kept a diary:

> July 1. Was troubled by a strong disinclination to getting up this morning . . . Of all the magnificent failures of the Army of the Potomac the administration of Genl. Hooker seems to me the greatest—one continued chapter of reverse and defeat—of Gen. Meade the best thing seems to be he is a new man.
>
> July 2. The clash of arms seems to have begun at last. The telegraph this morning brought news of a battle yesterday in the vicinity of Gettysburg and the result if not in our favor was not against us. Gen. Reynolds was killed, and we believe if we had a competent leader the rebel army would never see Richmond again. It begins to rain this afternoon.
>
> July 3 eve. Found father sitting up but mother had just gone to bed. Talked with him half an hour then came up to my room and am writing with the sound of running water in my ears. What memories and associations it calls up. I can hardly realize the years have gone by since it used to be the regular accompaniment of my sleeping hours . . . In the whole I have had a pleasant life. I have fond friends fond and true, but how fares it with the friends of these days that the running water calls to mind? Little Chucky, tenderly natured and delicate—have the long marches and the hardships of the campaign been too much for him? Where Charlie, has he come safely through another battle, or is he lying stark and dead, or groaning with ghastly wounds? God bless and protect them both and all of us.
>
> July 4. Well it is about the quietest 4th I ever saw . . . News from the army uncertain and doubtful, comes tonight, but on the whole quite favorable to the cause.
>
> July 5. Attended church this morning, there are many strange faces at church now.

July 6. Waited for the mail and got news of a great battle and a great victory. God grant that it may be so.

Gradually the news began to reach Vermont of great events at Gettysburg. July 2, a *Rutland Herald* headline: REPORTED BATTLE BETWEEN MEADE AND LEE. July 3, the *Herald:* SEVERE BATTLE IN PENNSYLVANIA; THE LOSSES HEAVY. That day the *Freeman* stated, "The enemy has been repulsed . . . several thousand prisoners taken."

July 4, the *Herald* reported, "Rumored Capture of Richmond."

Then on July 5, the *Herald:* HIGHLY IMPORTANT; TERRIFIC BATTLES; GLORIOUS VICTORIES. The *Freeman* said that day, "The most terrific fight of the war has taken place . . . The loss on both sides has been tremendous." (The latter must have been chilling news for the loved ones of the soldiers who had not written for days.)

On July 6, the *Free Press* editorialized, "It seems certain that Lee has been beaten and that the Army of the Potomac has won a signal victory." The paper also reported that the July 4 balloon ascent at Burlington had been something of a flop: "The strong winds that prevailed nearly all day rendered it hazardous to attempt inflation of the balloon, much to the disappointment of the people . . . It was so late in the eve, however, that few people witnessed the ascension, which reached 5,000 feet."

The *Free Press* on July 7 was full of state news:

—At Brimmer Crossing on the Southern Vermont Railroad near West Pownal Mr. Peter Rosenburg, who was entirely blind, lost his life by being run over by a train of cars.

— In the town of Charlotte recently a large rock is said to have been shivered in pieces by a thunderbolt.

— Mr. Ambrose Chase, of Bakersfield, while chopping in the woods last week, felled a tree, and with it came a nest of five WHITE crows.

— A severe freshet occurred at Worcester on Friday night by which Charles Hall was drowned.

—Mr. A.J. Morrill of West Charleston was riding out in a buggy when the foot mat took fire from a match used in lighting a cigar. He stopped his team and endeavored to throw the mat out, but the horse took flight and off. When stopped the buggy was nothing but a charred skeleton.

In Shoreham, the Northrup family's attentions were on the unknown fate of son Samuel in the 14th Vermont. "It is two weeks to the day since your last letter was written," his mother penned on July 7. "It is nearly a week since any letter has been received from any of your company, they say the mail is broken up in that vicinity . . . I hope soon to hear good news from you, but my mind is filled with the deepest anxiety. To say nothing of the dangers of the battlefield, your long marches in the heat must be very exhausting. It has been very warm for two weeks past but I think today has been the warmest of the season. How much the poor soldiers must have suffered from the heat, especially the sick and wounded. I hope you do not belong to either but I hardly dare to think what your situation at this time may be. I can do nothing but hope and pray for the best. I somehow hope the invasion may be speedily put down so that you can come home when your time is out which will be in two weeks from to day. We shall want to kill the fatted calf and have a day of general rejoicing."

She continued: "The interest and excitement of a year ago was nothing compared with the present. There has probably been no battle since the war commenced of more importance than the late ones in Pennsylvania. I do hope it will be the last one. My heart sinks within me to think of the dread battle fields. I hope we shall find a letter from you to night but do not much expect it. Your aunt Ruth says tell Sam to hurry home for she aches to make you more clothes. Your father is about to start for the post office and I must close. Remember you have a deep interest in our prayers and do not forget to pray for yourself."

That night, Private Northrup's brother Bert added a note to his mother's letter: "I never saw such a crowd at the post office as there was last night. Every body seems very anxious to hear the news."

The newspapers continued to report on a great battle. On July 8, the *Herald* stated, "A correspondent writing from Gettysburg after the late battles says Stannard's brigade of nine months Green Mountain Boys, after having repulsed the attack of the rebels, rushed in and took over 800 prisoners . . . Let Vermont ever hold them in grateful remembrance."

That same day both the *Freeman* and the *Free Press* ran a partial list of casualties from the Second Vermont Brigade. The *Freeman* said, "The people were publicly excited last night at the grand news from the seat of war. Flags were thrown out, bells rung, cannon fired, and every body felt good generally. The ringing of the bells continued long after nightfall."

Within a week after the fighting ended at Gettysburg, the home front began to realize that the Second Vermont Brigade had done something special, but at a considerable cost. On July 10, the full truth was revealed by the *Free Press,* which printed General Stannard's official report of the battle. It read, in part, "As soon as the change of the point of attack became evident I ordered a flank attack upon the enemy's column. Forming in the meadow in front of our lines, the 13th and 16th regiments marched down in column by the flank, changed front forward, and opened a destructive fire at short range . . . The movements I have briefly described were executed in the open under a heavy fire of shell, grape and musketry and they were performed with the promptness and precision of a battalion drill."

The *Free Press* that day also ran two accounts of Pickett's Charge from the *Richmond Sentinel* in the Confederate capital. Both noted the devastating effect of the Vermonters' flank attack. The first stated that as the Confederate advance neared the Union lines, "it swung around to the left and was exposed to the front fire and flanking fire of the Federals, which was very fatal. This swinging around unmasked a part of the enemy's force, five regiments being pushed out from their left to the attack." The other account reported, "A flanking party of the enemy, marching in column by regiments, was thrown out from the enemy's left on our extreme right, which was held by Kemper's Brigade, and by an enfilading fire forced the retirement of our troops."

That same day, the *Vermont Standard* wrote, "The 13th, 14th and 16th Vermont Regiments of Nine Months Men took part in the battle of Gettysburg and greatly distinguished themselves. Their loss in killed, wounded, and missing amounted to over three hundred and fifty, but they took over 800 prisoners . . . A dispatch was received in town this morning from Captain Paul of the 12th, dated Brattleboro 7 o'clock saying, 'We are all safe.'"

The *Standard* also carried a story about a man traveling through Vermont with a performing bear. A farmer somewhere got the man to give a show for his large family, and, at the end, the farmer asked the bear's owner what he was owed. The man said, "I can't take any thing, it is no more a sight for your family to see my bear than for my bear to see your family."

On July 10, the *Caledonian Record* reported, "At last we can say that a decisive battle has been fought and a glorious victory won. On the anniversary of our national independence the lightning flashed the glorious news across the country that, after a hard fought battle, the Army of the Potomac won a complete and overwhelming victory."

A week later, the *Record* editorialized: "Again have the noble sons of Vermont been tried amid the smoke and fire and carnage of the battle-field and found not wanting. The 1st Brigade won the admiration and praise of all loyal hearts by uncomplaining endurance of hardship in the Penninsula Campaign, by their bravery and daring on the bloody field of Antietam; and their steady courage and unfaltering heroism at the terrible battles of Fredericksburg. In the late battles of Gettysburg the 2nd Vermont Brigade showed the same courage, bravery, and daring as their older brothers in arms on the above memorable fields."

Another week passed, and on July 24 a complete list of the brigade's casualties filled half the *Record*'s front page.

In Brattleboro years later, Mrs. Levi K. Fuller recalled, "After every battle, a call was made for old linen, cotton, bandages, and money for supplies. The young women were the ones to solicit in different parts of the village, and we all had our beats. One friend, a school mate, and I, had part of our side of the brook, and I remember we collected $100 in an hour and a half two days after the Gettysburg battle, and we had been over the same ground a few weeks before." She also remembered that the opening of the Brattleboro military hospital, which Governor Holbrook had so vigorously sought, was a great relief to the local residents who had been housing wounded in their homes.

On June 29 from Benson on Lake Champlain went a letter from Sim Aiken to his brother Cpl. James Aiken in the 14th Vermont. "Have got over our hurry a little I finished shearing sheep last night, sheared for M.G. King. Have sheared 12 days in all the last day at home I cleaned off 40 sheep in good style. Have got don hoeing for the first time. Crops are looking pretty well. We need rain very much. I have been using Frank's rifle some lately. I could spot a Reb in the head EVERY time, at 100 yds. distance."

A reply came from Corporal Aiken in Brattleboro on July 22. "Father," it began, "Here I am once more in our dear old Green Mountain State alive and well & I assure you I am very thankful to return. It seems sad to think of our comrades who left here with us last summer and never will return. Alas, many of them are buried on the bloody field of Gettysburg. Since writing you last we have marched 250 miles & fought the bloodiest battle ever fought on this continent.

"I saw by last night's *Herald* that brother Sim was drafted—now I don't want to advise him contrary to wishes, or contrary to what seems to him to be his duty,—but—I DON'T want him to go to war. I think I am better able to judge what he ought to do than he is. Use any thing that belongs to me to keep him at home.

"I had rather turn & go back myself than to have him go.

"Remember me to the loved ones at home. I am most affectionately your returned soldier boy. J.H. Aiken."

Sad personal news of Gettysburg began to reach the Mead family in Hinesburg on July 6. The first to learn of Charles's death was his brother Elisha, living in Detroit. He received a telegram July 5 from a friend, E.B. Baldwin: "Your brother Charles was killed in battle the third (3)." But it was not until July 26 that the particulars were known, the facts having been ascertained by another brother, W.S. Mead, and written in a letter to brother Elisha. It stated, "The 14th Regiment is at Brattleboro some of the Hinesburg boys are here. Guy Boynton came here last Friday and gave us the particulars of our Brother's death it was at the time that the Rebbels were making one of their desperate charges upon our center. Guy said he had seen Charles and talked with him not two minutes before he was struck he said that Charles had just fired and loaded his gun when they were ordered to reserve their fire until the enemy came nearer. At that time he was struck and instantly killed, but not disfigured. They buried him under a large oak tree and set up a board with his name at the head of his grave . . . The last note in his diary is:

> Friday, July 3d. Heavy firing commenced at 4 AM. A shell struck a caisson within ten feet of where we lay feet on the ground.

"It is a great loss to us to lose our Brother. But we could not have chosen a better time, place or manner for his death. He fell in the front ranks in a great battle nobly doing his duty. Our national arms achieved a great victory and the Regiment and the Brigade to which he belonged covered themselves with lasting glory."

In Shoreham, the prayers of the Northrup family were answered as word was received that son Samuel, of the 14th, was safe and about to begin the long journey home.

★

26

The 12th Vermont reached Brattleboro on July 9. On that day Colonel Blunt and 200 of his men told Governor Holbrook of their willingness to return to New York and help put down the draft riots, but the governor declined their offer. Thus the entire regiment was on hand to welcome the 13th at the station and escort it to Camp Lincoln with a torchlight parade. Lieutenant Colonel Farnham sent the following telegram:

Bradford, July 9th 1863

By Telegraph from Brattleboro
To Mrs. Roswell Farnham

We reached here this morning—Come down today

ROSWELL FARNHAM

The Woodstock Company of the 12th, Capt. Ora Paul commanding, arrived home July 15. "At the foot of Central Street," the *Standard* reported, "was suspended the sentiment, worked in evergreen, 'Welcome Home.' Stretched across the street at the East end of the Phoenix Block was another sentiment 'Green Mountain Boys Ever True,' and near it was suspended a mammoth United States flag. At the entrance to the park an evergreen arch was erected bearing the words, 'Home Sweet Home' . . . From time to time through the day dispatches were received from the company indicating their progress, and when about four o'clock it was announced that they would be here in about an hour the jam in our streets was very great. A long procession of citizens was formed and headed by a volunteer band and mounted marshall and marched out about half a mile to receive them. Arriving in the village the procession marched through the west end of the park and then down the inside to the tables."

Captain Paul, who had once fired at Mosby's men down a dark Virginia road, responded to a brief welcoming speech. He noted that the company left Woodstock with 101 men, returning with 94. "Two have died, four have been discharged, and one has been transferred to another company," he said. "What they were ordered to do, they have done, where they were ordered to go, they have gone."

The paper then stated that "the company made a splendid charge on the

267

well-filled tables." After the feast, "[T]he drummer boy of the brigade band, which led the company into town, was then dragged upon the stand and gave us the long roll in splendid manner. The crowd then broke up and the company marched to the Town Hall for the transaction of a little business before separating. While in the hall the company gave nine cheers for Capt. Paul . . . Then they marched into the street and broke ranks for the last time. At sunset the brigade band discoursed from the piazza of Henry's Hotel the most charming music. The day was one of great rejoycing in Woodstock and one long to be remembered."

Private Jackson noted on July 15, "Took cars for Rut. Were well received by the citizens . . . and were treated to a good dinner at the Central House."

"Our first day in Camp Lincoln on our way home was a busy and happy one," Ralph Sturtevant wrote. "Our camp was full of citizens of Brattleboro and friends from up the state, men and women, boys and girls all the day long anxious to see the soldier boys of the bully 13th and hear them tell of the sanguinary struggle at Gettysburg . . . Our stay in Brattleboro for a week seemed much too long, for all were anxious to reach home . . . Our friends and relatives from up state were arriving on every train, the boys were going to the village and elsewhere in and about Brattleboro as pleased. Time began to hang heavy and each succeeding day seemed longer."

As they waited, Pvt. Samuel Hand rejoined the 13th. The oldest man in the regiment, thought to be nearly 60, he had served as a cook's helper in Virginia and was left behind as the long march began. He came through New York City on his way to Brattleboro, and a friend described him: "He was in a somewhat battered condition for on his way home he reached New York while the great riot was in progress and his uniform betrayed him to the fury of the mob, and he was roughly handled."

Sturtevant added more details: "The negligence of a few delayed the mustering out until Monday the 20th on which date each company was ordered to fall into line near their company quarters, and there the roll was called to ascertain if all present, and when Major Austine appeared accompanied by Colonel Randall and some of the staff and after the several officers in command of the respective companies announced all present or accounted for and then after a hasty examination of a final written report and personal inspection by looking up and down the line, said with a smile, 'You are released from further service. The discharge papers have been filled up and placed in the hands of your officers and will be delivered to you before leaving camp.' The paying off took more time, for each had to sign his name and receive what was due. Though the amount was small, each was glad to have it . . . Everything we purchased at Brattleboro had attached to it a big price, and a few greenbacks did not go far or last long. Each comrade, as they were now about to separate and go to their respective homes, wanted to treat his friends with lemonade, ice cream and cake, etc., before parting, and I am sure all did . . .

"The time had come, the last order had been made known to us, and now we began to realize the great family circle of our regiment must be broken, and each go his way not again to hear the reveille and tatoo and greet each other at the morning roll call nor open our hearts' dearest thoughts to tentmate and comrade during the lonely vigil of the picket line, and we were sad at the thought of parting . . . The friendships formed when associated together in the dangers of warfare are different and stronger than any other relation among men, but this we did not at the time fully realize, and yet each heart softened and eye moistened as we grasped hands on the day of separation, July 21st, 1863, and said good-by.

"The last company roll call was furnished and . . . the several companies of the regiment were marched to the parade grounds and formed a hollow square into which Colonel Randall and other officers of the Field and Staff entered for the parting ceremony. The Colonel said, as I remember, 'Boys, we are about to separate and take the cars for home . . . I appreciate your courteous conduct and loyalty to me as your colonel. I am sorry to part with you boys, for I feel you are all my friends, I shall never forget your friendship or faithfulness, and shall ever remember, I trust, with pride and pleasure how well and manfully you performed your duty from first to last, and especially your dash and courage in battle. I have good reason to be proud of what you did at Gettysburg . . . It is a wonder that many more were not left on the field when we consider the critical positions we occupied and desperate charges we made . . . It is my hope and expectation that in whatever sphere of life you may choose, you will prove as faithful and true and do your duty as well as you have while following the flag of your country. I do not wish to say good by, but would be pleased to have one and all come forward that I might take you by the hand before we start for home.'

"This rather informal reception so much enjoyed was soon over and all hastened to their respective quarters and soon returned ready to break camp and march to the depot and at the hour of about two o'clock in the afternoon started on that ever to be remembered and anxious journey for our homes dearer now than before . . . Our term of enlistment had expired, we had been duly mustered out and were free to go wherever it pleased us best. We still wore our uniforms and were proud that we had earned the right to do so."

On July 24, the *Freeman* reported the arrival of the 13th in Montpelier: "The Thirteenth Regiment—Colonel Randall, with many of the field and staff officers of the Thirteenth Regiment, and Captains Colburn and Slayton, arrived in town last (Thursday) evening at 8 o'clock. A large gathering of the people and the adjoining towns was at the depot, including quite a sprinkling of the Thirteenth boys who came in that morning. The train was greeted, on its arrival, with hearty cheers. There was no formal reception of the officers, the programme determined upon previously having been abandoned on account of the unexpected arrival of the soldiers the morning before. Fifteen guns, however, were fired, and the eager crowd compelled Col. Randall to appear on the balcony of the Pavilion, and saluted him with rousing cheers, to which the gallant colonel happily and briefly responded."

In Brattleboro, Private Williams in the 14th on July 22 wrote, "We were assembled at nine o'clock in the morning and addressed by the Colonel. All of us who desired were to be allowed to go home for six days, until arrangements were completed for our discharge from the service. After cleaning up our arms, we took the train for Rutland, reaching there at midnight. Slept in the cars until four o'clock in the morning.

"Thursday, July 23, 1863—Left Rutland at four o'clock in the morning and arrived at my uncle's house before they were up. Oh, the gracious welcome and kindness to me. After having something to eat, I bathed and cleaned and had clean clothes. Several came to see me. Had a good comfortable bed to sleep in."

Also in the 14th was Pvt. Edwin Pierce, whose best friend Billy Cairns had been killed beside him in the great artillery barrage before Pickett's Charge. He likely took the same train as Private Williams and got off at the Cuttingsville station some 10 miles south of Rutland in the early-morning darkness. Still tired from the long march and battle, Private Pierce no doubt hoped that a wagon would give him a lift the four uphill miles to his North Shrewsbury home. But he walked all the way, and saw the lights of home as he trudged the last few yards. As Pierce stepped through the front door, he collapsed from exhaustion.

Private Williams continued, "Tuesday, July 28, 1863—Returned to Brattleboro. Arrived there early in the afternoon.

"Wednesday, July 29—Rain in the morning. In the afternoon we gave up our arms.

"Thursday, July 30—Mustered out of the service in the morning. No reason for not returning home. A meeting in the evening in the town hall and the soldiers who were there acting like beasts."

Ironically, another member of the 14th, Pvt. Henry Dunn, enjoyed but a brief homecoming in Charlotte. On July 28, the *Burlington Times* reported:

"Murder in Charlotte—We learn that the neighboring town of Charlotte was on Sunday night the scene of a murder. The body of the wounded man, Henry Dunn, was found on the roadside, near Leavenworth's Mills, yesterday morning. It was perforated with buckshot, or perhaps a smaller size. An inquest was holden yesterday . . . The officers have arrested an Irishman named Burns as the suspected murderer."

Colonel Veazey's return to his beloved Julia must have been especially joyous, since their first child, a daughter, had been born just four days after the guns fell silent at Gettysburg. They christened the little girl Anne Gettysburg Veazey.

A soldier in the 16th Vermont was on a train with wounded from Gettysburg. He wrote to the *Freeman*, "Our division hospital was broken up on the 18th. The patients who were able had been previously sent to the village of Gettysburg, and from there they were sent to Baltimore and from thence disbursed . . . As we passed through Maryland and Pennsylvania we were greeted with unexpected cheers from the people who thronged the roadside in every village we passed and waved flags and handkerchiefs . . . Convalescent sick and wounded are every day reaching Brattleboro." Among those who also rode a train filled with wounded was Corporal Hitchcock, himself shot in the leg. "Sitting all night on the floor of a freight car with just a little hay spread under us," he recalled, "jolting and bumping along, for men whose wounds had reached a stage of extreme sensitiveness, was mild torture."

Some 25,000 wounded Union and Confederate soldiers remained in and around Gettysburg. A Vermonter and army physician, Maj. Henry Janes, the former town doctor in Waterbury, was sent to take charge of what would later be described as a "vast sea of human misery." Janes believed that no amputation should be performed until absolutely necessary. Among the wounded in his charge was a Vermonter too sick to travel. Newly promoted Corporal Doubleday was not doing well, his left leg smashed by a bullet. On August 4, according to his medical record, he was suffering from chronic diarrhea. On August 5, he was receiving injections of astringents and was fed arrowroot soup. His condition was listed as feeble.

A friend, or relative, named Avery went from Vermont to Gettysburg to help with his care. Doubleday managed to write one more letter to Asceneth:

> A good letter you sent me—strawberries O how good—taste to me. You don't know how glad I was to see Mr. Avery. He says he will stay with me until I can go home. he tend right to me. How I want to see you but don't make yourself sick worrying about me. We are expecting every day to be moved. We can't go to a worse place than this. Uncle Dan says I must not write any more, so good bye. Kiss the boys for me.

FROM YOUR EVER LOVING WILLIAM

On August 7, wine and brandy were added to Doubleday's diet, as the diarrhea persisted. Two days later, he developed dysentery. The next day, in a desperate attempt to reverse the decline, a surgeon amputated the lower third of the leg. On August 12, despite the administering of "stimulants and injections," the patient died at 6 PM.

Doubleday was listed by Adjutant General Washburn's office as having died from wounds and was thus counted as a war casualty. But other members of the Second Vermont Brigade who died as a result of their service were never counted among the official total of 5,224 Vermonters who perished in the Civil War.

Albert Barnard, 21, just discharged, reached home in Waitsfield exhausted. A comrade remembered, "Like so many others, those last marches and the battle proved to be more than he could endure, and he reached home sick and died August 12, 1863." His grieving parents had carved on the tombstone of their only son, "We have laid thee on our country's altar."

Marquis Emerson, at age 15, had left college to enlist in the 13th. "When the regiment arrived in Brattleboro, he was sick," said a fellow soldier, "though still able to attend to his arduous duties as orderly. The regiment was discharged July 21, and on his arrival at his home in Milton the following day, he went immediately to bed, from which he never rose. He lingered, most of the time delirious, until August 3d, when he died." The friend added, "He gave his life for his country's cause as surely as though his heart had been pierced by the enemy's bullet on the battlefield at Gettysburg."

Clark Cressey returned to Berlin but "his health was never good after his return from the war. He died in 1864 in Berlin," said a fellow soldier.

Sgt. Lorenzo Cutler died at home on July 24, after returning to Brattleboro and being admitted to the hospital there. "The Gettysburg campaign was too strenuous for his rather delicate condition," a fellow soldier recalled.

Pvt. John Baird was 20 when he came home to Fayston. "The hardships of our march to Gettysburg," a friend remembered, "together with the experiences of the battle and the march that followed it were too much for him . . . died Sept. 19, 1863."

"The close of the Gettysburg Campaign found him exhausted," said a friend of Sgt. Aretus Thayer. Soon after returning home to Warren, the 22-year-old was dead despite "the tenderest care."

William Hathaway had been ill since he contracted the measles in March. Discharged early, he never made it to Gettysburg, but died a few months after reaching his Moretown home. He was 19.

Pvt. Joel Robinson was 28 when he enlisted. He fought at Gettysburg and was discharged with his regiment in Brattleboro. But he was ill with typhus on his return to his upland home in Calais, and he died there on July 28. Within weeks, four other members of his family contracted the disease and died.

Those cases were all in the 13th regiment. How many from other regiments died at home of the effects of war? The 14th regiment's assistant surgeon, Dr. Lucretius Ross of Poultney, said many years after the war, ". . . the long march to Gettysburg, the terrible three days of battle and the week's march after the battle, and the journey home to Vermont, killed and disabled more men than all the rest of our service. More men died of disease directly after getting home than died during our service."

And how many family members died from diseases brought to Vermont by their soldier sons, brothers, fathers, and uncles?

In Warren, the young fiancée of Private Wilson (he had been shot during Pickett's Charge) was a tragic example of another kind of casualty. Pvt. Edward Fisk, a member of Wilson's company, wrote, "The missile that pierced his heart, like cases without number in the war, slew another in the home town, who was to become his wife on his return. She lived only a few months after the terrible news reached her."

There were lingering deaths from wounds. Captain Williams of the 13th, hit on the battle's third day, suffered for weeks at his Bakersfield home. A comrade in arms, Cpl. J.W. Hitchcock, who later became a minister, recalled: "Everything possible was done by devoted friends for his comfort and recovery; and for some time he was very hopeful. A fatal result was doubtless inevitable. After eleven weeks of suffering, patiently and heroically endured, death brought relief. He viewed death calmly and said he was ready to go, in hope of Christian immortality. He gave minute instructions for his funeral, requesting that Company G might be there, and that Rev. E.A. Titus preach the sermon. It was held at the Congregational Church in Bakersfield, attended by a very large gathering of citizens and soldiers, with impressive services, and many demonstrations of love and mourning. His body reposes in the now beautiful cemetery of his home town." Captain Williams was 23.

In late August, Pvt. Henry White was laid to rest in Woodstock. The *Vermont Standard* noted that services were held at the Methodist church, with the other two churches in the village closed for the occasion, though it was a Sunday. "More attended the services than the house could hold," the paper reported. "We understand that Mr. White, at the time he enlisted, was fitting for the ministry."

On July 24, the *Standard* had run the following news item:

GRAVES OF VERMONT WOUNDED

Robert R. Corson, Esq., state military agent at Philadelphia, has notified Adjutant General Washburn that the graves of the following Vermont soldiers, killed at Gettysburg, may be found 'under walnut tree in center of line near Emmitsburg Road.'

14th Regiment
Sergt. John Vaughan, Co. D, Manchester.
Dyer Rogers, D, Orwell.
G.S. Boseboom, D, Benson.
Wm. Green, G, Lincoln.
Corp. E.E. Mead, G, Hinesburgh.

16th Regiment
Jos. M. Martin, D, Jamaica.
Martin J. Cook, D, Windham.
Corp. Chas. Morse, H, Rochester.
Ira Emery, Jr., H, Bethel.
R.H. Tarbell, E, Chester.

The men who were well and able went back to their civilian occupations. Like many others in the brigade, Jabez Hammond and his brothers resumed work on their father's farm in West Windsor. James Scully, on whom the great flank movement had pivoted, became a dry goods clerk again.

In October, the *Burlington Times* noted that "only one of the colonels of the Second Vermont Brigade re-enters the service, Col. Randall of the 13th. Cols. Veazey and Proctor have opened a law office in Rutland. Col. Blunt has a machine shop in St. Johnsbury, while Col. Nichols resumes his law practice and goes to the State Senate."

Back at Gettysburg, treating the wounded and burying the dead continued. A tract of land was procured on Cemetery Hill for the burial of the Union dead, and they were dug up from the battlefield (some from under the walnut tree along the Emmitsburg Road) and near the hospitals from their shallow graves marked by hastily carved wooden headstones. They were carefully reburied in a great semicircle, by the state, on the gentle hillside where artillery fire had once rained in. November 19, 1863, was set for the cemetery dedication, and the most renowned orator of the time, Edward Everett of Massachusetts, agreed to speak. Later, President Lincoln accepted an invitation to deliver a few appropriate remarks.

Lieutenant Benedict, again editing the *Free Press,* traveled to Gettysburg for the occasion. He wrote of his trip for the paper, in a letter dated November 20: "We took at Wrightsville [Pennsylvania] a 'one horse' railroad to York, and then a one-and-a-half horse railroad to Gettysburg, reaching there through much delay and tribulation at ten o'clock at night—to find the hotels overflowing . . .

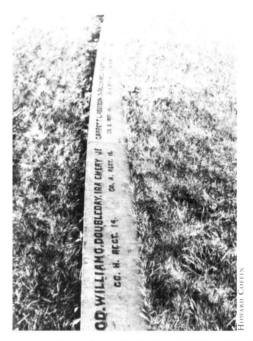

Vermont graves at Gettysburg, including William Doubleday's.

The next day I gave to the battle-field. I went to the scene of the first day's hard and costly fight. Guided by Maj. Rosengarten, then of Maj. Gen. Reynolds' Staff, I stood upon the spot where that brave and able general fell . . . We passed next to the south, along the ridge on which Lee formed his lines on the second day. The fields, then trampled by many thousand ill-shod rebels, have regained in that portion of the battle ground, in large measure, their former condition; the fences have been put up, and the plough and harrow have obliterated the deep cannon ruts . . . I reached the top of Round Top just as a fine national flag was flung to the breeze from a tall staff erected on its very summit. Then passing toward the centre, I stopped, of course, on the ground held by Stannard's men of the Vermont Second Brigade, and on which they flanked and shattered the rebel column . . . The battle ground here remains much as it was left at the battle's close—clothes, clothing, cartridge-boxes, bayonet sheaths, and soldiers' accoutrements by the thousands still strew the ground. The low breast-works of rails still remain, and the skeletons of horses covered by the skin, are scattered unburied as they fell."

His letter continued: "Thence to Cemetery Hill, on the left of which the grounds of the National Cemetery have been laid out. I found easily the position allotted to Vermont on the north-eastern slope of Cemetery Hill. NINETEEN of the bodies of our brave boys have been removed from the spots where they found hasty burial, and re-interred here, and the trenches are open for the remainder. Their remains are placed in plain wooden coffins in trenches walled with stone at the head and feet, and each body marked by a numbered stake, to be

274

replaced in due time I suppose by a suitable head board or stone. The work of re-interment is going on over the whole ground. About 1,200, hardly a third of the whole number of our dead, have thus far been collected; but it is intended the work shall be completed by winter."

Benedict concluded his letter, "I need not describe the proceedings of yesterday. Mr. Everett's polished discourse; President Lincoln's simple and touching dedicatory speech; the generals and governors and grandees present—all of this you have already had in the city papers . . ."

One wonders whether Benedict, a man of letters, was really present to hear the words of Lincoln and Everett. Perhaps he wandered the battlefield while the speaking went on. Why did he not note Everett's mention of Stannard's flank attack? The orator, during his two-hour address, gave an account of the three days of fighting and while describing the repulse of Pickett's Charge spoke of "Stannard's brigade of the First." Had he heard Lincoln's few appropriate remarks, he surely would have recognized the quality, and written more extended praise, of the "Gettysburg Address."

On Cemetery Hill the night of November 19, with the great crowd gone away, 19 Vermonters already reburied lay still in the now hallowed ground, the mightiest words the nation had yet brought forth, and likely ever would, having honored them. Among their number was Corporal Doubleday, at rest 500 miles from his mountain home and his beloved Asceneth and the boys. Eventually, 61 Vermonters would lie in Gettysburg National Cemetery.

★

Vermont has made a conscious effort to preserve its 19th-century countryside and streetscapes; thus, much of it would today be recognizable to many of the more than 34,000 lads who went forth to the Union armies. One community that particularly retains its Civil War look is Woodstock, in south-central Vermont. There lived Adjutant General Washburn, running the entire Vermont war effort from an office on the village square. His home still stands a few hundred yards away, across the Ottauquechee River at the corner of Mountain Avenue and River Street. His brick Greek Revival home, 50 years ago a hollow shell, has been restored and enlarged and is now a private home. You can retrace what must have been his route to work each morning, starting by his home and proceeding south across the reconstructed, covered Middle Bridge. Crossing it, you come to the boat-shaped village green upon which the townsfolk turned out to welcome home Captain Paul's company of the 12th Vermont.

On the green and along the village streets, Washburn marched his Woodstock Light Infantry Company as he drilled it before departing for Virginia to face fire in the war's first battle. He made that company the best in all Vermont. Across the green stands the antebellum Windsor County Court House, where the civilian Washburn, a prosperous Woodstock lawyer, certainly spent much time. As he turned and walked toward the village square, Washburn passed a row of stately white clapboard and brick houses, all of which survive. On the corner of the square stands a large white frame house that is reported to have brought shelter to escaped slaves before the Civil War, a stop on the Underground Railroad. Washburn himself was an abolitionist, firmly believing that the willingness of black soldiers to don the Union blue and risk life and limb for their freedom entitled them to full citizenship. In his lifetime he lamented that justice had not been done the supposedly freed slaves.

When death came to him in the winter of 1870, at age 56, during his term as governor, he was buried in River Street Cemetery, not far from his home. There rest many veterans of the Civil War, including Thomas Seaver, who won a Medal of Honor at Spotsylvania Court House and, later, uttered stirring words at the Vermont monuments' dedication at Gettysburg. Nearby are the small stones of several members of the 54th Massachusetts, the black regiment that earned glory in its brave storming of the walls of Fort Wagner. Vermont constructed one of the finest war records of all the Union states, and suffered the second highest number of men killed, per capita, among them. It was from Woodstock that the orders went forth that constituted and kept filled the units that held the vital crossroads in the Wilderness, stormed Marye's Heights at Fredericksburg, stopped the Confederate onslaught at Cedar Creek, and, of course, broke the flank of Pickett's Charge.

27

Though the nine-months Second Vermont Brigade had returned home, nearly two years of fighting remained in the Civil War. Having seen the worst of war, and no doubt feeling their duty done, most of the Vermonters resumed their civilian lives, resisting entreaties to reenlist in other units and resume military service.

Back in Vermont, Lt. Frank Kenfield of the 13th, recovered from his Gettysburg wounds, had been home but a short time when he received a message from Adjutant General Washburn summoning him to Woodstock. "I went and met him at his office," said Kenfield, "and he said he wished to raise two more regiments from that five that had just been mustered out. These to be the 17th and 18th, and he wished me to raise a company for the 17th. I told him I felt that it was quite an undertaking as I doubted if those men would be willing to reenlist."

On August 3, 1863, Governor Holbrook nonetheless directed that a new regiment, the 17th Vermont, be organized. Lt. Joel Lucia, who served in it, recalled, "The Second Vermont Brigade, composed of nine months men, having won glory and renown and made an enviable record, has recently been mustered out, and it was expected that many of these men, flushed with their great accomplishment would be eager to enlist in the new regiments. This did not prove to be the case, and recruiting was slow indeed."

The idea of an 18th Vermont was soon abandoned. But Colonel Randall accepted command of the 17th, while Lt. Col. Charles Cummings was appointed second in command. Some other members of General Stannard's brigade returned to service. Among them were John Yale, once cared for by his father as he lay near death in Virginia; Elden Hartshorn, forgiven by a court-martial for allegedly not fighting Mosby; and Kenfield, who had hurried to reach the brigade just before Gettysburg. But the 17th Vermont, with seven undermanned companies, did not go south until April 1864. Its first action was in the Battle of the Wilderness, where the regiment went in with just 313 men. The 17th served through the remainder of the war, fighting at Spotsylvania, at Cold Harbor, and in the long siege of Petersburg.

Colonel Randall returned home safely to resume lawyering, farming, and playing his violin. But Charles Cummings never got back to his Brattleboro newspaper office. In fighting on September 30 along the Petersburg lines, at Peebles

Farm, he was shot down in a Union attack. His men heard him shout, "Save the colors boys." Badly wounded, Cummings ended up behind enemy lines. Two days later a message came under a flag of truce that he had died, and several days after that his body was passed through the lines to be borne back to Vermont for a funeral in Brattleboro on October 26.

Pvt. Francis V. Crain, a Moretown lad nicknamed Cucumber, was shot dead in the Wilderness, as was Pvt. John Bowen, who had reenlisted as a sharpshooter. Stephen Brown joined the 17th. In fighting near the Wilderness's Widow Tapp clearing, he was hit in the left arm. Several days later it was amputated and he was out of the service for good. Also dead in the Wilderness was Pvt. Charles Carson, 21, of the 13th, remembered as stalwart and robust.

On July 30, a huge mine exploded under the Confederate lines at Petersburg, and a massive but delayed Union attack advanced into The Crater. In the ensuing battle Pvt. Thompson Stoddard, 19, once the popular laundryman of Company B of the 13th Vermont, was wounded and captured. He lived only until August 7. Lt. William Martin, a Marshfield lad who was remembered for keeping up the spirits of many men on the march to Gettysburg, also was killed.

Pvt. James Clark, wounded in the fight at Spotsylvania's Bloody Angle on May 12, 1864, recovered in time to charge The Crater, where he was shot dead.

The October 20 *Vermont Standard* noted, "Brigadier Gen. George J. Stannard, late of the 2nd Vermont Brigade, is now in command of the government forces in and about New York, of course subordinate to Gen. Dix, who commands the Eastern Department. Gen. Stannard has not yet sufficiently recovered from his wounds received at Gettysburg to ride a horse." Stannard recovered and returned to combat as a brigadier general at Cold Harbor, leading a heroic charge against Confederate entrenchments, and suffering another wound. Then on September 30, 1864, he led an attack against Fort Harrison, outside Richmond. The fort was taken, and Stannard led its defense against desperate attacks personally directed by Robert E. Lee. The fort held, but a bullet took Stannard's right arm.

Pvt. John Kusic, of Stowe, reenlisted in the 11th Vermont and was killed at Cold Harbor.

Pvt. Allen Frisbee, at home in Westfield, recalled, "I had a younger brother who was . . . mortally wounded at Spotsylvania Court House, Va., May 12, 1864 and another brother in the 9th Minnesota Volunteers taken prisoner and died in Andersonville Prison." A rebel prison at Richmond took the life of Pvt. Henry Wakefield, 21, formerly of the 13th, from East Montpelier, who was captured at The Crater. Pvt. Felix Valley, 23, of Plainfield, was also seized there and died in the Confederate prison at Salisbury, North Carolina, where he is buried.

Charles Tewksbury reenlisted in the 11th Vermont and served through the rest of the war. Late in life he said that he had seen plenty of dangerous service, including the battles of Cedar Creek and the siege of Petersburg, but nothing ever compared to Gettysburg.

Colonel Blunt returned to the service, and for many postwar years was superintendent of the military prison at Fort Leavenworth, Kansas.

Edwin Stoughton never returned to the military. He joined his uncle and namesake, a wealthy patent attorney in New York City, in the practice of law. The uncle was a man of influence who, though a Democrat, would in later years become a friend of Ulysses Grant and Rutherford B. Hayes. The latter, as president, named him minister to Russia. There was no such rosy future for the nephew. The former brigade commander was practicing law in New York in 1864 when a group of Confederates set fire to several buildings in an attempt to burn the city. The flames were soon extinguished, though P.T. Barnum's famous museum was leveled. Robert Cobb Kennedy, one of the arsonists, was captured and put on trial in New York. During his days at West Point, Kennedy, a Louisianan, had been one of Stoughton's many Southern friends. Thus he sought Stoughton's services as an attorney, and Stoughton agreed. A trial was held in New York, and Stoughton mounted an energetic defense as Kennedy steadfastly maintained his innocence. But Kennedy was sentenced to die on March 19, 1865. Stoughton visited him in his jail cell, and early on the morning of the appointed day walked to the gallows with his client and friend. As an army officer raised his sword to signal the hanging, the doomed man began to sing.

Stoughton must have been affected by the killing of Lincoln's assassin, John Wilkes Booth. Found in the pocket of the dead actor was a picture of Booth's lady love, Lucy Hale. She was the young woman whom Mary Farnham, in the winter of 1863, had seen Stoughton squiring around a Washington hotel, reporting that they were said to be in love.

Through the brief years after his military career ended in disgrace, Stoughton's health, none too good after his Richmond imprisonment, continued to fail. He was finally forced to give up the law and returned to Bellows Falls, where, at age 30, he died on Christmas Day 1868.

For other former members of the Second Brigade, though out of the service, the war was not quite over. Albert Wells returned to Enosburg and became a preacher. He and his wife happened to be in nearby Sheldon on October 19, 1864, when Confederates who had just robbed the banks in St. Albans rode through on their way to Canada. One of the raiders stopped his horse beside the Reverend and Mrs. Wells and asked them the way to the border. The former private replied, "You will find it quite a piece before you get there." Galloping away, a rebel dropped his pistol, and Wells picked it up and kept it.

Pvt. Charles Howard, formerly of the 13th Vermont, moved to Pennsylvania soon after his return home. In the spring of 1865, just after Abraham Lincoln's assassination, he was arrested and held for 24 hours because he fit Booth's description.

Before the war ended, George Benedict began assembling information on all the Vermont regiments. In January 1864, Colonel Proctor wrote to him of the 15th Vermont: "Now Benedict, though the 15th would have been 'historical' if kept with the Brigade & put into the fight, as it was we claim nothing more than to have obeyed orders and taken good care of the train." Proctor was elected governor in 1878, and the Vermont Legislature authorized him to appoint a state historian to compile a history of Vermont in the war of the rebellion. Proctor chose Benedict, who in 1886 published a detailed, two-volume *Vermont in the Civil War*. In 1895, he published a collection of his letters home from the war, *Army Life in Virginia*.

Artistic Pvt. William Jackson became a photographic retoucher in Burlington, often returning to Rutland to court the lovely Caroline Eastman. But in 1866 there was a lovers' quarrel and a saddened Jackson left Vermont. He went west and in the 1870s hooked up with the Hayden Survey, sent out by the government to chart the vast western landscape still largely unseen by most Americans. Undeterred by his unwieldy box camera, Jackson produced thousands of images of the central Rockies, the Tetons, Yellowstone, and much more. His photos helped convince Congress to set aside great areas of the West for permanent protection as national parks. He became one of the finest photographers America has yet produced.

Corporal Williams and Sergeant Palmer came through the war unscathed and converted their wartime diaries into books. Palmer's, published in 1864, noted that during the fury of Gettysburg, he was reminded of the following lines from Milton's *Paradise Lost:*

> From those deep-throated engines belche'd, whose roar
> Embowel'd with outrageous noise the air,
> And all her entrails tore, disgorging foul
> Their devilish glut, chain'd thunderbolts and hail
> Of iron globes; which on the victor host
> Level'd with such impetuous fury smote
> That, whom they hit, none on their feet might stand,
> Though standing else as rocks, but down they fell
> By Thousands.

Palmer was three times elected to the Vermont Legislature and became superintendent of Vermont's public schools. He died in 1914.

Soon after Gettysburg, a controversy erupted concerning just who was responsible for ordering the Vermonters' flank attack on Pickett. General Hancock insisted that it was his doing; Stannard resolutely maintained that he had given the order before hearing anything from Hancock or his staff. Not long before his death, according to Benedict, Hancock somewhat softened his claim; after he died a handwritten memorandum stated, "I had seen the importance of it and probably General Stannard had also, and may have given similar directions. This is quite probable for General Stannard was a cool and reliable officer, in whom I had great confidence, from earlier associations."

After the war, against the advice of friends, Stannard accepted the position of collector of customs for the District of Vermont. In charge of a large payroll and with the power to make appointments, he apparently showed much favor to old army friends. He resigned in 1872, with a sizable shortfall in his accounts, though he was never accused of any wrongdoing. In 1881, nearly broke, Stannard became doorkeeper for the US House of Representatives, sadly and silently keeping watch at the entrance to the ladies' visitors gallery. He died in Washington in 1891; on his deathbed he repeated his assertion that he, not Hancock, had ordered the great flank attack. His body came back to Vermont for a funeral in Burlington. The *Free Press* carried an account, probably written by G.G. Benedict, that began, "For nearly an hour before the procession formed hundreds were gathering in the City Park and on all sides of the square, awaiting the time when

Statue of George Stannard atop the Vermont monument at Gettysburg.

the funeral cortege should take up the line of march. The scene was one of deep interest,—the great multitide awaiting in hushed expectation, flags drooping from their staffs at half mast, public and private buildings draped in black, stores and places of business all around closed . . . As the troops forming the military escort began to assemble, the measured tramp of many feet, the tap of muffled drums, the low command, the reverent bearing of the troops, all conspired to enhance the deep solemnity of the occasion."

Stannard rests in Lakeview Cemetery, beneath his bronze statue with empty sleeve. Nearby are Major William Wells (later Brigadier General), who led the Vermont Cavalry at Gettysburg, and Maj. Gen. Oliver Otis Howard, who commanded the entire Union force at Gettysburg before relinquishing command to Hancock. It was Howard who had selected Cemetery Ridge and Cemetery Hill as the Union position. The old general lived the last 15 years of his life in Burlington, to be near his officer son, who was stationed at nearby Fort Ethan Allen.

Benedict died in 1912, having long presided over the family newspaper and serving for 40 years as a University of Vermont trustee. An obituary noted that he walked with a military bearing until the end.

Even before the war had ended, the five regiments of the Second Vermont Brigade began to hold regimental reunions. At a gathering of the 13th Vermont, Ralph Sturtevant was elected historian and set about assembling a detailed chronicle. The 897-page work, *Pictorial History, 13th Regiment, Vermont Volunteers*—one of the best of all the regimental histories from the Civil War—appeared in 1913.

The veterans gathered at the State House on October 22, 1868, and heard an address by the man who had administered the war effort from Woodstock. Former Adj. Gen. Peter Washburn delivered the keynote address. In recounting the history of Vermont in the war, he noted the great moment of the Second Brigade: "The tornado ceased, and the veteran division of Pickett was hurled against them . . . then was the time for the Second Brigade. Changing front upon the battle-field with the precision of a parade, they assailed the rebel column in flank and it disappeared before the impetuous charge."

As the years passed, the reunions became occasions for stirring rhetoric. Washburn set a considerable standard that autumn day: "The names of your deceased comrades, whose memories are kept 'green and sacred' in your hearts, yet fresh in your recollection, are known and honored throughout the State . . . May they never be forgotten. Patriotic towns have erected monuments to the patriot dead; and in every grave yard throughout the state are grassy mounds, whose marble headstones mark the resting place of the soldier, where he awaits the final reveille. Let these monuments stand, while time shall endure, not merely as the votive offerings of a grateful people to commemorate brave deeds and men, but perpetual remembrances of the great principle of the universal equality of man, illustrated by its defenders in their lives, but rendered sacred by their sacrifice,—so that, when your children's children, to the remotest generation, shall gaze reverently upon them, when your name and deeds shall have faded even from tradition, they shall say, each to the other,—these men died that we might be free."

And Washburn went on, in the spirit of Lincoln at Gettysburg, to speak of tasks unfinished. "The national faith and the national honor, to be preserved at all

Veterans of the 14th Vermont at the dedication of their regimental monument.

hazards, demand," he said, "not only that slavery, but that every incident and result of slavery, shall cease to exist; that the loyal colored men of the South shall retain inalienably the right to maintain by the ballot the privileges for which they were willing and were deemed worthy to contend with the bayonet and the bullet."

Veterans of the 14th met in Fair Haven in 1887 to mark the 25th anniversary of their entry into the service. A highlight was the reading of a lengthy letter sent by Gen. Abner Doubleday, which included the following story: "My brother, at present residing in North Carolina, was conversing recently with one of Pickett's men who was made prisoner in the charge. He gave his experience as follows, 'I told my Captain that the Yankees were on our flank, but he said we had nothing to do with that. Those in the rear would attend to them. All we had to do was go forward. He said, Follow me! and I tried to do so when I suddenly felt the muzzle of a revolver pressed against my head and heard a Vermonter say, "wall naouw, I guess you won't go any farther in that direction!" and I didn't.'"

Doubleday wrote, "The country will never cease to honor the men who in the most critical period of the Battle of Gettysburg, flung themselves with the steadfast courage of veterans, upon the flanks of the elite troops of the enemy . . . It was one of the most brilliant episodes of the war and did much to gain victory."

In 1886, the Vermont Legislature appointed a state commission to draft plans for appropriate monuments at Gettysburg. Among the commissioners were George Benedict, Wheelock Veazey, and Redfield Proctor. They decided to erect five monuments—two to the Vermont sharpshooters; one to the First Vermont Brigade; one to the First Vermont Cavalry; and a grand state monunent, 55 feet high, a copy of Lord Nelson's column in Trafalgar Square, to be topped by a statue of General Stannard. To stand on Cemetery Ridge near where the Second Vermont Brigade was positioned on July 3, the general would be depicted in bronze with an empty sleeve (though his arm was not lost until well after Gettysburg). The monuments were dedicated on October 9, 1889, with a large crowd present from Vermont. Veazey spoke: "It was here that the Second Vermont Brigade stood in what turned out to be the pivotal point of the battle." Poet Julia Dorr, of Rutland, composed a lengthy poem for the occasion, which was read by one Prof. James Churchill. It concluded:

> Oh beautiful one, my Country
> Thou fairest daughter of Time,
> To-day are thine eyes unclouded
> In the light of faith sublime!
> No thunder of battle appals thee;
> From thy woe thou has found release;
> From the graves of thy sons steals only
> This one soft whisper,—'Peace!'

Col. Thomas Seaver, a member of the commission, who had won a Medal of Honor at Spotsylvania with the Old Brigade, then spoke, presenting the monu-

Stephen Brown (left front) and fellow veterans of the 13th Vermont at the dedication of the regimental monument at Gettysburg, which depicts Lieutenant Brown.

HOWARD COFFIN

Stephen Brown, with his famous hatchet at his feet,
atop the 13th Vermont monument, facing the Codori farm

ments to the Gettysburg Battlefield Association on behalf of the state of Vermont. "We hope that in all the coming years," he said, "as our children in their pilgrimages from the distant states shall visit this spot, they may find in the contemplation of this structure and the mighty events here enacted, something that will remind them of the value of their country, and of the cost at which its dignity was preserved, and so shall be sealed their own devotion to its honor and its flag."

The 13th, 14th, and 16th regiments raised funds for, and erected, monuments of their own along Cemetery Ridge, close to the tall Stannard column. The 16th's was dedicated on September 23, 1892. The 13th's and 14th's were presented on October 19, 1889, and Ralph Sturtevant was there. "As we approach this place," he said, "many for the first time since those July days in '63, with what emotions we are filled in contrasting the present peaceful time with the tumult and carnage of the scenes enacted thirty-six years before."

His regiment's monument was a bronze statue of Stephen Brown, with captured Confederate sword in hand, looking across the shallow valley toward Seminary Ridge. The original plan was for Brown to be wielding a hatchet in one hand, a sword in the other. But the Gettysburg Monument Commission vetoed that design, apparently because of the insubordination it implied, so the hatchet was placed, in bronze, at his feet.

Colonel Randall died in Northfield in 1885 after having served for a time as vice president of Norwich University. Veterans of his regiment gathered in the village cemetery in June 1893 to dedicate a memorial at his grave. Albert Clarke spoke: "The memory that lives is the memory that leads. The service which connects with an undying cause, and which o'erleaps the bounds of mere duty and perils all for the utmost, transmits a voice, as by a phonograph, which will go ringing through the halls of time. When Randall, being asked by Hancock if he could retake a battery, replied, 'We will do it or die trying,' the keynote of his success was sounded, and we hear it still. And so in future emergencies, when something dangerous or great awaits the doing, long may our children and our children's children, to the remotest generations, rise to the dignity of their inheritance and say, 'We will do it or die trying.'"

Former Lt. Carmi Marsh became wealthy after acquiring a large interest in the Kendall Spavin Cure business. He had nearly died of meningitis in the service, and was nursed back to health in the home of a Virginia woman, Mrs. Wilcoxson. In 1898 Marsh was visiting Washington and decided to seek out his former nurse. After a long search, he found her in Manassas, an elderly lady now known as Mrs. Selecman. She lived four more years, and each year Marsh visited her. Four times a year he sent a check. When he heard that she was dying, Marsh headed south to see her one last time.

Late in the century, three members of the brigade were notified that they had been authorized to receive the Medal of Honor for service at Gettysburg. Captain Lonergan's citation noted his gallantry in recapturing four cannon and a number of prisoners. Lieutenant Benedict's noted that he "passed through a murderous fire of grape and canister in delivering orders and re-formed the crowded lines." Colonel Veazey's stated that he "rapidly assembled the regiment and charged the enemy's flank; changed front forward under heavy fire, and charged and destroyed a Confederate battery, all with his new troops in their first battle."

Veterans of the Second Vermont Brigade proved to be ambitious, and several achieved political prominence. As George Benedict once noted, "From their number, in the 25 years after the close of the war, three governors, two lieutenant governors, two judges of the supreme court, a congressman, a secretary of state, a United States district attorney, an adjutant general and quartermaster general, fourteen state senators, and many town representatives were selected in the state of Vermont, and others in other states." Roswell Farnham served as Vermont governor from 1880 to 1882, Capt. Ebenezer Ormsbee, also of the 12th, from 1896 to 1898. William Grout, who commanded the men of the brigade in their last skirmish, served five terms as a congressman from Vermont. Adj. Gen. Peter Washburn was elected governor in 1869, but died in office.

For a time, Wheelock Veazey and his friend Redfield Proctor practiced law together in Rutland. But Proctor soon left to enter the marble business, founding the Vermont Marble Company and becoming its first president. Veazey stayed in law, though he dabbled in politics and eventually was elevated to the Vermont Supreme Court. Then he was appointed to the US Commerce Commission. The position he treasured most, though, was his election as commander of the national Union veterans association, the Grand Army of the Republic.

Proctor's long and distinguished career included service as Vermont governor and US secretary of war, appointed by Benjamin Harrison. During that

Redfield Proctor and veterans of the Second Vermont Brigade, at Gettysburg

term, in 1889, a former secretary of war, Jefferson Davis, passed away. It had long been the custom that the flag at the War Department be flown at half-staff on the death of a former secretary. But in the case of the Confederate president, Proctor refused. The citizens of Tupelo, Mississippi, in Davis' home state, promptly hanged him in effigy.

As secretary, Proctor once received a letter from a Vermont soldier, Cornelius Palmer, asking that his war record be set straight. At long last, Cornelius wanted it officially recorded that he, and not his brother Simeon, had served in the 13th. Proctor wrote to Palmer: "The enclosed discharge is probably the last one which will ever be issued to a volunteer soldier who served in the War of the Rebellion."

The 15th regularly held reunions, which Proctor attended faithfully. The regiment's 13th gathering was held November 15, 1876, in the House of Representatives at the State House. Proctor was a speaker: "The war is over," he said in his conclusion, "but let not its lessons soon be forgotten. We preserve in these corridors the battle-torn flags that tell their silent story. I would that by enduring monuments in the daily haunts of men the memory of the fallen might be perpetuated, and the lessons of their lives and glorious sacrifices be kept ever before the people. The war is over, and let us trust its marks and scars may soon be healed; but never at the cost of any of the dearly-bought principles for which you fought. The duties of peace are crowding upon us, in which it is sometimes more difficult to guide our steps aright, than in the rougher paths of war." The St. Albans Glee

14th Vermont monument on Cemetery Ridge

Club then sang "The Battle Hymn of the Republic."

At the 16th reunion, held in Brandon, Proctor said, "The Green Mountains, termed the back-bone of the State, suggested the thought that the Vermonter, narrow, and bigoted and prejudiced as he might sometimes seem, never lacked that saving quality of back-bone; he always had spine and some to spare, even if he sometimes lacked the most perfect breadth of soul."

Proctor's career in the Senate, to which he was appointed in 1891, included an impassioned speech in 1898 that tipped the scales in favor of war with Spain. Proctor's powerful report of Spanish barbarism in Cuba caused Speaker of the House Reed to attack him as "The Marker King—a war will make a large market for gravestones," a caustic reference to Proctor's 1894 contract for supplying marble head- and footstones for Civil War battleground cemeteries.

In 1904, Senator Proctor invited the families of the 15th to his hometown of Proctor, where the family marble business thrived, to celebrate his 75th birthday. A grand luncheon was held, and the 275 guests toured the marble plant. They then walked up the hill to the burial spot of Proctor's warhorse, Old Charlie, who had given many of the men a welcome ride on the long march to Gettysburg. There they parted, though many returned three years later, among the crowd of 10,000 gathered for Proctor's funeral. He died in Washington, still a senator.

Lt. Albert Clarke was successful in the newspaper and railroad businesses, then was elected to Congress from Massachusetts. But he faithfully returned to Vermont for reunions of the 13th regiment and once hosted his old comrades at reunions on Boston Common and Nantucket Island.

Jabez Hammond, a lister and road commissioner in West Windsor for many years, like many members of the brigade was elected to the Vermont House. He was a member of the local Methodist church for 44 years and farmed his father's land all his life. He and his wife had six sons. On June 17, 1910, the *Vermont Journal* of Windsor printed the following item, written in the Hammond family style: "This community was shocked and saddened to learn early Sunday morning of the death of Jabez H. Hammond one of the most respected and best known citizens of this town. His death was the result of an accident. It appears he was trying to get his manure spreader under the shed at his home early Saturday evening which was down a steep incline about 100 feet from the place he started at. The supposition is that he tried to bear down on the pole of the spreader to steady it. It carried him 25 feet all right, when either the pole or forward wheels hit some cobble stone and threw him off. He received a blow on his head which probably stunned him and as there was no evidence of a struggle, he probably died instantly . . . He was a soldier in the Civil War where he served as a Sergeant in Co. A of the 12th Vermont Regiment. Mr. Hammond will be greatly missed as he was a respected citizen and a good neighbor and friend."

James Scully, like many of his comrades, became involved in Republican politics and once served as a delegate to the Republican National Convention. He ran a successful dry goods business in Burlington, and was a fixture at regimental reunions and patriotic events, always admired, in Benedict's words, as "the pivot of the pivotal movement of the pivotal battle of the war." Late in life he also received appointment as a doorkeeper of the US House and was serving there when he died in Washington.

In October 1902, the 13th veterans returned to Virginia and sought out the places where they had camped. They went south from Washington by train. Henry Meigs remembered: "Leaving Alexdandria we soon crossed Hunting Creek, a familiar name to the 13th Vermont. On the left in the distance is the site of Old Camp Vermont and near by is Fort Lyon, which we with pick and shovel constructed. We remembered around it, in almost every direction, the plains and hill slopes were white with tents . . . At Fairfax Court House we . . . repaired to the front yard of the house wherein our doughty General Stoughton had his head-quarters and from whence he started on his enforced excursion to Richmond with Mosby and his men as escort. Then in the front yard our regimental association held a meeting."

There it was noted that Antonia Ford, always suspected of complicity in the capture of Stoughton, had eventually married a Vermonter. He was Henry H. Willard, a native of Westminster, who as a lad of 16 had worked for a time in a store in Stoughton's home village of Bellows Falls. Willard was said to have become Washington's wealthiest citizen, the founder and co-owner of fashionable Willard's Hotel.

John McMahon, the brigade wrestling champion who had helped drag re-captured cannon back within Union lines at Gettysburg, became a world champion collar and elbow wrestler, though as he grew older he told Sturtevant, "The malaria of the Occoquan has settled in my bones and I am disabled by rheumatism."

In 1886, Roswell Farnham and Mary built Bradford's first house with central heat. He worked as a company lawyer and was active in politics. He was chosen a delegate to the Republican National Convention in 1876 and then elected governor. In 1898 he fell from a railroad platform, badly injured his head, and never fully recovered. He died at home in 1903, with Mary at his side.

John Lonergan's wild Irish spirit never stilled; he became active in the Fenian movement. Then he served as a federal customs inspector, lived for a time between Democratic administrations on a mountainside farm in Lincoln, then moved to Montreal, where he died in 1902. He was buried with honors in St. Joseph's Catholic Cemetery in Burlington. Written on his tombstone is a reminder that this son of Ireland was a recipient of the Medal of Honor for his deeds at Gettysburg. The epitaph says that Lonergan died "believing in future life and in the destiny of this dear land."

Shortly before he died, Stephen Brown donated to the Vermont Historical Society the Confederate sword he had captured with upraised hatchet, along with a letter that defended his disobeying of Stannard's orders against stopping for water. "I have never been called upon to do an act that caused me so much distress as I felt in disobeying his order," he wrote. ". . . Impelled by an overwhelming sense of high Duty (as I understood it) I got that water for the men. In comparison of the discharge of that duty the artillery fire on the afternoon of July 3, the shock of Pickett's Charge that struck our centre and recoiled, and the capture of that Johnnie in hand to hand encounter, were pleasant pastimes that a golf player might have envied." Brown was buried in a Swanton village cemetery, next to Cpl. William Church, whose horribly mangled body had been brought home from the battlefield. Brown's grave was marked by an elegant granite carving of an angel pointing to heaven. Sometime later, the pointing finger broke away, leaving the angel with an upraised fist.

In the fall of 1909, veterans of the 13th and their families toured the Gettysburg battlefield. Everyone went by train to Washington and the White House the next day to be greeted by President Theodore Roosevelt. The president said it was a great pleasure to meet the Vermonters for, on a visit to Gettysburg several years earlier, he had learned of what they had done for their country. Roosevelt added that he was once in a war himself: "It was not big," he said, "but it was all there was."

In that same year a Civil War monument was erected in the northwestern Vermont town of Milton, and many veterans of Stannard's Brigade turned out to hear Henry Clarke, a former member of the 13th. "We look back upon our part and it seems all a dream now," he said, "but vacant chairs and empty sleeves and this monument remind us that it was no dream then. When we place ourselves in imagination upon those fields of valor, well may we say with the martyred Lincoln: 'The world will little note nor long remember what we say here, but it can never forget what we did here.'"

To Gettysburg in late June and early July of 1913 came 50,000 Union and Confederate veterans for the 50th anniversary of the battle. The Vermont Legislature appropriated a total of $10,000 to pay the travel expenses of any Vermont veterans wishing to go, and more than 500 accepted the offer. A special train departed Burlington, reaching Gettysburg on June 29 after a two-day journey. Thomas Cheney, who accompanied the veterans, said of the trip, "One would be led to think as he listened to their jokes and laughter, they were boys instead of men that had passed the allotted time of human life."

On arrival, the Vermonters encountered acres of white tents erected to house the old soldiers. "The Vermont camp . . . was about one mile from Gettysburg village, lying on Seminary Ridge and on a portion of the field where the first day's fight occurred. It was on high ground and a fine location," Cheney wrote.

The Vermonters found themselves camped next to Confederate veterans. Cheney added, "They had a band and many of them wore the gray uniform. As they marched down the avenue with the band playing, the Confederate flag was seen to fly beside Old Glory. No one seemed to care for the gray uniforms, but many of the boys that wore the blue took exception to the Confederate flag." Still, he wrote, "The Johnnies were frequent visitors to our camp, and they seemed to enjoy the company of the Vermont Yanks."

President Woodrow Wilson spoke at the ceremonies, as did the commanders of the Grand Army of the Republic and the United Confederate Veterans. Some of the Vermonters were amazed that the Confederate commander was none other than Bennett Young, who led the rebel raiding party that robbed the banks in St. Albans.

One veteran of the 13th Vermont was especially popular at Gettysburg, for in his tent he had a chest from which he willingly dispensed what he called "medicine." Confederates as well as Yankees came by to sample the wares, and one day the Vermonter admired a reunion badge an old rebel was wearing. The conversation went something like this:

"Johnny, I want one of those badges for a souvenir."

"Can't sell 'em."

"Why not?"

"Because I can't get another."

"What if you lose one?"

"If we can prove we lost it, we can get another."

As the Confederate left the tent, a badge fell to the ground.

The reunion ended on July 4. The veterans departed the next day after a long wait in the hot sun, boarding a train bound for Vermont. As the train pulled away, a torrential rain erupted, just as it had 50 years before on the day after battle.

Among those who attended was Edwin Pierce, whose best buddy was shot dead by his side in the great barrage that preceded Pickett's Charge. On departing his home in North Shrewsbury, he got only a short way down the road before hurrying back to get his false teeth. Late in his life his grandaughter, Marjorie Pierce, often saw him rocking in his favorite chair before the fire on the family farm. He rocked and softly sang the old songs of the war. She particularly recalls "We Are Tenting Tonight on the Old Camp Ground."

Some of the boys of Stannard's brigade lived to a great age, including Albert Harwood of Brattleboro, once of the 12th Vermont, and George Peck of Montpelier, formerly of the 13th. Harwood died on April 1, 1939, at age 99; Peck expired at 97 on January 22, 1940. Photographer William Jackson was still climbing into the Rockies past age 90, to take scenic photographs with modern Kodak cameras. He lived to 99, recalling much of the nation's history, including the return of an uncle from the Mexican War and news of Pearl Harbor. Jackson died in Washington on June 30, 1942, and was buried with honors in Arlington National Cemetery.

The central experience of their nine months plus of service stayed with the men who endured it as long as they lived, and in many ways. Pvt. Samuel Benjamin was hit at Gettysburg by an iron ball that entered his body near the spinal column, where it was a source of pain and discomfort for 36 years. In the summer of 1899 it was finally located and removed, eight inches below its entry point, and Benjamin at last had some relief from his suffering.

Pvt. Burton Dean had gone home to Highgate very ill not long after the 13th Vermont arrived in Virginia. A comrade said of him more than 40 years later, "He still lives, but has never seen a well day since he was a soldier . . . He is a feeble-minded harmless old man."

Pvt. Myron Scullin, a mechanic from Essex, had his wounded foot amputated soon after Gettysburg. The doctor told him he had preserved the foot in alcohol and that Scullin could have it. He declined. Years later, according to Scullin, "He said that he would have it mounted and send it to the Medical Museum in Washington, and there I found it."

Pvt. Octave LaFleur died on June 29, 1906, in Montgomery. A friend said, "He was a good husband and kind father, a good worker and a good provider. His only fault was he got on a spree once in a while."

Pvt. Torrey Sibley, wounded at Gettysburg, recovered, lived for a while in Boston, then set up a hardware business in Essex Junction. He wrote at age 64

William Henry Jackson with an unidentified man at the 75th reunion of the Battle of Gettysburg

for Sturtevant's history, "I know the final call is at hand and I hope to be buried in sight of old Mansfield, which mountain from earliest recollections commanded my love and admiration . . . We shall see each other when gathered on that eternal camping ground where all is peace and love."

Pvt. Amos Whiting, who once jumped from a train derailed by Mosby, said late in life, "Many of my Company C have gone over the river. They sleep beneath the shadows of the clouds, careless alike of the sunshine or storm, each in the windowless palace of rest."

Pvt. Nelson Goodspeed of Berkshire, just 22 when sickness claimed his life in Virginia in 1863, had been dead 46 years when Sturtevant compiled his history. Yet a comrade remembered him well: "On each recurring Memorial Day the flag he loves is raised on his lowly grave and the early flowers of spring are

293

LIMOGE COLLECTION

Ralph Orson Sturtevant as he completed
his 13th Vermont regimental history

scattered above his resting place as tokens of love and affection."

In 1917, a daughter of Walcott Mead presented his Civil War letters to the Vermont Historical Society, with an accompanying message: "The old fields where daisies grow are covered thick with stones and lettered monuments that mark the place where brave men strove, and won or lost. It is well that it is so. These same old battle grounds are dotted thick with rotting caissons and bronze cannon that will never be unlimbered again . . . Again, it is well that it is so."

The men of the Second Vermont Brigade remained friends as long as they lived. Ralph Sturtevant became a lawyer, with a practice in Swanton. He worked for years on his regimental history, but died on May 28, 1910, before its publication. A former comrade in arms, Eugene Ranslow, also of Swanton, added to the regimental history a tribute to its author. "He was no deserter either on the field of war or of friendship," Ranslow wrote. "In this poor fickle world, one such light shines a long way. The esteem in which our comrade was held and the wide circle of his friends was evinced by the throngs who came from far and near to pay honor at his bier. They did not come because he was among the great and rich and those powerful to help: they came because they could not stay away . . . May is the month when all nature puts on new life and 'the exuberant burgeon seemed to mock the sere and desolate winter of our sorrow'; but it was only in the seeming, for we thought of another world where in it is always Spring and where we, soldiers of '61–'65, who have come to a mellow autumn, shall put on a new life forevermore."

Among those at the funeral was Pvt. James Judkins, of nearby Highgate, a shoemaker by trade, who had strived to keep his comrades' footwear in good repair while they were on duty. Sturtevant had been close to the completion of his history (and his life) when he saw Judkins on the street one summer day. "He is an old man, 85 years past," said Sturtevant, "and yet he walks off just as when he appeared on the march, quick, steady and strong. I saw him here in Swanton only a few days ago . . . and his memory of the old days was fresh and life in the army was spoken of with pleasure, and when I remarked to him, 'We shall soon pass away and be forgotten,' 'Yes,' said he, 'but what we did will remain, and for us it does not matter.'"

★

MAIN CHARACTERS

Albert Clarke. A Montpelier lawyer, Clarke served as a lieutenant in the 13th Vermont. His brief history of the 13th Vermont is in *Peck's Roster,* and his reminiscences of soldier life are in Ralph Sturtevant's history of the 13th. (The 13th also included an Albert Clark, a sergeant from Georgia, Vermont, who is quoted.)

George Benedict. Junior editor of the *Burlington Free Press,* Benedict enlisted as a private in the 12th Vermont, then was promoted to lieutenant and made an aide to George Stannard, brigade commander. He also served as war correspondent for the *Free Press.* After the war he wrote Vermont's official history of the Civil War and several shorter works, including *Army Life in Virginia*—a story of his nine months in the Second Vermont Brigade. His papers are preserved at UVM's Special Collections.

Asa Blunt. Elected commander of the 12th Vermont, the St. Johnsbury man served as brigade commander in Stoughton's absence. After the war he commanded Leavenworth military prison. Benedict's writings contain the best information on Blunt.

Stephen Brown. A part-time schoolteacher from Swanton, Brown was a company commander in the 13th Vermont and served with distinction at Gettysburg, where his bronze likeness now tops the regimental monument. His wartime recollections are included in the 13th Vermont's regimental history, and some of his papers survive at the Vermont Historical Society.

Charles Cummings. Lieutenant colonel of the 16th Vermont and a newspaper editor in Brattleboro, he was killed late in the war in fighting around Petersburg. His wartime letters are at the Vermont Historical Society.

Samuel Dana. A private in the 13th Vermont from Warren, his letters from the war to his family are reprinted here courtesy of Elizabeth Bordeaux of Waterbury, Vermont.

William Doubleday. A private, then corporal, in the 14th Vermont, Doubleday left his wife, Asceneth, and their sons in Pittsfield to enlist in the 14th. He died of wounds suffered at Gettysburg and is buried in the national cemetery there. His letters appear courtesy of a descendant, Hazen "Doc" Doubleday, of Hartland, Vermont.

Mary Farnham. The wife of the second in command of the 12th Vermont, schoolteacher Mary Farnham joined her husband in camp during the winter of 1862–63. The University of Vermont and the Vermont Historical Society preserve her letters, while UVM has a copy of her wartime diary. The Bradford Historical Society has photographs of Mary, her husband, and family.

Roswell Farnham. Second in charge of the 12th Vermont, he commanded it while Colonel Blunt led the brigade. Farnham, a lawyer and schoolmaster, was elected governor of Vermont after the war. His papers are at the University of Vermont and the Vermont Historical Society.

Jabez Hammond. A sergeant from West Windsor, Hammond wrote letters home to his father, Daniel Hammond, a farmer and jack-of-all-trades, who replied. Three other brothers served with Hammond in the 12th Vermont. The letters between Jabez and his father are reprinted courtesy of Sidney Hammond of Hartland, Vermont.

Benjamin Hatch. A private in the 12th Vermont from Hartland, Hatch's letters to his wife, Lucina, are preserved at the University of Vermont.

Frederick Holbrook. The only Vermont governor to serve two full one-year terms during the Civil War, the Massachusetts native sent more regiments to the war than the two other wartime governors combined. He wrote reminiscences of his governorship for the *Brattleboro Phoenix*, which are preserved at the Brooks Memorial Library in Brattleboro and at the Vermont State Library in Montpelier.

William Henry Jackson. A young artist working in Rutland, Jackson enlisted in the 12th Vermont and made the long march almost to Gettysburg. Employed as an artist and map maker by his regimental commander, he later became a famed photographer, particularly of the American West. His wartime diary is in the New York Public Library and his wartime sketches are preserved at the Scotts Bluff National Monument in Gering, Nebraska.

John Lonergan. The captain of Company A of the 13th Vermont was a native of Ireland and won a Medal of Honor for his service at Gettysburg. The story of his Civil War service is told in the 13th Vermont's regimental history and in Benedict's writings and papers.

George Mason. An elderly Virginian and owner of a plantation at Alexandria called Spring Bank. This house was used, for a time, as headquarters of the Second Vermont Brigade. Mason's letters to the brigade commander are contained in the Farnham papers at the Vermont Historical Society.

Charles Mead. A member of a well-to-do family in Hinesburg, he enlisted against his parents' wishes and served in the 14th Vermont. The family papers are preserved at the University of Vermont.

Walcott Mead. A private in the 14th Vermont from Shoreham. Mead's Civil War letters are preserved at the Vermont Historical Society.

John Singleton Mosby. Legendary cavalry commander known as the Gray Ghost of the Confederacy. The story of his capture of General Stoughton is told in his own words in his memoirs.

William Nichols. Commander of the 14th Vermont, he is dealt with at length in Benedict's writings and in the 14th's regimental history. His views on Pickett's Charge are in the Benedict papers at the University of Vermont.

Edwin Palmer. A Dartmouth graduate, this young Waterbury attorney enlisted in the 13th Vermont and later wrote a book based on his wartime experiences, titled *Second Vermont Brigade or Camp Life*.

Ora Paul. Captain of a company in the 12th Vermont that advanced against J.E.B. Stuart's raiders. Paul's service is dealt with in Benedict's writings, and the return of his company to Woodstock is described in the *Vermont Standard*.

Redfield Proctor. Proctor began the war as a major in the Third Vermont. He came home to raise men for the Second Vermont Brigade and was elected

Colonel of the 15th Vermont. Later he became a Vermont governor, US senator, and secretary of war. His letters are in the family papers at the Proctor Free Library in Proctor, Vermont.

Francis Randall. A lawyer, Randall was elected commander of the 13th Vermont and led it to glory at Gettysburg. Two of his sons served with him. Sturtevant details his service in his regimental history.

Lyman Seeley. A private in the 13th from Cambridge, Seeley wrote letters to the *Lamoille News Citizen.*

Joseph Spafford. From Reading, Spafford served in the Third Vermont, then came home to enlist in the 16th Vermont, serving as a lieutenant. His letters to his family are preserved at the Vermont Historical Society.

George Stannard. The second commander of the Second Vermont Brigade. The Benedict papers at the University of Vermont provide a wealth of information on him, as do Benedict's books and the 13th Vermont's history. Excerpts from his wartime diary are found in the official records and in the writings on Gettysburg of John Bachelder.

Edwin Stoughton. Member of a prominent Vermont family, Edwin Stoughton of Bellows Falls graduated from West Point and served as commander of the Fourth Vermont. Breveted a brigadier general, he was given command of the Second Vermont Brigade but left the army soon after his capture by Mosby. The story is detailed by Mosby in his memoirs; the 13th's regimental history also contains many accounts of the capture, as do dozens of soldier letters. His military records are at the National Archives. The book *The Man Who Tried to Burn New York* tells the story of his legal defense of a Confederate friend from his West Point days.

Ralph Sturtevant. Enlisted as a private in the 13th Vermont and fought at Gettysburg. Late in life, he compiled the *Historical and Biographic History of the 13th Regiment Vermont Volunteers*—the best single source of information on the Second Vermont Brigade.

Wheelock Veazey. Commander of the 16th Vermont and winner of a Medal of Honor, he had previously commanded the Third Vermont Regiment. A lawyer in Springfield before the war, his letters to his wife, Julia, are preserved at the Vermont Historical Society; some wartime letters are in the William F. Smith papers at the University of Vermont.

Peter Washburn. A veteran of the Mexican War and of the First Vermont Regiment, Washburn was elected adjutant general of the state and administered Vermont's war effort from offices in Woodstock. Some of his papers are preserved at the University of Vermont's Special Collections. Considerable information about the adjutant general's office is contained in contemporary Vermont newspapers, particularly the *Vermont Standard* at the Norman Williams Public Library in Woodstock.

John Williams. A corporal in the 14th Vermont from Danby, Williams kept a wartime diary and converted it into a book called *Life in Camp.*

John Williams. A private in the 14th Vermont from Fair Haven, Williams's letters—in Welsh—are at the Vermont Historical Society, with translations.

Andrews, C.C. *Minnesota in the Civil and Indian Wars, 1861–65.* St. Paul, Minn., 1891.

Aiken, Cpl. James H. *Civil War Letters.* Courtesy of Brad and Sue Limoge, Morrisville, Vt.

Bachelder, John B. *Gettysburg Papers,* Vols. I, II, and III, New Hampshire Historical Society.

————. Excerpts from diary of General Stannard.

————. General Hancock's description of Vermonters' battlefield position.

————. Col. Edwin Bryant's account of Stannard's flank attack.

————. G.G. Benedict's accounts of Vermont troop positions and of troop movements of the 14th Vermont.

————. Wheelock Veazey's account of Vermont Brigade troop movements.

Barber, James G. *Alexandria in the Civil War.* Lynchburg, Va.: H.E. Howard and Co., 1988.

Barnett, George. Civil War letters. Vermont Historical Society, Montpelier.

Basset, T.D. Seymour. *The Growing Edge: Vermont Villages 1840–1880.* Vermont Historical Society, Montpelier, 1992.

Bellows Falls Sentinel. 1862–1863. Vermont State Library, Montpelier.

Benedict, George Grenville. *Vermont in the Civil War.* Burlington, Vt.: Free Press Printing Co., 1908.

————. *Army Life in Virginia.* Burlington, Vt.: Burlington Free Press Association, 1895.

————. *The Battle of Gettysburg and the Part Taken Therein by Vermont Troops.* Burlington, Vt.: Free Press Printing Co., 1867.

————. *A Short History of the 14th Vermont Regiment.* Bennington, Vt.: Press of C.A. Pierce, 1887.

————. Family papers. Special Collections, Bailey/Howe Library, University of Vermont, Burlington.

Benton, Guy Potter. *Memorials of Vermonters.* New York, 1917.

Bostwick, Lucius H. Civil War letters. Special Collections, Bailey/Howe Library, University of Vermont, Burlington.

Bowie, Chester W. *Redfield Proctor: A Biography.* Doctoral thesis. University of Wisconsin, Madison, 1960.

Boynton, Joseph. Letter in the Reuben Savage papers. Special Collections, Bailey/Howe Library, University of Vermont, Burlington.

Brandt, Nat. *The Man Who Tried to Burn New York.* Syracuse, N.Y.: Syracuse University Press, 1986.

Brattleboro Phoenix, 1862–1863. Bailey/Howe Library, University of Vermont, Burlington, and Brooks Memorial Library, Brattleboro, Vt.

Brown, Stephen. Papers including accounts of hatchet incident and affidavit concerning assisting a battery on Cemetery Hill. Vermont Historical Society, Montpelier.

Buono, Anthony. "The First Vermonter to Enlist in the War." *America's Civil War,* July 1996.

Burlington Free Press, 1862–1912. Bailey/Howe Library, University of Vermont, Burlington, and Vermont State Library, Montpelier.

Bushnell, Sidney. Wartime diary. Special Collections, Bailey/Howe Library, University of Vermont, Burlington.

Cabot, Mary R. *Annals of Brattleboro.* Brattleboro, Vt.: Press of E.L. Hildreth & Company, 1922.

Caledonian Record, 1862–1863. Vermont State Library, Montpelier.

Chamberlin, Edson E. *A Vermonter in the Rebellion: Amos Leavitt.* Randolph, Vt.: Beacon Printing, 1992.

Chamberlin, J.B. Civil War letters. Special Collections, Bailey/Howe Library, University of Vermont, Burlington.

Cheney, Thomas C. *Vermont at Gettysburg, July 1863 and 50 Years Later.* Rutland, Vt.: Marble City Press, The Tuttle Co., 1914.

Clark, B.G. Civil War reminiscence. Papers of G.G. Benedict. Special Collections, Bailey/Howe Library, University of Vermont, Burlington.

Clarke, Albert. *The Thirteenth Regiment.* Handwritten reminiscence, Vermont Historical Society, Montpelier.

Clark, Edmund Payson. Civil War letters. Missouri Historical Society, St. Louis.

Clark, Myron. Civil War diary. Courtesy of Clifford J. Heustis, Bridport, Vt.

Cobb, Hiram. Civil War diary. Courtesy of Gordon Tuthill, Woodstock, Vt.

Coddington, Edwin B. *The Gettysburg Campaign: A Study in Command.* New York: Charles Scribner's Sons, 1968.

Coffin, Charles Carleton. *The Boys of '61.* Boston: The Page Company, 1890.

Cooling, Benjamin Franklin III and Owen H. Walton II. *Mr. Lincoln's Forts: A Guide to the Civil War Defenses of Washington.* Shippensburg, Pa.: White Mane Publishing Company, 1988.

Cross, David. "Wheelock Graves Veazey." *Rutland Historical Society Quarterly,* Vol. XXV, No. 2, 1995.

Cummings, Charles. Civil War letters. Vermont Historical Society, Montpelier.

Dana, Samuel J. Civil War letters. Courtesy of Elizabeth Bordeaux, Waterbury, Vt.

Davis, Burke. *Jeb Stuart: The Last Cavalier.* New York: The Fairfax Press, 1988.

Dix, Henry F. Civil War letter. Vermont Historical Society, Montpelier.

Dog River Crier: Northfield Historical Society Newsletter, Northfield, Vt., Winter 1995.

Doubleday, William O. Civil War letters and medical records. Courtesy of "Doc" Doubleday, Hartland, Vt.

Downey, Fairfax. *The Guns at Gettysburg.* New York: Collier Books, 1958.

Dudley, Henry. Civil War letters. Redfield Proctor papers. Proctor Free Library, Proctor, Vt.

Farmer, Alonzo. Civil War letters. Vermont Historical Society. Montpelier.

Fairbanks, Charles. *The American Conflict as Seen from the European Point of View: A Lecture.* Boston: Press of George C. Rand & Avery, 1863.

Farnham, Mary E. Civil War diary. Special Collections, Bailey/Howe Library, University of Vermont, Burlington.

Farnham, Roswell, and Mary E. Farnham. Civil War letters. Vermont Historical Society, Montpelier.

———. Academy Record Book, 1854–1860. Vermont Historical Society, Montpelier.

Faust, Patricia L., ed. *Historical Times Illustrated Encyclopedia of the Civil War.* New York: Harper & Row, 1986.

Fisher, John R. *Louis Barttro: A Vermont Franco-American in the Civil War.* Privately printed, 1980.

Foot, Solomon. Speech on the Vermont war effort. *Green Mountain Freeman,* 1980.

Foote, Shelby. *Fort Sumter to Perryville.* New York: Random House, 1958.

———. *Fredericksburg to Meridian.* New York: Random House, 1963.

Freeman, Douglas Southall. *Robert E. Lee: A Biography,* Vol. 4. New York: Charles Scribner's Sons, 1934.

Fuller, Mrs. Levi K. Address before the Brattleboro Chapter of the Daughters of the American Revolution. Vermont Historical Society, Montpelier.

Gale, Frederick. Civil War letters. Special Collections, Bailey/Howe Library, University of Vermont, Burlington.

The Gettysburg Papers, Vols. I and II. Compiled by Ken Bandy and Florence Freeland. Dayton, Ohio: Press of the Morningside Bookshop, 1978.

Glover, Joel. Civil War letters. Special Collections, Bailey/Howe Library, University of Vermont, Burlington.

Green Mountain Freeman, 1862–63. Vermont State Library, Montpelier.

Hagar, George. Civil war letters. Special Collections, Bailey/Howe Library, University of Vermont, Burlington.

Hammond, Jabez. Civil War letters. Courtesy of Sidney Hammond, Hartland, Vt.

Harrison, Kathleen R. Georg. *A Common Pride and Fame: The Repulse of Pickett's Division at Gettysburg.* Library, Gettysburg National Military Park.

Haskell, Frank. *The Battle of Gettysburg.* Boston: Houghton Mifflin Co., 1957.

Hatch, Benjamin Franklin. Civil War letters. Special Collections, Bailey/Howe Library, University of Vermont, Burlington.

Herrick, William. Diary, 1863. Fairbanks Museum, St. Johnsbury, Vt.

Hoar, Jay. *New England's Last Civil War Veterans.* Arlington, Tx.: Seacliff Press, 1976.

Hoyt, William. Wartime diary. Special Collections, Bailey/Howe Library, University of Vermont, Burlington.

Irwin, Richard. Civil War letters. Special Collections, Bailey/Howe Library, University of Vermont, Burlington.

Jackson, William Henry. Civil War diary. New York Public Library, New York City.

———. Sketches. Courtesy of Scott's Bluff National Monument, Gering, Neb.

Keith, Unite. Civil War letters. *Morrisville News Citizen,* Morristown Centennial Library, Morrisville, Vt.

Keyes, Elmer. Civil War letter. Courtesy of Lawrence and Allan Keyes, Rutland, Vt.

Leetch, Margaret. *Reveille in Washington.* London: Harper & Brothers Publishers, 1941.

Lonergan, John. Letter on the death of Lt. Sinnott. Benedict Papers, Bailey/Howe Library, University of Vermont, Burlington.

McKeen, Siles. *A History of Bradford, Vermont.* Montpelier, Vt.: J.D. Clark & Son, 1875.

Marshall, Jeffrey D. Vermonters in the Civil War. Special Collections, Bailey/Howe Library, University of Vermont, Burlington.

Martin, Charles. *Gettysburg the Second and Third Days.* Unpublished manuscript, courtesy of Charles Martin, Montpelier, Vt.

Mason, George. Letter complaining of military restrictions at his Virginia home. Roswell Farnham Papers, Vermont Historical Society, Montpelier.

McPherson, James. *Battle Cry of Freedom.* New York: Oxford University Press, 1988.

Mead, Charles E. Civil War letters. Mead family letters, Special Collections, Bailey/Howe Library, University of Vermont, Burlington.

Mead, Walcott. Civil War letters. Vermont Historical Society, Montpelier.

Meigs, Henry B. "A Day in Virginia." Pamphlet. Burlington, Vt.: The Thompson Printing Co., 1903.

Moore, Kenneth A. "Frederick Holbrook." *Vermont History,* April 1965: 65–77.

Morgan, Gen. C.H. General Hancock at the Battle of Gettysburg. Prepared at St. Paul, Minn., May 1872. Reminiscence. Benedict Papers, Special Collections, Bailey/Howe Library, University of Vermont, Burlington.

Morrisville News Citizen, 1862–1863. Morristown Centennial Library, Morrisville, Vt.

Mosby, J.S. *The Memoirs of John S. Mosby.* Boston: Little, Brown & Co., 1917.

———. My Guerrilla Operations. *Sunday Magazine,* August 1908.

Nichols, William. Gettysburg reminiscence and map. Benedict Papers, Special Collections, Bailey/Howe Library, University of Vermont, Burlington.

Northrup, Samuel. Letters from his family in Shoreham. Special Collections, Bailey/Howe Library, University of Vermont, Burlington.

Palmer, Edwin. *The Second Brigade or, Camp Life.* Montpelier, Vt.: E.P. Walton Co., 1864.

Parker, David. Letter to Ethelbert Barksdale (son of Gen. Barksdale). Barksdale Papers, University of Mississippi Library.

Peck, Theodore S. *Revised Roster of Vermont in the Civil War.* Montpelier, Vt.: Watchman Publishing Company, 1892.

Pfanz, Harry W. *Gettysburg the Second Day.* Chapel Hill: The University of North Carolina Press, 1987.

Pierce, Edwin. Information courtesy of Marjorie Pierce, North Shrewsbury, Vt.

Post, Herman A. Civil War diary. Special Collections, Bailey/Howe Library, University of Vermont, Burlington.

Proctor, Redfield. Papers. Proctor Free Library, Proctor, Vt.

————. 1864 letter to George Benedict. Special Collections, Bailey/Howe Library, University of Vermont, Burlington.

Rosenblatt, Emil and Ruth, eds. *Hard Marching Every Day: The Civil War Letters of Private Wilbur Fisk.* Lawrence: University Press of Kansas, 1992.

Rutland Daily Herald, 1862–1863. Vermont State Library, Montpelier.

Sandburg, Carl. *Abraham Lincoln: The Prairie Years and the War Years.* New York: Harcourt, Brace & Co., 1954.

Scott, George H. *Vermont at Gettysburgh.* Proceedings of the Vermont Historical Society, Montpelier, 1930.

Sixteenth Regiment Vermont Volunteers Reunions and Rosters. Montpelier, Vt.: Patriot Printing, 1889.

Smith, James O. Civil War diary. Special Collections, Bailey/Howe Library, University of Vermont, Burlington.

Spafford, Joseph. Civil War letters. Vermont Historical Society, Montpelier.

Stearns, John W. Civil War letters. Special Collections, Bailey/Howe Library, University of Vermont, Burlington.

Stewart, George R. *Pickett's Charge.* Boston: Houghton Mifflin Co., 1959.

Stoughton, Edwin. Military records. National Archives, Washington, D.C.

Sturtevant, Ralph Orson. *Pictorial History: The Thirteenth Vermont Volunteers, 1861–1865.* Compiled by Eli N. Peck, secretary of the Thirteenth Vermont Regiment Association. Burlington, Vt., 1911.

Trimble, Tony L. "Paper Collars: Stannard's Brigade at Gettysburg." *The Gettysburg Magazine,* January 1990.

Tucker, Mary. Civil War diary. Special Collections, Bailey/Howe Library, University of Vermont, Burlington.

Turner, William Harrison. Civil War letters. Courtesy of Richard Turner of Berlin, Vt., and Vernon Turner of Amherst, Mass.

The War of the Rebellion: Official Records of the Union and Confederate Armies. Government Printing Office, Washington, D.C., 1889.

Vermont Standard, 1862–65. Norman Williams Public Library, Woodstock, Vt.

Wallace, John. Civil War letters. Vermont Historical Society, Montpelier.

Washburn, Peter. *An Oration before the Reunion Society of Vermont Officers, in the Representatives Hall, Montpelier, Vermont, Oct. 22, 1868.* Montpelier, Vt.: J.M. Poland Printers, 1869. Brad and Sue Limoge collection.

Wert, Jeffrey D. *Mosby's Rangers.* New York: Simon & Schuster, 1990.

White, Pvt. Henry. Civil War letters. Courtesy of Timothy White, Woodstock, Vt.

Williams, J.C. *Life in Camp.* Claremont, N.H.: Claremont Manufacturers Co., 1864.

Wills, Garry. *Lincoln at Gettysburg: The Words That Remade America.* New York: Touchstone, 1992.

Wilson, James. *Under the Old Flag,* Vol. 1. New York, 1912.

Yale, John L. An account of his illness. Yale family papers. Special Collections, Bailey/Howe Library, University of Vermont, Burlington.

INDEX

Please remember that this is a library book,
and that it belongs only temporarily to each
person who uses it. Be considerate. Do
not write in this, or any, library book.